Code Optimization:
Effective Memory Usage

CODE OPTIMIZATION: EFFECTIVE MEMORY USAGE

KRIS KASPERSKY

alist

A-LIST, LLC
295 East Swedesford Rd.
PMB #285
Wayne, PA 19087
702-977-5377 (FAX)
mail@alistpublishing.com
http://www.alistpublishing.com

This book is printed on acid-free paper.

Code Optimization: Effective Memory Usage
By Kris Kaspersky

ISBN 1-931769-24-9

Printed in the United States of America

03 04 7 6 5 4 3 2 1

A-LIST, LLC, titles are available for site license or bulk purchase by institutions, user
groups, corporations, etc.

Book Editor: Julie Laing

Contents

Introduction to Optimization

Expediency of Optimization

Is optimization worth spending time on nowadays? Isn't it better to concentrate on learning Microsoft Foundation Classes or .NET technology? Are modern computers so powerful that even the newest operating systems, such as Windows XP, cannot slow them down?

The newest generation of programmers is skeptical about optimization. However, it is not wise to go from one extreme to another. Even contemporary processors are not powerful enough to solve all tasks. The list of difficult tasks is long: modeling various real-world physical processes, multimedia information processing, optical character recognition, and so on. Even developing an efficient data-compression utility is a challenge.

Processor power is growing at a rapid rate. Nevertheless, the requirements of PC users keep pace with it. In contrast to the early days of data processing, when people were willing to start a program and wait for its execution, most users now expect all operations to be accomplished instantly or within a few minutes. The amount of data being processed also has increased. Now, files often exceed a couple of hundred megabytes. Do you recall the time when the entire hard-disk capacity was ten times smaller?

The target defines the means used to achieve it. This thesis will drive the direction of this book. Therefore, you should apply the following recommendations to all optimizing algorithms:

1. *Optimization should be as hardware-independent as possible, and it should be portable to other operating systems without additional effort or significant loss of efficiency.* In other words, inline assembler functions are seldom acceptable. You should stay within the limits of high-level programming languages. Furthermore, it is best to avoid nonstandard language capabilities and extensions that only are applicable to specific compilers.

2. *Optimization should not increase the labor intensity of the development process (including testing) by more than 15%.* Ideally, all crucial algorithms should be implemented as a separate library that requires no additional labor.

3. *The optimizing algorithm should provide a performance improvement of no less than 20%.* Optimization methods that provide a gain of less than 20% will be considered rarely in this book. Attention will be focused on algorithms that allow performance to at least double without additional efforts from the programmer. However fantastic this might seem, such algorithms exist!

4. *Optimization should provide the possibility of painless code modification.* Many optimization techniques can "kill" a program, because even a minor change can negate the optimization. All variables may be distributed carefully among registers, the microcode may be parallelized, and all functional capabilities may be employed. These can't compensate for the loss of the code flexibility. The execution speed of such a program can't be increased by even one clock, and its size can't be reduced by just 1 byte. Therefore, I will discuss only those optimization techniques that are not sensitive to correct changes introduced to the program structure.

The key concept that I will try to prove here is as follows: The common opinion that it is better to purchase a newer and more powerful processor than to spend time and effort on optimization is incorrect. In addition, optimization is not as labor-consuming as most individuals consider it to be. For example, this book provides many universal solutions that do not require individual tuning of each task. In this book, I have made an attempt to describe portable optimization at the system level and to avoid using assembly language without special need. It is impossible, however, to do without the assembler, especially in the chapters that discuss profiling techniques and machine-optimization algorithms. Nevertheless, I hope that the comments throughout the code will make it understandable, even to readers who have no experience in assembly-language programming.

Intended Audience

This book describes the organization, architecture, and mechanisms of interaction between various hardware components. It focuses on efficient programming and code-optimization techniques, at the level of machine code and of data structures.

The book is oriented toward application programmers with some experience in C/C++ programming, as well as toward system programmers with knowledge of the assembly language. However, the optimization techniques described here are not bound to any high-level programming language. Thus, knowledge of C is required only for understanding the source code provided in this book.

I also hope that this book will be useful to hardware specialists and technicians — especially those who build and fine-tune computers. I tried to provide detailed descriptions of the hardware operating principles and discuss the bottlenecks of the most common hardware components.

Most materials provided in this book are based on my experience. All information has been tested and checked carefully. However, I can't guarantee that it is free of errors. (After all, "there is always one more bug.")

The materials of the book are mainly applicable to the *AMD Athlon* and the *Intel Pentium II, Pentium III,* and *Pentium 4* microprocessors. Earlier processors are mentioned and considered when necessary.

Optimization Foundations

Programmers (even highly skilled ones) often automatically tackle problematic functions in the assembly language. This is not the right approach! As I will demonstrate in *Chapter 4*, in most cases, the performance difference between machine and manual optimization is negligible. There often may be nothing to optimize or improve except cosmetic elements. In most cases, a compiler provides an ideal result, and no efforts can improve it more than by a few percent. It would be unfortunate if this circumstance became evident only after one or more functions have been rewritten in the assembly language. Time and effort would have been wasted, and that's a pity.

Thus, before proceeding with manual optimization, it makes sense to find out if the code generated by the compiler really is nonoptimal and to what degree. It is also expedient to evaluate the existing performance reserve. However, it is not wise to go to the other extreme and assume that the compiler always generates optimal code. Everything depends on how well the implemented computational algorithm corresponds to the context of the high-level programming language. Some tasks that require the entire group of C or Pascal operators can be solved by a single machine instruction. It is naive to assume that the compiler would replace this group of instructions with the appropriate machine command. (On the contrary, it will translate each instruction into one or more machine commands.)

Therefore, consider some basic optimization rules.

Rule 1

Before proceeding with code optimization, develop a reliable, nonoptimized version of the same code. This means that before you start optimizing code, make sure that the program works correctly.

It is impossible to create optimized code in the course of software development. This specifically affects command scheduling. Introducing even a tiny change into the algorithm almost always results in a radical rewrite of the code. Therefore, do not start to optimize the code before you make sure that the algorithm implemented in the high-level programming language works correctly. Furthermore, if software bugs are revealed, optimized code fragments are the first suspects. (Optimized code is rarely readable and understandable, and debugging such code is a tedious project.) A nonoptimized but carefully debugged version will be helpful: If the optimized code is replaced by the nonoptimized version, and the errors are not reproduced, then the optimized code contains the bug. If the errors persist, then look for bugs elsewhere.

Rule 2

Use algorithmic optimization, rather than features of the system, to achieve the greatest performance gain. No optimization can significantly improve the efficiency of algorithms such as bubble sorting or linear searching. At best, correct command scheduling and other programming tricks will improve the program performance by a couple of percent. Conversely, implementation of a quick sort and a binary search will improve the speed at least ten times, regardless of the awkwardness of the source code implementation. Therefore, if your program is too slow, try to use more efficient algorithms instead of optimizing an inefficient one.

Rule 3

Don't confuse code optimization with assembly implementation. If you detect hotspots in your program during the profiling session, don't rush to rewrite them using the assembly language. First, take every step possible in the high-level programming language: Remove resource-consuming arithmetical operations (especially the division and calculation of the remainder), minimize branches, unroll loops with a small number of iterations, and so on. In extreme cases, try to change the compiler. (The quality of compilation can differ greatly.)

Rule 4

Before you try to rewrite a program in the assembly language, review the assembly code generated by the compiler and evaluate its efficiency. Perhaps the compiler is not responsible for poor performance of your application; it may be caused by the processor or memory subsystem. This is especially true for scientific applications that perform numerous calculations and for graphical software that require large amounts of memory. Simply shifting the program to the assembly language does not increase the throughput of the memory subsystem or make the processor to perform calculations faster. Produce the assembly listing of the code generated by the compiler. (For example, on Microsoft Visual C++, use the `/FA` command-line option.) Then, scan the listing for blunders such as `MOV EAX, [EBX] \MOV [EBX], EAX`. As a rule, it is easier to improve the code generated by the compiler than to create the assembly implementation from scratch. The former requires much less time, and the quality of the results will be comparable.

Rule 5

If the assembly listing produced by the compiler is perfect, but the program still runs slowly, load it into a disassembler. There, you may make discoveries, such as that compilers have an inaccurate approach to the alignment of jumps. Your compiler may not align jumps properly. Aligning jumps by addresses that are multiples of 16 would give the best performance. It would be even better to fit the entire loop body within one cache line (i.e., 32 bytes). However, I have digressed. Techniques of machine-code optimization are a different topic. The best advice I can give you is to study carefully the documentation released by the leading processor manufacturers: Intel and AMD.

Rule 6

If the available processor commands allow you to implement the algorithm more efficiently, leave the compiler alone and start implementing assembly code. However, this situation is rare. Furthermore, you are not living on a deserted island. There are tons of high-performance, carefully debugged, and highly optimized libraries available. Why should you reinvent a library if you can purchase one?

Rule 7

When developing assembly code, create an elegant and efficient solution, free of bells and whistles. Yes, undocumented features, nontraditional styles, and other tricks exist. However, none of these approaches are portable, free of problems, or clear to all individuals.

(Honestly, can you easily understand a source code that you wrote ten years ago?) I have shot myself in the foot more than once by using my own old tricks. The most painful thing about it was that these tricks were unnecessary; they were used out of love for the "art." Therefore, don't neglect comments, and place all assembly functions in a separate module. Avoid inlining assembly functions in your code: They seldom are portable, and they often have negative side effects when moved to another platform or compiler.

Assembly tricks are justified only in software copyright protection. However, this is the topic of another, and quite different, discussion.

Common Misperceptions

Erroneous statements about optimization are numerous. These often cause professionals to smile, but they can harm beginners. In this section, I'd like to debunk a few of these myths.

Myth 1

My compiler will optimize everything for me.

Belief in the almighty power of compilers has no foundation. Even a good optimizing compiler can translate efficiently only well-designed code.

If the source code is lame, no compiler will be able to correct its faults. Therefore, do not delegate all performance- and efficiency-related tasks to the compiler! A better approach is to help the compiler accomplish these tasks. Specific methods of achieving this goal deserve a separate discussion, which you will find in *Chapter 4*.

Myth 2

Maximum efficiency can be achieved only when programming in the pure assembly language; programming in a high-level language doesn't allow such a result.

Moving a program to the assembly language rarely improves its performance. The results of translating high-quality source code using manual optimization are only 10% to 20% better than the results shown by optimizing compilers. This is a significant difference, but it isn't large enough to justify the difficulties and labor of programming in naked assembly language.

Detailed information on this topic, including a comparison of the quality of machine and manual optimization, will be provided in *Chapter 4*.

Myth 3

Humans, unlike an optimizing compiler, are unable to account for all of the features of processor architecture.

Only compilers developed by Intel can generate code that the processor's microarchitecture would consider optimal. In *Chapter 1* (see *Practical Profiling Session Using VTune*), I'll illustrate this statement with practical example.

Nevertheless, contemporary processors can optimize code passed for processing. Attempts at manual optimization are bound to be unsuccessful: no code is optimal for all existing processor architectures, and the features of processors such as PII, P4, AMD-K6, and Athlon are strikingly different.

The exception is a limited range of specific tasks (such as password cracking) with critical performance requirements. In these exceptions, manual optimization is justified and will produce better results than any compiler.

Myth 4

The x86 processors are not worth using; PowerPC must be used to understand what true performance is.

Each architecture has its own advantages and drawbacks. I do not optimize anything for PowerPC, but I am acquainted with individuals who develop optimizing compilers for it and are disappointed by some of its "features."

The x86 family of processors also has many limitations and problems. However, this cannot serve as an excuse for programmers who write awkward code and never attempt to improve it.

For now, this family of processors has one of the most sophisticated system of commands, and provides system programmers with almost unlimited capabilities. Application programmers cannot even imagine what kind of experiences are stolen from them by compilers!

Chapter 1: Program Profiling

Throughout this book, I will use the term *profiling* to describe the process of analyzing the performance both of an entire program and of its particular fragments in order to detect *hotspots* — sections of the program that require the longest time to execute.

According to the well-known "Ninety-Ninety Rule,"[1] 10% of a program's code often consumes as much as 90% of the system resources. If the time required to complete each machine instruction is represented graphically in relation to the growth of the instructions linear addresses, the resulting diagram will show several distinct peaks rising from a flat plain that contains a multitude of low "hills." (See Fig. 1.6 in *Practical Profiling Session Using VTune*.) These peaks are hotspots.

Why is the topology of the graph line for different sections of the program so varied? This is because most number-crunching algorithms are organized as *loops* (i.e., multiple repetitions of the same code fragment). Often, these loops are not processed

---

[1] "The first 90% of the code accounts for the first 90% of the development time. The remaining 10% of the code accounts for the other 90% of the development time." This humorous aphorism is attributed to Tom Cargill of Bell Labs, and was popularized by Jon Bentley's September 1985 *Bumper-Sticker Computer Science* column in *Communications of the ACM*. In that column, it was called the "Rule of Credibility," a name which seems not to have stuck.

sequentially, but form hierarchies with multiple levels of nesting. As a result, loops with the deepest level of nesting occupy the lion's share of the program's execution time. Consequently, it is optimization of these loops that will yield the greatest improvement in performance.

Note that the optimization of bulky and slow, but rarely called, functions is practically pointless; the resulting improvement in performance will be virtually negligible (except, perhaps, when these functions are written too awkwardly).

If the program implements a simple algorithm and its source code is limited to a few hundred lines, hotspots can be easily located by examining a listing visually. However, as the size of the source code grows, this task becomes more complicated. The program being analyzed might comprise several thousand sophisticated functions that interact with each other in a complicated manner. (Some of these functions might be called from external libraries or from the APIs of the operating system.) When analyzing such a program, it is difficult to determine which of these functions is responsible for poor performance. In this case, the solution is to use specialized software tools.

The *profiler* is the primary tool for optimizing programs. "Blind" optimization rarely produces good results. According to a popular proverb, the pace of a squadron is the pace of its slowest vessel. Software code behaves in the same way: The performance of an application is determined by its "bottlenecks." Sometimes this happens because of a single machine instruction (for example, a division instruction executed repeatedly within a loop with a deep level of nesting). The programmer, having spent enormous efforts to improve other sections of code, might well be surprised to discover that all of his or her work has yielded an increase in the application performance by a mere 10% or 15%.

Hence, the first rule is as follows: *The elimination of hotspots that are not the "hottest" yields practically no improvement in the application's performance.* To return to the metaphor, speeding up the second-slowest vessel rarely increases the pace of the squadron as a whole. Whether or not the second-slowest vessel's pace has any influence on that of the slowest is a topic for another discussion. Because it requires a sound knowledge of profiling techniques, this topic will not be considered in this book.

Goals and Objectives of Profiling

The main goal of profiling is *the investigation of the applications' run-time behavior in all it spots.* Depending on the level of detail, the term *spot* can be used to designate either a single machine command or an entire fragment of code written in a high-level programming language. (For example, this could be a function, a loop, or a single line of source code.)

Most contemporary profilers support the following set of basic operations:

☐ Determining the total execution time for each program spot (total spots timing)
☐ Determining the type of execution time for each program spot (spots timing)
☐ Determining the reasons behind and/or the sources of conflicts and penalties (penalty information)
☐ Determining the number of calls to each spot (count)
☐ Determining the program coverage (coverage)

Total Execution Time

Gathering information about the time required by an application to execute each spot enables you to detect the "hottest" sections in that application. It is important to note that direct measurement will show that 99.99% of the total program's execution time is consumed by the main function. However, it is obvious that the main function is not a hotspot. The genuine hotspots are the functions called by the main function! To avoid confusion among programmers, profilers usually subtract the time required to execute child functions from the total execution time of each function within a program.

As an example, consider the result generated by the profile.exe profiler supplied as part of the Microsoft Visual C++ compiler (Listing 1.1).

Listing 1.1. Profiling Results from the profile.exe Tool Supplied with Visual C++

Func time	%	Func+Child time	%	Hit count	Function
350,192	95.9	360,982	98.9	10000	_do_pswd (pswd_x.obj)
5,700	1.6	5,700	1.6	10000	_CalculateCRC (pswd_x.obj)
5,090	1.4	10,790	3.0	10000	_CheckCRC (pswd_x.obj)
2,841	0.8	363,824	99.6	1	_gen_pswd (pswd_x.obj)
1,226	0.3	365,148	100.0	1	_main (pswd_x.obj)
98	0.0	0,098	0.0	1	_print_dot (pswd_x.obj)

The second column (Func+Child Time) lists the total execution time for each function. The most time is taken up by the main function (as would be expected). Second place goes to the gen_pswd function (99.6%), followed by the do_pswd function

(98.9%) and the CheckCRC function (3.0%). The CalculateCRC function, which takes a humble 1.6% of the total time, at first, may seem unimportant. Thus, a quick examination of the collected data reveals the following three hotspots: main, gen_pswd, and do_pswd (Fig. 1.1).

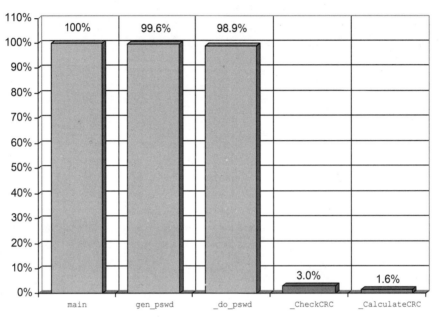

Fig. 1.1. A diagram showing the total execution time for each function. At first, there may seem to be three hotspots. However, this is not the case

In reality, the main function should be dismissed at once. It is obvious that this function is not responsible for performance degradation. The gen_pswd and do_pswd functions remain for consideration. If these were two independent functions, then they would represent two hotspots. This, however, is not the case. If you subtract the total execution time of the child function (do_pswd) from the total execution time of the parent function (gen_pswd), the resulting figure for the parent function is only 0.8% — less than 1% of the total execution time.

The leftmost column of the profiler table (Func time) proves these assumptions: There is one hotspot in this program: do_pswd. The way to improve the application's performance considerably is to optimize the performance of this hotspot (Fig. 1.2).

Assume that the "hottest" function has already been detected. Now, its performance needs to be optimized. To achieve this goal, it would be useful to be able to locate the hotspots within the function itself. Unfortunately, the profile.exe profiler (and other similar tools) cannot help; its resolution is limited to functions.

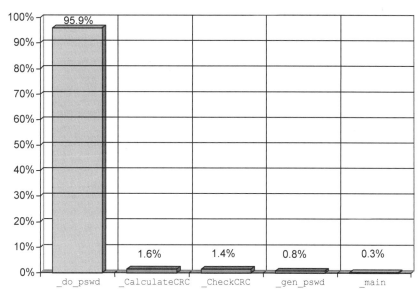

Fig. 1.2. A diagram illustrating the net execution time of each function (i.e., without child functions). The program being profiled has only one hotspot, but it's significant

Fortunately, there are other, more advanced profilers specifically for resolving particular lines of code and even individual machine commands. One example of this type of tool is the VTune profiler from Intel. Here, it has been used to investigate the do_pswd function. (More details on the techniques of working with this profiler will be provided in *Practical Profiling Session Using VTune*.) The results of this investigation are shown in Listing 1.2.

Listing 1.2. "Temperature" Distribution within do_pswd, Generated Using VTune

Line	Clock ticks	Source	Temperature
105	729	while((++pswd[p])>'z'){	████████████████ >>>
106	14	pswd[p] = '!';	██████
107	1	y = y | y << 8;	█
108	2	x -= k;	█
109		k = k << 8;	█
110	3	k += 0x59;	▒
111	2	p++;	█
112	1	}	█

Now, you can see an entirely different picture. It is immediately clear which code fragments need to be optimized, and which parts of the program have been optimized extensively. Hotspots are concentrated around the pswd[p] construction, which runs too slowly. Why? The source code doesn't provide an answer to this question. Therefore, what should be done to decrease the "temperature" of the hot spots is unclear.

For this reason, it is necessary to investigate pure machine commands. (Fortunately, VTune provides this capability.) Consider what the compiler has done to the innocent-looking pswd[p] = '!' assignment operator (Listing 1.3).

Listing 1.3. Commands within the pswd[p] = '!' Assignment Operator

Line	Instructions		Cycles	Count	Temperature
107	mov	edx, DWORD PTR [ebp+0ch]	143	11	████████████
107	; The *pswd* pointer is loaded into the *EDX* register.				
107	add	edx, DWORD PTR [ebp-4]	22	11	░░
107	; The *p* variable is added to the *EDX* register.				
107	mov	BYTE PTR [edx], 021h	33	11	████
107	; The 0x21 value ('*!*') is written by the resulting offset.				

Fancy that! A single line of source code initiates three attempts to access the memory. First, the pswd pointer is loaded into the EDX register, then it is added to the p variable, also located in the memory. Only after this has been accomplished is the '!' (021h) constant written to the memory.

Why such a long time is required to load the pswd pointer remains unclear. One explanation might be that some process constantly removes pswd from cache, forcing the processor to access RAM. This is clearly not the case here. This program works with a small number of variables, which easily fit within L2 cache.

Type of Execution Time

If the execution time of a spot within a program is not constant but varies within certain limits (for example, depending on the type of the data being processed), then the profiling results become ambiguous, and the result itself is unreliable. To produce more accurate results from the analysis, it is necessary to take the following measures:

Find out if the program contains such "floating" spots and, if it does, *determine their execution times in the best, average, and worst cases.*

Few profilers are capable of measuring execution times for individual machine commands, measured in *clocks*. (Pentium-processor architectures use the term *retirement cycles*.) Fortunately, VTune is capable of doing this. Consider the log of dynamic assembly analysis that it has generated (Listing 1.4). In all likelihood, this will help solve the problem of the slow loading of the pswd pointer.

Listing 1.4. Execution Times for Machine Commands within the Profiled Code

Line	Instructions	Dyn-retirement cycles
107 pswd[p] = '!';		
107	mov edx, DWORD PTR [ebp+0ch]	13
107 ;	The *pswd* pointer is loaded into the *EDX* register.	
107	add edx, DWORD PTR [ebp-4]	2
107 ;	The *p* variable is added to the *EDX* register.	
107	mov BYTE PTR [edx], 021h	3
107 ;	The *'!'* value is written to *(pswd+p)*.	
109 y = y | y << 8;		
109	mov eax, DWORD PTR [ebp-28]	2
109 ;	The *y* variable is loaded into the *EAX* register.	
109	shl eax, 08h	1
109 ;	*EAX* is shifted left eight positions.	
109	mov ecx, DWORD PTR [ebp-28]	(0,7.3,80)
109 ;	The *y* variable is loaded into *ECX*.	
109	or ecx, eax	1
109 ;	*ECX = ECX | EAX (tmp = y | y)*	
109	mov DWORD PTR [ebp-28], ecx	1
109 ;	The result is written to *y*.	
110 x -= k;		
110	mov edx, DWORD PTR [ebp-24]	0

```
110 ;      The x variable is loaded into the EDX register.

110        sub     edx, DWORD PTR [ebp-36]       1  ▊
110 ;      The k variable is subtracted from the EDX register.

110        mov     DWORD PTR [ebp-24], edx       1  ▊
110 ;      The result is written to x.
```

The same difficulty has reappeared. The command loading the pswd pointer has consumed 13 processor clocks, but all other commands easily fit within a couple of clocks. Some commands are even completed with the previous instruction, thus requiring no clocks.

With the exception of the command that loads the contents of the y variable to the ECX register, the execution time of all commands is constant (i.e., it doesn't vary with the time). The command under consideration (mov ecx, DWORD PTR [ebp-28]) can take up to 80 clocks, depending on a number of yet unclear circumstances. This, of course, makes it the hottest spot of this code fragment. Eighty clocks is excessive! Although its average execution time is only seven clocks, and the minimum value is 0, it is necessary to find out why, for what purposes, and under which circumstances so many CPU cycles are required.

Penalty Information

The existence of the hotspot is evidence that something is wrong with the program. This might simply be an algorithmic error, which can be detected without using specialized tools. (As an example of this type of situation, the application's bottleneck might be the result of bubble sorting.) However, there may be no apparent reason why CPU time is being consumed. In the worst case, these leaks may not occur systematically; rather, they might take place under specific conditions that cannot be determined.

Now, return to the original question: Why does the pswd pointer load so slowly? Under which circumstances does its loading time increase so dramatically — from 7 clocks to 80? The most probable explanation is that something is wrong with two machine commands (MOV EDX, DWORD PTR [EBP+0ch] and MOV ECX, DWORD PTR [EBP-28]). Because of this, the processor has penalized them by temporarily delaying their execution. Is it possible to find out when this happened, and why? Without fully emulating the processor, it is unlikely (although contemporary x86 processors provide the possibility of collecting this information with some minor limitations).

Leading manufacturers, such as Intel and AMD, long ago released platform-specific profilers, which include full-featured emulators for their respective processors. These emulators allow the programmer to visualize the finest details of execution for each machine instruction.

For example, when working with VTune, if you simply click the mov ecx, DWORD PTR [ebp-28] line, the profiler will provide the following information:

Listing 1.5. Penalties for mov ecx, DWORD PTR [ebp-28], Displayed by VTune

---

```
Decoder Minimum Clocks = 1        ; Minimum time of decoding: 1 clock
Decoder Average Clocks = 8.7      ; Effective time of decoding: 8.7 clocks
Decoder Maximum Clocks = 86       ; Maximum time of decoding: 86 clocks


Retirement Minimum Clocks = 0     ; Minimum time of retirement: 0 clocks
Retirement Average Clocks = 7.3   ; Effective time of retirement: 7.3 clocks
Retirement Maximum Clocks = 80    ; Maximum time of retirement: 80 clocks


Total Cycles = 80 (00.65%)        ; Total time of execution: 80 clocks


Micro-Ops for this instruction = 1; Number of micro-ops per instruction: 1

The instruction had to wait 0 cycles for its sources to be ready.



Dynamic Penalty:  IC_miss
The instruction was not in the instruction cache, so the processor loaded
the instruction from L2 cache or the main memory.
Occurrences =  1                  ; This happened once.



Dynamic Penalty:  L2instr_miss
The instruction was not in L2 cache, so the processor loaded the instruc-
tion from the main memory.
Occurrences =  1                  ; This occurred once.



Dynamic Penalty:  Store_addr_unknown
The load instruction stalled because of the address calculation of the pre-
vious store instruction.
Occurrences =  10                 ; This occurred ten times.
```

Thus, the investigation turns into a sort of detective story, with enough complications to make Agatha Christie proud. If the obtained results are processed using even the simplest mathematical methods, the result will look like nonsense. Consider the situation: The total number of CPU cycles required for the instruction to execute is 80. You know that the instruction has been executed 11 times. (See the `Count` column in the profiler's report in Listing 1.3.) In the worst-case scenario, the instruction will require 80 clocks to execute. The longest period for decoding is even worse — 86 clocks. This means that *the longest of period of instruction decoding exceeds the total execution time*. As if these discrepancies weren't enough, the instruction loses at least one clock per iteration (this occurred ten times) because the address block was busy. Sorting this out is enough to cause brain damage.

The reason for such discrepancies lies in the concept of the relativity of the time. If you thought that this concept important only to the theories of the likes of Einstein, then you were mistaken. In pipelined processors (Pentium and AMD-K6/Athlon in particular) there is no such concept as "instruction execution time." (See *Pipelining, or Throughput vs. Latency*.) Because several instructions can be executed in parallel, a simple arithmetic total of their execution times will produce a larger result than these instructions require.

This topic will be covered in detail later. For now, just note that because the instruction is missing from cache (it resides on the boundary of two cache lines), it is necessary to load it from the main memory. Therefore, during the first iteration of the loop, it executes much slower than during all subsequent iterations. Hence, 80 cycles are required.

With more iterations (which can be quite numerous), you can ignore the time required for initial loading. But stop! The profiler has executed the body of this loop only 11 times. As a result, the average execution time for this instruction was 7.3 cycles, which doesn't correspond to reality.

Hmm... This "hotspot" is not a hotspot at all. There is nothing to optimize here. If the number of profiler runs is increased at least four times, the average run time for the instruction will drop to 1.8 clocks, making it one of the "coldest" spots in the program. This spot ultimately will have a value of absolute zero, because the effective run time of this instruction is zero clocks (i.e., it completes simultaneously with the previous machine command). Trying to optimize the program in this way is like trying to nail jelly to a tree.

This experience yields the following rule: *Before you start optimization, make sure that the number of runs is sufficient to mask the initial loading overhead.*

Now, briefly consider why such a situation occurred. By default, VTune runs the profiled fragment 1,000 times. Is this too many? Before you answer, realize that the intricate loop is organized to gain control every `'z'` - `'!'` == 0x59 iterations. During the entire interval of analysis, it will be executed only `1,000/89` == `11` times (Listing 1.6). This is not an artificial example. On the contrary, it occurs rather frequently.

Listing 1.6. Code with Infrequent-Run Fragments That Distort Profiling Results

```
while((++pswd[p])>'z')   // This loop was run 1,000 times by the profiler.
{
pswd[p] = '!';           // This instruction was run only 11 times.
...
}
```

Therefore, *having detected the hotspot for the first time, make sure that the number of times it runs is sufficient.* Otherwise, it is likely that the result will be incorrect. At this point, it is time to proceed with the discussion of the number of calls to each spot in the program.

The second hotspot still needs to be considered, as well as the surprisingly slow loading of the `pswd` pointer. Experienced programmers probably have guessed the reason for this delay.

The `pswd[p] = '!'` line is the first line of the loop body. It gains control every 0x59 iterations, which significantly exceeds the depth of the dynamic branching-prediction algorithm used by the processor to prevent the execution pipeline from becoming blocked.

Consequently, this branching is always predicted incorrectly, and the processor must start execution of this instruction from scratch. Note that the processor pipeline is rather long, so you must wait while it is filled. In reality, it is not the `mov edx, DWORD PTR [ebp+0ch]` command that is responsible for the drop in performance — any other command in its place would also run with similar inefficiency. The cause, which, like a soldering iron, makes this spot so "red-hot," resides somewhere else.

Move up a level to the conditional-jump instruction immediately preceding this command, and double-click it. VTune will provide the following information:

Listing 1.7. Penalties for the Conditional-Jump Instruction Preceding
`mov edx, DWORD PTR [ebp+0ch]`, **Displayed by VTune**

```
Decoder Minimum Clocks = 0      ; Minimum time of decoding: 0 clocks
Decoder Average Clocks = 0      ; Effective time of decoding: 0 clocks
Decoder Maximum Clocks = 4      ; Maximum time of decoding: 4 clocks

Retirement Average Clocks = 1   ; Effective time of retirement: 1 clock

Total Cycles = 1011 (08.20%)    ; Total time of execution: 1,011 clocks (8.2%)
```

```
Micro-Ops for this instruction = 1 ; Number of micro-ops per instruction: 1

The instruction had to wait (8,11.1,113) cycles for its sources to be ready.


Dynamic Penalty: BTB_Miss_Penalty ; Dynamic penalty of the BTB_Miss_Penalty type
This instruction stalled because the branch was predicted incorrectly.
Occurrences =  13                 ; This happened 13 times.
```

The hypothesis has been fully proven. This branching was predicted incorrectly 13 times, which the evidence generated by VTune confirms. Why, you might ask, does VTune indicate that this has occurred 13 times, when the loop body has been executed only 11 times? Yes, it runs only 11 times, but the processor couldn't predict this beforehand. It has attempted twice to pass control to this loop. After these attempts failed, it ceased its attempts to pass control to this branch.

So, one puzzle has been solved, and the problem has been located. However, there remains a more important question: How will the problem be solved? Fortunately, the unpredictable conditional jump is located close to the hotspot. This is not always the case. Frequently, the "responsible" instruction is located in different modules of the program. This needs no further comment, but it does warrant one recommendation: When profiling, always use a complex approach and your brain. This is the best advice you can take.

Note about the Number of Calls

As just demonstrated, determining the number of calls to the hotspot being profiled is necessary to determine if the measured data are reliable. It also is possible to evaluate the hotspot's "temperature" by the frequency of calls or by its execution time.

Suppose that you have two hotspots, both of which are consuming the same processor time. The first hotspot is called 100 times, but the second is called 100,000 times. It is at once clear that by optimizing the performance at the second hotspot by even 1%, you will see considerable overall performance growth. On the other hand, even if you manage to halve the run time of the first hotspot, there will be only a 25% increase in the speed of the program.

Often, it makes sense to inline frequently called functions (i.e., directly insert their code into the body of the other function, thus saving a certain amount of time).

Almost all profilers are designed to determine the number of calls. Therefore, this problem is not one that deserves special consideration.

Coverage Level

Strictly speaking, determining the coverage level has no direct relationship to program optimization. This is a secondary function of profilers. Nevertheless, because it is present, it should be considered at least briefly.

Coverage is the percentage of the program code executed during the profiling session. Who might need this information? For the most part, this information is of use to beta-testers. They need to make sure that the application code has been fully tested and no "dark" spots remain in it.

In addition, when you are optimizing a program, it is important to know which parts of the program were profiled and which were not. Otherwise, you might overlook most hotspots simply because their respective branches never gained control.

As an example, consider how the function-coverage protocol generated by profile.exe might look (Listing 1.8) for a test program: pswd.exe. (Details on the test program are in *Practical Profiling Session Using VTune.*)

Listing 1.8. Function-Coverage Protocol Generated by the profile.exe Profiler

---

```
Program Statistics                    ; Statistics on the profiled program
------------------

    Command line at 2002 Aug 20 03:36: pswd     ; Command line
    Call depth: 2                     ; Data on the call depth: 2
    Total functions: 5                ; Total number of functions: 5
    Function coverage: 60,0%          ; Functions covered: 60%


Module Statistics for pswd.exe        ; Statistics on the pswd module
------------------------------

    Functions in module: 5            ; Number of functions in the module: 5
    Module function coverage: 60,0%   ; Functions covered: 60%


Covered Function                      ; List of covered functions
----------------

    .      _DeCrypt (pswd.obj)
    .      __real@4@4008fa00000000000000 (pswd.obj)
    *      _gen_pswd (pswd.obj)
    *      _main (pswd.obj)
    *      _print_dot (pswd.obj)
```

This listing shows that only 60% of the functions gained control during the program's execution, meaning that the remaining 40% were not called. Clearly, it makes sense to find out if these functions are ever called or, conversely, if they are so-called dead code that can be deleted from the program, which may almost halve its size.

If these functions are given control under specific circumstances, it is necessary to analyze the source code to find out what circumstances result in calls to those functions. Reproducing these circumstances will enable the profiler to run other sections of the program. All of the names of covered and uncovered functions are listed in the `Covered Function` section. Covered functions are marked with the * character; uncovered ones are marked with the . character.

Generally, there are many specialized applications (such as NuMega Code Coverage), designed to solve this particular problem. These applications solve code-coverage problems much better than any profiler does.

Fundamental Problems of Microprofiling

Throughout this book, the term *microprofiling* will refer to measuring the run time for small code fragments (sometimes simply single commands).

Microprofiling brings with it a range of serious inherent problems that are difficult to eliminate. A lack of understanding about these problems often results in serious errors when interpreting the profiling results, and, consequently, in loss of time and poor optimization.

Pipelining, or Throughput vs. Latency

Pipelined systems have no concept such as "single command execution time." To illustrate this statement, consider the following analogy. Suppose that a factory produces 600 memory chips per hour. How long does it take to produce a single chip? Six seconds? No! The complete technological cycle takes months, rather than days or even seconds. This is not apparent because of the manufacturing pipeline, which divides the whole manufacturing process into individual stages. At any moment, at least one memory chip is passing through one of the individual stages.

The number of manufactured items produced by the pipeline per time unit is known as its *throughput*. It is simple to show that, generally, throughput is proportional to the inverse function of the duration of one production stage. The shorter each individual step, the more products manufactured. The number of these steps (the length of the pipeline) doesn't affect this aspect. Note that for almost all manufacturing processes, each stage represents an elementary operation. This is not because human beings perform routine work better than machines — on the contrary, they hate it.

This is for the simple reason that elementary operations take very little time, thus ensuring maximum throughput for the pipeline.

Processor manufacturers exploit the same approach. One visible trend is that the pipelines become longer with each new model. In the first models of Pentium processors, this length was only five stages. That number rose to 14 for Pentium II and, with Pentium 4, it has grown to 20. This shift was generated by a rapid growth in the processor's clock speed and, consequently, by the necessity to make the pipeline operate at this higher frequency.

This is all very well — the pipeline operates at an incredible speed, processing up to six micro-operations per clock. Does its length matter? It does! Returning to the factory analogy, suppose that the manufacturer wants to introduce a new model. When will it be able to produce the first items? The new model clearly won't be ready after six seconds nor after an hour of waiting. The manufacturer will have to wait until the whole technological cycle has been completed.

Latency — the time interval required to complete the production cycle — may have little influence on the technological process. (After all, new chips don't appear every day.) However, it has significant influence on the performance of a CPU that processes heterogeneous code comprising various, dissimilar fragments. The advancement of machine instructions along the pipeline faces several basic problems: The operands might not be ready, the executive device might be busy, an unexpected conditional jump might be encountered (similar to the reorientation of a factory to manufacture a new model), and so on. As a result, instead of continuous and smooth operation, lengthy downtime will occur. Occasionally, it will be interrupted by short spurts of action, immediately followed by another lengthy interval of idleness.

In the ideal case, the time required to execute a single instruction is determined by the pipeline throughput. In the worst case, the same value depends on the pipeline's latency. Since throughput and latency are values of different scales, it doesn't make any sense to speak about the average run time for an instruction. If you calculate this value, it will not correspond to reality. An unpleasant consequence of this is that it is impossible to determine the actual run time of a compact code section (unless processor emulation is used). *Until the execution time of the code section exceeds the pipeline's latency (30 clocks for P6), you won't be able to determine anything about the code, its execution time, or the pipeline.*

Measurement Inaccuracy

One of the fundamental differences between digital and analog devices is that the upper limit of measurement accuracy for digital devices is determined by the precision of the measuring instrument. (The precision of measurement by an analog instrument, on the contrary, increases with the number of measurements.)

How can you measure the run time of individual sections of a program? The IBM PC AT family provides two such mechanisms: a *system timer* (with a default frequency of 18.2 clocks per second, or 55 msec, and a maximum frequency of 1,193,180 clocks per second, or 0.84 nsec), and a *real-time* clock (a frequency of 1,024 clocks per second, or 0.98 msec). Additionally, processors in the Pentium family have a *Time Stamp Counter*, a register whose contents are incremented by 1 with each clock of the processor core.

Consider all of these mechanisms in detail. The system timer (including the time required to read measurements) provides an accuracy of about 5 msec, which means more than 2,000 clocks in a 500 MHz system. For the processor, this is an eternity. During this time, it is capable of processing enormous volumes of data, such as sorting about 1,500 numbers. Because of this, the *system timer is not suitable for profiling individual functions*. Do not, in particular, expect to find bottlenecks of the quick-sort function using this approach. Why do I bring up bottlenecks? Because, when the number of processed values is small, it cannot reliably determine even the total time required for sorting.

In addition, the system timer is not directly accessible under the right operating system. The minimum time interval that can be resolved by the `clock()` standard C function is only 0.01 sec. This interval is suitable only for measuring the run time of the whole program.

The precision of the real-time clock not comparable to that of the system timer (reprogrammed, of course).

Therefore, the Time Stamp Counter remains the only hope. After their initial acquaintance with it, most people are delighted: "Finally, Intel has given me something that I have dreamed about for so long." Consider for yourself: The operating systems of the Windows family (including Windows NT) provide unrestricted access to the `RDTSC` machine command, which reads the contents of this register. Because this register is increased incrementally with each clock, the programmer gets a *false impression* of the possibility of correctly determining the run time of each processor command.

As you know, in pipeline systems, there is no concept of command run time. Therefore, either throughput or latency has been encountered. The following question immediately arises: In reality, what value is measured using `RDTSC`? Original documentation from Intel doesn't answer this question directly. According to the available information, `RDTSC` reads the contents of the timer register at the instant when the instruction in question passes through the respective executive device. However, `RDTSC` is not an ordered command (i.e., it can be completed before the commands that precede it). This will be the case when the preceding command is idle because it is waiting for an operand.

Consider an extreme case that measures the run time for the minimum portion of code (Listing 1.9). (One machine command is required to save the value read during the first iteration.)

Listing 1.9. Attempt to Measure Execution Time of a Single Machine Command

---

```
RDTSC                      ; The time register value is read
                           ; and placed into the EDX and EAX registers.

MOV [clock], EAX           ; The lower double word or the time register
                           ; is saved in the clock variable.

RDTSC                      ; The time register is read again.

SUB EAX, [clock]           ; The difference between the first and
                           ; the second measurement is calculated.
```

When this example is run on PIII, the result will be 32 clocks. This, in turn, results in a reasonable question: "Why so many?" I'll return to the problem of processor clock leakage later. For now, try to measure the run time for a machine command (such as INC EAX, which incrementally increases the EAX value by 1). Place this command between two RDTSC instructions and recompile the program.

Surprisingly enough, the test run produces the same result — 32 clocks. Strange. Add an extra INC EAX command. Once again, the test produces the same result — 32 clocks. How can this be? If you add *three* INC EAX instructions, the run time will be increased by 1 clock — and the result will be 33 clocks. Four and five INC EAX instructions will produce the same result, but after you add a sixth instruction, the measurement result again will be increased by one clock.

However, the Pentium processor has only one Arithmetic Logical Unit (ALU); therefore, it cannot execute more than one additional operation per clock. The obtained result — three commands per clock — represents the rate of their *decoding*, rather than the rate of their execution. To confirm this statement, launch the following loop for execution:

Listing 1.10. Time Required To Execute 6x1000 INC Machine Commands

---

```
MOV ECX,1000      ; The 1000 value is placed into the ECX register.

@for:             ; Label marking start of the loop

INC EAX           ;
INC EAX           ; First group of profiled instructions
INC EAX           ;

INC EAX           ;
```

```
INC EAX             ; Second group of profiled instructions
INC EAX             ;

DEC ECX             ; The EAX value is decreased by 1.
                    ; (Here, EAX is used as loop counter.)

JNZ @xxx            ; A jump is made to the @for label,
                    ; as long as ECX does not reach zero.
```

When this loop is run on PIII, the execution of Listing 1.10 will require 6,781 clocks per machine instruction, rather than the approximately 2,000 clocks as expected. Consequently, when measuring the time required for the execution of several machine commands, the RDTSC instruction prematurely reports the expected result, rushing like a willing horse before the cart.

Thus, it would be useful some method existed for delaying the execution of the RDTSC command until all preceding machine instructions have been completed. There is such a method! Simply place one of the ordered execution commands before RDTSC. Ordered execution commands are processed only after the last preceding unordered command leaves the pipeline. Until the ordered command is completed, all of the commands following it will wait.

Most ordered commands are *privileged commands* (for example, I/O port reading instructions). Only a few of them are available at the application level. The CPUID instruction, in particular, belongs to this set of commands.

Most manuals (such as *How To Optimize for the Pentium Microprocessors* by Agner Fog and Intel's official document titled *Using the RDTSC Instruction for Performance Monitoring*) suggest using the following code:

Listing 1.11. Official Recommendation for Calling RDTSC To Measure Run Time

```
XOR EAX, EAX        ; The CPUID machine command is called
CPUID               ; to ensure that all preceding commands
                    ; have left the pipeline
                    ; and, therefore, cannot influence
                    ; the measurement results.

RDTSC               ; The RDTSC instruction is called,
                    ; which returns to the EAX register
                    ; the lower double word of the current value
                    ; of the Time Stamp Counter.

MOV [clock], EAX    ; The obtained result is saved
```

```
                          ; to the clock variable.

// ...                    ;
// profiled code          ; Here, the profiled code is run.
// ...                    ;

XOR EAX, EAX              ; The CPUID command is executed again
CPUID                     ; to ensure that all preceding instructions
                          ; have left the pipeline.

RDTSC                     ; The RDTSC instruction is called to read
                          ; the new value of the Time Stamp Counter.

SUB EAX, [clock]          ; The difference is calculated between
                          ; the first and the second measurements,
                          ; thus defining the actual time
                          ; required to execute the code fragment.
```

Unfortunately, this officially recommended code is not suitable for measuring the run time of individual instructions; it produces the *full run time* of the instruction (i.e. its latency), rather than the throughput.

 Note

The example program in Listing 1.11 doesn't contain an explicit specification of the argument that CPUID expects to read from the EAX register. This argument must be specified before the CPUID instruction. Because an instruction's run time depends on its argument, the run time of the profiled fragment is not constant. Rather, it depends on the state of the registers at the input and output. Listing 1.10 explicitly initializes EAX, preventing various side effects that can affect the profiler.

There is another, more serious problem: One of the basic rules of quantum physics is that any measurement of an object's properties inevitably introduces changes into that object. The changes, in turn, distort the result of the measurements. As a further complication, these distortions cannot be eliminated by simple calibration because they can be both quantitative and qualitative.

If the profiled code exploits the same processor units as the RDTSC and CPUID commands, its measured run time can differ considerably from the actual value. No sophisticated measures can achieve the precision of measurement of one or two clocks.

Because of these factors, in my experience, the minimum time interval that can be measured with any certainty is no less than 50 to 100 clocks.

Hence, it is impossible to measure the execution time of an individual command using standard processor tools.

Hardware Optimization

Forget computers for a moment. Instead, try to answer the following question: Is it possible to measure the thickness of a normal paper sheet using a standard ruler or measuring tape? At first, it may seem that this task cannot be completed without special tools. However, if you take a stack of about 50 sheets of paper... You get the point. Even if the measurement error is ±1 mm, the precision of measurement for an individual sheet will be no worse than ±0.02 mm, which is a sufficient margin of error for most calculations.

Why can't this approach be used to measure the run times of individual machine commands? The run time of a single command is so small that there is no way to measure it. (See *Measurement Inaccuracy*.) However, if you take a few hundred or, even better, a few hundred thousand of such commands, then... Eureka! However, note that the nonuniformity of the pipeline results in a nonlinear dependency between the number of commands and their run times.

You might think that contemporary processors are too intellectual to interpret literally the code being processed. This is not the case. They are creative and inventive when performing this task. Consider a situation in which the processor encounters the following sequence of commands: MOV EAX, 1; MOV EAX, 1; MOV EAX, 1. Each command places the value of 1 into the EAX register. The processor is not "dumb" enough to execute all three commands. Because the results of first two assignments are not used, the processor will dismiss these commands as unneeded. Thus, it will spend time only on command decoding, saving a lot of time in execution.

Code optimization performed by the processor at the hardware level considerably improves overall system performance, decreasing the actual run time of machine commands. The precise amount of time can be measured that it took the processor to execute a code fragment comprising a thousand specific commands. However, you need to interpret the results carefully in relation to the evaluation of the run time of an individual command.

Low Resolution

The throughput of most instructions takes one clock, and that the minimum time interval that can be measured is about 50 to 100 clocks. Therefore, the resolution limit for profilers without emulation is 50 commands.

From this point on, the term *resolution* will refer to the length of the hotspot, more or less reliably recognized by the profiler. Strictly speaking, profilers without emulation detect a lengthy area to which the hotspot belongs, rather than the hotspot.

Fundamental Problems of Macroprofiling

The term *macroprofiling* is used in this book to designate measurements of the run time of structural program units (functions, repeatedly executed loops, etc.), and sometimes, even that of the entire program.

Macroprofiling has inherent problems. These include inconsistency of run time, the necessity of a "second pass," and various side effects.

Run-Time Inconsistencies

If you have some experience with the profiling of applications, you likely have encountered run-time inconsistencies. The results of run-time measurements vary from run to run, and sometimes can differ greatly.

There are at least two reasons for these differences: *software inconsistency* (in multitasking operating systems, particularly Windows, the profiled program is influenced strongly by an extremely varied environment), and *hardware inconsistency* (caused by the internal "multitasking" of the hardware).

Both these reasons will be covered in detail because of their significant effect on profiling results.

Software Inconsistency

In a multitasking environment, of which Windows — today's most popular operating system — is a good example, no program has exclusive access to all system resources; it has to share them with other tasks. This means that the speed of execution of the profiled program is not constant, but depends heavily on the existing environment. In practice, the resulting dissipation can effect the values by 10% to 15% and sometimes more, especially if other resource-consuming tasks are running simultaneously.

Still, this doesn't present a problem. It is enough just to make several test runs within each profiling session, and then *choose the measurement with the shortest run time*. The idea of this approach is as follows: Performance measurements are not normal instrumental measurements, and typical rules of measurement are not applicable here. The processor never makes errors, and each obtained measurement result is accurate. It is, to some degree, distorted by side effects. Therefore, *the fastest run* (the one with minimum run time) *represents the result least distorted by side effects*.

By the way, most manuals recommend that, before profiling, you disconnect from the network (so the machine won't receive network packets), close all applications (except the profiler), and even reboot. This is overkill! I often profile programs while working in Microsoft Word, receiving mail, downloading files from the Internet, etc. The profiling results I obtain during these activities are always satisfactory. Of course, it makes sense to close applications running in parallel if you don't need them. However, there is no need to make the situation absurd by attempting to ensure an absolutely "sterile" environment.

Hardware Inconsistency

This might seem strange, but at the hardware level, the run time of the same operations is not constant. The run time is subject to dispersions, which are sometimes significant and can exceed software inconsistency. In contrast to software inconsistency, which can be eliminated (for example, by running the program in a single-user mode), *hardware inconsistency cannot be eliminated.*

Why does this problem arise? There are various reasons. If the system bus frequency doesn't match the frequency of the RAM chips, the chipset will have to wait a random time interval for the arrival of the leading front of the next clock pulse. Depending on the type of RAM chips, each burst cycle takes approximately five to nine clocks, and it is necessary to synchronize both the start and the end. A simple calculation show that, in the worst case, the discrepancy will be 25% to 40%.

The most interesting fact here is that hardware inconsistency can differ greatly from system to system. Unfortunately, I haven't had any success in determining a reason for this. Nevertheless, I know that on Pentium III 733/133/100/I815EP, the hardware inconsistency rarely exceeds 1% to 2%, despite the difference in system bus frequency and RAM frequency. Therefore, in this case, it is negligible.

The situation is different for AMD Athlon 1050/100/100/VIA KT 133. This processor produces an enormous discrepancy, which sometimes more than doubles the time during operations with RAM. On such a system, it is impossible to profile programs. In particular, sequential measurements of the time required to copy a 16 MB memory block might appear as follows (after discarding extreme values):

Listing 1.12. Time Required To Copy a 16 MB Memory Block

```
Run № 01: 84445103  clocks
Run № 02: 83966665  clocks
Run № 03: 73795939  clocks
Run № 04: 80323626  clocks
Run № 05: 84381967  clocks
Run № 06: 85262076  clocks
Run № 07: 85151531  clocks
```

```
Run № 08: 91520360   clocks
Run № 09: 92603591   clocks
Run № 10: 100651353  clocks
Run № 11: 93811801   clocks
Run № 12: 84993464   clocks
Run № 13: 92927920   clocks
```

Here, the discrepancy between the minimum and maximum run times is at least 36%. This means that you will be unable to detect hotspots of a lower "temperature." Furthermore, you won't be able to evaluate the influence of specific optimizing algorithms unless there is at least a twofold improvement in performance.

Hence, the following conclusions: Not every system is suitable for profiling and optimizing applications, and if sequential measurements produce significant discrepancies, simply replace the system. (In this case, the term *system* designates computer hardware, rather than the operating system.)

Processing the Measurement Results

As previously shown, "raw" measurement results obtained for program run time require processing before they can be used. It is necessary at least to discard marginal values caused by unexpected side effects (such as when the OS starts to flush data to the disk at the most vital moment of profiling). Then, a difficult choice arises: Either use the result with the shortest run time (as the result least influenced by multitasking), or calculate the typical run time (as the real-world result, rather than one generated under ideal laboratory conditions).

I have successfully tested and used a mixed approach, combining both methods. I recommend working on the basis of an average minimal run time. The general algorithm is as follows: Perform N runs of the profiled program, then discard the $N/3$ maximum and $N/3$ minimum measurement results. For the remaining $N/3$ measurements, it is necessary to calculate the average value, assumed to be the realistic result. The value of N varies with the situation. Usually, 9 to 12 runs are sufficient because a larger sample of runs doesn't improve the accuracy of the result appreciably.

One possible implementation of this algorithm is shown in Listing 1.13.

Listing 1.13. Calculating the Typical Average Execution Time

```
unsigned int cycle_mid(unsigned int *buff, int nbuff)
{
int a, xa=0;
if (!nbuff) nbuff=A_NITER;
```

```
buff = buff + 1;    nbuff--;   // The first element is excluded.

if (getargv("$NoSort", 0)==-1)
qsort(buff, nbuff, sizeof(int), \
      (int (*)(const void *, const void*))(_compare));

for (a = nbuff/3; a < (2*nbuff/3); a++)
   xa += buff[a];

xa /= (nbuff/3);

return xa;
}
```

Second-Pass Problem

To achieve an acceptable level of precision in the measurement results, it is necessary to run the profiled application at least nine times. (See *Run-Time Inconsistencies.*) Note that each run must be performed under similar circumstances and a similar environment. This raises a problem: Without developing a full-featured emulator of the whole system, this requirement practically cannot be fulfilled. The disk cache, the CPU caches of both levels, the Translation Look-aside Buffer (TLB), and the branch history complicate program profiling, because the repetition of runs greatly reduces the run time.

If you profile a loop that is repeated several times, you can ignore this factor; the time required to load data and/or code into cache usually has little effect on the total run time of the loop. Unfortunately, this is not always true. (See *Penalty Information.*)

Sometimes, however, you may wish to optimize the application initialization. Although it is executed once per session, it is an annoyance if a program's startup procedure lasts several minutes or longer. It is possible to reboot the system, but this will stretch out the process of profiling unnecessarily.

The solution — clearing the data cache — is an easily performed task. All you need to do is read a memory block that greatly exceeds the cache size. It also makes sense to write a large block to flush all of the write buffers. (See *Working Principles of Cache.*) This operation, by the way, will also clear the TLB — the buffer-storing memory pages for quick access. Similar procedures can be used to clear the code's cache or TLB. It is enough to generate a large function, with a size of 1 MB to 4 MB, that doesn't do anything. (For example, you can fill it with NOP commands.) All of these steps will reduce the previously described negative effects. Unfortunately, it is impossible to eliminate these negative effects completely; some phenomena can't be controlled directly or indirectly (at least, at the application level).

If you are optimizing an individual function (such as a string reverse function), then its first run won't generate any useful results. This is because the efficiency of the function's code or algorithm determines the performance. Overhead related to loading machine instructions into cache, assigning and mapping of pages by the operating system, loading functions into cache, etc., in real programs, usually is eliminated beforehand (even if the function is called only once).

Run the following experiment. Take the function in Listing 1.14, and run it ten times sequentially, measuring the execution time during each run.

Listing 1.14. Function That Accesses Only Once Each Cell Loaded into Cache

```
#define a (int *)((int)p + x)
A_BEGIN(0)
#define b (int *)((int)p + BLOCK_SIZE - x - sizeof(int))
for (x = 0; x < BLOCK_SIZE/2; x+=sizeof(int))
{
    #ifdef __OVER_BRANCH__
        if (x & 1)
    #endif
        *a = *a^*b; *b = *b^*a; *a = *a^*b;
}
A_END(0)
```

On Pentium III 733/133/100/I815EP, for memory blocks that fit within L1 cache, the following result is obtained:

Listing 1.15. Results from the Function for Memory Blocks That Fit in L1 Cache

__OVER_BRANCH__ not defined	__OVER_BRANCH__ defined
68586	63788
17629	18507
17573	18488
17573	18488
17573	18488
17573	18488
17573	18488
17573	18488

Note that the time required for the first run of this function (do not confuse it with the run time of the first loop iteration) is almost four times as long as all subsequent runs. Measurement results can vary unpredictably from 62,190 to 91,873 clocks, meaning the margin of error is about 50%. If this loop is only executed once, does it make sense to try to optimize it? Yes, it does! As an example, get rid of this XOR crankiness and exchange these two array elements using a temporary variable, as most practical people would do. This will reduce the time of the first run to between 47,603 and 65,577 clocks, improving the efficiency by 20% to 40%.

Nevertheless, stable repetition of the results begins only from the third run. The first run is slow for obvious reasons (loading data into cache, etc.). Why is the second run also slow, and what prevents it from being faster? In practice, these are branches. During the first run, the dynamic branch prediction mechanism has not collected sufficient information. Therefore, during the second run, it still produces mistakes. However, beginning with the third run, it finally understands the situation and begins to work as expected.

Thus, when profiling functions that run repeatedly, the results of the first two or three runs must be discarded. You should never use them when you are calculating an average value.

On the contrary, when profiling functions that run once within the profiled program, it is necessary to pay attention only to the run time of the first run and discard all other results. In subsequent runs, it is necessary to clear all types of cache and all buffers, which distort the actual performance.

Side Effects

When specific errors are corrected, others often are introduced. Therefore, after any code modification, regardless of how insignificant it might seem, it is necessary to repeat the whole profiling session.

Listing 1.16 illustrates this. Consider a situation where the optimized program contains a function similar to the one presented here.

Listing 1.16. Fragment in which Discarding Redundant Code Might Significantly and Unexpectedly Degrade Performance

---

```
ugly_func(int foo)
{
    int a;
    ...
    ...
    ...
    if (foo<1) return ERR_FOO_MUST_BE_POSITIVE;
```

```
for(a=1; a <= foo; a++)
{
    ...
    ...
    ...
}
}
```

If you attempt to pass 0 or a negative value to this function, the `for_a` loop will never be executed and, consequently, the forced argument check (highlighted in bold within the listing) makes no sense. When `foo` values are large enough, the overhead is irrelevant. Can this line be removed without slowing the function?

This isn't a crazy question, and it isn't a theoretic abstraction. It is possible that the removal of this line will produce an effect opposite of the one expected. Instead of function optimization, it will reduce the speed of the function's execution.

How can this be? It's simple: If the compiler doesn't align loops in memory (this applies to Microsoft Visual C++), a cache conflict, subject to penalty, likely will occur. (See *Working Principles of Cache.*) Nevertheless, there might be situations when this conflict simply doesn't occur. This matter may as well depend on the phases of the moon. Perhaps this senseless argument check (executed only once) saved the whole loop from penalty delays that arise in *each* iteration.

These factors relate not only to the elimination of the redundant code, but also to any code modification that changes the code size. During optimization, the code performance can change drastically. It can both decrease and improve unexpectedly, without any visible reason. The most inconvenient circumstance is most compilers do not have the capability to manage code alignment. Thus, if the loop fits into "inconvenient" memory addresses (from the processor's point of view), the only solutions are to add an extra code fragment to the program that moves the loop out of unfavorable conditions, or simply to change the program code by choosing a better combination.

If you think this situation is idiotic, you're probably right. Fortunately, compilers such as Microsoft Visual C++ align functions by addresses that are multiples of 0x20 (which corresponds to the length of a single cache line in processors such as P6 and K6). This eliminates the mutual influence of functions and limits the area of command change to a single function.

The same relates to the size of processed data blocks, the number and types of variables, etc. A decrease in the amount of required memory often results in conflicts of specific types, which, in turn, result in a degradation of performance. Note that when dealing with global and/or dynamic variables, you are not limited to the range of a specific function; rather, you are limited to the effect on the program as a whole. (See *Strategy of Data Distribution over DRAM Banks.*)

Three rules must be observed when profiling large programs, especially those ones developed independently by a number of individuals. Imagine a situation in which you notice that, after you introduce several "improvements," the performance of your code fragment drops significantly and unexpectedly. Nothing you do (including a rollback to the previous version) brings back the performance provided by earlier versions. The next day, however, the performance level has been restored without any visible explanation. Perhaps a colleague has changed his or her module, and this has influenced your part of the program.

The three rules are as follows:

❏ Never optimize a program "blindly," relying only on common sense and intuition.
❏ Test each modification that you introduce using the profiler. If the application's performance drops unexpectedly, instead of improving, investigate. Ask the following questions: Which code fragments are responsible? What is the reason? Don't limit yourself to your code; investigate the whole application.
❏ After you have completed the optimization of the local code fragment, perform a test profiling of the whole program. Try to detect new hotspots that can appear where they are least expected.

Problems of Code Optimization on Individual Machines

Most programmers, especially freelancers, usually have a couple of machines on which the whole software-development cycle takes place — from initial design to debugging and optimization. The hardware configurations of these computers usually are different. The code optimized for one platform can be inefficient on other. Data-flow planning illustrates this point. (See *Planning Data Flows.*) Consider the specific features of data prefetching in the VIA KT 133 chipset, which result in an unexpected performance drop when several proximate processes are executed simultaneously. This difficulty is not reflected in the documentation and cannot be predicted by calculation. Instead, it can be detected experimentally.

Profiling a program on a single machine will not allow you to detect all the bottlenecks of the algorithm. At minimum, it is necessary to cover three or four typical configurations, paying attention not only to processors, but to chipsets as well. By doing so, you will provide some kind of insurance against surprises, such as the previously mentioned "features" of the VIA KT 133 chipset.

It is impossible to find a combined solution that fits all existing platforms.

Brief Overview of Contemporary Profilers

Profilers are not numerous. Therefore, programmers don't face many problems in choosing a profiler.

If optimization isn't your main field of interest, and efficiency isn't crucial, then you will be satisfied with any available profiler — such as the one supplied with your compiler of choice. More sophisticated profilers will be a burden, because you won't be using their full capabilities and potential, which requires a sound knowledge of processor architecture and computer hardware.

However, if the performance of your programs and the quality of their optimization is of primary interest to you and you plan to dedicate a lot of time to profiling, Intel VTune and AMD Code Analyst are far and away the best options. Pay specific attention to the previous statement: "Intel VTune *and* AMD Code Analyst," rather than "Intel VTune *or* AMD Code Analyst." Each profiler supports only its native processor. Thus, using only one of them, you won't be able to optimize the code for both platforms (i.e., each of them will do no more than half of the job).

Intel VTune

VTune is the most powerful profiler to date for the IBM PC platform. It shouldn't be classified simply as a profiler; VTune is an intellectual tool with functions beyond hotspot detection. Beside detecting hotspots, VTune is capable of providing helpful tips and offering advice about the elimination of hotspots. Additionally, VTune provides a powerful code optimizer that is capable of increasing the performance of programs compiled with Microsoft Visual C++ 6.0 by approximately 20%. This is clearly a welcome improvement.

The list of advantages provided by VTune is so comprehensive that it should be considered the market leader, with practically no alternative. Nevertheless, no program is free of drawbacks.

One of the main disadvantages of VTune is its enormous size (version 6, the most recent at the time of writing, takes about 150 MB of space). Its price is also rather high.

Another shortcoming is that VTune isn't always stable; sometimes it can crash the system. I often encounter the following situation: After activating some performance counters, Windows crashes and displays the "Blue Screen of Death." (The most common error message is `IRQL_NOT_LESS_OR_EQUAL`.) Nevertheless, if you think over each of your actions carefully, stability should not be a problem.

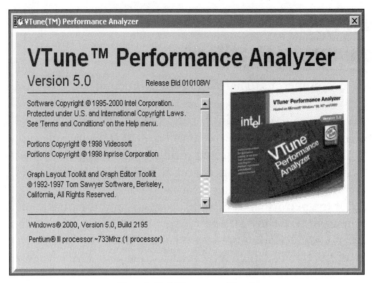

Fig. 1.3. VTune profiler logo

Further, VTune is rather complicated. Sometimes it might seem that it is impossible to master it and achieve a sound understanding of all its features. Even the built-in help system occupies more than a thousand pages (A4 format). Careful reading will take you at least a month! However, you should consider this problem from another point of view. What instrument do you need: a powerful tool, or a toy for beginners? If you need a tool, then the more powerful instrument you choose, the more sophisticated it will be. In my opinion, VTune is no more complicated than the most popular development environments, such as Visual C++ or Delphi. Hence, the problem is the lack of comprehensive literature on profiling in general — and this product in particular — rather than that VTune is complex and difficult to master. Therefore, this book includes a short, self-study guide on VTune, which you will find in this chapter under *Practical Profiling Session Using VTune.* I hope that this information will be helpful to you.

AMD Code Analyst

Code Analyst is inferior to its nearest competitor — VTune — on several counts. I wouldn't recommend it as a main profiler. Although I'm exposing myself to the risk of being attacked by aggressive AMD fans, the following is a list of the chief drawbacks of Code Analyst:

❑ Code Analyst requires that debugging information be present in the program being profiled. It will refuse to load a program without debug information. However, the majority of compilers never place debugging information into optimized programs. This is because optimization introduces key changes into the source code, destroying the direct mapping between numbers of code lines and generated machine instructions. In practice, the program before optimization and the program after optimization are two different programs, with different, although intersecting, subsets of hotspots. *Profiling a nonoptimized version of the program doesn't allow you to detect and eliminate all of the bottlenecks in the real application.* (When optimization is disabled, you might find nonexistent hotspots.)

❐ The resolution of Code Analyst's diagrams is limited by the lines of source code, rather than by machine commands (in contrast to VTune). Further, although, in principle, Code Analyst can measure the time required to execute each instruction, it doesn't provide any mechanisms for detecting hotspots at this level. The detection of "heavy" machine commands must be done manually, by viewing the Cycle per Instruction (CPI) column. Even relatively small code sections can have several thousand machine commands. This tedious analysis method can consume a lot of time.

Fig. 1.4. AMD Code Analyst logo

❐ Code Analyst doesn't provide any tips about the elimination of detected bottlenecks. This is unsatisfactory for most programmers.

❐ This profiler is inconvenient to use. It has a limited set of context menus, a rather ascetic interface that lacks configuration capabilities, and little capability for saving the profiling history.

Despite these drawbacks, Code Analyst has some advantages. It is small. (At the time of writing, its latest version, 1.1.0, required only 16 MB, approximately ten times less than VTune.) It is reliable and stable. Most importantly, it provides a fully functional emulator for AMD processors such as K6-2, Athlon (with external and on-die cache types), and Duron, including their mobile implementations. Furthermore, it allows manual selection of bus and core frequencies. This feature is useful for assessing the influence of the bus frequency on performance, which is especially important for applications that work intensely with RAM. (VTune lacks this feature.) Code Analyst also has a clearly written help system. It describes a processor's bottlenecks briefly, but in clear and readily understandable language. And unlike VTune, it is, for now, freeware.

In the long run, however, it doesn't matter whether you like or dislike this profiler. You must use it to optimize your applications if you want them to run on Athlon processors, which occupy a large segment of the market.

Microsoft's Profile.exe

The next profiler, Microsoft's profile.exe, is so simple and unsophisticated that it doesn't even have a product name. Throughout this book, I will refer to it using the name of its executable file. Profile.exe is a small profiler that provides minimum functionality. It is considered in this overview only because it is included with Microsoft Visual C++ compilers (Professional and Enterprise Editions). Thus, most programmers using Visual C++ compilers get this profiler along with their development environment; other profilers must be purchased or downloaded from the Internet.

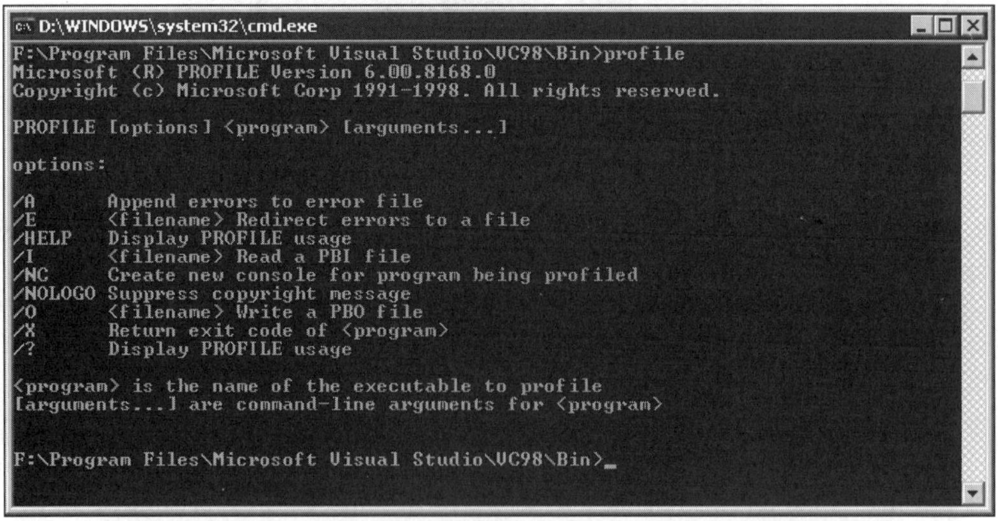

Fig. 1.5. Copyright information displayed by Microsoft's profile.exe

Writing Your Own Profiler

Why do you need to develop your own profiler if such tools are supplied with most compilers? If the functions provided by built-in profilers prove to be insufficient, you can use Code Analyst and VTune, right?

Unfortunately, the built-in profiler supplied with Microsoft Visual Studio (like most similar profilers) uses a system timer for time measurement; therefore, its sensitivity is usually insufficient. VTune is large and expensive; the Code Analyst freeware is inconvenient (and may cease to be a freeware program in the future). All of these factors prevent me from using these profilers as my main instrument, and you may feel the same way.

The program I recommend — DoCPU Clock — can't be classified as a profiler in the general sense of this term. It doesn't detect hotspots, doesn't calculate the number of calls, and can't even work with executable files. DoCPU Clock is nothing more than a small set of macros intended for inclusion in the source code of a program. These macros determine the time required to execute profiled code fragments. For the purposes of this book, these limited capabilities are sufficient. All that is needed here is an evaluation of the influence of specific optimizing algorithms on program performance.

Practical Profiling Session Using VTune

Almost any instrument will be useless if you don't know how to work with it. The VTune profiler can't be classified as an intuitive product that you can master simply by trying to use it. VTune is a professional instrument, which requires special training for proper usage. Otherwise, most of its capabilities will remain unnoticed, possibly leaving the developer asking in astonishment: "Why do people like VTune?"

This section isn't a detailed guide, but it should help you to take your first steps in mastering VTune and get acquainted with its main functional abilities. Besides this, you should decide whether you are going to work with VTune or choose a simpler profiler.

As a test program for experiments with profiling and optimization, I will use a simple password cracker. Why a password cracker? First, it is an illustrative and realistic example. Second, such applications have the highest performance requirements. Although I anticipate indignation from some readers, I'd like to mention this example will not deal cracking real ciphers and passwords. The algorithm implemented in this program is never used in the real world. Besides this, it is vulnerable to quick and efficient attacks that crack the ciphertext within a few seconds.

This book is interested in hotspot detection and elimination, rather than in password cracking. Because of this, even those who consider all investigators to be hackers, and all hackers to be criminals, can type in the following source code without injuring their puritan sensibilities:

Listing 1.17. [Profile/pswd.c] Password Cracker before Optimization

```
//----------------------------------------------------------------------
// This example illustrates the worst practices of software development!
// It contains many of errors that have a negative effect on performance.
// Profiling will eliminate all of them.
// ----------------------------------------------------------------------
// CONFIGURATION
#define ITER 100000           // Maximum number of iterations
#define MAX_CRYPT_LEN  200    // Maximum length of the ciphertext

// Decrypting ciphertext using the found password
DeCrypt(char *pswd, char *crypteddata)
{
int a;
int p = 0;            // Pointer to the current position within the data

// * * * MAIN DECRYPTION LOOP * * *
do {
    // Decrypting the current character
    crypteddata[p] ^= pswd[p % strlen(pswd)];

// Decrypting the next character
} while(++p < strlen(crypteddata));
}

// Calculating the password checksum
int CalculateCRC(char *pswd)
{
int a;
int x = -1;           // CRC calculation error

for (a = 0; a < strlen(pswd);  a++) x += *(int *)((int)pswd + a);
return x;
```

```
}
// The CRC calculation algorithm is awkward.
// This was done intentionally to demonstrate misalignment.

// Checking the password CRC
int CheckCRC(char *pswd, int validCRC)
{
 if (CalculateCRC(pswd) == validCRC)
    return validCRC;
 // else
    return 0;
}

// Processing the current password
do_pswd(char *crypteddata, char *pswd, int validCRC, int progress)
{
 char *buff;

 // Displaying the current state on the terminal
 printf("Current pswd : %10s [%d%%]\r", &pswd[0], progress);

 // Checking the password CRC
 if (CheckCRC(pswd, validCRC))
 {                                // CRC match

    // Copying ciphertext to the temporary buffer
    buff = (char *) malloc(strlen(crypteddata));
    strcpy(buff, crypteddata);

    // Decrypting
    DeCrypt(pswd, buff);

    // Displaying the decryption results
    printf("CRC %8X: try to decrypt: \"%s\"\n",
             CheckCRC(pswd, validCRC), buff);
 }
}

// Password generation procedure
```

```
int gen_pswd(char *crypteddata, char *pswd, int max_iter, int validCRC)
{
int a;
int p = 0;

// Generating passwords
for(a = 0; a < max_iter; a++)
{

    // Processing the current password
    do_pswd(crypteddata, pswd, validCRC, 100*a/max_iter);

    // * Main loop of password generation *
    // Using the "counter" algorithm
    while((++pswd[p])>'z')
    {
        pswd[p] = '!';
        p++; if (!pswd[p])
        {
            pswd[p] = ' ';
            pswd[p+1] = 0;
        }
    }                   // end while(pswd)

    // Returning the pointer to initial position
    p = 0;
}                       // end for(a)
return 0;
}

// Displaying the number, using DOT as a delimiter
print_dot(float per)
{

// * * * CONFIGURATION * * *
#define N 3           // Separating three positions
#define DOT_SIZE 1    // Size of the DOT delimiter
#define   DOT "."     // Delimiter
int     a;
char    buff[666];
```

```
    sprintf(buff,"%0.0f", per);
    for(a = strlen(buff) - N; a > 0; a -= N)
    {
        memmove(buff + a + DOT_SIZE, buff + a, 66);
        if(buff[a]==' ') break;
            else
        memcpy(buff + a, DOT, DOT_SIZE);
    }

    // Displaying on the screen
    printf("%s\n", buff);
}


main(int argc, char **argv)
{

    // Variables
    FILE *f;             // For reading the source file (if present)
    char *buff;          // For reading data from the source file
    char *pswd;          // Currently tested password (needed by gen_pswd)
    int validCRC;        // For storing the original password CRC
    unsigned int t;      // For measuring the execution time
    int iter = ITER;     // Maximum number of passwords
    char *crypteddata;   // For storing the ciphertext

    // built-in default crypt
    // Those who read this text have discovered a great secret. ;)
    char _DATA_[] = "\x4B\x72\x69\x73\x20\x4B\x61\x73\x70\x65\x72\x73\x6B"\
    "\x79\x20\x44\x65\x6D\x6F\x20\x43\x72\x79\x70\x74\x3A"\
    "\xB9\x50\xE7\x73\x20\x39\x3D\x30\x4B\x42\x53\x3E\x22"\
    "\x27\x32\x53\x56\x49\x3F\x3C\x3D\x2C\x73\x73\x0D\x0A";

    // Title
    printf("= = = VTune profiling demo = = =\n"\
            "================================\n");

    // Help
    if (argc==2)
    {
            printf("USAGE:\n\tpswd.exe [StartPassword MAX_ITER]\n");
            return 0;
    }
```

```
// Memory allocation
printf("memory malloc\t\t");
buff = (char *) malloc(MAX_CRYPT_LEN);
if (buff) printf("+OK\n"); else {printf("-ERR\n"); return -1;}

// Getting the ciphertext for decryption
printf("get source from\t\t");
if (f=fopen("crypted.dat", "r"))
{
   printf("crypted.dat\n");
   fgets(buff, MAX_CRYPT_LEN, f);
}
else
{
   printf("built-in data\n");
   buff=_DATA_;
}

// Calculating CRC
validCRC=*(int *)((int) strstr(buff, ":")+1);
printf("calculate CRC\t\t%X\n", validCRC);
if (!validCRC)
{
   printf("-ERR: CRC is invalid\n");
   return -1;
}

// Extracting the encrypted data
crypteddata=strstr(buff,":") + 5;
// printf("cryptodata\t\t%s\n", crypteddata);

// Allocating memory for the password buffer
printf("memory malloc\t\t");
pswd = (char *) malloc(512*1024); pswd+=62;
// The consequences of misaligned data, when requesting blocks
// of a chosen size, are demonstrated. The malloc function
// always aligns the address by the desired 64 KB.

memset(pswd,0,666);            // Initialization

if (pswd) printf("+OK\n"); else {printf("-ERR\n"); return -1;}
```

```
// Parsing command line arguments, and getting the
// initial password and maximum number of iterations
printf("get arg from\t\t");
if (argc>2)
{
    printf("command line\n");
    if(atol(argv[2])>0) iter=atol(argv[2]);
    strcpy(pswd,argv[1]);
}
    else
{
    printf("build-in default\n");
    strcpy(pswd,"!");
}
printf("start password\t\t%s\nmax iter\t\t%d\n", pswd, iter);



// Starting password enumeration
printf("===================================\ntry search... wait!\n");
t=clock();
    gen_pswd(crypteddata,pswd,iter,validCRC);
t=clock()-t;

// Output of the number of passwords per second
printf("                                        \rPassword per sec:\t");
print_dot(iter/(float)t*CLOCKS_PER_SEC);

return 0;
}
```

Compile this code with maximum optimization and run it to check how the machine optimizer did its job.

A test run of this program on Pentium III 733 will produce the cracking speed of about *30,000 passwords per second*. This is almost useless. How long will it take to crack the ciphertext at this rate? Where is the leak?

The VTune profiler can be used to detect the bottlenecks in this program. So, start it. (Under Windows 2000 and Windows NT, you must log in as administrative user.) While the PC is blinking with the hard-disk LED, create the *symbol table*. (Don't confuse it with the debug information.) Without this table, no profiler will be able to determine which part of the executable code relates to which function. To create the symbol table, specify the `/profile` key in the linker command line. This might look as follows: `link /profile pswd.obj`. If everything has been done correctly, the pswd.map file will be generated and will contain approximately the following:

Listing 1.18. [Profile/pswd.c] Contents of the pswd.map File

```
0001:00000000          _DeCrypt                    00401000 f    pswd.obj
0001:00000050          _CalculateCRC               00401050 f    pswd.obj
0001:00000080          _CheckCRC                   00401080 f    pswd.obj
```

Now, VTune is ready for profiling and waiting for instructions. You have the following options: *Open the existing project, start the New Project Wizard,* or *perform a quick analysis of the application's performance* by choosing the **Quick Performance Analysis** option. As you have nothing to open and may not understand all of the settings of the wizard, the final option is the best choice. In the next dialog box, specify the path to the pswd.exe file and click on the **GO** button. VTune will start the profiled application automatically and begin to collect the run-time information for each of the program's points. The progress indicator will entertain you during the process. If you are lucky and the system doesn't freeze, then, after a couple of seconds, VTune will open a full-screen window filled with various information. Some of it is valuable; other information is useless. Fig. 1.6 shows this data in more detail. In the left part of the screen, you'll see the *project navigator*, which lets you navigate quickly between various parts of the project. For the moment, you don't need this. Therefore, concentrate your attention on the central part of the screen, displaying the diagram's windows.

The top window maps the detected hotspots to their addresses. The bottom window contains information about the relative run times of all modules in the system. Note that the pswd.exe module (marked by an arrow in the diagram) isn't in the first position on this list. The most resources are consumed by another module. This gives the false impression that optimizing pswd.exe is useless.

The top window, which shows how long it took to execute each point, allows you to detect hotspots (i.e., the code fragments that took the longest time to execute). In this example, the profiler has detected 187 hotspots (as shown in the right pane of the profiler window). Pay special attention to the two peaks located to the right of the center of the screen. These two peaks aren't just "hot;" they are "white hot," because they consume the majority of the program's performance. It is a must to begin with the optimization of these points.

Move the cursor to the highest peak. VTune will immediately tell you that it belongs to the `output` function. Stop! Why is it `output`? You didn't call this function, or anything like it. Who called this annoying function? (You may have already guessed that it was the `printf` function, but pretend that you haven't guessed this; it isn't always easy to determine the culprit.)

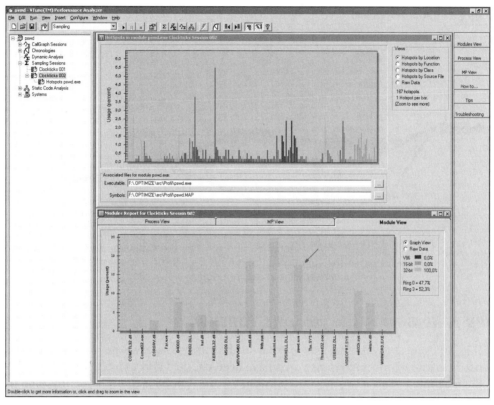

Fig. 1.6. Contents of the VTune window immediately after initial analysis of the application

To avoid pointless examination of the entire code, employ an instrument provided by the profiler, *Call Graph*, that displays the class hierarchy in a user-friendly form.

From the **Run** menu, select the **Win32* Call Graph Profiling Session** command and relax while VTune profiles the application. When the profiling is complete, two more windows will appear. The contents of the top window — in the form of a spreadsheet — are intuitive. Look at the bottom window more carefully. On a light background, there are two bright rectangles, labeled `Thread 400` and `mainCRTStartup`. Double-click the latter, and VTune will immediately display a long tree of child functions called on by the application's source code. Among them, find the `main` function (this function will be highlighted) and double-click it again. Proceed in this manner until you have opened all child functions of the `main` procedure.

You will discover that the `printf` function calls the `output` function. The `printf` function, in turn, is called from the `do_pswd` function. You should recall that this function was used for the output of the current password. From this, the cause of performance degradation is clear.

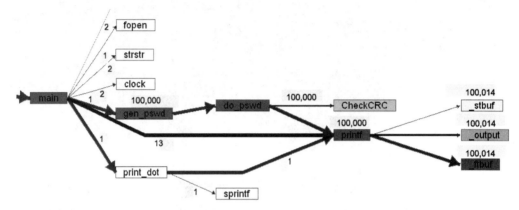

Fig. 1.7. Hierarchy of "hot" functions generated by the Call Graph wizard (shading symbolizes the function's "temperature;" the numbers specify how many times each function was called)

Step 1: Removing the `printf` Function

It is impractical to eliminate the display of the current state of the program. (The user needs to know how many passwords have been checked and to have some control over the machine just to make sure that it hasn't frozen.) Rather than displaying each password, you can carry out this operation for each 600th or, better still, each 6,000th password. The overhead caused by calling `printf` will be reduced drastically; it may even drop to zero.

Rewrite the code fragment responsible for the output of the current state as shown in Listing 1.19.

Listing 1.19. Reducing the Number of Calls to the `printf` Function

```
static int x=0;
// Output of the current state to the terminal
if (++x>6666)
{
    x = 0;
    printf("Current pswd : %10s [%d%%]\r", &pswd[0], progress);
}
```

Wow! After recompiling the program, its lightning speed *exceeds 1.5 million passwords per second*. The program has become so fast that the "sensitivity" of the `clock` function becomes insufficient, and it is necessary to increase drastically the number of iterations. As you will soon learn, this is not the limit of performance growth.

Step 2: Moving the `strlen` Body outside the Loop

After restarting has been performed, the updated program under the profiler shows that the number of hot spots has decreased from 187 to 106. This is good, but hotspots remain. If you go to the **Views** pane in the right corner of the **HotSpots** window, and set the **Hotspots by Function** radio button, you'll learn that about 80% of the total run time of the program is consumed by the `CalculateCRC` function, followed (after a gap) by `gen_pswd` (which consumes about 12%). The next positions in the list (which consume about 3%) are shared by the `CheckCRC` and `do_pswd` functions.

This, then, is no-go. Some nasty function (`CalculateCRC`) is consuming most of the program's run time. If only you could find out, *which* of its parts is most responsible for this performance degradation. Fortunately, VTune allows you to do this.

Double-click the tallest rectangles to zoom in. You'll find the `CalculateCRC` function contains 18 hotspots (Fig. 1.8), 3 of which are especially "hot" (about 30%, 25%, and 10%). Start with the hottest. Double-click on the tallest rectangle. VTune will beep and show the following message: "No source found for offset `0x69` into F:\.OPTIMIZE\src\Profil\pswd.exe. Proceed with disassembly only?" Because the program was compiled without debug information, VTune is unable to understand which byte of assembler code corresponds to which code line. The compiler won't provide this information because, in the optimized program, the correspondence between the source code and machine code generated by the compiler is ambiguous.

You can profile nonoptimized program, but what would be the point? This would be another program with *different* hotspots. High-quality optimization is impossible without knowledge of the assembler; therefore, click **OK** to work with assembler code and without source code.

VTune will immediately draw your attention to the `REPNE SCANB` instruction. You don't need to be a guru to recognize the `strlen` core. But was `strlen` in the source code of the program? Yes, it was! The call to `strlen` in the loop header produced a negative effect. The compiler didn't recognize it as invariant and didn't move it outside the loop. As a result of this mistake, the length of the same string has been calculated at each iteration.

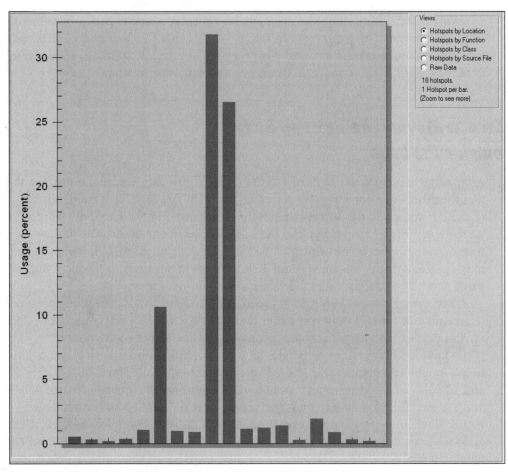

Fig. 1.8. "Temperature" distribution within the `CalculateCRC` function
(with a snapshot taken at high resolution)

Listing 1.20. Call to `strlen` in the Loop Header Produces a Negative Effect

```
int CalculateCRC(char *pswd)
{
int a;
int x = -1;            // CRC calculation error
for (a = 0; a < strlen(pswd);   a++)
    x += *(int *)((int)pswd + a);
return x;
}
```

It appears that the compiler hasn't moved the call to strlen outside the loop body, although its argument — the pswd variable — wasn't modified within the loop. If the compiler didn't do it, you can do it yourself. Rewrite this code fragment as follows:

Listing 1.21. Moving the strlen Function outside the Loop

```
int length;
length=strlen(pswd);
for (a = 0; a < length;   a++)
```

After recompiling the program, you will notice that its performance has mushroomed to *3.5 million passwords per second.*

Step 3: Aligning Data

Still, profiling shows that the number of hotspots hasn't been reduced. On the contrary, a new hotspot has appeared. Why? The algorithm used to calculate the number of hotspots accounts for the relative run times of program fragments, rather than their absolute values. As you eliminate the highest peaks, small hills will appear.

Despite optimization, the CalculateCRC function remains the leader in resource consumption; it still occupies more than 50% of the total run time for the entire program. Now, the following two commands become the "hottest" spots:

Listing 1.22. "Hottest" Spots After Moving the strlen Function outside the Loop

```
mov      edi, DWORD PTR [eax+esi]
add      edx, edi
```

What's wrong with these commands? It is clear that memory is being accessed (x += *(int *)((int)pswd + a)), but the password being tested must be in L1 cache. Consequently, accessing it must take only one clock. Has someone discarded this data from cache, or has some conflict occurred? Trying to guess the answer could take forever, because this code isn't causing the problem; it comes from a different branch of the program.

Now, it is time to employ one of the most powerful functions of VTune: *dynamic analysis*. This allows you not only to detect the leak, but also to find the reason behind it. Dynamic analysis isn't carried out on the "live" processor; rather, it is done on its soft emulator. This allows you to save financial resources. To perform software optimization, you don't need to purchase the whole line of processors — from Intel 486 to Pentium 4; you just need to purchase VTune. After that, you'll be able to optimize your programs for Pentium 4 with only Pentium II or Pentium III at your disposal.

Before starting dynamic analysis, you'll need to specify which part of the program you are going to profile. In particular, it is possible to choose whether you'll profile the entire `CalculateCRC` function or a specific hotspot of that function. Because the example function contains many hotspots, I'll describe the first approach.

Scroll the window up and move the cursor to the line labeled `CalculateCRC` string. (Labels are displayed in the second column from the left.) If you don't find this line, click the **Scroll to Previous Portal** button on the toolbar. (Its icon looks like a triangle with the point turned upward.) Now, establish the **Dynamic Analysis Entry Point** by clicking the button with the right-arrow. Proceed in a similar manner to specify the **Dynamic Analysis Exit Point**: Scroll the screen down, find the last line of the `CalculateCRC` function (it contains a single command, `ret`), click it, then click the toolbar button with the left-arrow. Now, choose the following commands from the menu: **Run/Dynamic Analysis Session**. In the dialog box that appears, select the processor model to be emulated (PIII, in this example) and click **Start**. The profiler will restart the program. After running it for a couple of minutes, the profiler will display a screen similar to the one in Fig. 1.9.

Address	Label	OpCodes	Instructions	Pe p~	Dyn-Count %	Dyn-Total Cycles Count	Dyn-Retiremen	Dyn-Penalties
1:4c		90	nop	1				
1:4d		90	nop	1				
1:4e		90	nop	1				
1:4f		90	nop	1				
1:50	CalculateCRC	56	push esi	3	1000 (03,18%)	9007 (16,06%)	(0,9,0,13)	1*IC_miss:4, 1*L2instr_miss:84,
1:51		8B742408	mov esi, DWORD PTR [esp+08h]	1	1000 (03,18%)	1084 (01.93%)	(1,1,1,85)	1*DC_rd_miss:3, 1*L2data_rd_miss:84,
1:55		57	push edi	3	1000 (03,18%)	1008 (01.80%)	(1,1,0,9)	
1:56		8BFE	mov edi, esi	1	1000 (03,18%)	0		
1:58		83C9FF	or ecx, -1	1	1000 (03,18%)	1 (00,00%)	(0,0,0,1)	
1:5b		33C0	xor eax, eax	1	1000 (03,18%)	999 (01,78%)	(0,1,0,1)	
1:5d		83CAFF	or edx, -1	1	1000 (03,18%)	0		
1:60		F2AE	repne scasb	*	2910 (09,25%)	6019 (10,73%)	(1,2,1,111)	1*IC_miss:20, 1*DC_rd_miss:3, 1*L2data_
1:62		F7D1	not ecx	1	1000 (03,18%)	7000 (12,48%)	7	1000*Partial_Stall:(11,11,1,123).
1:64		49	dec ecx	1	1000 (03,18%)	1000 (01,78%)	1	
1:65		780A	js CalculateCRC+21 (1:71)	1	1000 (03,18%)	1000 (01,78%)	1	
1:67	CalculateCRC+17	8B3C30	mov edi, DWORD PTR [eax+esi]	1	2910 (09,25%)	20117 (35,89%)	(0,6,9,104)	1*DC_rd_miss:4, 2000*DC_mcalign:0,1*
1:6a		03D7	add edx, edi	1	2910 (09,25%)	2002 (03,57%)	(0,0,7,1)	
1:6c		40	inc eax	1	2910 (09,25%)	908 (01,62%)	(0,0,3,1)	
1:6d		3BC1	cmp eax, ecx	1	2910 (09,25%)	0		
1:6f		7EF6	jle CalculateCRC+17 (1:67)	1	2910 (09,25%)	2002 (03,57%)	(0,0,7,1)	5*BTB_Miss:(12,26.4,42), 1*IC_pend:12,
1:71	CalculateCRC+21	5F	pop edi	2	1000 (03,18%)	926 (01,65%)	(0,0,9,9)	
1:72		8BC2	mov eax, edx	1	1000 (03,18%)	90 (00,16%)	(0,0,1,1)	
1:74		5E	pop esi	2	1000 (03,18%)	910 (01,62%)	(0,0,9,1)	
1:75		C3	ret	4	999 (03,18%)	1999 (03,57%)	(2,2,0,3)	999*RET_not_ind:(20,28,9,122).
1:76	CalculateCRC+26	90	nop	1				
1:77		90	nop	1				
1:78		90	nop	1				
1:79		90	nop	1				
1:7a		90	nop	1				

Fig. 1.9. Dynamic analysis of the program, which determines the "temperature" of each machine instruction and explains the reasons for its "heat"

Here is the hotspot. (In Fig. 1.9, it is highlighted with the cursor.) If you double-click it with the mouse, VTune will display the following dialog, which provides detailed description of the problem:

Listing 1.23. Dynamic Analysis Results for the Chosen Hotspot

---

```
Decoder Minimum Clocks = 0,        ; // Minimum decoding time: 0 clocks
Decoder Average Clocks = 0.7       ; // Average decoding time: 0.7 clock
Decoder Maximum Clocks = 14        ; // Maximum decoding time: 14 clocks

Retirement Minimum Clocks = 0,     ; // Minimum retirement time: 0 clocks
Retirement Average Clocks = 6.9    ; // Average retirement time: 6.9 clocks
Retirement Maximum Clocks = 104    ; // Maximum retirement time: 104 clocks

Total Cycles = 20117 (35.88%)      ; // Total execution time: 20,117 clocks

Micro-Ops for this instruction = 1 ; // Decoding occurs in one micro-operation

The instruction had to wait (0,0.1,2) cycles for its sources to be ready.

Warnings: 3*decode_slow:0          ; // No decoder conflicts

Dynamic Penalty: DC_rd_miss
The operand of this load instruction was not in the data cache. The
instruction stalls while the processor loads the specified address location
from L2 cache or the main memory.
Occurrences =  1                   ; // This happened once.

Dynamic Penalty: DC_misalign
The instruction stalls because it accessed data that was split across two
data-cache lines.
Occurrences =  2000                ; // This happened 2,000 times.

Dynamic Penalty: L2data_rd_miss
The operand of this load instruction was not in L2 cache. The instruction
stalls while the processor loads the specified address location from the
main memory.
Occurrences =  1                   ; // This happened once.

Dynamic Penalty: No_BTB_info
The BTB (Branch Target Buffer) does not contain information about this branch.
The branch was predicted using the static branch prediction algorithm.
Occurrences =  1                   ; // This happened once.
```

What a goldmine of information! It proves that cache has nothing to do with the problem. (A cache miss occurred only once.) The main cause of the problem is access to misaligned data. (This occurred 2,000 times, equal to the number of program runs.) This means that this type of event took place on each iteration of the loop — hence the performance degradation.

Can you find out where within the program the pswd pointer is initialized? Listing 1.24 shows the fragment of the main function. (It is clear why static analysis of the CalculateCRC function was unable to provide something useful.)

Listing 1.24. Aligning the Password Buffer To Avoid Penalty from the Processor

```
pswd = (char *) malloc(512*1024);
pswd += 62;
```

Remove the pswd += 62 line and recompile the program. The result is *4.5 million passwords per second.* Now, that's lightning speed!

Step 4: Removing the `strlen` Function

Return to Fig. 1.9, and note that the access to the misaligned data is not the only hot-spot in the CalculateCRC function. After a small gap, the CalculateCRC function is followed by the PUSH instruction, which temporarily stores registers in the stack, and the strlen function, which was encountered previously.

Calculation of the password length by its duration is comparable to calculation of its CRC. But why do you need to calculate the length of *each* password? Password checking isn't chaotic. On the contrary, passwords are generated in a strict order. This method increments passwords by one character; but it isn't used frequently. Therefore, perhaps it would be better to delegate this task to the gen_pswd function. Let this function determine the length of initial password, then, as the string length is incremented, increment the global variable length by one character. Rewrite the gen_pswd code as follows:

Listing 1.25. Eliminating `strlen` by Manually Incrementing the Password Length

```
int a;
int p = 0;
length = strlen(pswd);  // Determining the initial password length
...
if (!pswd[p])
```

```
{
    pswd[p]=' ';
    pswd[p+1]=0;
    length++;      // "Manually" increasing the password length
}
...
```

The code of the `CalculateCRC` function must be rewritten as follows:

Listing 1.26. Using a Global Variable To Determine the Password Length

```
for (a = 0; a <= length;  a++)
```

As a result of these simple transforms, the speed has increased to *8 million passwords per second*. Is this sufficient? Just wait. The most interesting part of your job has not begun yet.

Step 5: Eliminating the Division Operation

Now, the `gen_pswd` function, which consumes more than 50% of the total program run time, becomes the leader.

After the `gen_pswd` function, by a large margin, follow two other functions: `CalculateCRC` (about 21%) and `CheckCRC` (about 15%). About 40% of the total time required to execute `gen_pswd` is concentrated in a single hotspot. Clearly, this function requires optimization!

Double-click the highest peak, and you'll come to the `IDIV` instruction, which performs integer division. But where was integer division used in the `gen_pswd`? Here it is:

Listing 1.27. Integer Division in the `gen_pswd` Function

```
do_pswd(crypteddata, pswd, validCRC, 100*a/max_iter);
```

These lines of code calculate the percentage of completed work. Curiously, this operation takes approximately the same time as the work itself. Therefore, you can get rid of these "bells and whistles." Remove the division command, substitute 0 or any other numeral for the progress indicator, and recompile the program. Now, its speed is *14.5 million passwords per second*.

Step 6: Removing Performance Monitoring

Despite the checking speed, the gen_pswd function still takes about 22% of the total execution time, which isn't a positive situation.

Double-click this function, and you'll notice that a single peak towers over the other peaks of approximately equal height. Disassembling will reveal that this hotspot hides a previously encountered construction.

Listing 1.28. Well-Known Construction Hidden between Hotspots in gen_pswd

---

```
if (++x>66666)
{
    x = 0;
    printf("Current pswd : %10s [%d%%]\r", &pswd[0], progress);
}
```

For the sake of performance, you can forego monitoring of the current state. Actually, you can discard this code fragment altogether.

As a result, the speed will be increased by *5 million passwords per second*. This result isn't too impressive; therefore the necessity of this step is doubtful.

Step 7: Combining Functions

Here is a new hotspot: The ESI register is saved somewhere deep within the CalculateCRC function. The compiler carefully prevents any modifications from being introduced. The number of variables used in this program is not large, and memory access could be avoided by placing all of the variables in the registers. However, the compiler is unable to do so because it optimizes each function separately.

You can sacrifice the structured architecture and unite all intensely used functions (gen_pswd, do_paswd, CheckCRC, and CalculateCRC) within a single "super-function."

Its implementation might look as follows:

Listing 1.29. Integrating the gen_pswd, do_paswd, CheckCRC, and CalculateCRC Functions within a Single Super-function

---

```
int gen_pswd(char *crypteddata, char *pswd, int max_iter, int validCRC)
{
int a, b, x;
int p = 0;
char *buff;
```

```
int length = strlen(pswd);
for(a = 0; a < max_iter; a++)
{
    x = -1;    for (b = 0; b <= length;  b++) x += *(int *)((int)pswd + b);
    if (x == validCRC)
    {
        buff = (char *) malloc(strlen(crypteddata));
        strcpy(buff, crypteddata); DeCrypt(pswd, buff);
        printf("CRC %8X: try to decrypt: \"%s\"\n", validCRC, buff);
    }

    while((++pswd[p])>'z')
    {
        pswd[p] = '!';    p++; if (!pswd[p])
        {
            pswd[p]=' '; pswd[p+1]=0; length++;
        }
    }; p = 0;
}
return 0;
}
```

Compile and start the redesigned program. You may not believe your eyes — now you have achieved a speed of *35 million passwords per second*. Before this, it seemed that there were no more performance reserves. Now, who would dare say that Pentium is a slow processor? The generation of the next password, its checking, and the calculation of its CRC take about 20 clocks.

Nevertheless, there is still something to work on.

Step 8: Reducing the Number of Memory-Access Operations

As profiling has shown, the main part of the hotspots is now concentrated within the loop of the CRC calculation; it consumes more than 80% of the total program run time, among which 50% is used by a conditional jump that closes the loop. (Pentium processors can't stand short loops and conditional jumps.) The remaining 50% is used to access cache memory. This fact needs to be clarified.

There is a common belief that reading nonsplit data from cache memory requires one clock — the same as reading data from a register. However, after careful investigation, you would discover that "one cell per clock" represents the throughput of cache memory, and the total time required to load the data (and account for latency) is at least three clocks. When reading dependent data from cache (as in this example), the total time required to access the cell is determined by latency, rather than by the throughput. Besides this, P6 processors are equipped with a single-load memory unit. Therefore, even under favorable conditions, they can load only one cell per clock. The data stored in registers are not subject to this limitation.

Thus, to increase the performance, you need to remove the loop and reduce to a minimum the number of memory-access operations. Unfortunately, you cannot efficiently remove the loop because you don't know the required number of iterations beforehand. There is a similar situation with variables: When programming in assembly language, you could easily place the password buffer in general-purpose registers. (A 16-character password is the longest one that can be reasonably determined using a password cracker.) This fits within four registers; other variables fit within the remaining three registers. However, this method isn't available to application programmers who have mastered only one high-level programming language, and they have to search for other solutions.

Such solutions exist. Up to this point, the program speed has been increased by restricting or discarding resource-consuming operations. Nothing has been changed in the basic algorithms. This approach has improved performance considerably, but it has reached its limit. Further optimization is only possible at the *algorithmic* level.

There are no universal approaches or commonly accepted solutions to algorithmic optimization; each case must be considered individually, in the context of a specific environment. Returning to the example, think over the following question: Is it necessary to calculate checksums for each new password? Obviously, the CRC calculation algorithm used in this program is weak. You can replace it with an equivalent, but faster, option.

Because the lower byte of the password is summed only once, when going to the next password, CRC usually is increased by 1 byte. I say "usually," because, when changing the second and subsequent bytes of the password, the changed byte is summed at least two times. This significantly complicates the algorithm. However, this is much better than the less effective method of constantly calculating the CRC, which was used previously.

Thus, the improved implementation of the password cracker might look as follows:

Listing 1.30. Algorithmic Optimization of the CRC Calculation Algorithm

```
int gen_pswd(char *crypteddata, char *pswd, int max_iter, int validCRC)
{
    int a, b, x;
    int p = 0;
    char *buff;
    int y=0;
    int k;
```

```
int length = strlen(pswd);
int mask;

x = -1;
for (b = 0; b <= length;  b++)
   x += *(int *)((int)pswd + b);

for(a = 0; a <  max_iter ; a++)
{

   if (x==validCRC)
   {
   buff = (char *) malloc(strlen(crypteddata));
   strcpy(buff, crypteddata); DeCrypt(pswd, buff);

   printf("CRC %8X: try to decrypt: \"%s\"\n", validCRC, buff);
   }
   y = 1;
   k = 'z'-'!';
   while((++pswd[p])>'z')
   {
      pswd[p] = '!';

      // Next character
      y = y | y << 8;
      x -= k;
      k = k << 8;
      k += ('z'-'!');

      p++;
      if (!pswd[p])
      {
            pswd[p]='!';
            pswd[p+1]=0;
            length++;
            x = -1;
            for (b = 0; b <= length;  b++)
               x += *(int *)((int)pswd + b);
            y = 0;
            pswd[p]=' ';
      }
      // printf("%x\n", y);
```

```
    } // end while(pswd)
    p = 0;
    x += y;
  } // end for(a)

  return 0;
}
```

What is the result of algorithmic optimization? It is *83 million passwords per second*, or about 1/10 of a password per clock. Amazing!

Additionally, the program has been written in pure C. What's the most interesting is that a good performance reserve remains.

Step 9: VTune as Your Personal Coach

Now, I'll discuss a lesser-known feature of the VTune profiler — the *Coach*.

Realistically, the Coach is nothing more than a high-class, interactive optimizer that supports a range of programming languages, including C, C++, Fortran, and Java. It analyzes the source code of the program, searches for weak points, then provides detailed instructions on their elimination.

Naturally, the IQ of this program can't be compared to that of the human programmer. Furthermore, as you will discover later, the Coach is not as smart as it might seem. (Some might even say that it is submoronic, with a less-than-room-temperature IQ.) Still, it would be useful to consider it closely.

Although the Coach is oriented toward beginners (an has a simple style for its help system), it sometimes can be useful for professionals, especially when you need to optimize code written by someone else and you can't afford a detailed investigation of that code (or are simply short of time).

However, without debugging information, the Coach cannot work with the source code. It goes to the level of pure assembly language. (See *Step 10: Conclusion*.) However, this circumstance doesn't present serious inconveniences because the source code is *analyzed*, rather than profiled. Therefore, don't be surprised that the inclusion of debugging information into the executable file automatically disables all optimizing options of the compiler. When the Coach works with machine code, it won't even touch the compiled machine code.

Recompile the demonstration example with the /Zi option in the compiler's command line, and link it with the /DEBUG command line option of the linker. Then, load the resulting file into VTune, wait until the profiler displays the **HotSpots** diagram, then double-click the highest rectangle. As you already know, this corresponds to the gen_pswd function, where the program spends most of its run time.

Now, holding the left mouse button, highlight the fragment that you want to analyze. (It would be most logical to select the entire gen_pswd function.) Then, locate the toolbar button with the icon that depicts the Coach and click on it. The Coach will request information about the file used to compile the program. You can choose between the following options: make-file, pre-processor file, and, as in any professional program, manual input. Because you didn't set specific compiler options and have no make-file, choose the **Manual Entry** option and click **OK**. Ignore the "No source options were specified" message displayed on the screen, then click **OK** again.

VTune will immediately start the analysis. After several seconds, it will display the following type of message: "There are 9 recommendations identified for the selected code. Double-click on any advice for additional information." It shows that the program (which has been optimized) contains no less than nine weak points. What's more important, these weak points are so problematic that they can be detected by trivial search using the template. No worries; you have done a good job. Now, look at what VTune has found. The Coach's recommendations are written directly over the program code. The first one is as follows:

Listing 1.31. First Recommendation from the Coach

```
84  for (b = 0; b <= length;  b++)
85     x += *(int *)((int)pswd + b);
The loop at line 84 can be unrolled 4 times.
```

VTune isn't quite right. This loop is executed once during each run of the program. Therefore, optimization of this loop will have little effect on the program's performance. You may wonder: "What is loop unrolling, and how can I accomplish it?" Double-click the highlighted line, and the Coach will display the following:

Loop unrolling

Examples: C, Fortran, Java

The loop contains instructions that do not allow efficient instruction scheduling and pairing. The instructions are few or have dependencies that provide little scope for the compiler to schedule them in such a manner as to make optimal use of the processor's multiple pipelines. As a result, extra clock cycles are needed to execute these instructions.

Advice

Unroll the loop as suggested by the Coach. Create a loop that contains more instructions, but is executed fewer times. If the unrolling factor suggested by the Coach is not appropriate, use an unrolling factor that is more appropriate.

To unroll the loop

− Replicate the body of the loop the recommended number of times.

− Adjust the index expressions to reference successive array elements.

− Adjust the loop control statements.

Result

− Increases the number of machine instructions generated inside the loop.

− Provides more scope for the compiler to reorder and schedule instructions so that they pair and execute simultaneously in the processor's pipelines.

− Executes the loop fewer times.

Caution

Be aware that increasing the number of instructions within the loop also increases the register pressure.

This is quite a detailed instruction on loop unrolling! Nevertheless, if you still can't understand how the loop is unrolled, you can click on the **Examples** link and view a specific example written in C, Java, or Fortran. Choose C and view further instructions provided by VTune.

Listing 1.32. Further Instructions Provided by the Coach (C Language Example)

Original Code	Optimized Code

```for(i=0; i<n; i++)```
```a[i] = c[i] ;```
	```for(i=0; i<n-(n%3); i+=3)```
	```{```
	``` a[i] = c[i] ;```
	``` a[i+1] = c[i+1];```
	``` a[i+2] = c[i+2];```
	```}```
	```for(i; i < n; i++)```
	```a[i] = c[i];```

Despite VTune's recommendations, do not unroll this loop. Rather, go further and consider the second tip. This tip also recommends that you unroll the loop, but this time, the loop to be unrolled is nested within the while loop. Because this loop gains control only when the checked password is lengthened by one character (which does not happen frequently), it also has little influence on the program's performance. For these reasons, send both these recommendations to /dev/null.

The third tip criticizes the innocent-looking instruction p++, which increases the p variable by 1:

Listing 1.33. Third Tip Provided by the Coach

```
114 p++;
115 if (!pswd[p])
116 {
117    pswd[p]='!';
118    pswd[p+1]=0;
119    length++;
120    x = -1;
121    for (b = 0; b <= length;  b++)
122        x += *(int *)((int)pswd + b);
```

The loop whose index is incremented at line 114 should be interchanged with the loop whose index is incremented at line 121, for more efficient memory access.

Obviously, the Coach went crazy because of the processor's overheating. These are *different* loops. They have *different* indexes. They are not related in any way. Furthermore, the loop that starts at line 121 is executed so rarely that it is an enigma. So why doesn't VTune like it?

Perhaps the additional information provided by the Coach will explain everything. Double-click line 114 to read the following:

Loop interchange

Loops with index variables referencing a multidimensional array are nested. The order in which the index variables are incremented causes out-of-sequence array referencing, resulting in many data cache misses. This increases the loop execution time.

Advice

Do the following:

– Change the sequence of the array dimensions in the array declaration.

– Interchange the loop control statements.

Result

The order in which the array elements are referenced is more sequential. Fewer data cache misses occur, significantly reducing the loop execution time.

What? Where are multidimensional loops or cache misses? There is nothing of the sort! Presumably, this is an error by the Coach. (After all, a template search is no more than a template search.) However, consider the example provided by the Coach. Perhaps, there is a misunderstanding.

Listing 1.34. Example Provided by the Coach for the Third Tip

```
Original Code                        Optimized Code
int b[200][120];                     int b[200][120];
void xmpl17(int *a)                  void ympl17(int *a)
{                                    {
  int i, j;                            int i, j;
                                       int atemp;

  for (i = 0; i < 120; i++)            for (j = 0; j < 200; j++)
   for (j = 0; j < 200; j++)            for (i = 0; i < 120; i++)

   b[j][i]=b[j][i]+a[2*j];               b[j][i]=b[j][i]+a[2*j];
}                                    }
```

Well, this is correct. The code fragment provided by VTune illustrates that it is better to process two-dimensional arrays by rows, rather than by columns. (See *Working Principles of Cache.*) However, the example in this book has no two-dimensional arrays. Therefore, there is no need to observe these instructions from the Coach.

The fourth tip relates to the CRC calculation loop. What has attracted the Coach's attention in this loop?

Listing 1.35. Fourth Tip Provided by the Coach

```
121        for (b = 0; b <= length;  b++)
122            x += *(int *)((int)pswd + b);
123        pswd[p]=' ';
124        y = 0;
125    }
126 } // end while(pswd)
```

Use the Intel C/C++ Compiler vectorizer to automatically generate highly optimized SIMD code. The statement on line 122 and others like it will be vectorized if the following program changes are made (double-click on any line for more information):

==> Simplify the pointer expression to indicate contiguous array accesses.

==> Restructure the loop to isolate the statement or construct that

interferes with vectorization.

==> Try loop interchanging to obtain vector code in the innermost loop.

==> Simplify the pointer expression to indicate contiguous array accesses.

The recommendation to simplify the addressing (which is primitive enough) has been repeated. In addition, you won't succeed in efficiently vectorizing this loop using Intel C/C++, let alone other compilers.

Still, view the built-in help system; perhaps it will provide yo with some interesting information.

Intel C++ Compiler Vectorizer

The Coach has identified an assignment or expression that is a candidate for SIMD technology code generation using Intel C++ Compiler vectorizer.

Advice

Use the Intel C++ Compiler vectorizer to automatically generate highly optimized SIMD code wherever appropriate in your application. Use the following syntax to invoke the vectorizer from the command line: `prompt> icl -O2 -QxW myprog.cpp`.

The `-QxW` command enables vectorization of source code and provides access to other vectorization-related options.

Result

The Intel C++ Compiler vectorizer optimizes your application by processing data in parallel, using the Streaming SIMD Extensions of the Intel processors. Since the Streaming SIMD Extensions that the class library implements access and operate on 2, 4, 8, or 16 array elements at one time, the program executes much faster.

Vectorization is a useful approach; it allows you to increase the program's speed considerably. However, there are two obstacles that prevent it from being adopted widely: First, most x86-compilers cannot vectorize code, and migration to Intel's compiler isn't always acceptable. Second, vectorization will only be efficient if the program was optimized initially to use this technology. Finally, although code vectorization is well-known in the world of mainframes, for x86 programmers, it is still something exotic.

Now, consider what the Coach has produced for its fifth tip.

Listing 1.35. Fifth Tip from the Coach That Is Correct but Impractical

---

```
91          if (x==validCRC)
92          {
93          // Copying encrypted data into temporary buffer
94          buff = (char *) malloc(strlen(crypteddata));
95          strcpy(buff, crypteddata);
96
97          // Decrypting
98          DeCrypt(pswd, buff);
99
```

The argument list for the function call to _malloc on line 94 appears to be loop-invariant. If there are no conflicts with other variables in the loop, and if the function has no side effects and no external dependencies, move the call out of the loop.

The Coach is right, from a formal point of view. Moving invariant functions outside the loop body is a good programming practice. When the function resides within the loop body, it is called many times, but, because of its independence on the loop parameters, it gives the same result any time it is called. Isn't it simpler to allocate memory once, when entering the function, and then simply store the pointer returned by malloc in special variable for future use?

The first objection to this approach is as follows: What will be gained? This branch is called only when the checksum of the current password matches the reference checksum, which is a rare event. In the best case, this happens a few times during the entire run of the program.

The second objection is the branch of the program that has allocated the memory block must release it, unless this unexpectedly degrades performance.

Thus, you will not move anything outside the loop, despite the tips provided by the Coach.

The sixth recommendation is almost identical to the previous one; however, this time, the Coach recommends moving the DeCrypt function. Yes, it considers this function to be invariant and suggests moving it outside the loop, despite the following facts: The code of this function was principally at its disposal ("principally" because the Coach was instructed to analyze only the gen_pswd function), and the DeCrypt function takes the pswd pointer as an argument. This pointer is explicitly changed within the loop! Because of this, DeCrypt cannot be invariant. Isn't the Coach ashamed of giving such advice? I hope so.

With the seventh tip, the Coach notes: "The value returned by DeCrypt() on line 98 is not used." It provides the following recommendation: "If the return value is being ignored, write an alternate version of the function which returns void."

This recommendation is based on the Coach's assumption that a function that doesn't return any value will execute faster than a function that does. This statement is disputable. Returning of the value doesn't take a long time, and the creation of two instances of the same function is much more costly than the overhead for returning an unnecessary value.

Therefore, ignore this tip and proceed further.

The Coach's eighth tip claims another function is invariant — `printf`, which prints the contents of the buffer just returned by the `DeCrypt` function. Hmm... Didn't VTune developers inform the Coach about the semantics of main library functions? The `printf` function can never be moved outside the loop, whether it is invariant or not. I don't think that it is necessary to explain why.

The ninth tip notes that the value returned by the `printf` function isn't used.

Overall, such instructions cannot be considered satisfactory. None of the nine tips improved the program's performance. Still, the Coach shouldn't be considered useless program; it explains interesting and efficient optimization techniques, most of which are unknown to beginners.

Some experienced programmers may argue that this result was obtained because it was loaded with the highly optimized program; therefore, the Coach was forced to dig into minor details. Load the initial version of the program, and make the Coach analyze the entire source code. It will provide 33 warnings, none of which are useful.

Step 10: Conclusion

The remaining 17 hotspots represent overhead for accessing cache memory and penalties for unsuitable (from the processor's point of view) command grouping. I'll leave memory access alone for you to think over. (Why do passwords need to be generated if their checksums are calculated without accessing them?) This section will concentrate on the scheduling the optimal command flow.

Employ another powerful tool provided by the VTune profiler — the *automatic optimizer*, which has the pathetic name of *assembly coach*. (Don't confuse it with the source Coach.) Press and hold down the left mouse button, highlight the entire `gen_pswd` function, then find the **Coach** button on the toolbar. Click this button.

You'll have to choose between three types of optimization in the **Mode of Operation** list: **Automatic Optimization**, **Single Step Optimization**, and **Interactive Scheduling**. The first two modes are of no particular interest. However, the quality of the third mode, **Interactive Scheduling**, is very high. Select **Interactive Scheduling** and click the **Next** button to the right of the drop-down list.

The screen contents will change immediately (Fig. 1.10): The left pane will display the original assembly code; the right pane will display the code to be optimized. The bottom pane will display the so-called assumptions for resolving issues, which the optimizer will address the programmer. For the moment, this window contains the following assumption: "Offsets: 0x55 & 0x72: Instructions may reference the same memory." Here are the instructions residing at these offsets:

Listing 1.36. Instructions Residing at the Offsets Specified by VTune

```
1:55 mov      ebp, DWORD PTR [esp+018h]
1:72 mov      DWORD PTR [esp+010h], ecx
```

Despite the visible difference in operands, they address the same variable because there are two PUSH machine commands between them. These commands decrease the value of the ESP register by 8. Thus, this assumption is correct, and you can confirm it by clicking the **Apply** button.

Now, concentrate on the instructions in gray (in Fig. 1.10) and marked with traffic lights. These are poorly planned instructions fined with penalties by the processor.

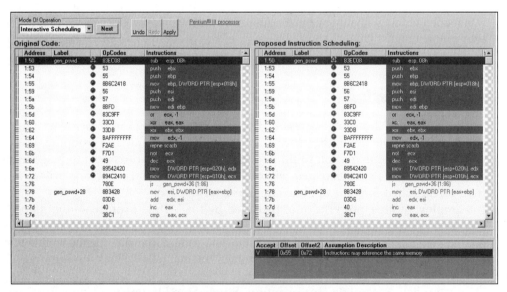

Fig. 1.10. Using the assembly coach to optimize
the planning of machine commands

Click the lowest stop light in the column, and see how VTune regroups the commands. Things have improved! No instructions are highlighted, which indicates that there are no conflicts and no penalties. What has changed in the optimized code? First, the PUSH commands (which push registers into the stack) have been separated from the command that modifies the register pointing to the stack top. This eliminates the dependence of data. (It is incorrect to push new data into the stack until you know the position of its top.)

Second, arithmetic commands have been distributed evenly and interleaved with the register read/write commands. Because Pentium processors only have one Arithmetic Logical Unit (ALU), this organization almost doubles performance.

Third, Pentium processors only contain one fully functional x86 decoder; therefore, the declared speed of decoding (three instructions per clock) is achieved only when instructions follow a strict order. Instructions decoded only by a full-featured x86 decoder should be located at the starting positions of each triplet. The triplet "tail" can be filled with commands that can be decoded by the other two decoders. As should be clear, the Microsoft Visual C++ compiler generates code that is far from optimal (from the Pentium processor's point of view), and VTune recombines the commands to optimize the code.

Listing 1.37. Assembly Code Optimized by Microsoft Visual C++ 6.0 in the Maximum Optimization Mode (*Left*) and Improved by VTune (*Right*)

```
sub      esp, 08h                        sub      esp, 08h
push     ebx                             or       ecx, -1
push     ebp                             push     ebx
mov      ebp, DWORD PTR [esp+018h]       push     ebp
push     esi                             mov      ebp, DWORD PTR [esp+018h]
push     edi                             xor      eax, eax
mov      edi, ebp                        push     esi
or       ecx, -1                         push     edi
xor      eax, eax                        xor      ebx, ebx
xor      ebx, ebx                        mov      edx, -1
mov      edx, -1                         mov      edi, ebp
repne scasb                              repne scasb
not      ecx                             mov      DWORD PTR [esp+020h], edx
dec      ecx                             not      ecx
mov      DWORD PTR [esp+020h], edx       dec      ecx
mov      DWORD PTR [esp+010h], ecx       mov      DWORD PTR [esp+010h], ecx
```

Click **Next** again and proceed with an analysis of the next block of instructions. Now, VTune eliminates the data dependence by separating the commands for reading and adding the ESI register, placing the command for incrementing the EAX register between them.

Listing 1.38. Data Dependence Produced by Microsoft Visual C++ 6.0 (*Left*) and Eliminated by VTune (*Right*)

mov	esi, DWORD PTR [eax+ebp]		mov	esi, DWORD PTR [eax+ebp]
add	edx, esi		inc	eax
inc	eax		add	edx, esi
cmp	eax, ecx		cmp	eax, ecx

You must proceed the same way until the entire code is optimized. At this point, you will encounter a new problem. Unfortunately, VTune doesn't allow you to place the optimized code into the executable file. It probably assumes that an assembly programmer can type this code in easily from the keyboard. However, not everyone is a qualified assembly programmer.

Where should you retype the code — into the "live" binary file? Of course not! This following approach is far from perfect, but I have yet to find a better one: Move the cursor to the pane containing the optimized code then select the **Print** command from the **File** menu. In the **Field Selection** window, clear all checkboxes except for **Labels** and **Instructions**, then print the code to a file or clipboard.

While printing goes on, prepare an assembly listing of the program by specifying the /FA option in the compiler command line. (This option might differ for different compilers.) The result will be the pswd.asm file. This file can be compiled (ml /c /coff pswd.asm), linked (link /SUBSYSTEM:CONSOLE pswd.obj LIBC.LIB), and started for execution. What a nuisance! The speed will be about 65 million passwords per second. (Compare this result to the 83 million passwords per second achieved when proceeding in the normal way.) As it turns out, Microsoft Visual C++ doesn't insert the alignment directives into the assembly code. This complicates the quality evaluation of the code optimization achieved by VTune. Take these 65 million passwords per second as a base, and see how VTune improves this result.

Open the file created by the profiler, and you'll encounter another problem. Its syntax is incompatible with the syntax of popular assembly translators.

Listing 1.39. Fragment of the Assembly File Generated by VTune

Label	Instructions	
gen_pswd	sub	esp, 08h
	js	gen_pswd+36 (1:86)
gen_pswd+28	mov	esi, DWORD PTR [eax+ebp]

First, the labels are not followed by colons. Second, the invalid + sign occurs in the labels. Third, the conditional jumps contain a extra trailing address enclosed in brackets.

In other words, there is a lot of work to do manually. After you accomplish this work, the code fragment will look as follows:

Listing 1.40. Corrected File Fragment for Translation by TASM or MASM

```
Label           Instructions
gen_pswd:         sub       esp, 08h
                  js        gen_pswd+_36  (1:86)
gen_pswd+_28      mov       esi, DWORD PTR [eax+ebp]
```

Now it only remains to enclose it in the following construction and translate using a TASM or MASM assembler (whichever you prefer):

Listing 1.41. Enclosing Code for the Assembly File (Optimized Code of the _gen_pswd Function Must Be Nested for Further Translation)

```
.386
.model FLAT

PUBLIC      _gen_pswd

EXTERN      _DeCrypt:PROC
EXTRN       _printf:NEAR
EXTRN       _malloc:NEAR

_DATA   SEGMENT
my_string       DB 'CRC %8X: try to decrypt: "%s"', 0aH, 00H
_DATA   ENDS

_TEXT   SEGMENT

_gen_pswd PROC NEAS
// The code of the gen_pswd function
_gen_pswd ENDP

_TEXT   ENDS
END
```

In relation to the pswd.c program, it is necessary to declare `gen_pswd` as an external function. This can be done as follows:

Listing 1.42. Declaring the External `gen_pswd` Function in a C Program

---

```
extern int _gen_pswd(char *crypteddata,
        char *pswd, int max_iter, int validCRC);
```

Now, it is possible to assemble the entire project:

Listing 1.43. Final Build of the Password Project

```
ml /c /coff gen_pswd.asm
cl /Ox pswd.c /link gen_pswd.obj
```

A test run of the optimized program shows a speed of *78 million passwords per second*, about 20% better than the speed before optimization. VTune provides pretty good code optimization. Still, the result is inferior to the speed achieved in the previous step. The fact that this is due to compiler, rather than profiler, is of no consolation. Nevertheless, this problem doesn't effect the optimization of assembly programs.

Results and Predictions

Now, it is time to analyze the results. If you discard the first version of the program with the repeated calls to `printf`, you could say that you have improved the performance of the program from 1.5 million passwords to 84 million passwords per second. You certainly can be proud of this result. Although it is far from the theoretical limit (for example, it is possible to check several passwords in parallel using vector MMX commands), application profiling is clearly the best approach for avoiding performance overhead.

Curiously, every step in the optimization process resulted in almost exponential growth of the application's performance (Fig. 1.11). You cannot always expect exponential performance growth, but the common trend is clear: The most difficult problems are deeply nested, and it is almost impossible to solve them without digging into the code.

This chapter has considered only the basic functional capabilities of VTune (and even this was done briefly). Its capabilities are not limited to these features. VTune represents an entire world, which, among other useful features, has a built-in programming language and even its own API, allowing the programmer to call VTune functions from add-on custom modules (i.e., create custom plug-ins for this profiler).

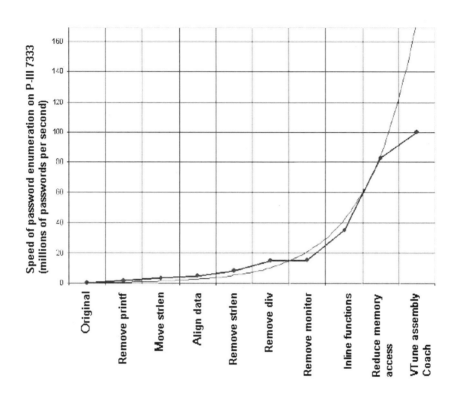

Fig. 1.11. Chronology of the password cracker optimization

By carefully studying this example, you will be able to take the first step in mastering VTune. Later on, you'll be able to study its features on your own. In conclusion, I'd like to provide you with some useful advice. The built-in help system in VTune is extensive and inconvenient to use; therefore, most of its topics remain unknown to most users. Because of this, it is better to use any help-decompiler to convert the HLP file to RTF format. The resulting RTF file can be opened using any text processor (such as Microsoft Word) and printed or read on-screen. (The helpfile comprises more than 1,000 pages.)

Chapter 2: RAM Subsystem

Introduction to RAM

Billions of bit cells, packed within a tiny chip that fits easily in your palm... Today, when RAM is measured in hundreds of megabytes, programmers are relieved of the "pleasure" of optimizing programs for speed and size simultaneously. Even if a program requires 1 GB of RAM, the system will allocate it at the expense of the hard disk.

However, memory subsystem performance is far from perfect. The current situation is even worse than it was 10 or 15 years ago. Typical PC configurations of the 1980s and early 1990s were equipped with 10 MHz processors and RAM with a typical access time of 200 nsec. Today, a typical PC configuration is 1,000 MHz to 2,000 MHz and 20 nsec. It isn't difficult to see that the performance ratio between the memory and the processor has decreased by a factor of hundred.

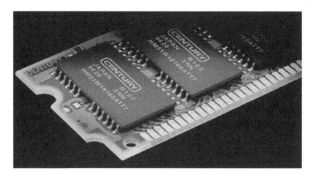

Fig. 2.1. Billions of bit cells, packed within a tiny chip that
fits easily in your palm, form contemporary RAM

Despite the rapid growth of the RAM throughput in the past few years, the gap between the CPU and the memory has increased at a frightening pace. Curiously, this isn't the first time such a situation has occurred: About 40 to 50 years ago, during the age of mainframes with fast (for that time) processors and horribly slow drum or ferrite memory, the relationship between memory and processor speeds was similar to that of today.

Efficient work with memory of all levels is impossible without understanding its physical and architectural features. At the minimum, the programmer must ensure that frequently used data fit within cache. To achieve the best performance, it is necessary to match carefully requests to the memory with the features of all its subsystems. This book focuses on the problems associated with this type of matching.

RAM Hierarchy

What is RAM — an existing, real-world object, or an abstraction that has no physical association? Don't answer this question too quickly. Consider the problem logically. If you take a screwdriver and remove several screws from the case of your computer's system unit, among the other chips located on the motherboard, you will find some vertically installed memory chips. These chips make up the computer's Random Access Memory (RAM). Thus, *RAM appears to be a physical device*.

However, if address this same question to any serious programmer, you will most likely hear that *memory is a set of cells combined into address space with predefined properties*, or something similar. Did you notice the difference? Not a word about a physical device. A system programmer can easily place the value 0x666 into a cell numbered 0x999 and, if required, retrieve this value later. Software developers, however, tend to have a vague understanding of cell numbering. High-level programming languages operate with *variables*, rather than with memory cells. It is commonly accepted that variables reside in the memory and that each variable fits within one or more memory cells. In practice, however, this is far from being the case! The compiler might decide that it is necessary to store variables in registers. Sometimes, it might decide not to store them (for example, if it finds out that the variable value isn't used in the program, or that it can be calculated at compile time).

So, the question remains: What is RAM? From the hardware specialist's point of view, it is a chip. From the programmer's point of view, RAM is an abstract data storage place. It doesn't make sense to try to determine which side is right; both the hardware specialist and the programmer are *wrong*. RAM is neither a chip nor an abstraction. It is a computer subsystem comprising a variety of interacting physical components that, together, create a complex hierarchy of logical abstractions.

▶ *Note*

Years ago, when computers could run without operating systems and no one had even heard about multitasking, programs had to be loaded manually. After it was loaded, each program monopolized the computer's resources, including the main memory.

With the arrival of multitasking operating systems came the problem of how to share resources (especially the main memory) between several applications. The protection of the "property" of a specific application from the influence of other applications was no less important. In addition, it was necessary to ensure an application's independence from the loading address and, at the same time, to make several concurrently running programs fit within a limited amount of RAM.

The solutions to these problems required developers to create a multilevel memory hierarchy. As a result, direct memory access had to be sacrificed.

The greatest advantage of an abstraction is that it reduces the level of basic knowledge required to work with hardware, eliminating a range of minor architectural features. For example, is it necessary to know that reading a dynamic memory cell destroys its contents? This fact remains unnoticed only because the system automatically restores this information by rewriting the destroyed data after the read operation has been accomplished.

Another useful property of abstractions is as follows: Without abstractions, no program would be portable. Abstractions emulate a virtual machine, reducing or eliminating the effect of physical hardware implementation on the program-implementation algorithm.

However, I have been distracted from the main topic. Abstract main memory is uniform; physical memory is not. An abstract model of RAM has no idea about the numerous traps and design limitations that can prevent the programmer from achieving maximum performance. To win this struggle, all abstraction layers must be sequentially bypassed so that the work occurs at the hardware level.

This does not mean that you will have to write programs in assembly language and work directly with computer hardware. It is sufficient to schedule memory access that accounts for the features of specific hardware. For efficient programming, you can choose any language — C/C++, Pascal, or Perl. Nothing limits your choice of programming language.

The need for scheduling may be best illustrated by an analogy. Suppose that letters are collected from the mailbox at 9 a.m. daily. To speed up the arrival of your letters, you need to leave them before that time. If a letter is placed in the box at 9:05 a.m., the delay in delivery will be 24 hours.

Now, remove the cover from the "black box" labeled *memory subsystem of the IBM PC* and find out what is inside.

At the top of the hierarchy (Fig. 2.2) are the *memory management libraries* that implement a unified interface to the *heap manager* of the operating system. (Some operating systems, particularly MS-DOS, have no adequate heap manager. In this case, the heap manager functions are delegated to the application library.)

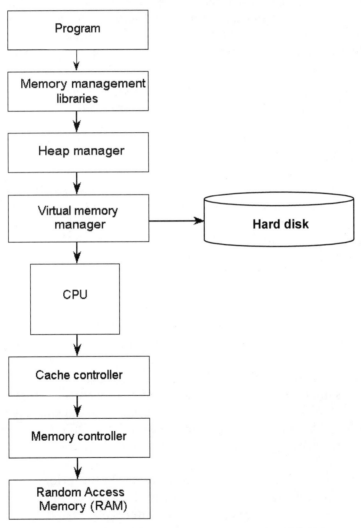

Fig. 2.2. Memory hierarchy in Windows 9x/NT/2000 and UNIX operating systems

The heap manager (or dynamic memory manager) supports basic operations with memory blocks (block allocation, block release, changing the size of allocated memory block, etc.).

The *virtual memory manager* resides one level lower. In close coordination with the processor, it implements the following:

❏ *Virtual address spaces.* The virtual memory manager abstracts from physical addresses, allowing arbitrary addresses to be assigned to memory cells. Because of this capability, several concurrently running applications can be loaded by the same logical (virtual) addresses, and the address spaces of these applications won't intersect. Applications, like the inhabitants of parallel worlds, will never "see" one another if they do not use shared memory regions created specially for this purpose (or other methods of interprocess communication).

❏ *Virtual memory.* Virtual memory is an extension of the ideas of virtual address space. Any cell of virtual memory can reside both in the main memory and on the hard disk. This allows practically unlimited amounts of memory, up to dozens of gigabytes, to be allocated. In practice, operating systems of the Windows family provide each process with 2 GB of memory space. The exception is the Windows NT Enterprise Server, which doesn't impose limits on the programmer's appetite. (See the *Very Large Memory* description in the Platform SDK documentation.)

Functions of the virtual memory manager require certain privileges to be established, because this module interacts directly with the CPU and the hard-disk driver.

The *processor* doesn't interact directly with the memory and the hard disk. Rather, this interaction is accomplished via the *memory controller* and the *disk controller*. In contemporary computers, both of these controllers are integrated within the *chipset*, a set of chips (also known as the system logic set) whose intellectual capabilities determine overall system performance.

The *system memory* of contemporary PCs usually is based on rather slow (by today's standards) Dynamic RAM (DRAM) chips. Therefore, to speed up access to commonly used data, a small amount of high-speed cache memory resides within or close to the CPU.

Cache memory is unavailable formally to the programmer: It is not included in the address space, and its contents cannot be directly read or modified.

Cache memory management is performed by the *cache controller*, rather than by the CPU. (In contemporary processors, the cache controller is usually integrated within the CPU. Nevertheless, this doesn't change the working principle.) The cache controller is mainly responsible for accumulating important data within cache memory and clearing away the "garbage" data that are no longer required.

Thus, the memory subsystem has at least seven levels, each of which is implemented by specific hardware. Each level also is subdivided into several nested levels. For example, the chipset includes the Bus Interface Unit (BIU), the query arbiter, several query queues, the memory controller, and a clipboard.

Therefore, Fig. 2.2 should be interpreted as a tour route of the memory subsystem.

Random Access Memory

Just like ten years ago, the RAM of contemporary PCs is based on relatively cheap Dynamic Random Access Memory (DRAM). Over this decade, several generations of the interface logic, which connect the memory core with the "outside world," have been introduced. Rather than evolution, this was succession — each new generation of memory inherited most of the architecture of its predecessor, including its limitations. The memory core has not undergone any principal changes (with the exception of improved silicon fabrication technologies, such as the integration level). Even the "revolutionary" Direct Rambus DRAM (RDRAM) contained no innovative features and holds a place on the genealogical tree of the memory family.

For this reason, the best way to study memory organization and working principles is to trace this genealogical tree. I'll start with the oldest memory models and proceed through newer variants to the most recent technologies at the time of writing.

It is important to note that this chapter only provides the information on RAM organization necessary for software optimization. I strongly recommend that you not limit yourself to this required minimum. You can find detailed information on memory chips by reading the specifications and technical documentation supplied by leading memory manufacturers. In my opinion, the best documentation on this topic can be downloaded from the following Web sites: **http://www.ibm.com**, **http://www.samsung.com**, **http://www.intel.com**, and **http://www.amd.com**.

RAM Design and Working Principles

In the Core

The DRAM chip core comprises a set of cells, each storing a single bit of information. Physically, the cells are joined into a rectangular matrix, whose horizontal lines are known as *rows*, and whose vertical lines are called *columns* or *pages*.

Lines are normal electric conductors. At their intersection is the "heart" of the cell — a simple device comprising a *transistor* and a *capacitor* (Figs. 2.3 and 2.4).

The capacitor provides immediate information storage. However, the amount of data that it can store is small — only 1 bit. If the capacitor plate holds no charge, the bit contains a logical 0; the presence of the charge corresponds to a logical 1. The transistor plays the role of the *key*, preventing the capacitor from discharging. In a normal state, the transistor is closed. Several moments after an electric signal is supplied to the respective line of the array (the time interval depends on the design and chip quality), it will open to connect the capacitor plate with the corresponding column.

The *sense amplifier* (sense amp), connected to each of the array columns, reads the entire page by reacting to a weak flow of electrons through open transistors from the capacitor plates. *The page represents the minimal portion of data exchange with the DRAM core.* The reading or writing of a separate cell is impossible! Opening of a single row will open all transistors connected to it and, consequently, discharge all related capacitors. Therefore, you must read the entire row for every read operation.

The reading of a cell is destructive because the sense amp discharges the capacitor while reading its charge. Therefore, DRAM is *single-use memory*. To avoid information loss, it is necessary to rewrite the row immediately after it has been read. Depending on design features, this mission is delegated to the programmer, the memory controller, or to the memory chip. Most contemporary chips take on this task. Those that delegate this responsibility to the controller are rare, and no chips delegate the rewrite operation to the programmer.

Fig. 2.3. 1,024-bit core of a UNIVAC computer (approximately life-size)

Because of a small capacitance, a capacitor only can hold information for a short time — hundredths or thousandths of a second. The reason for this lies in the self-discharging nature of the capacitor. Despite high-quality dielectric materials with enormous resistance, the charge is lost quickly because few electrons can be accumulated by the capacitor on its plate. To overcome the memory's "forgetfulness," it must be periodically refreshed. The refresh process consists of periodical read-and-rewrite operations. Depending on the memory implementation, the regenerator might reside within the controller or within memory chip. For example, in XT/AT computers, memory was refreshed by a timer interrupt every 18 msec via a special Direct Memory Access (DMA) channel. Any attempt to freeze hardware interrupts resulted in the loss or corruption of the data stored in RAM. This degraded overall system performance because RAM was inaccessible during refresh. Today, the regenerator is usually built into the memory chip. Furthermore, before refreshing occurs, the contents of the regenerated row are copied to a special buffer, preventing the blocking of data access.

Conventional DRAM (Page Mode DRAM)

Now that you understand the design and working principles of the memory core, I'll proceed to its interface. Physically, the memory chip is a rectangular piece of ceramic or plastic "bristled" with a multitude of *leads* (also referred to as contact fingers or connectors) on two (less commonly, on four) of its sides.

Before I can explain the leads, I must distinguish between *address lines* and *data lines*. Address lines, as their name implies, are used to choose a specific memory cell. Data lines are used to read and write the contents of the chosen cell. The required operation mode is determined by the state of a specific outlet — *Write Enable* (WE).

A low level of the WE signal prepares the chip for reading the state of data lines and writing this information into the respective cell. A high level of the same signal makes the chip read the contents of the data cell and output them to the data line.

This trick greatly reduces the number of chip leads, helping decrease its size. The smaller the size, the higher the maximum clock frequency. Why is this the case? First, because of the limited speed of electric-signal propagation, the lengths of the conductors connected to individual chip leads must not differ widely. If this requirement is not observed, the signal from one outlet will pass ahead of the signal from another. Second, the conductors themselves must not be too long. Otherwise, the delay in signal propagation will cancel out the operating speed. Third, any conductor acts as both a receiving and a transmitting aerial, and the negative effect of these dual roles sharply increases with the growth of clock frequency. Several methods can be used to overcome this effect (such as shifting the signals to adjacent bits). However, reducing the lengths and number of conductors remains the most efficient approach.

Finally, each conductor is characterized by its *electric capacitance.* Capacitance is incompatible with data-transmission speed. Here is one illustrative example: The first transatlantic cable for the telegraph was successfully laid in 1858. When the voltage was supplied to one end of the cable, it didn't appear immediately at the other end. The voltage at the receiving end gradually reached a stable value. When the power to the cable was shut off, the voltage at the receiving end didn't drop sharply; it decreased slowly. The cable was accumulating electricity like a sponge absorbs water. This property is known as electric capacitance.

Thus, multiplexing the chip outlets increases the throughput of data exchange with memory, but it doesn't allow read and write operations to be accomplished in parallel. (Running a few steps ahead, note that on-die cache memory, because of its tiny size, is not subject to this limitation. Therefore, it is capable of reading one cell while writing to another.)

The same approach is used to combine the rows and columns of the memory array into multiplexed address lines. For the square array, the number of address lines is halved. The maximum clock frequency is inversely proportional to the number of address lines raised to the 4th power because row and column numbers must be transmitted sequentially. How can you know what is on the address line — row number, column number, or neither? The solution to this problem introduced two extra outlets that signal the presence of rows or columns on the address lines. These outlets are known as *Row Address Strobe* (RAS) and *Column Address Strobe* (CAS). When no information is on the address lines (quiet state), a high-level signal can be found at both outputs, which informs the chip that no action should be taken.

Assume that the programmer needs to read the contents of a specific memory cell. The controller transforms the physical address into a pair of numbers — row number and column number, then sends the first of them to the address lines. After waiting until the signal stabilizes, the controller resets the RAS signal to the low level, informing the memory chip that there is information on the address line. The chip reads this address and selects the appropriate row of the array. All transistors connected to this row open, and about a million electrons that accumulated at the capacitor plates flow to the inlets of the sense amp. The sense amp decodes the row by converting it into a sequence of ones and zeroes, then stores the resulting information in a special buffer. This entire operation (depending on the chip design and quality) takes 20 nsec to 100 nsec.

During this time, the memory controller pauses. When the chip has read the row and is ready to receive information, the controller supplies the column number to the address lines. After the signal stabilizes, the controller resets the CAS signal to the low level. When this occurs, the chip transforms the column number to the cell offset within the buffer. All that remains is to read the cell contents and supply them to the data lines. This takes time, during which the controller waits for the requested information. At the final stage of data-exchange cycle, the controller reads the state of the data lines and deactivates the RAS and CAS signals by setting them to the high level. The chip precharges its internal circuitry and restores the row by rewriting it (if restore operations are delegated to the chip).

The delay between supplying row and column numbers is known as the *RAS-to-CAS delay* time (^tRCD). The delay between supplying the column number and receiving the cell contents at the output is known as the *CAS delay* time (^tCAC). The delay between reading the last cell and supplying the new line number is called the *RAS precharge* time (^tRP). From this point, I will use the full terms, which are more illustrative and better correspond to their respective *Basic Input/Output System* (BIOS) settings.

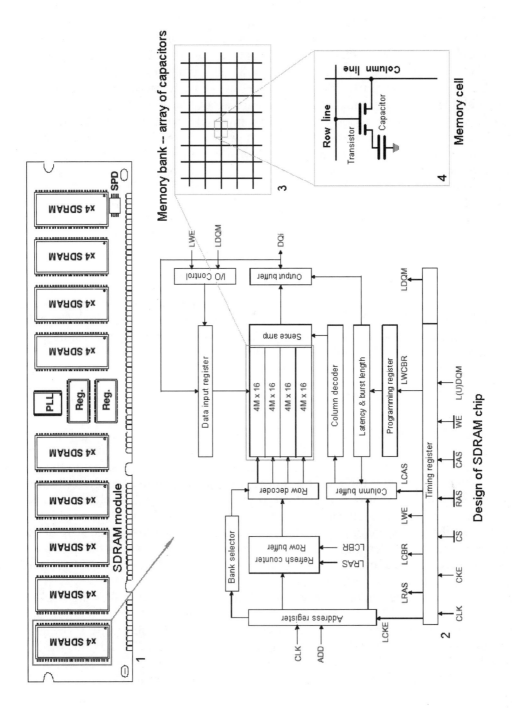

Fig. 2.4. Designs of a RAM module (*1*), a memory chip (*2*), a RAM array (*3*), and a memory cell (*4*)

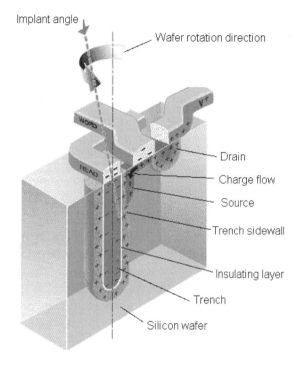

Fig. 2.5. Memory cell of a contemporary DRAM chip

DRAM Evolution

In memory chips manufactured until the mid-1990s, the sum of all three delays (RAS-to-CAS delay, CAS delay, and RAS precharge) was about 200 nsec. This corresponded to 2 clocks in a 10 MHz system and 12 clocks in a 60 MHz system. With the arrival of the Intel Pentium 60 (1993) and the Intel 486DX4 100 (1994), it became evident that DRAM required improvement; its operation speed had become inadequate.

Fast-Page Mode DRAM (FPM DRAM)

The first improvement was introduced with *Fast-Page Mode* (FPM) DRAM in 1995. It differed from the chips of the previous generation chiefly in its support of *short addresses* (i.e., one RAS signal obtains an entire row). If the next cell that will be requested resides in the same row as the previous cell, its address is determined by the column number. (It isn't necessary to transmit the row number). How is this done? Consider Fig. 2.6. In previous-generation DRAM (top diagram), the RAS signal was deactivated after the data was read, preparing the chip for the new work cycle. In FPM DRAM (center diagram), the controller holds RAS at the low level, eliminating the need to retransmit the row number.

During sequentially reading of memory cells or processing of small structures (of 1 KB or 2 KB), access time is reduced 40% or more because the row being processed resides in the chip's internal buffer. It isn't necessary to reaccess the RAM array!

Nevertheless, chaotic access to memory and cross-references to cells from different pages are not aided by fast-page memory access. When performing such operations, FPM DRAM functions like conventional DRAM. If the cell requested next lies outside the current row, the controller is forced to deactivate RAS, hold the RAS precharge pause required to recharge the chip, transmit the row number, then hold the RAS-to-CAS delay. Only after it has accomplished all these operations can the controller proceed with transmitting the column number.

The situation in which the requested cell resides in the open row is a *page hit*. Otherwise, a *page miss* occurs. Because misses result in overhead, performance-crucial program modules must account for specific features of the FPM DRAM architecture.

Another problem arises: Access-time inconstancy complicates measurements of memory-chip performance, as well as procedures for comparing the measurement results. In the worst case, the time (in nanoseconds) required to access a memory cell equals *RAS-to-CAS delay + CAS delay + RAS precharge*; in the best case, it equals the time of the CAS delay. Chaotic but subdued memory access (that gives the memory time to refresh) requires at least *RAS-to-CAS delay + CAS delay* (in nanoseconds).

Because the RAS-to-CAS delay, CAS delay, and RAS precharge are not interrelated and can take any values, a reliable evaluation of memory-chip performance requires at least three parameters. However, chip manufacturers, looking to generate the best results, usually provide only two parameters: *RAS-to-CAS delay + CAS delay* and *CAS delay*. The first parameter (also known as full access time) is the time required to access an arbitrary cell; the second parameter (known as work-cycle time) is the time taken to access the next cells residing in the open row. The time required to recharge the chip (i.e., the RAS precharge) is excluded from the full access time. (However, technical documentation, including documents published on the Internet, usually provides all parameters and all timing values.)

Memory Timing

By the mid-1990s, the average value of RAS-to-CAS delay was 30 nsec, CAS delay was about 40 nsec, and the RAS precharge was less than 30 nsec. Thus, at a system bus frequency of 60 MHz (i.e., about 17 nsec), six clocks were needed to open and access the first cell of the page. Accessing other cells of the open page took three clocks. This layout can be described by the following *memory timing*: 6-3-x-x.

Memory timing simplifies the comparison of different chips. However, to obtain reliable comparison results, it is necessary to know the prevailing type of memory access — sequential or random. How can you determine whether a 5-4-x-x or 6-3-x-x chip is better? The form of the question is senseless. Better for *what tasks*? For streaming algorithms with sequential data processing, the latter memory type is better. Otherwise, the comparison doesn't make any sense, because reading two nonadjacent cells will not take 5-5-x-x and 6-6-x-x clocks for each chip. Rather, the number of clocks will equal *5+RAS precharge*-5-x-x and *6+RAS precharge*-6-x-x, respectively. Because the precharge time for the chips won't necessarily match, the 6-3-x-x chip may prove to be better both for sequential and irregular access. Therefore, the only practical approach is to compare the work-cycle time. By improving the memory core, manufacturers reduced this parameter, first to 35 nsec and later 30 nsec, achieving almost a sevenfold growth in performance over the previous generation of chips.

Extended Data Output DRAM (EDO DRAM)

The invention of FPM DRAM didn't solve the performance problem; it simply gave manufacturers a break. The clock frequencies of newer processors were growing rapidly, nearing the 200 MHz barrier. The market demanded a radical new solution instead of a tedious struggle for each nanosecond. Engineers at most leading manufacturers were laboring to find a solution when (around 1996) someone came up with a brilliant idea: If the chip is equipped with special trigger-latched data lines that are available after the CAS fades away, it will be possible to deactivate CAS *before* the data are read, thus preparing the chip to accept the next column number.

According to the timing information provided in Fig. 2.6, in FPM chips, the low level of the CAS signal is retained until the data is read. Then, CAS is deactivated and a short pause is used to recharge the internal circuitry. Only after this is the column number of the next cell supplied to the address bus. In the newer memory type, *Extend Data Output* (EDO) DRAM, the CAS signal is deactivated in the course of data reading while the internal circuitry is recharged. Therefore, the next column number can be supplied *before* the data line is read. The duration of the EDO DRAM work cycle (depending on the chip quality) was 20 nsec to 30 nsec, which corresponded to two clocks on a 66 MHz system. Technological advances reduced the total access time. At the 66 MHz frequency, the best chips had timing of 5-2-x-x. Simple calculation can determine that the peak performance growth achieved by migrating from FPM to EDO was about 30%.

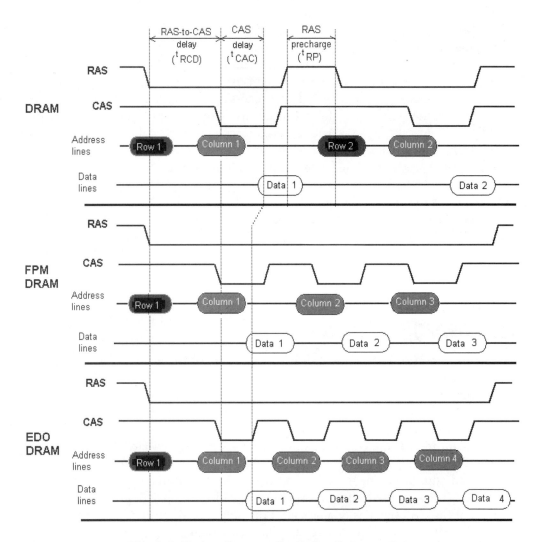

Fig. 2.6. Timing diagrams illustrating the operation
of specific DRAM types

Burst EDO DRAM (BEDO DRAM)

Twofold performance growth was achieved only in *Burst EDO* (BEDO) DRAM. By
adding the column-count generator the chip, the designers eliminated CAS delay,
reducing the work cycle to 15 nsec. After accessing a random cell, the BEDO chip

automatically increased the column number by one without requiring it to be transmitted explicitly. Because the address counter had a limited length (only 2 bits), the maximum packet length could not exceed four cells ($2^2 = 4$).

Note that because of the burst mode, Intel 80486 and Pentium processors never process more than four adjacent cells per operation. (Detailed information on this topic will be provided in *Interaction between the Memory and the Processor*.) Regardless of the order of data access, BEDO always operates at maximum speed. For a 66 MHz frequency, its timing is 5-1-1-1, approximately 40% faster than EDO DRAM.

Despite its speed characteristics, BEDO enjoyed little popularity. The main miscalculation was that BEDO, like all of its predecessors, was asynchronous memory. This imposed stringent limitations of 60 MHz to 75 MHz on the maximum clock speed. Suppose that the work cycle is 15 nsec (one clock in a 66 MHz system). Because the clock of the memory controller is not synchronized with that of the memory chip, there is no guarantee that the starting point of the chip's work cycle will coincide with the starting clock pulse of the controller. As a result, the minimum wait is *two* clocks.

To be precise, *the start of the work cycle and the clock pulse never coincide.* Several nanoseconds are taken for the controller to form the RAS or CAS control signal. Several more nanoseconds are required to stabilize the signal so that it can be understood by the chip. It is impossible to predict how long this will take; the time depends on the ambient temperature, length of conductors, noises on the line, and many other factors!

Synchronous DRAM (SDRAM)

With the arrival of microprocessors operating at bus frequencies of 100 MHz, it became evident that memory-management mechanisms needed to be reconsidered carefully. As a result, *Synchronous DRAM* (SDRAM) was developed. As its name implies, SDRAM and the controller operate synchronously, which guarantees that the exchange cycle will be accomplished within predefined terms. Besides this, row and column numbers are supplied in a way that ensures the signals are stabilized and ready to be read when the next clock pulse arrives.

SDRAM implements an improved burst-exchange mode. The controller can request adjacent memory cells and even an entire row, if necessary. This became possible with the implementation of a full-sized address counter. (In BEDO, this counter was limited to 2 bits.)

Another improvement was in the number of memory arrays (banks); in SDRAM, the banks were increased from one to two, and then to four. This provided the possibility of accessing the cells from one bank while the internal circuitry was recharged in another (the so-called ping-pong access), increasing performance approximately 30% (if data flows were correctly planned, as described in *Strategy of Data Distribution over DRAM Banks*).

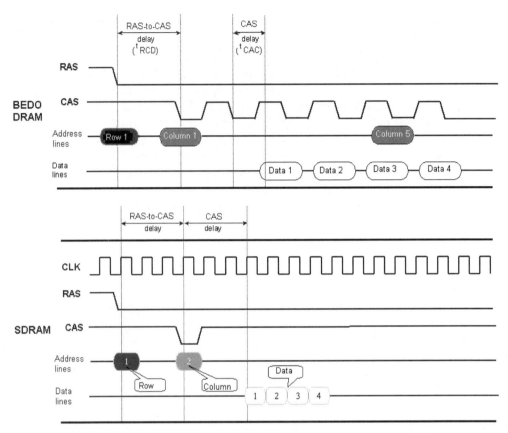

Fig. 2.7. More timing diagrams illustrating the operation of specific DRAM types

It also became possible to open two or four memory pages simultaneously. The opening of one page (i.e., the transmission of the row number) could occur while information was read from another page, which allowed a new column to be accessed in each clock cycle.

In contrast to FPM\EDO\BEDO DRAM, which recharged the internal circuitry when they closed the page (i.e., when they deactivated the RAS signal), SDRAM performs this operation automatically, allowing pages to be held as long as necessary.

Finally, the bit capacity of the data lines was increased from 32 bits to 64 bits, which doubled their performance.

Usually, the read timing of an arbitrary cell from the closed row for SDRAM is 4-1-x-x. For the open row, this timing changes to 2-1-x-x.

At the time of writing, most PCs were equipped with SDRAM, which has maintained its market position despite the rapid development of new technologies.

Double Data Rate SDRAM (DDR SDRAM), or SDRAM II

Further advances in synchronous memory technologies came with the arrival of *Double Data Rate* (DDR) SDRAM. The data rate was doubled because data was transmitted on both the leading and trailing fronts of the clock pulse. (In SDRAM, data are transmitted only on the leading front.) The effective frequency was doubled, so that the performance of 100 MHz DDR SDRAM equaled the performance of 200 MHz SDRAM. (In practice, this statement is not entirely accurate, as I will explain in *Calculating the Full Access Time.*) For marketing purposes, manufacturers of DDR chips started to denote them by the maximum throughput (measured in MB per second), rather than by clock frequency. Thus, if your memory chip is labeled DDR-1600, it doesn't operate at 1.6 GHz (so far, an unattainable ideal); it operates at the frequency of 100 MHz. Accordingly, DDR-2100 operates at 133 MHz.

Memory-bank management also has changed. The number of banks has increased from two to four. In addition, each bank is equipped with a personal controller. (Do not confuse this with the memory controller.) As a result, it seems that rather than a single chip, four chips are operating independently.

Direct Rambus DRAM (Direct RDRAM)

The closest competitor to DDR SDRAM was developed by Rambus. Contrary to popular opinion, the architecture of *Direct Rambus DRAM* (Direct RDRAM) is ordinary and does not incorporate any revolutionary ideas. Three main features distinguish this memory from previous-generation chips:

❏ Increased clock frequency because of the use of a high-speed 16-bit data bus, known as the Rambus channel
❏ Parallel transmission of a cell's row and column numbers
❏ Increased number of banks, which strengthens parallelism

The increased clock frequency causes a sharp amplification of all possible noises, particularly *electromagnetic interference*. Generally, the intensity of electromagnetic interference is proportional to the frequency value squared. At frequencies exceeding 350 MHz, this dependence is best approximated by the cubic parabola. This circumstance places stringent limitations on the topology and quality of the chip's printed circuit boards, complicating the production technology and base cost of this memory. The peak-to-peak noise level can be reduced considerably by decreasing the number of conductors (i.e., by reducing the chip's bit capacity). This approach was implemented by Rambus. The company has compensated for the frequency increase up to 400 MHz (taking into account DDR technology, the effective frequency is 800 MHz) by reducing the data-bus width to 16 bits (plus 2 bits for the Error Correction Code). Thus, Direct RDRAM tops DDR-1600 in frequency by a factor of four, but it is defeated by it in width to the same degree.

The second feature of RDRAM is the parallel transfer of a cell's row and column numbers. When considered closely, this proves to be a minor improvement. It doesn't reduce the read latency of the arbitrary cell (i.e., the time between address transmission and data reception) because this value is dependent on the core speed. (RDRAM is based on an old core.) According to the RDRAM specification, access time is 38.75 nsec. The access time for 100 MHz SDRAM is 40 nsec. Is this gain worth all that fuss?

The answer is yes: The large number of banks theoretically allow the achievement of ideal pipelining of requests to memory. Although data are supplied to the bus with a 40 nsec delay after the query (which corresponds to 320 clocks in an 800 MHz system), the data flow is continuous.

For streaming algorithms of sequential data processing, the gain is worthwhile. In all other cases, Direct RDRAM has no advantages over DDR SDRAM or even standard SDRAM operating on a modest frequency of 100 MHz. Additionally (as will be shown in *Working Principles of Cache*), the amount of cache memory in contemporary processors allows most queries to be processed locally, without accessing the main memory or, in the worst case, with a delay of this access until a better time. The performance gain associated with Direct RDRAM only becomes noticeable when vast amounts of data are processed (such as when top-quality images are edited in Adobe Photoshop).

Thus, there is little justification for using Direct RDRAM in home or office computers. For high-end workstations, DDR SDRAM remains the best choice because it keeps pace with Direct RDRAM in performance but is much less expensive.

This doesn't mean that I suggest you go from one extreme to another and label Rambus memory "unworthy." Engineering experience attained in the development of this extremely high-tech memory will find applications in advanced technologies. Take Babbage's Analytical Engine, the first attempt at a digital computer, as an example: Despite the advanced idea (described by its inventor, Charles Babbage, in 1837), the parameters of its implementation were considerably lower than those of basic calculation tools (such as the abacus). This is similar to the situation with Direct RDRAM. Less sophisticated approaches can be used to achieve a throughput of 1.6 GB/sec.

Comparing Different Memory Types

From the PC user's point of view, the most important memory parameter is its speed. At first glance, it seems nothing could be easier than measuring speed; it seems sufficient to calculate the throughput capability of the memory per time interval (such as megabytes per second). However, if you try to use this approach, you won't succeed! As you already know, memory-access time is not constant. Depending on the type of access, it can vary greatly. The highest speed is achieved during sequential reading; the lowest speed occurs during irregular access. In addition, contemporary memory modules have several independent banks; therefore, they can process several queries in parallel.

If the queries follow each other in a continuous flow, the answers also are generated continuously. The delay between the arrival of the query and the reception of the corresponding answer can be lengthy, but this doesn't matter; the latency (i.e., the value of this delay) is masked by pipelining. Thus, memory performance is determined exclusively by its throughput. An analogy can be found in automobile production. Assume that the assembly of a single car takes one month. If a large number of cars are assembled at the same time, the factory can produce a hundred cars every day, and its throughput is determined mainly by the quality of assembly pipelines, rather than by the time required to assemble each car.

Most RAM manufacturers mark their products using the throughput value (Table 2.1). Strange as this might seem, the rapid growth in throughput (Fig. 2.8) doesn't produce an adequate growth in application performance. Why is this so?

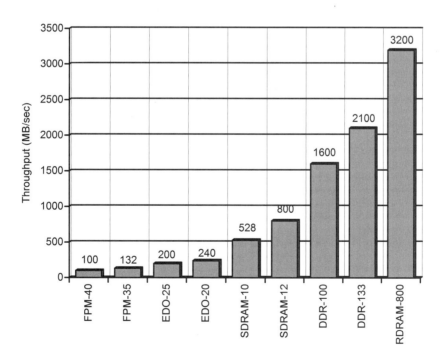

Fig. 2.8. Maximum performance of various memory types

A fundamental problem has been encountered: data dependence. (See *Eliminating Data Dependence*.) Consider the following situation: Cell No. 1 stores the pointer to cell No. 2, which contains the data to be processed. Before the contents of cell No. 1 have been obtained, a query cannot be sent to read the contents of the cell No. 2 because its address is unknown. Consequently, memory performance will depend on latency, rather than on throughput. I do not mean the latency of the memory chip; I mean the latency of the entire memory subsystem — the cache controller, system bus, system logic, etc. The latency of this subsystem adds up to about 20 clocks of the system bus, which is many times larger than the full access time for a specific memory cell. Thus, when processing the dependent data, the memory-operation speed doesn't play an important role. This means that different memory types, such as SDRAM-PC100 and RDRAM-800, will deliver identical results.

This situation isn't artificial; on the contrary, it is normal. The most basic data structures (such as trees or lists) are highly dependent on data because they reference their elements via pointers. Most performance gain from the increased speed of memory chips is negated by this data dependence.

Table 2.1. Characteristics of the Main Types of Memory

Memory type	Frequency (MHz)	Memory organization (bits)	Access time (nsec)	Working cycle (nsec)	Throughput (MB/sec)
FPM	25, 33	32	70, 60	40, 35	100, 132
EDO	40, 50	32	60, 50	25, 20	160, 200
SDRAM	66, 100, 133	64	40, 30	10, 7.5	528, 800, 1064
DDR	100, 133	64	30, 22.5	5, 3.75	1600, 2100
RDRAM	400, 600, 800	16	30	2.5	1600, 2400, 3200

Interaction between the Memory and the Processor

Contrary to a common fallacy, the processor doesn't interact directly with RAM. This interaction is via a special controller connected to the system bus in a manner similar to other peripheral-device controllers. From the processor's point of view, the mechanism for accessing input/output ports is identical to the process of accessing a memory cell. First, the processor sends the required address to the address bus.

At the next clock, it specifies the type of request: an attempt to access the memory, an attempt to access I/O ports, or an interrupt confirmation. In some aspects, RAM can be considered a set of I/O registers, each storing specific value.

The processing of requests from the CPU is delegated to the system logic set (also known as the chipset), which, along with other components, includes the memory controller. The memory controller is "transparent" to the programmer. Nevertheless, knowledge of its architecture will simplify the process of optimizing data exchange with the memory.

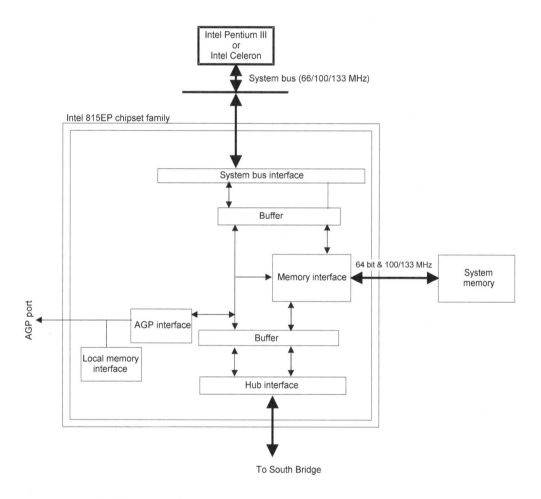

Fig. 2.9. North Bridge design of the Intel 815EP chipset (which contains the memory controller, labeled *Memory interface*)

Consider the mechanism of interaction between the memory and the processor in the Intel 815EP chipset (Fig. 2.9). When the processor needs to retrieve the contents of a specific memory cell, it waits until the bus is ready, and then uses the arbitration mechanism to catch the bus (which takes one clock). In the first clock, the signals define the transaction type in enough detail to begin a request. In the second clock, the signals carry additional information to define the complete transaction type. This phase of the query takes three clocks of the system bus. (More information on this topic can be found in the P6 and EV6 bus specification.)

Regardless of the size of the cell to be read (byte, word, or double word), the query length always equals the size of the L2 cache line: 32 bytes for K6, PII, and PIII processors; 64 bytes for Athlon; and 128 bytes for P4. (For more information on this topic, see *Working Principles of Cache.*) This approach significantly improves memory performance when cells are read sequentially and causes little reduction in performance for irregular read operations. This is not surprising, because the chipset latency exceeds the data-transmission interval several times.

The *system bus controller* (also known as the Bus Interface Unit) is planted on the North Bridge of the chipset. It receives the query from the processor, then passes it to appropriate *agent* (such as the memory controller) or places it into the *queue* if the agent is busy. The queue allows the processor to send the next query without waiting until the processing of the previous one has been completed.

If the query is passed to the memory controller, it takes one clock to decode the obtained address to the physical row or column number of the cell. Then, it transmits this information to the memory module, according the scenario described in *RAM Design and Working Principles.*

Depending on its architecture, the memory controller might work with memory only at the frequency of the system bus (a synchronous controller), or it might support memory operating at any frequency (an asynchronous controller). Synchronous controllers limit a PC user's choice of memory modules, but asynchronous controllers are less efficient. Why is this so? First, because of frequency mismatch, it is impossible to pass the data directly to the bus controller. Instead, the data first must be stored in the temporary buffer, from where bus controller extracts them at the speed it requires. (A similar situation exists for write operations.) Second, if the relation between the system bus frequency and the memory frequency cannot be represented as a relation between integer numbers, then it is necessary to wait until the current clock pulse has been completed before starting the data exchange. There are two such delays (in technical jargon, these are known as penalties): The first delay takes place when the cell address is passed to the memory chip, and the second when the data is passed to the bus controller. All of these factors increase the latency of the memory subsystem (the time from when the query is sent until the data is received). Thus, an asynchronous controller operating with SDRAM PC-133 at a 100 MHz system bus is less efficient than a synchronous controller operating at the same bus with SDRAM PC-100 memory.

When the requested data are ready, the memory controller notifies the bus controller. Having received this notification, bus controller waits until the bus is ready, then passes the data to the processor in the burst mode. Depending on the bus protocol, one to four data packets can be passed during one clock. In K6, PII, and PIII processors, one transfer occurs per clock; in an Athlon processor, two transfers occur; and in P4, four transfers occur.

At this time, the data is passed to cache and becomes available to the processor.

 ### *Note*

Most contemporary chipsets comprise two chips — the North and South Bridges. The North Bridge (which received its name because of its traditional position on design drawings) includes the controller of the system bus, the memory controller, the optional AGP controller, and the PCI controller or internal bus controller for communicating with the South Bridge. The South Bridge is responsible for input and output. It includes the DMA controller, the interrupt controller, a timer, hard disk controllers, the floppy disk controller, and controllers for various ports (COM, LPT, and USB).

Fig. 2.10. Appearance of the Intel 815EP chipset

Up to this point, the bus controller and memory controller have been described as black boxes. The time has come to remove the covers from these boxes and carefully study their interiors. Because the previous discussion used Intel products as examples, I'll now discuss the design of the AMD 750 chipset (Fig. 2.11). Note that in the quality of accompanying documentation for its chipsets, AMD surpasses its competitors.

The system bus controller, or *Bus Interface Unit* (BIU), is responsible for query processing and data movement between the processor and the chipset. It comprises the following functional components: the *Processor Source Synch Clock Transceiver*,

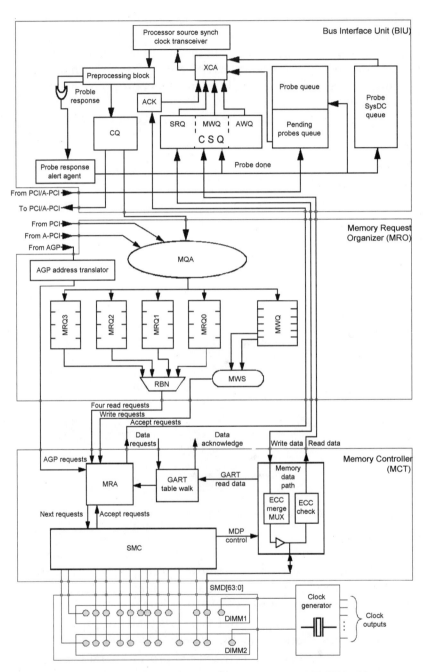

Fig. 2.11. Memory interaction mechanism in the AMD 750 chipset

the *Command Queue* (CQ), the *Control System Queue* (CSQ), and the *External Communications Adapter* (XCA). All other components of the bus controller in Fig. 2.11 support probe debugging unrelated to the topic under discussion.

The clock transceiver is the basic bus controller, which understands the bus protocol and takes responsibility for all interactions with the processor. Queries received from the processor are sent to the CQ, then passed to respective agents as the agents become free.

The answers of the agents are stored in three separate queues: the *SysDC Read Queue* (SRQ), the *Memory Write Queue* (MWQ), and the *PCI/A-PCI Write Queue* (AWQ). Note that this deals with read and write operations into the processor, rather than data written by the processor into the system memory.

The XCA retrieves the contents of the queues and transforms them into command packets. These are passed to the clock transceiver to be sent to the processor. If all queues are empty, the NOP command is sent to the processor.

The *Memory Request Organizer* (MRO) receives queries for reading and writing the memory simultaneously from three devices: the bus controller, the PCI bus, and the AGP port. The MRO tries to serve each client efficiently, which is not always simple. (The system memory must be shared.)

The *Memory Queue Arbiter* (MQA) places all clients into a *round-robin* (RBN) queue and processes one transaction per clock. In addition, the arbiter translates the physical address to a DRAM bank, row number, and column number. Processed transactions are placed in one or more queues. In the AMD 760 chipset, there are five such queues: four read queues, each comprising four entries (MRQ0 through MRQ3), and one write queue, containing six entries (MWQ). In this case, the "read" term means reading data from the memory (and "write" means writing data to the memory).

Each read queue stores queries intended exclusively for its memory bank. As the RBN agent samples data from the queues, the memory bank is regenerated while the other queries are processed.

The *Memory Controller* (MCT) is responsible for physically supporting RAM modules installed on the computer. (In the AMD 760 chipset, this task is delegated to the *SDRAM Memory Controller* (SMC). Newer chipsets can work with DDR and Rambus memory). The same module is responsible for initializing, regenerating, and reconfiguring memory chips — including the settings for parameters such as RAS-to-CAS delay, CAS delay, RAS precharge, and the selection of the operating clock frequency.

The *Memory Request Arbiter* (MRA) receives read and write queries from the MRO and AGP, then passes them to the SMC. Transmission of one query takes one clock.

The data written to the memory are retrieved from the SRQ of the system bus controller. The data read from the memory are sent to the MWQ, then sent to the processor.

Calculating the Full Access Time

Now that you are acquainted with the mechanisms of interaction between RAM and the processor, you can calculate real throughput when reading dependent data. Review the following data-exchange mechanism stages:

1. The processor receives a request to read a cell. It carries out arbitration and passes the address and length of the requested memory block to the chipset. If the bus is ready, this operation takes four clocks.

2. The bus controller, having received the query, places it into the queue. If the memory controller is ready, the bus controller passes it the query at the beginning of the next clock.

3. During the next clock, the memory controller decodes the address and places it into its internal queue of memory-read requests.

4. At the next clock, the request is retrieved from the queue. The controller passes the cell address to the memory chip. (When necessary, it waits until the start of the clock pulse.)

   I. If the requested page is open and the memory bank is not in process of regeneration, the chipset sets the CAS signal and passes a short cell address to the line. After two or three clocks of the *memory frequency*, the first packet of the retrieved data appears on the bus.

   II. The memory controller reads it within one clock.

   III. At the beginning of the next clock, a synchronous memory controller transmits the retrieved data to the bus controller. Further data transfer is carried out while data is read (with a one-clock delay).

   An asynchronous memory controller, because of frequency mismatch, cannot transfer and read data in parallel. Instead, it must accumulate the data to be transmitted in the internal buffer, and a burst-read cycle occurs. When the beginning of the next pulse arrives, the memory controller starts transferring the temporary buffer contents to the bus controller at the required frequency.

> **Note**
>
> Some low-priced chipsets, such as VIA KT 133 and VIA KT 266, only perform data transfer within the chipset at the beginning of the pulse. This eliminates the advantages of the EV6 bus used in Athlon processors: The effective frequency of the EV6 bus (defined by the system's bottleneck) equals only from 100 MHz to 133 MHz.

> **Note**
>
> If the query length exceeds the packet length, regardless of the type of memory controller, data transfer will proceed via the temporary buffer.

IV.   Depending on the length of the packet's tail, three to seven clocks of RAM frequency are needed to read it.

V.   If the query length exceeds the packet length, return to Step I.

VI.   The bus controller receives the read data, requests that the data be sent from the chipset to the processor, and places this request into the queue. (This operation takes one clock.)

VII.   If nothing else is placed into the queue and the bus is ready, the bus controller retrieves the query from the queue and sends it to the bus. Only one, two, or four data packets can be moved per operation (for K6/PII/PIII, Athlon, and P4, respectively).

VIII.   As soon as requested cell is passed to the processor, it becomes available, even if the packet-burst cycle is not yet complete.

IX.   The latency of all cache controllers is added to the latency of the processor.

5.   If the requested DRAM page is closed but the banks are not being regenerated, the memory controller passes to the memory row address. It carries RAS signal, waits two or three clocks until the chip is ready, and then goes to Step I.

6.   If the bank is being regenerated, the controller has to wait one to three clocks until regeneration is complete.

This is only an outline; it doesn't account for the design of various chipsets. For example, Nvidia chipsets are equipped with two independent memory controllers, each working with a dedicated memory module. (The memory module should not to be confused with the memory chip previously discussed in this chapter.) As a result, queries from the AGP and queries from the processor are executed in parallel, reducing chipset latency. The most interesting variant is the Dynamic Adaptive Speculative Pre-processor (DASP), which recognizes regular templates of memory access and prefetches the required cells to an internal buffer, which is located near the bus controller.

Thus, it doesn't make sense to try and derive a general formula for calculating the latency of a chipset. To accomplish this task, it is necessary to know the chipset's basic characteristics (rarely provided in accompanying documentation). Nevertheless, it can be useful to know influence specific factors have on the system's performance. Because of this, I will provide such a program (and mention its limitations).

The complete source code of this program is in the Memory/speed.exactly.c file on the companion CD-ROM. Here is its key fragment (Listing 2.1).

Listing 2.1. [Memory/speed.exactly.c] Calculating Memory Throughput and Accounting for CPU and Chipset Latency

---

```
// Calculating RAM throughput, taking into account chipset latency

C = (N * BRST_LEN)
// N is the memory digit capacity in bytes.
// BRST_LEN is the packet length in iterations.

(
    2/FSB                                          // Arbitration
  + 1/FSB                                          // Pass the cell address
  + 1/FSB                                          // Pass a transaction identifier
  + 1/FSB                                          // BIU latency
  + 1/FSB                                          // Address cell decoding by MCT
  + 1/FSB                                          // MCT latency
  + Chipset_penalty/Fm                             // Mem/FSB frequency-match penalty
  + BRST_NUM*CAS_latency/Fm                        // CAS delay
  + (fSrl?BRST_LEN/Fm:1/Fm)                        // Pass data from DRAM to
                                                   // BUFF/BIU
  + Chipset_penalty/FSB                            // Frequency-match penalty
  + (fMCT2BIUparallel?BRST_LEN/FSB:1/FSB)          // Pass data from BUFF to BIU
  + 1/FSB                                          // BIU latency
  + (fImmediately?1/FSB:BRST_LEN/Ftransf)          // Pass data from BIU to CPU
  + CPU_latency/Fcpu                               // CPU latency
  + X_CACHE*BRST_LEN/Fcpu                          // Pass data from L2 to L1 cache
  + CPU_penalty/Fcpu                               // CPU/FSB frequency-match penalty
  + RAS_latency/((LEN_page*K/(N*BRST_LEN))*Fm)     // Page-opening delay
  + (fInterleaving?0:RAS_precharge/Fm)             // Bank-recharging delay
);
```

It is immediately apparent that the value of the RAS-to-CAS delay has little influence on performance when memory cells are accessed sequentially. Therefore, in this case, the delay can be ignored. The time needed to recharge the bank (RAS precharge) is masked by the interleaving of the banks. Therefore, when memory cells are accessed sequentially, this time is irrelevant.

The value of the CAS delay is much smaller than the total chipset latency. Therefore, it has little influence on the system performance — especially on AMD Athlon, where eight data packets are read from the memory during one CAS delay. (On Pentium II/III, only four packets are read during the same period.)

Thus, the main factors that influence the system's performance (besides the chipset architecture) are the memory operation frequency and the system bus frequency. (This is true if the data within the chipset travel at a speed no less than this value. Otherwise, the system bus frequency plays no role.)

Mapping Physical DRAM Addresses to Logical Addresses

From the processor's point of view, RAM is a uniform data array whose cells are accessed using 32-bit pointers. At the same time, the address space of physical RAM is highly heterogeneous; it is divided into banks, page addresses, and column numbers (and memory-module numbers, if there is more than one module). The chipset is responsible for coordinating the RAM and processor interfaces. This coordination process is known as *mapping* physical DRAM addresses to logical processor addresses.

The specific address-mapping method depends both on the type of memory installed and on the chipset's design. Programmers are isolated from the details of the technical implementation of these algorithms and cannot work directly with physical memory. Does the physical location of a specific cell (its row and column) make any difference to a programmer? It is enough to know that the cell exists. Abstracting from the hardware is an excellent method for making a program run on any hardware platform. But how can you determine whether it will operate efficiently?

In *Optimizing Memory Operation*, I will show you that it is impossible to ensure the efficient processing of large data arrays without taking into account specific features of the DRAM architecture. You must hold an idea about the physical address that memory cells are read from or written to.

Fortunately, the address-mapping method is similar in most cases (Fig. 2.12). Low-order bits of the logical address represent the cell offset relative to the start of the burst cycle. They are never passed to the bus. Depending on the processor model, the length of the burst cycle varies from 32 bytes (K6, PII, and PIII) to 64 bytes (Athlon), and even to 128 bytes (P4). Consequently, the allocated area for storing the offset within the packet is different: 4 bits (K6, PII, and PIII), 5 bits (Athlon), and 6 bits (P4).

31	30	29	28	27	26	25	24	23	22	21	20	19	18	17	16	15	14	13	12	11	10	9	8	7	6	5	4	3	2	1	0

High-order bits of the column number   Page number   DRAM bank selection   7 low-order bits of the column number   Offset within the burst cycle

Fig. 2.12. Typical technique for mapping processor addresses to physical addresses in DRAM

The next portion of bits specifies the cell offset within the DRAM page. (In other words, these bits represent the column number.) Depending of the design features of the DRAM chip, the page length might equal 1 KB, 2 KB, or 4 KB. Therefore, the number of bits required for addressing differs. Chipset developers suffer from an inconvenience: Because it is necessary to implement several different methods of address mapping, they can't make everyone happy. Most existing chipsets only support memory modules with 2 KB DRAM pages, which corresponds to 7 address bits. More advanced chipsets (particularly, Intel 815) can process larger pages by mapping high-order bits of the column number to the "end" or the processor address. Thus, programmatic length of DRAM pages in almost all systems equals 2 KB, a circumstance that often proves useful.

The following one or two bits are responsible for memory-bank selection. All memory modules with capacities exceeding 64 MB have four DRAM banks; therefore, they use 2 bits to map logical address space ($2^2 = 4$).

The remaining bits represent the number of DRAM pages. Their number depends on the capacity of the memory module.

Optimizing Memory Operation

This section will concentrate on the optimization of large memory blocks and streaming memory-intensive algorithms. These are the situations in which intensive memory access is inevitable. (The processing of compact data structures with repeated access to each cell represents a topic for a separate discussion. This is covered in detail in *Optimizing Cache and Memory Access.*)

Despite the significant growth in memory throughput and the dramatic reduction of access time, RAM remains one of the bottlenecks suppressing overall system performance. This is annoying; the theoretical level of throughput claimed by manufacturers is never achieved because of features of the IBM PC architecture.

Typical data-processing algorithms barely use one-third of RAM performance, and performance is often far below this level. Surprisingly, most programmers don't suspect that this problem exists. One explanation may be that few people measure the performance of their programs in megabytes of processed memory per second. Even if a programmer performs such an assessment, low throughput usually can be explained as the result of bulky calculations, despite the fact that time spent on calculations plays minor role here.

A competently organized data exchange is usually much faster. Remarkably, efficient memory access is not limited to assembly language; it can be achieved using most programming languages (including interpreted languages).

The algorithms and optimization techniques suggested here are hardware-independent and can be implemented on most platforms and operating systems.

Note

Generally, performance gain is achieved exclusively by taking into account specific features of the hardware platform. However, in terms of portability, most contemporary systems are based on DRAM. The working principles of various models of dynamic memory have much in common. Furthermore, nothing revolutionary appears to be on the horizon in this field. The optimization techniques for DDR and Rambus memory adhere to the rules of continuity and provide significant performance growth, exceeding that for standard SDRAM. Do you need more confirmation of this portability?

Recommendations

Here is a brief list of recommendations that will have the greatest influence on memory performance:

- ❏ Unroll loops that read memory
- ❏ Eliminate data dependence
- ❏ Send several queries to the memory controller simultaneously
- ❏ Request data for reading with increments of no less than 32 bytes
- ❏ Use all requested pages
- ❏ Process data with an increment that eliminates hits to the same DRAM page
- ❏ Create virtual data flows
- ❏ Process data in double words
- ❏ Align the addresses of data sources
- ❏ Combine code execution with memory reads
- ❏ Group read and write operations
- ❏ Access the memory only when necessary
- ❏ Never optimize a program for a specific platform

In the following few sections, each tip will be covered in detail.

Unrolling Loops

Unrolling loops is a simple and efficient optimization technique. Pipelined microprocessors are oversensitive to branching, which greatly reduces the speed of program execution (and loops are a type of branching). Figuratively, the processor is a racer, and the software code is a road. The racer must reduce his speed at each turn (i.e., each branching). Fewer turns in the road (and, consequently, longer straightaways) means less time is required to accomplish the race.

In general, unrolling loops reduces the number of loop iterations but creates a loop containing duplicate instructions. As an example, consider the following loop:

Listing 2.2. Source Loop without Optimization

```
for(a = 0; a < 666; a++)
   x+=p[a];
```

From the processor's point of view, this loop is a set of turns, pits, and bumps without any straightaways. Unrolling this loop will improve the situation partially. To reduce the number of branches twice, you should reorganize this loop as follows:

Listing 2.3. Twofold Loop Unrolling

```
for(a = 0; a < 666; a+=2)
{
// Note that when the loop is unrolled,
// the step is increased.

   x+=p[a];
   x+=p[a + 1];
 // This is the duplicated loop body.
 // The loop-counter value is corrected.
}
```

Fourfold loop unrolling will be even more efficient. However, this cannot be achieved directly because the number of loop iterations is not a multiple of four. One way of solving this problem is to approximate the number of iterations to the nearest multiple of four (or to the nearest multiple of the repetition factor of the loop unrolling), and place the remaining iterations outside the loop body.

The code optimized in such a way might look as follows:

Listing 2.4. Fourfold Loop Unrolling (Loop Iterations Are Not a Multiple of Four)

```
for(a = 0; a < 664; a+=4)
{
// This shows the approximate number of
// loop iterations to the nearest multiple of four.

   x+=p[a];          // The body
   x+=p[a + 1];      // of the loop
```

```
    x+=p[a + 2];        // is duplicated
    x+=p[a + 3];        // four times.
}
x+=p[a];                // The two remaining iterations
x+=p[a + 1];            // are added to the end.
```

What if the number of iterations is unknown at compile time? (In other words, the number of iterations is a variable, rather than a constant). In this situation, it is advisable to use bitwise operations.

Listing 2.5. Number of Loop Iterations Is Unknown at Compile Time

```
for(a = 0; a < (N & ~3); a += k)
{
// This shows the approximate number of iterations before
// the number representing the repetition factor is reached.

    x+=p[a];
    x+=p[a + 1];
    x+=p[a + 2];
    x+=p[a + 3];
}
for(a = (N & ~3)); a < N; a++)
x+=p[a];
// The remaining iterations are added to the end.
```

As you can see, the expression (N & ~3) is the approximate number of iterations before the value is reached that represents a multiple of four. Why four? Does the speed of loop execution depend on the unrolling depth? The optimization efficiency depends both on the depth of loop unrolling and on the type of data processing. For this reason, memory-reading loops and memory-writing loops must be tested separately. Start with the read operations.

Listing 2.6. [Memory/unroll.read.c] Unrolling Depth Affects the Execution Time of the Memory-Reading Loop

```
; /*------------------------------------------------------------
;  *                    Nonoptimized version (reading)
```

```
;  ------------------------------------------------------------------------*/
for (a = 0; a < BLOCK_SIZE; a += sizeof(int))
  x += *(int *)((int)p + a);

; /*--------------------------------------------------------------------
;  *                    Fourfold unrolling (reading)
;  ------------------------------------------------------------------------*/
for (a = 0; a < BLOCK_SIZE; a += 4*sizeof(int))
{
  x += *(int *)((int)p + a );
  x += *(int *)((int)p + a + 1*sizeof(int));
  x += *(int *)((int)p + a + 2*sizeof(int));
  x += *(int *)((int)p + a + 3*sizeof(int));
}
```

The test results are encouraging: Deep unrolling of the loop cuts its execution time by more than half. However, make sure that you don't go too far with loop unrolling! An excessive unrolling depth will result in a dramatic increase of the loop size and won't justify the time gain. For example, 64-fold duplication of the loop body looks uncanny. Even worse, such a monster cannot fit within cache, which will degrade performance.

As shown in Fig. 2.13, the most expedient is 8- or 16-fold loop unrolling. Further increase of the repetition factor produces negligible performance gain.

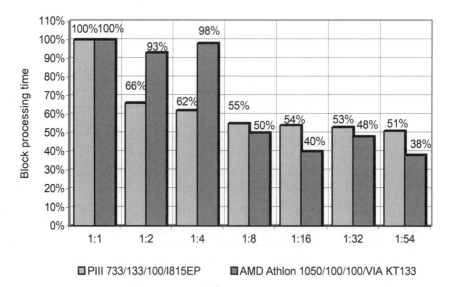

☐ PIII 733/133/100/I815EP   ■ AMD Athlon 1050/100/100/VIA KT133

Fig. 2.13. Efficiency of unrolling memory-reading loops (in which the loop-processing time sharply decreases with the unrolling depth)

The situation with write operations is different (Fig. 2.14). I won't provide here the listing of test program; it has much in common with the previous one, and the differences are minor. On a Pentium III processor with a Intel 815EP chipset, the time required to execute the memory-write loop is independent of the depth of unrolling. The unrolled loop executes approximately 2% *slower* because the code is less compact. In practice, this value is negligible. To improve the efficiency of this program for an Athlon processor with a VIA KT 133 chipset, it is advisable to unroll the memory-writing loop 16 times.

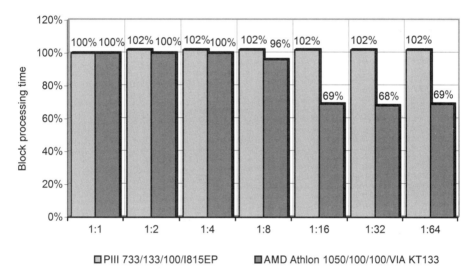

Fig. 2.14. Efficiency of unrolling memory-writing loops (in which the loop-execution time is independent of the unrolling depth)

If mixed loops access the memory both for reading and writing, it is also advisable to unroll such loops 8 to 16 times. (Details on this topic will be provided in *Grouping Read and Write Operations*.)

Unrolling Loops Using a Macro Assembler

Before concluding this discussion, I should mention one unfavorable circumstance: The C preprocessor doesn't support loop macros. Therefore, it does not provide the capability of implementing efficient loop unrolling. Programmers must manually perform the tedious and error-prone job of repeatedly duplicating the loop body and correcting the counter.

Assembly programmers are in a more favorable position. Advanced macro tools provided by MASM and TASM enable programmers to delegate all routine work to the translator. Writing a macro that unrolls the loop any number of times is an easy task. This capability simplifies program debugging and optimization considerably.

An example of such a program is provided in Listing 2.7. Note that the READ_BUFF macro allows the loop to be unrolled any number of times. You must agree, it is physically impossible to produce an elegant solution for this task using ANSI C/C++.

Listing 2.7. Unrolling a Loop Using a Macro Assembler

```
; /*-------------------------------------------------------------------
; *                    Macro that duplicates its body N times
; ------------------------------------------------------------------*/
READ_BUFF MACRO N
MYN = N
MYA = 0

WHILE MYA NE MYN
; Duplication loop
    MOV EDX, [EBX + 32 * MYA]
    MYA = MYA + 1
    ; Loop body, which the macro processor
    ; will duplicate a specified number of times
ENDM
ENDM


UNROLL_POWER  EQU 8
; Repetition factor

Loop:
READ_BUFF UNROLL_POWER
; Note that repetition factor is specified
; by the preprocessor constant.
; No manual work is needed.

ADD EAX, EDX
ADD EBX, 4 * UNROLL_POWER
; Correction of the number of iterations

DEC ECX
JNZ Loop
```

Unrolling Loops Using the C Preprocessor

Although there is no way to unroll a loop automatically using preprocessor directives of ANSI C/C++, routine work can be eliminated. You only need to think creatively.

One idea would be to modify the loop counter within the macro, rather than within the loop header. This would eliminate the need to correct the counter manually. All copies of the loop body would become identical replicas that could be moved to the preprocessor macro. This is the best approach in C language.

Listing 2.8. Unrolling a Loop Using C Preprocessor Directives

```
#define BODY x+=p[a++];
// Loop body

for(a=0; a < BLOCK_SIZE;)
{
   BODY; BODY; BODY; BODY;
   BODY; BODY; BODY; BODY;
// Unrolling the loop eight times
}
```

Eliminating Data Dependence

If requested RAM cells have address-data dependency (i.e., one cell contains the address of another cell), the CPU cannot process them in parallel and has to wait until it receives the addresses. Consider this situation on the following example: `while(next=p[next])`.

Until the processor gets the value of the `next` variable, it won't know the address of the next cell and won't be able to start loading it. Execution time of such a loop is mainly determined by the memory subsystem latency and rarely depends on its throughput. All types of memory, including SDRAM, DDR SDRAM, and even high-speed Direct RDRAM, will produce a similar result. Even users of EDO DRAM would laugh at this result, were this not obsolete memory! In contemporary PCs, the latency of the memory subsystem takes approximately 20 clocks of the system bus, which corresponds to a full access time of 200 nsec.

The opposite of this cycle is `while(a=p[next++])`. The processor requests the chipset to load the `p[next]` cell, and immediately increases `next` by one. Without waiting for an answer (because the address of the next cell is known), the processor sends another request to the chipset, then another one, and so on. The processor continues to send requests until the number of unprocessed requests reaches its maximum value. (For P6, this value is four.) Because requests follow one after the other with minimum delay, they can be considered *processed in parallel*. The time required to load N dependent cells generally can be expressed as follows:

$$t = N(T_{ch} + T_{mem})$$

Here, T_{ch} is the chipset latency, and T_{mem} stands for the memory latency. Therefore, loading the same number of independent cells will require the following:

$$t = \frac{N}{C} + T_{ch} + T_{mem}$$

In this formula, C is the throughput of the memory subsystem.

Thus, when processing independent data, the negative effect of the memory subsystem latency is reduced considerably, and performance mainly depends on the throughput. This approach won't allow you to achieve the throughput declared by the memory manufacturer. (The number of requests processed in parallel is limited; therefore, this technique doesn't allow you to achieve full parallelism.) Nevertheless, the result will be praiseworthy.

The fragment of the test program in Listing 2.9 provides an illustrative comparison of the processing speeds of dependent and independent data.

Listing 2.9. [Memory/dependence.c] Efficiency of Processing Dependent and Independent Data

```
; /*------------------------------------------------------------------
;  *                  Loop for reading dependent data
;  *                       (nonoptimized version)
;  -------------------------------------------------------------------*/
for (a=0; a < BLOCK_SIZE; a += 32)
// The loop is unrolled to speed up the processing.

{
   x = *(int *)((int)p1 + a + 0);
// The cell is read.

   a += x;
// The address of the next cell is calculated using the value of
// the previous cell. Therefore, the processor cannot send
// the next request to the chipset until it receives this cell.
// The code proceeds in a similar manner...
```

```
    y = *(int *)((int)p1 + a + 4);
    a += y;

    x = *(int *)((int)p1 + a + 8);
    a += x;

    y = *(int *)((int)p1 + a + 12);
    a += y;

    x = *(int *)((int)p1 + a + 16);
    a += x;

    y = *(int *)((int)p1 + a + 20);
    a += y;

    x = *(int *)((int)p1 + a + 24);
    a += x;

    y = *(int *)((int)p1 + a + 28);
    a += y;
}


; /*-----------------------------------------------------------------
;  *                  Loop for reading independent data
;  *                          (optimized version)
; -----------------------------------------------------------------*/
for (a=0; a<BLOCK_SIZE; a += 32)
{
    x += *(int *)((int)p1 + a + 0);
    y += *(int *)((int)p1 + a + 4);
    x += *(int *)((int)p1 + a + 8);
    y += *(int *)((int)p1 + a + 12);
    x += *(int *)((int)p1 + a + 16);
    y += *(int *)((int)p1 + a + 20);
    x += *(int *)((int)p1 + a + 24);
    y += *(int *)((int)p1 + a + 28);
// The processor could send the next request to the chipset
// without waiting for the previous request to be completed,
// because the cell address is not related to the data being processed.
}
```

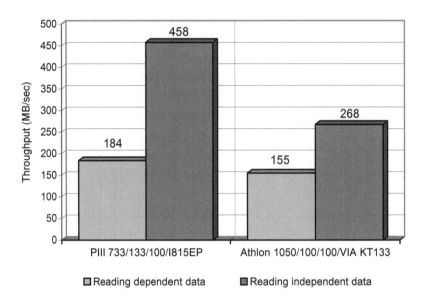

Fig. 2.15. RAM throughput test for linear reading of dependent and independent data

The result of testing on two computers is shown in Fig. 2.15. The first thing that attracts attention is the gap in times required for processing of dependent and independent data. On Pentium III/733/133/100/I815EP, the loop for reading independent data is executed 2.5 times faster than the loop for reading dependent data. The result for AMD Athlon 1050/100/133/VIA KT 133 is worse, at 1.7 times the dependent data speed. This can be explained by serious design defects of this chipset: Inadequate throughput of the channel connecting the memory controller and the Bus Interface Unit (both are mounted in the North Bridge of the chipset) results in permanent jams, which limit the number of simultaneously processed requests. (See *Calculating the Full Access Time.*) Nevertheless, reading of independent data is more efficient on any hardware. The only problem that needs to be solved *how* these data should be processed.

Linear reading (also known as sequential reading) of memory cells is not the best idea. PIII did not achieved 60% of the theoretical throughput of 800 MB/sec. (Athlon's value is even less — about 30%.) This is "fabulous" performance, isn't it? Why and how does this happen? Is the PC architecture so imperfect that it doesn't deal well with such an easy thing as RAM? If you think this is so, you won't be the first one to arrive at this conclusion: Most application developers believe that the PC and high performance have nothing in common. Still, do not rush to change it for Cray.

Parallel Data Processing

Thus, processing is much faster for independent than dependent data. But how fast is it? Unfortunately, if you migrate from relative values to absolute ones, your delight will wane.

The highest throughput that can be achieved during linear reading of independent data is no more than 40% to 50% of the declared throughput for the type of memory. At the same time, the memory subsystem is optimized for linear access, and random reads are much slower. What can be faster than linear access? Looking for answers to such questions is the starting point for investigating the true nature of this subject.

In most cases, an attempt to read two adjacent cells simultaneously initiates one request to the memory subsystem (rather than two, as might be expected). The byte does not represent an elementary unit of data exchange with the memory; an entire packet is the basic unit. The length of this packet, depending on the processor type, can vary from 32 bytes to 128 bytes.

Thus, *linear reading of independent data doesn't ensure parallel processing of this information.* Return to the program in Listing 2.9. Suppose that the processor needs to get the contents of the following cell: `*(int *) ((int) p1 + a)`. The processor formulates the query and sends it to the chipset. At the same time, it starts processing the next command: `x += *(int *)((int)p1 + a + 4)`. The CPU doesn't discover data dependence. This is good! Nevertheless, this cell will return with the previous requested block. Therefore, there is no need to send just another request. (The chipset won't operate faster.) The execution of this command is delayed. The next command, `x += *(int *)((int)p1 + a + 8)`, is also delayed because it attempts to read a cell from the previously requested block. Thus, the processor only accumulates data until the chipset returns the processed query (during linear data reading). Then, as the operands become ready, the processor unfreezes and executes commands.

Finally, the processor encounters another command, which accesses the cell directly following the end of the last requested block. Unfortunately, if the processor encountered this cell earlier, it would send two simultaneous requests to the chipset.

A more efficient data processing algorithm is as follows: During the first pass, the memory is read at the increments of 32 bytes (64 bytes or 128 bytes if the program is optimized exclusively for Athlon or P4). This makes the processor generate requests to chipset at each attempt to access the memory. As a result, several overlapping queries and responses are always on the bus, and these requests or answers are processed almost in parallel. During the second pass through the loop, the processor reads the addresses of all remaining cells. (These addresses are not multiples of 32.) When the first pass is completed, they are already in cache; therefore, access to these cells will not cause significant delays (Fig. 2.16).

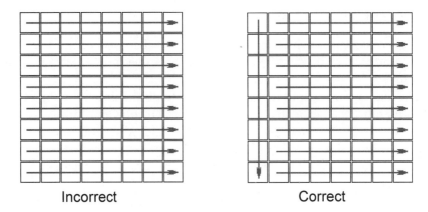

Incorrect   Correct

Fig. 2.16. Avoid linear reading of memory cells. Instead, during the first pass, read the cells at an increment equal to the multiple of the packet-exchange cycle. Process the remaining cells as usual

Consider the improved version of the program fragment that performs parallel reading of independent data:

Listing 2.10. [Memory/parallel.test.c] Achieving Maximum Throughput Using Parallel Memory Reading

```
; /*-------------------------------------------------------------------
; *                Measuring throughput during parallel reading
; -----------------------------------------------------------------*/
#define BLOCK_SIZE (32*M)        // Size of the processed block
#define STEP_SIZE L1_CACHE_SIZE  // Size of the processed block part

for (b=0; b < BLOCK_SIZE; b += STEP_SIZE)
{

for (a = b; a < (b + STEP_SIZE); a += 128)
// First pass through the loop, during which
// parallel data loading is accomplished
{
    x += *(int *)((int)p + a + 0);
    // The first cell is loaded.
    // Because it is not present in cache,
    // the CPU sends the reading request
    // to the chipset.
```

```
x += *(int *)((int)p + a + 32);
// The next cell is loaded.
// Because there is no data dependency,
// the processor can complete this command
// without waiting for the result of the
// previous one. However, the processor
// detects that this cell will not be returned
// with the block that it has just requested.
// Therefore, it sends another request to the chipset
// without waiting for the previous one to be completed.

x += *(int *)((int)p + a + 64);
// Now there are three queries on the bus.

x += *(int *)((int)p + a + 96);
// The fourth query is sent to the bus.
// The first query still may be incomplete.
}

for (a = b; a < (b + STEP_SIZE); a += 32)
{
    // There is no need to read the next cell
    // because it was read in the first loop:
    // x += *(int *)((int)p + a + 0);

    x += *(int *)((int)p + a + 4);
    x += *(int *)((int)p + a + 8);
    x += *(int *)((int)p + a + 12);
    x += *(int *)((int)p + a + 16);
    x += *(int *)((int)p + a + 20);
    x += *(int *)((int)p + a + 24);
    x += *(int *)((int)p + a + 28);
    // These cells will be present in cache.
    // Therefore, they can be loaded very quickly.
}
}
```

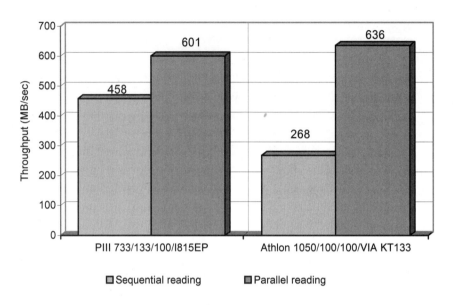

Fig. 2.17. Efficiency of parallel reading

Using this trick on PIII, it is possible to achieve a throughput of 601 MB/sec (Fig. 2.17). This is 31% faster than the linear-reading algorithm, and only 33% slower than the theoretical throughput of 800 MB/sec. Testing on Athlon produces an even better result, only 25% less than the ideal one.

The chipset latency has been nearly counterbalanced, and the system is almost flying! These results are achieved without any tricks. The test program is written in native C without any "hacks" or components written in the assembly language. This means that there are opportunities for further performance improvement.

Optimizing Reference Data Structures

Likely, you do not want a program to crawl at the speed of a snail. On the contrary, you want it to benefit from the advantages provided by high-speed memory. Therefore, it is necessary to eliminate data dependency. How can you achieve this?

For example, if you have a BMP file, parallel processing can be easily achieved because this file is a uniform data array of a fixed size. The situation is different for binary trees, lists, and other reference structures that store dissimilar data.

Splitting Lists (Trees)

Consider the list that binds a couple of megabytes of variable-length text strings. How can you optimize the procedure of traversing the list if address of the next element is not known beforehand and the list is highly fragmented? The first idea that comes to mind is to split the single list into several independent lists that would be processed in parallel. With this approach, which splitting strategy is optimal? To find out, develop a test program that sequentially traverses the lists with different splitting ratios: 1:1, 1:2, 1:4, 1:6, and 1:8. For brevity, the fragment of my program in Listing 2.11 implements 1:1 and 1:2 combinations. All other splitting ratios are implemented in a similar way.

Listing 2.11. [Memory/list.split.c] Finding an Optimal Strategy for Splitting Lists

```
#define BLOCK_SIZE (12*M)     // Size of the processed block

struct MYLIST{                // List item
    struct MYLIST *next;
    int val;
};

#define N_ELEM    (BLOCK_SIZE/sizeof(struct MYLIST))

; /*------------------------------------------------------------------
; *                   Processing a single list
; -----------------------------------------------------------------*/
// Initialization
for (a = 0; a < N_ELEM; a++)
{
   one_list[a].next = one_list + a + 1;
   one_list[a].val  = a;
} one_list[N_ELEM-1].next = 0;

// Tracing
p = one_list;
while(p = p[0].next);

; /*------------------------------------------------------------------
; *                   Processing two split lists
; -----------------------------------------------------------------*/
// Initialization
for (a = 0; a < N_ELEM/2; a++)
{
   spl_list_1[a].next = spl_list_1 + a + 1;
   spl_list_1[a].val = a;
```

```
    spl_list_2[a].next = spl_list_2 + a + 1;
    spl_list_2[a].val  = a;

} spl_list_1[N_ELEM/2-1].next = 0;
  spl_list_2[N_ELEM/2-1].next = 0;

// Tracing
p1 = spl_list_1; p2 = spl_list_2;
while((p1 = p1[0].next) && (p2 = p2[0].next));
// Attention: This tracing method assumes that both lists
// contain equal numbers of items. Otherwise, the code
// needs to be modified — for example, as follows:
// while(p1 || p2)
// {
//    if (p1) p1 = p1[0].next;
//    if (p2) p2 = p2[0].next;
// }
//
// This would make the code less illustrative.
// Therefore, the first variant is used in the listing.
```

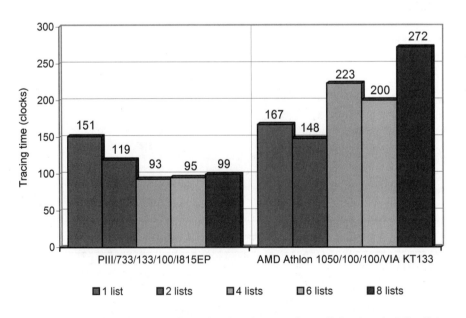

Fig. 2.18. Dependence of processing time on the splitting level of the list

On Pentium III 733/133/100/I815EP, there is a visible trend of *decreasing list traversal time as the splitting ratio approaches 1:4* (Fig. 2.18). As the number of lists increases from one to four, the performance increases 1.6 times. Further increase of the splitting level only degrades the result. When more than four data flows are processed in parallel, DRAM pages are opened and closed repeatedly. These open and close operations invalidate the gain obtained from parallelism. (More on this topic will be provided in *Planning Data Flows*.)

On AMD Athlon 1050/100/100/VIA KT 133, the situation is different. Both the Athlon processor and VIA KT133 chipset are optimized to work with a single data flow. Therefore, parallel processing of split lists decreases the performance considerably. Splitting a single list provides insignificant performance gain. Therefore, the optimal strategy splits one list into six independent lists. This number provides the best result when a program is optimized for different processors simultaneously.

This technique is not limited to lists. Splitting is efficient for binary trees and other data structures, including ones that are not based on references.

Fast Addition of Items

To avoid traversing the entire list when adding a new item to its end, store the reference to the last element in a special field. This will improve program performance.

More information on this topic will be provided in *Optimizing C String Library Functions*. How are strings related to lists? Strings are like lists that doesn't store the reference to the next element; instead, they forcefully arrange them in the memory in such a way that they strictly follow one after the other.

Reducing the Data Structure Size

Suppose a data structure (such as a list) contains a fixed number of elements. If each element is processed once, how important is the choice of memory-reading increment? Because the minimum data unit used during data exchange with the memory is at least 32 bytes, and list items are often much smaller, the processing speed is inversely proportional to the processing increment. When reading memory with an increment of 1 (byte, word, or double word), half of the loaded cells are never accessed. When reading memory with an increment of 4 (bytes, words, or double words) only 25% of loaded cells are used; the other loaded cells do not serve any purpose. Hence, *data in the memory must be packed as densely as possible*. (See *Data Alignment* and *Data Alignment Efficiency*.)

Separated Data Structures

Classic list representation (Fig. 2.19) is far from optimal from the point of view of the IBM PC memory subsystem. Why is this so? The reason is that, when tracing the list (i.e., traversing the list without accessing the values of its elements), the processor is forced to load all cells, not just references to the next elements. If the tracing operation is repeated many times, performance losses may be large.

Reorganize the data structure by placing the pointers to the next item and values of the list items in two separate arrays (Fig. 2.20). Now, performing list tracing (or most other basic list operations, such as calculating the number of list items, searching the last item, or closing and breaking lists) will use all loaded cells. Consequently, processing efficiency will be improved.

Notice how method of accessing list elements changes. In the classic list, access to elements may be as follows: `_list[element].next=xxx; _list[element].val=xxx;`. Access to the optimized list will change to the following: `_mylist.next[element]=xxx; _mylist.val[element]=xxx`. This doesn't cause any difficulties or inconveniences, but it can confuse novice programmers who have no previous experience with C.

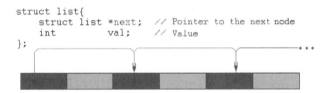

Fig. 2.19. Arrangement of a classic list

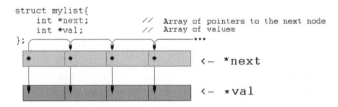

Fig. 2.20. Arrangement of an optimized list

Twofold splitting of the list reduces the amount of memory allocated during its tracing. This is not the limit! With less than 50,000 list items (a common situation), it makes sense to cease using 32-bit pointers and migrate to 16-bit *indexes* (Fig. 2.21). This algorithm is not advanced, but it can be improved easily. After all elements in the memory are aligned by even addresses, the least significant bit of the pointer can be reserved for "internal use." If it is set to zero, then the pointer length is 32 bits. If the value of this bit is one, the compact 16-bit relative pointer is used for address representation. Because the distance between two adjoining list elements is usually short, it is not always necessary to reference them using an absolute address. This saves 16 bits per element.

Fig. 2.21. Floating-length pointers should use
the minimal number of bits to reduce the amount of required memory

Improving on this idea, it is possible to introduce support for certain situations, such as "the next element is located directly at the end of the current one" or "the next element is located in another list." The goal is the same: Replace the fixed-length pointers with floating-length pointers, which take the minimum number of bits.

When list splitting is combined with decreasing the bit capacity of pointers, it will reduce the size of the reference array according to following formula: `sizeof(struct list)/sizeof(index_next)`. In this example, the reference array will becomes four times smaller. Quite good, isn't it? How many times will it improve the performance? The program fragment in Listing 2.12 implements both classic and optimized versions of the list and comparing the time required for their processing.

Listing 2.12. [Memory/list.separated.c] Tracing Efficiency of Split Lists

```
; /*-------------------------------------------------------------------
; *                     Processing the classic list
; -------------------------------------------------------------------*/
struct list{            // Classic list
struct list    *next;   // Pointer to the next node
int     val;            // Value
};

struct list *classic_list, *tmp_list;

// List initialization
for (a = 0; a < N_ELEM; a++)
{
   classic_list[a].next= classic_list + a+1;
   classic_list[a].val = a;
} classic_list[N_ELEM-1].next=0;
```

```
// List tracing
tmp_list=classic_list;
while(tmp_list = tmp_list[0].next);

; /*-------------------------------------------------------------------
; *                    Processing the optimized list
; -----------------------------------------------------------------*/
struct mylist{             // Optimized, separated list
short int *next;           // Array of pointers to the next node
int *val;                  // Array of values
};

struct mylist separated_list;

// List initialization (note the position of the square brackets)
for (a=0; a<N_ELEM; a++)
{
   separated_list.next[a] = a+1;
   separated_list.val[a] = a;
} separated_list.next[N_ELEM-1]=0;

// List tracing
while(b = separated_list.next[b]);
```

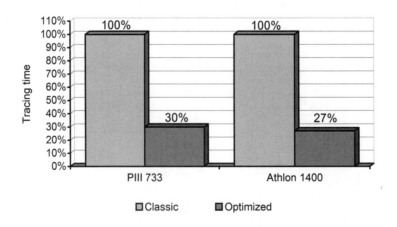

Fig. 2.22. Efficiency of processing separated lists using short pointers

The results produced by this program will look approximately as shown in Fig. 2.22.

As expected, the optimized version is faster. The theoretical limit has not been reached. (The processing of 16-bit values is inefficient on contemporary processors). Nevertheless, you can be proud of such a result. If the loop is unrolled and references are processed in parallel (see *Parallel Data Processing*), the gain will be even greater.

Complex Cases and Whims of Separated Optimization

Suppose that a structure contains body of some object (obj_body) and object attributes (obj_attr). Assume that the object body takes several kilobytes, and its attributes require about 50 bytes. Additionally, suppose that a function is needed to process the attributes of all objects without touching the object bodies.

Listing 2.13. Nonoptimized Structure Containing an Object Body and Attributes

---

```
struct list_of_obj {
struct list_of_obj *next;
int        obj_attr[14];
int        obj_body[8000];
}
```

Would it make sense to place the elements of such a structure into separate arrays? The length of the burst cycle usually is 32 bytes (K6, PII, or PIII) or 64 bytes (Athlon). The sum of the length of the obj_attr and obj_body fields is 60 bytes. Consequently, only about 10% of the loaded cells will remain unused. This loss is small and can be ignored. However, before accepting this result, compare optimized and nonoptimized fragments of the program.

Listing 2.14. [Memory/list.obj.c] Efficiency of Optimizing the Structure

---

```
; /*-----------------------------------------------------------------
; *                  Processing the classic list
; -------------------------------------------------------------------*/
struct LIST_OF_OBJ {                    // Nonoptimized list
struct   LIST_OF_OBJ *next;             // Pointer to the next object
int obj_attr[ATTR_SIZE];                // Object attributes (compact)
int obj_body[BODY_SIZE];                // Object body (enormous)
};

struct LIST_OF_OBJ *list_of_obj, *tmp_list_of_obj;
```

```
// Memory allocation
list_of_obj = (struct LIST_OF_OBJ*)
    _malloc32(N_ELEM*sizeof(struct LIST_OF_OBJ));

// List initialization
for (a = 0; a < N_ELEM; a++)
 list_of_obj[a].next = list_of_obj + a + 1; list_of_obj[N_ELEM-1].next = 0;

// List tracing
tmp_list_of_obj = list_of_obj;
do {
 for(attr = 0; attr < ATTR_SIZE; attr++)
    x += tmp_list_of_obj[0].obj_attr[attr];
} while(tmp_list_of_obj = tmp_list_of_obj[0].next);

; /*-------------------------------------------------------------------
; *                    Processing the optimized, separated list
; -------------------------------------------------------------------*/
struct LIST_OF_OBJ_OPTIMIZED {          // Optimized list
 struct LIST_OF_OBJ_OPTIMIZED *next;    // Pointer to the next object
#ifdef PESSIMIZE
    int *obj_attr;                      // Pointer to the attributes
                                        // (That's too bad!)
#else
    int obj_attr[ATTR_SIZE];            // Object attributes
                                        // (This is good!)
#endif

 int *obj_body;                         // Pointer to the object body
};

struct LIST_OF_OBJ_OPTIMIZED    *list_of_obj_optimized,
    *tmp_list_of_obj_optimized;

// Memory allocation
list_of_obj_optimized = (struct LIST_OF_OBJ_OPTIMIZED*)
    _malloc32(N_ELEM*sizeof(struct LIST_OF_OBJ_OPTIMIZED));

// List initialization
for (a = 0; a < N_ELEM ; a++)
{
   list_of_obj_optimized[a].next = list_of_obj_optimized + a + 1;
```

```
#ifdef PESSIMIZE
    list_of_obj_optimized[a].obj_attr = malloc(sizeof(int)*ATTR_SIZE);
#endif
    list_of_obj_optimized[a].obj_body = malloc(sizeof(int)*BODY_SIZE);
}   list_of_obj_optimized[N_ELEM-1].next = 0;

// List tracing
tmp_list_of_obj_optimized = list_of_obj_optimized;
do {
 for(attr = 0; attr < ATTR_SIZE; attr++)
   x+ = tmp_list_of_obj_optimized[0].obj_attr[attr];
} while(tmp_list_of_obj_optimized = tmp_list_of_obj_optimized[0].next);
```

The optimized version is almost 60% faster than the classic version (Fig. 2.23). This is impressive performance gain, isn't it? Unfortunately, the optimized version is rather capricious. For example, if the optimized structure is changed to its closest analog (the pessimized version in Fig 2.23), the difference between the optimized and nonoptimized versions will be about 30% on PIII.

Listing 2.15. Optimized Structure Containing an Object Body and Attributes

```
struct list_of_obj_optimized {
   struct list_of_obj_optimized *next;
   int       obj_attr[ATTR_SIZE];
   int        *obj_body;
};
```

Listing 2.16. Closest Analog of the Optimized Structure

```
struct list_of_obj_optimized {
   struct list_of_obj_optimized*next;
   int           *obj_attr;
   int           *obj_body;
};
```

Why is `int *obj_attr` worse than `int obj_attr[ATTR_SIZE]`? Even more surprising is the performance gain achieved with the latter. At what expense has it been achieved? There is something mystical about it; the number of loaded memory cells must be the same.

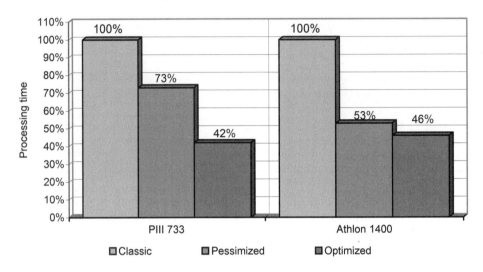

Fig. 2.23. Efficiency of different approaches that optimize the structure

Page-Memory Organization

For the moment, tear yourself away from this little puzzle. Instead, investigate the dependence of the list-tracing time on the memory-reading increment. At first, it might seem that there is nothing surprising here. However, consider the shape of the curve obtained using the Memory/list.step.c program on the companion CD-ROM, and try to explain it. A fragment of this program is in Listing 2.17.

Listing 2.17. [Memory/list.step.c] Dependence of the List-Tracing Time on the Memory-Reading Increment

```
for(a = STEP_FACTOR; a < MAX_STEP_SIZE; a += STEP_FACTOR)
// Various values of memory-read increment are checked

{
#ifdef UNTLB
for (i=0; i<=BLOCK_SIZE; i+=4*K) x += *(int *)((int)p + i+32);
#endif
// Pages are loaded into the Translation Look-aside Buffer.

L_BEGIN(0);      // Measurement of the execution time is started.
```

```
i=0;
for(b = 0; b < MAX_ITER; b++)
{
    x += *(int *)((int)p + i);
    i += a;
}
// Memory is read with the increment of a.

L_END(0);          // Measurement of the execution time is stopped.
}
```

The behavior of the curve is interesting (Fig. 2.24). Despite all predictions, the tracing time doesn't remain constant; rather, it increases with the step. This growth is not infinite. After passing the limit of 32 KB (for PII and PIII) or 64 KB (for Athlon), the curve hits the saturation point and turns into plateau. The difference between height of the plateau the plain is too high and cannot be ignored. What causes the growth of processing time? RAM is not uniform, and the time required to access it isn't constant, but can it be so nonuniform?

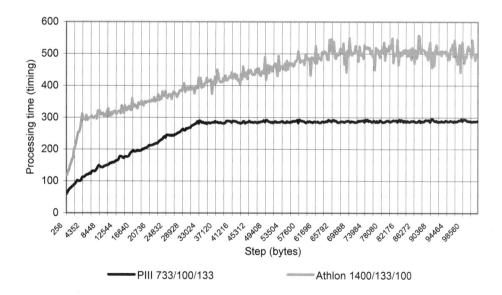

Fig. 2.24. Dependence of the block-processing time
on the value of the reading step

What reality is reflected by the 32 KB point (for Athlon, the 64 KB point)? Structures of such a size do not appear to be in the memory. Still, the processing time grows with the step. Why? You could abandon all attempts to solve this problem. (When I contacted a technical-support service to ask this question, I received the following answer: "You know, the processor is so complicated.") However, it will remain as a thorn in your side. Aren't you going to solve problems, seek high-quality solutions?

Modify the program by making it display the time required to access each cell. (See Memory/memory.way.c on the companion CD-ROM.) It will become evident that the curve has formidable peaks repeating every 4 KB (Fig. 2.25). Each peak takes thousands of clock cycles. No, this isn't a misprint. It occurs because most contemporary operating systems (including Windows and UNIX) use page-memory organization.

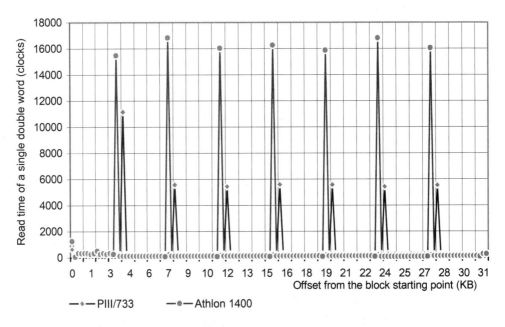

Fig. 2.25. Time required to access the memory cell depends on
the cell address for linear reading

Each page has a related 32-bit data structure that contains the page attributes and its base address. When accessing the page for the first time, the processor reads these data from the physical memory into its internal buffer, the Translation Look-aside Buffer (TLB). All further attempts to access the same page occur without delays until this information is removed from the TLB. (For technical details, see the *3.6: Paging* section in the *Intel Architecture Software Developer's Manual*, Volume 3: *System Programming Guide*.)

This is a clue to the problem: *The minimum unit of data used when interacting with the memory is not a 32-byte burst cycle; rather, it's an entire page.* The delays that occur when accessing the page for the first time are slightly smaller than the time required to read the entire page. This means that, no matter how many bytes of the page are read, processing takes the same time amount as if it were read as a whole. Hence, streaming algorithms must minimize the number of accessed pages. Therefore, try to place the data within pages as densely as possible and avoid unused spaces.

But wait. In this situation, saturation must take place at the 4 KB step. Page attributes are loaded at each iteration (i.e., the loop is executed extremely inefficiently). The curve, after passing the 4 KB point, becomes less sharp (on PIII, this is unnoticeable but present), then grows steadily. Why?

This happens because page attributes are not randomly distributed over the entire memory space. Instead, they are combined into special structures known as *page tables.* Each element of the page table takes 1 double word. However, the minimum unit of data exchange with the memory exceeds this value. When the processor accesses one page, it loads the attributes of seven more pages. (For Athlon, this number is 15.) It stores this information in cache memory. This is the answer! Multiply 8 (or 16) elements by 4 KB (the page size); you'll find that 32 (or 64) KB limit the curve's growth.

Now it becomes clear why placing `obj_body` into a separate array increased the speed of list processing. Elements such as `*next` and `obj_attr` have been packed densely; therefore, they fit within a smaller number of pages.

It is more difficult to understand why the separation of `obj_attr` decreased the performance. The number of pages will be only slightly greater. The first version of the structure will be 64 KB (16 pages), according to the following formula:

```
(sizeof(*next) + sizeof (int) * ATTR_SIZE + sizeof(*obj_body)) * N_ELEM
```

The second version will be 76 KB (19 pages), according to the following formula:

```
(sizeof(*next) + sizeof(*obj_attr) + + sizeof(*obj_body)) * N_ELEM

+ sizeof(int) * ALIGN_ATTR_SIZE * N_ELEM
```

Assume that a couple of extra pages will be required to compensate for rounding. The general ratio between the performance values for the first and the second versions will be 21/16 = 1.3; the ratio will equal 1.4 for Athlon and 1.8 for PIII.

The memory-allocation strategy employed by the `malloc` function works in the following way: When the CPU requests small blocks, each allocated block has an address smaller than that of the previous block. Thus, elements of page catalog are read in the reverse order. The burst cycle reads elements in the direct order. Consequently, the processor has to wait for the attributes of requested page, and performance drops. The following rule can be used: To achieve maximum performance, it is necessary to use the accessed pages entirely. Furthermore, the pages must be requested in the ascending order of their linear addresses.

Strategy of Data Distribution over DRAM Banks

The rule formulated at the end of the previous section is exclusively for streaming algorithms that only access each cell (and each memory page) once. What happens when memory pages are accessed multiple times? Is the order of their processing important? At first, it seems that if the processed pages are already in the TLB, the data reading step has no meaning. Check this assumption! To do so, add the following loop to the test program shown in Listing 2.17 (the Memory/list.step.c program on the companion CD-ROM):

```
for(i = 0; i <= BLOCK_SIZE; i += 4*K) x += *(int *)((int)p + i + 32)
```

This loop will force the system to map all pages and load them into the TLB before it starts to measure execution time. (Just remove the comment from the UNTLB definition.) You will obtain the graph similar to the one shown in Fig. 2.26.

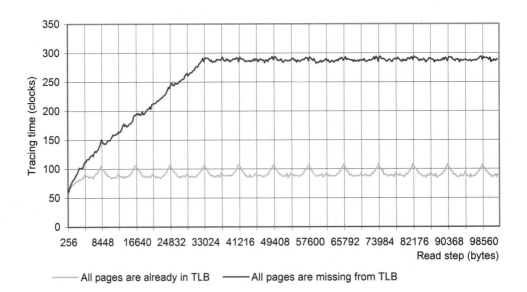

Fig. 2.26. Dependence of the data-block processing time
on the read step, with ripples caused by DRAM-bank recharging

The list-tracing time has been decreased dramatically. The dependence of the processing speed on the step apparently has been eliminated. However, if you study the graph carefully, you should notice small waves. The periodicity of these waves is evidence of a regular pattern, rather than a measurement error. What is the nature of this regular pattern? The performance drop at the crests of these waves reaches approximately 30%. Therefore, these decreases cannot be attributed simply to side effects.

Specific features of the RAM organization explain the nature of the curve. As you know, memory access time is a variable that depends on a range of factors. Maximum performance is achieved when the following conditions are satisfied: *Requested cells reside within currently open DRAM pages*, and *neither a memory page nor a memory bank are in the refresh state at access time*. Now, try to answer the following question: How does access time change, depending on the reading step?

Start with the first statement. Generally, access time grows proportionally with the increase of the step because pages are opened more frequently. This behavior lasts until the step length has reached the length of a single DRAM page. (The typical length of such a page is 1 KB, 2 KB, or 4 KB.) After this point, pages will open with *each* attempt to access the cell. Consequently, the curve will reach saturation and become nearly horizontal. You can verify this assumption with the test in Memory/dram.wave.c on the companion CD-ROM, a fragment of which is shown in Listing 2.18. (The scale of the graph in Fig. 2.26 is not suitable for accurate measurements.)

Listing 2.18. [Memory/dram.wave.c] Investigation of the DRAM Waves

```
// Heading for Microsoft Word
printf("STEP");
for(pg_size=STEP_SIZE; pg_size<=MAX_PG_SIZE; pg_size+=(STEP_SIZE*STEP_FACTOR))
 printf("\t%d",pg_size); printf("\nTime");

// Main loop and various read steps
for(pg_size=STEP_SIZE; pg_size<=MAX_PG_SIZE; pg_size+=(STEP_SIZE*STEP_FACTOR))
{
// Starting the measurement of the execution time
A_BEGIN(0)

    // Loop that reads memory with the specified step
    for (b=0; b<pg_size; b+=STEP_SIZE)
    for(a=b; a<BLOCK_SIZE/sizeof(int); a+=(pg_size/sizeof(int)))
        x+=p[a];
    // Physical memory is limited, and with a large step,
    // all cells will fit in cache. Therefore, a trick
    // is needed that represents memory as a circular array.
```

```
    // Generally, the code of this algorithm is self-evident.

A_END(0)
// Ending the measurement of the execution time

printf("\t%d", Ax_GET(0));

    // Printing execution time
PRINT_PROGRESS(100*pg_size/MAX_PG_SIZE);
}
```

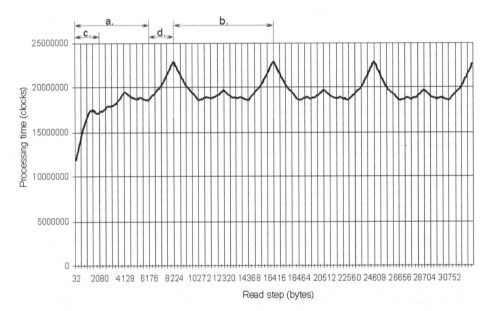

Fig. 2.27. Memory waves reveal the design of memory chips, including the distance between the end of one DRAM page and the start of another (*a*), the size of each DRAM bank (*b*), and the size of a DRAM page (*c* and *d*)

Look at Fig. 2.27: The ascending branch of the curve behaves as predicted. However, it doesn't reach saturation; rather, it turns into a cross-country trail, pocked with pits and bumps. The cell access time changes with the growth of the step. Fortunately, the graph demonstrates periodicity, which gives some hope of decrypting the dependence. This graph provides a lot of information, revealing the internal structure and organization of the memory chips used in a specific hardware configuration.

Where there is periodicity, there is always some structure. Therefore, the memory is not just a long chain of cells; it is something more complex and nonuniform. Yes, memory is composed of pages, but this is insufficient for explaining the curve's shape. Something else is required.

Do memory banks and their regeneration affect this situation? Access time to the cell without regeneration takes seven clock cycles: *2* (RAS-to-CAS delay) + + *2* (CAS delay) + *1* + *1* + *1*. If regeneration is included, the cell access time will be nine clock cycles: *2* (RAS precharge) + *2* (RAS-to-CAS delay) + *2* (CAS delay) + *1* + *1* + *1*. This is almost 1.29 times greater than the previous calculation. In Fig. 2.26, the peak of the block-processing time is 22,892,645 clock cycles, while the foot is 18,610,240 clock cycles. Thus, the ratio of 22,892,645: 18,610,240 equals 1.23. The results nearly coincide. Thus, the assumption concerning recharge is correct (although as a cautious investigator, it would be better to say *probably* correct).

It is possible to derive several recommendations for most memory models. Observance of these rules won't increase performance drastically, but it will help you to avoid a decrease of 20% to 30%.

Fine-Tuning Optimization

This section will concentrate on the method of mapping physical memory cells to the processor's address space. (See *Mapping Physical DRAM Addresses to Logical Addresses.*) It also will consider other characteristics and technical details, such as the number and size of DRAM banks and page length.

The wave's crest shows when each memory access hits the recharging bank. Therefore, *the distance between two neighboring crests equals the product of the length of a DRAM page and the number of memory banks* (about 8 KB in Fig. 2.27). This satisfies the following combinations: *1* (DRAM page length in kilobytes) × *8* (banks), *2 × 4*, *4 × 8*, and *8 × 1*. Is it possible to determine which specific memory type is being used? This is possible. The key to this problem is the width of the slope. (In Fig. 2.27, it is marked as *d*.) It is easy to prove that the *slope width equals the length of a DRAM page.* Suppose that χ is the length of a page, and N is the number of banks. The distance between the end of one page and beginning of another in any bank equals:

$$(N-1) \times \chi$$

Accordingly, the distance between two pages of the same bank equals:

$$N \times \chi$$

The distance between beginning of one page and the end of another equals:

$$(N+1) \times \chi$$

The following corresponds to the foot of the peak: if the read step is less than the result of $(N-1) \times \chi$, the next requested cell will reside in another bank, regardless of the cell offset within a page. What if the step is increased at least by 1? When the last cell of one DRAM page is read, the next cell will belong to the next page of the same bank. (If this is unclear, try to represent it graphically.) Increasing the step further will involve more cells, steadily decreasing performance. This will continue until the reading step reaches $N \times \chi$. At this point, the reverse process begins: More cells will dart to the pages of the neighboring bank ready for processing the query.

Consequently, the slope width can be found as follows: $N \times \chi - (N-1) \times \chi$. Opening the parentheses gives the following: $N \times \chi - N \times \chi + \chi = \chi$. This was what needed to be proved. Knowing χ, it will be easy to calculate the value of N: *The number of banks equals the relation of the distance between two peaks to the width of the slope of one peak.* Therefore, the graph in Fig. 2.27 corresponds to four-bank memory with a page length of 2 KB.

Undoubtedly, this method is promising for the development of test programs. (It is interesting to know what equipment is at your disposal.) Would it help in program optimization? Because there are many memory models, the value of the optimal (or nonoptimal) memory-read step at the software-development stage is unknown. This value must be determined dynamically at run time, then optimized for a specific hardware configuration.

These considerations are not limited to tracing lists and other reference structures. They also are applicable to the parallel processing of several data flows. As an example, consider the following code:

Listing 2.19. Nonoptimal Code in Which Parallel Processing May Be Impossible

```
int *p1, int p2;
p1=malloc(BLOCK_SIZE*sizeof(int));
p2= malloc(BLOCK_SIZE*sizeof(int));
...
if (memcmp(p1,p2, BLOCK_SIZE*sizeof(int)) ...
...
```

Can this code fragment be considered optimal? If you say "yes," you are mistaken. No one can guarantee that the memory blocks returned by the `malloc` function will start from different banks. The opposite situation is more probable. If the block size is above 512 KB (as it is during the processing of such vast memory arrays as those discussed here), it can't fit within the heap. Therefore, the required memory must be allocated using a Win32 API function — `VirtualAlloc`. Unfortunately, the address returned by this function is always aligned by the 64 KB boundary (i.e., the value that is a multiple of all reasonable combinations of $N\chi$). Simply speaking, all memory blocks allocated by the malloc function always start from the same bank. It is not difficult to check if this assumption is correct. Develop a small program that allocates memory blocks of different sizes and analyzes the values of the 11th and 12th bits. (These bits are responsible for DRAM bank selection.) Such a program is Memory/bank.malloc.c, which can be found on the companion CD-ROM. A fragment of this program is in Listing 2.20.

Listing 2.20. [Memory/bank.malloc.c] Initial Banks of Memory Blocks Allocated by the malloc Function

```
#define N_ITER     9                    // Number of iterations
#define STEP_FACTOR   (100*1024)        // Increment of the memory step
#define MAX_MEM_SIZE (1024*1024)

#define _one_bit    11                  // These bits are responsible
#define _two_bit    12                  // for bank selection.

#define MASK         ((1<<_one_bit)+(1<<_two_bit))

#define zzz(a) (((int) malloc(a) & MASK) >> _one_bit)
main()
{
int a, b;
PRINT(_TEXT("= = = Determining the numbers of DRAM banks = = =\n"));
PRINT_TITLE;

printf("BLOCK\n SIZE-  -  -  n BANK -  -  -\n");
printf("----!-------------------------------------------------------\n");
for(a = STEP_FACTOR; a < MAX_MEM_SIZE; a += STEP_FACTOR)
{
   printf("%04d:", a/1024);
   for (b = 0; b < N_ITER; b++)
      printf("\t%x", zzz(a));
   printf("\n");
}

}
```

The result produced by this program will look as follows:

Listing 2.21. Output of the Program Determining the Numbers of DRAM Banks

```
BLOCK
  SIZE (K) -   -   -   n BANK -   -   -
----!------------------------------------------------------------
0100:   0   2   0   2   0   2   0   2   0
0200:   0   0   0   0   0   0   0   0   0
0300:   0   2   0   2   0   2   0   2   0
0400:   2   2   2   0   0   0   0   0   0
0500:   2   0   2   0   2   0   2   0   2
0600:   0   0   0   0   0   0   0   0   0
0700:   0   0   0   0   0   0   0   0   0
0800:   0   0   0   0   0   0   0   0   0
0900:   0   0   0   0   0   0   0   0   0
1000:   0   0   0   0   0   0   0   0   0
```

Until the size of the allocated blocks is below 512 KB, both favorable and unfavorable combinations occur. However, beginning with 512 KB, all allocated blocks start from the same bank.

What is the solution? Develop a custom implementation of `malloc`? This is not a way out! A better approach is to detect the values of N and χ dynamically, then check the appropriate bits in the addresses returned by `malloc`. If they happen to be equal, it is sufficient to increase any of these addresses by the value of χ. (The size of the requested block should have been increased by the same value.) As a result, 1 KB to 4 KB of available memory will be exchanged for a performance gain of 20% to 30%.

This is one of the rare situations in which "magic" enables the programmer to increase the performance of code written by someone else by adding a line of code to it. Notice that you don't even need to analyze the source code.

Now, forgive a small digression: I once was commissioned with the task of optimizing a program that, according to the customers, was fully optimized already. In this program, the main part of processor time was consumed by exchange with RAM, rather than by calculations. The size of the data that needed to be processed was minimal, and the customers were sure nothing else could be optimized. In their presence, I performed a brief context search over the source code. Without starting the profiler, I simply added several code lines, each of which looked approximately as follows: `p += 4*1024`. The program speed increased by approximately one-third.

They repeatedly asked if I was sure that this result was not obtained by chance and if the program would run on any hardware platform under any operating system. I was sure that the program, modified in such a way, would run under any Windows operating system on most hardware. Supported memory chips include 2x4, 4x2, and

4x4 memory; on Intel 815 (and similar chipsets), all types of memory would be supported. These chipsets map the 8th and 9th bits of the column number to the 25th and 26th bits of the linear address, instead of 11th and 12th bits, as would be expected.

The programmatic length of DRAM pages on such chipsets always equals 2 KB. All 64 MB or greater memory modules have at least four banks. *On all such modules, shifting a pointer by 4 KB will prevent hits to the same DRAM bank.*

Note that exploiting such hardware "features" is a bad style of programming. Therefore, if you develop a program intended for a long life, don't be lazy. Instead of using this technique, implement automatic calculation of the DRAM page length, or at least provide an option for changing this value as necessary.

Planning Data Flows

The previous section discussed the problems that accompany the parallel processing of several memory blocks (also known as data flows). This section will consider this topic in more detail. The key rule is as follows: *Data flows must start from different DRAM banks.* (Do not worry about the TLB; during parallel processing, all required pages will be already there.) Because most contemporary memory modules have a four-bank organization, working with five or more memory flows in parallel is pointless.

This is only the tip of the iceberg. As an example, consider the following statement from the VIA KT 133 chipset manual: "Supports maximum 16-bank interleave (i.e., 16 pages open simultaneously)." Does this mean that on VIA KT 133 (and similar chipsets), up to 16 data flows can be processed in parallel? Not quite; the keyword here is "maximum." If one DIMM module with four-bank organization is installed, no tricks will allow the chipset to hold five or more DRAM pages open. The memory chip will have only one RAS outlet; therefore, to open one more page in the same bank, this signal must be deactivated (i.e., an active page must be closed).

Thus, processing more than four data flows in parallel will lead to problems with the performance.

Suppose that it is necessary to process more than four data flows simultaneously, but it is undesirable to do so at the expense of performance and pay penalties for continuously opening and closing DRAM pages. Is this a dead-end? Certainly not!

The first idea that comes to mind is migrating to Direct RDRAM. Combined with the Intel 850 chipset, this will allow eight open pages, which means eight data flows can be processed. Are you satisfied with such a solution? This really is a satisfactory way out. Unfortunately, it is not suitable in all cases. Direct RDRAM is not the cheapest product on the market; therefore, it is not widespread.

However, even on the typical SDRAM, it is possible to process practically unlimited number of data flows without penalties. After all, no one demanded that you process *physical* data flows. Therefore, create one physical data flow and split it into several logical (virtual) data flows. In other words, use interleaved address translation.

The following mapping will be set up between the addresses of logical and physical data flows:

```
p[N][a]  == a*MAX_N + N
P[a]     == a mod MAX_N
```

❑   p — Array of pointers to the starting addresses of logical data flows
❑   P — Pointer to the starting address of the physical data flow
❑   N — Index of the logical flow
❑   a — Index of the Nth logical flow
❑   MAX_N — Number of logical flows

An example of interleaved address translation is shown in Fig. 2.28. Before optimization, two isolated memory blocks (*a* and *b*) each stored eight memory cells (designated *a0, a1, ..., a7* and *b0, b1, ..., b7*). In the optimized version of the program, these blocks are joined into a single, continuous block composed of 16 interleaved cells (*a0, b0, a1, b1, ..., a7, b7*). Now, when the *a* and *b* logical flows are processed in parallel, the requested data are merged into a single physical flow. This provides several advantages: First, it is possible to avoid constantly opening and closing DRAM pages. Second, it ensures that contiguous cells of the *a* and *b* flows won't belong to different pages of the same DRAM bank, which is recharged at access time. Third, it simplifies the process of hardware prefetching (if present), because most such systems are optimized for a single flow. (One flow is easier to implement. Furthermore, it only is efficient to increase the burst cycle for sequential access.)

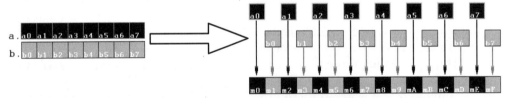

Fig. 2.28. Several source flows (*left*) are combined to form
one physical flow (*right*), constructed according to the address-interleave principle

Note that these benefits are practically free and do not overload the algorithm. However, there is one detail to consider: The transition from the physical address of the flow to the logical address inevitably involves calculation of the remainder. Therefore, the elimination of the DIV machine command, which accomplishes integer division, should be considered. Division is a slow operation, whose execution time is comparable to the time required to close an active DRAM page. If the number of flows equals a power of 2, you can use quick bitwise operations. Another approach would be to replace the remainder calculation with multiplication. (See *Arithmetic Operations*.)

Now, consider the efficiency of flow optimization with a large number of such flows. For this purpose, a fragment of a small program is provided in Listing 2.22. Consider the results of its execution.

Listing 2.22. [Memory/stream.virtual.c] Effect of Virtual Flows

```
#define BLOCK_SIZE    (2*M)       // Maximum virtual flow size
#define MAX_N_DST 16              // Maximum number of virtual data flows
#define MAIL_ROOL(a)     for(a = 2; a <= MAX_N_DST; a++)
                                 // Starting with two virtual flows


int a, b, r, x=0;
int *p, *px[MAX_N_DST];

// Header
printf("N DATA STREAM"); MAIL_ROOL(a) printf("\t%d", a); printf("\n");

; /*-------------------------------------------------------------------
; *                 Classic (nonoptimized) flow processing
; --------------------------------------------------------------------*/
// Allocating memory for all flows
for (a = 0; a < MAX_N_DST; a++) px[a] = (int *) _malloc32(BLOCK_SIZE);

printf("CLASSIC");
MAIL_ROOL(r)
{
// Starting the measurement of execution time
 A_BEGIN(0)
    for(a = 0; a < BLOCK_SIZE; a += sizeof(int))
       for(b = 0; b < r; b++)
          x += *(int *)((int)px[b] + a );
          // All flows are checked, one after the other.
          // It is easy to ensure that the cells of all flows
          // reside within different DRAM pages. If more than
          // four flows are processed, DRAM pages will open
          // and close constantly, reducing performance.
          // Note that the a and b loops can be exchanged,
          // which will improve performance.
          // However, this example is intended to
          // show parallel processing of flows.

// Stopping the measurement of execution time
 A_END(0)
```

```
// Printing the time of flow processing
printf("\t%d", Ax_GET(0));
} printf("\n");


; /*-----------------------------------------------------------------
; *                Optimized processing of virtual flows
; ------------------------------------------------------------------*/
// Allocating memory to the physical flow
p = (int*) _malloc32(BLOCK_SIZE*MAX_N_DST);

printf("OPTIMIZED");
MAIL_ROOL(r)
{
// Starting the measurement of execution time
 A_BEGIN(1)
    for(a  =  0; a < BLOCK_SIZE * r; a += (sizeof(int)*r))
    // What has changed? The increment now
    // equals the number of virtual flows.

        for(b = 0; b < r; b++)
            x += *(int *)((int)p + a + b*sizeof(int));
            // Now, the cells of all flows are adjacent.
            // Therefore, their processing time is minimal.

 // Ending the measurement of execution time
 A_END(1)

 // Printing the flow processing time
printf("\t%d", Ax_GET(1));
} printf("\n");
```

The optimized version was expected to perform better than the classic implementation, but who could imagine how greatly it would do this (Figs. 2.29 and 2.30)? On Pentium III 733/133/100/I815EP/2x4, as long as the number of flows in the classic version did not exceed four (the maximum number of active DRAM pages), the optimized wersion was slightly ahead of the classic one (Fig. 2.29).

However, when the number of flows passed five, the execution time of the nonoptimized version blasted up like a rocket. For the optimized version, the number grew nearly linearly. (The small oscillations can be explained by specific features of the cache subsystem, which will be covered in *Chapter 3*.)

Thus, with 16 flows (a realistic number for typical calculations), optimization provided more than fourfold growth in the execution speed. The results were achieved without introducing any crucial changes into the basic algorithm. Flow optimization mustn't necessarily be thought of at the design stage; on the contrary, it can be considered at any time.

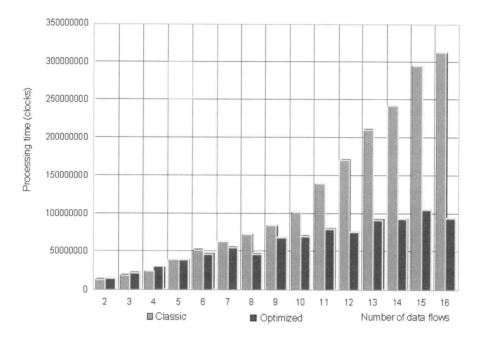

Fig. 2.29. Efficiency of virtual flows on Pentium III 733/133/100/I815EP/2x4

This is far from the performance limit. The program speed can be improved considerably if you use parallel data processing. (See *Parallel Data Processing*.)

Now, look at the results for AMD Athlon 1050/100/100/VIA KT 133/4x4 (Fig. 2.30). Strangely, the optimized version has surpassed the classic one in all cases, even when processing only two flows. How could this happen? The VIA KT 133 manual previously referred to promised "four cache lines (32 quad words) of CPU to DRAM read prefetch buffers." To decrease the latency, VIA engineers decided to take a daring step — implement the read-ahead from RAM. The prefetching algorithm must be able to recognize regular templates of data access and, based on them, predict with high probability which cells will be accessed next. Otherwise, the prefetching algorithm will cause nothing but losses because RAM will be unavailable during the read operation. Instead of decreasing the latency, it is possible to multiply it!

Unfortunately, the documentation provides no information on the prefetching scenario. However, you can guess. It appears that the read-ahead algorithm in KT 133 doesn't even attempt to recognize the strategy of memory access. It simply loads the next 32 quadruple words when accessing each cell. As a result, when working with several data flows, the contents of the prefetching buffer will be flushed before an attempt is made to access them. The prefetching data algorithm thrashes, and performance is degraded. Because of this, it is not recommended that you work with more than one physical data flow on VIA KT 133 and similar chipsets. Note that performance gain obtained by using virtual flows exceeds even the system based on PIII: Ten flows shows a more than fivefold gain. VIA KT 133 is quite a good chipset, isn't it

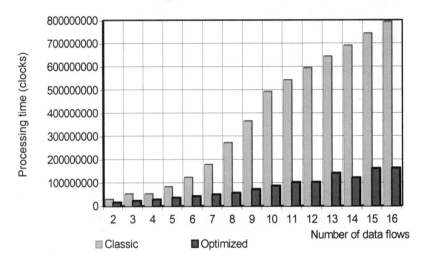

Fig. 2.30. Efficiency of virtual flows on AMD Athlon 1050/100/100/VIA KT 133/4x4

Special Cases of Virtual Flows

Digging deeper, try to answer the following question: What is minimum distance data flows can reside from each other? The common-sense answer is the smaller this distance, the better. However, if you give such an answer, you'll be wrong. The buffering features of some chipsets (actually, implementation errors of the buffering mechanism and/or a dumb prefetching algorithm) can cause a large performance drop when closely located cells (from the chipset's point of view) are accessed alternately. Consider the following example:

Listing 2.23. Inefficient Code That Doesn't Account for Some Buffering Features

```
for(a=0; a<BLOCK_SIZE; a+=STEP_FACTOR)
{
  x += *(int *)((int)p + a );
  y += *(int *)((int)p + a + DELTA_SIZE + STEP_FACTOR/2 );
}
```

On the Intel Pentium III 733/133/100/I815EP/2x4 system, the block-processing time rarely depends on the distance between data flows (DELTA_SIZE) (if the same bank is not hit repeatedly). However, this problem has been covered already. (See *Strategy of Data Distribution over DRAM Banks.*) At first, there are no other surprises. Nevertheless, consider the upper line on the graph, illustrating behavior of the AMD Athlon 1040/100/100/VIA KT 133/4x4 system (Fig. 2.31).

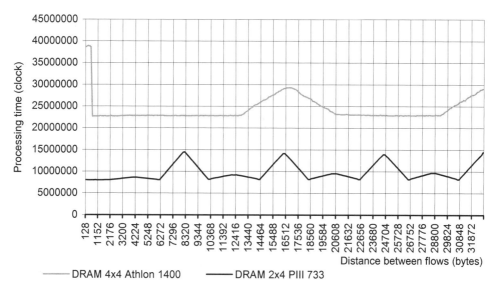

Fig. 2.31. Features of the buffering mechanism on the VIA KT 133 chipset

Parallel processing of the data flows located less than 512 bytes from each other incurs more than twofold increase of the execution time. This is also due to the prefetching mechanism implemented in the VIA KT 133 chipset. It is possible to simply declare: "It is strongly recommended that you use the Intel chipset to achieve maximum performance." However, any developer that wants clients should never limit freedom of choice, including that of a hardware manufacturer. If your customers like VIA, support them. To achieve maximum performance, simply shift the starting point of each virtual flow by 512 bytes from the previous flow. If the number of required flows is small, several kilobytes can be lost. Otherwise, hits to the banks being recharged will occur, and performance will decrease. Is there a graceful way out? Unfortunately, there are no universal solutions.

However, a sophisticated address-translation mechanism can be implemented by placing the data flows as follows: *p0, 512+p1, p2, 512+p3,* and so on. If the flows are processed according to the strict queue order, each access won't incur overhead. If the data are accessed alternately from the p1 and p3 flows, the execution speed will drop. To avoid this situation, you'll have to modify the address-translation mechanism to match the flow-processing algorithm (or simply abandon attempts to optimize the program for VIA).

The problem of minimum distance has been solved. Is there a maximum reasonable distance between data flows? It is easy to discover that it is $(N - 1) \times \chi$. (It even could be $(N - 2) \times \chi$ if the blocks are processed randomly. Careful planning of data flows avoids this problem.) Hence, one physical flow can comprise no more than the number of logical flows equal to $(N - 1) \times \chi$ divided by *sizeof(element)*, where *sizeof(element)* refers to flow elements. For arrays comprising _int32 elements, the maximum reasonable number of virtual flows will be 1,536: $(4 - 1) \times 2,048 / 4$. This number is more than sufficient for all conceivable tasks, isn't it?

The maximum reasonable number of physical flows remains equal to 1. All DRAM banks are employed, and when accessing the second physical flow, you may hit the banks being recharged. Still, everything depends on the mechanism used to work with data flows. It is possible to coordinate the operation of four physical flows, each containin about 1,500 virtual flows. But this totals about 6,000 virtual flows. It is difficult to imagine a task that needs so many flows, even in clustering technologies. I have encountered even larger numbers of data blocks processed in parallel — in a calculation system intended for modeling star movement in galaxies that would take scientists one step closer to revealing the mystery of dark matter. However, such processes currently are not modeled on PCs.

Processing Memory in Bytes, Double Words, and Quadruple Words

In their daily work, programmers encounter a variety of data types: bytes, double words, quadruple words, etc. Which of them is the most efficient? Programmers have no common opinion on this matter. Some manuals recommend processing large memory blocks in double words and advise forgetting about bytes. Others lure you into using commands for multimedia data processing, which are capable of "swallowing" at least 64 bits (an entire quadruple word) per operation. The first recommendation is closer to ideal, although with several reservations.

A simple test program (see Memory/dword.c on the companion CD-ROM) serves as a convincing example that reading memory in double words is approximately 30% to 40% faster than reading in bytes (Fig. 2.32). Reading in quadruple words (the MOVQ command) on Pentium III 733/133/100/I815EP is approximately 26% slower than reading in double words. Although on AMD Athlon 1050/100/100/VIA KT 133, this gap in performance between quadruple and double words is only about 4%, it doesn't change the problem: Reading a large memory block in quadruple words is inexpedient. (Small memory blocks are another matter. See *Working Principles of Cache.*)

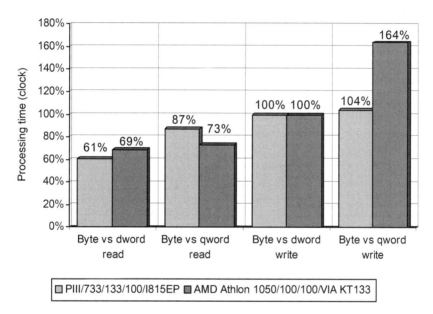

Fig. 2.32. Efficiency of reading and writing large memory blocks in double and quadruple words (when the byte-processing time equals 100%)

An interesting situation exists with memory writing: Bytes and double words are equally efficient. Therefore, when writing data, you can choose any data type (meaning the one best suited for the specific algorithm). Writing memory in quadruple words, as you have probably guessed, is less advantageous. Curiously, in contrast to memory reading, the largest performance gap exists on Athlon, where memory writing in quadruple words is approximately 64% slower that the same operation accomplished in double words.

Processing Byte Streamsin Double Words

In some cases, byte streams of data can be processed directly in double words (using some tricks). This can improve the performance of the application processing such byte streams.

Consider a simple example that encrypts bytes with the XOR operation using a constant mask:

Listing 2.24. Byte-Stream Processing

```
simple_crypt(char *src, int mask, int n)
{
int a;
for (a = 0; a < n; a++)
    src[a]^=mask;
}
```

Because all bytes are processed uniformly, why not to try to process 4 bytes in a single command? To achieve this result, it is sufficient to duplicate the encryption mask by copying it into the remaining 3 bytes of 1 double word.

You'll also need to provide the capability of processing blocks whose sizes are not multiples of four. This can be accomplished easily: Just calculate the remainder by dividing the block size by four, then encrypt the tail manually (i.e., by bytes).

This can be achieved as follows:

Listing 2.25. Optimized Processing of the Byte Stream in Double Words

---

```
optimized_simple_crypt(char *src, int mask, int n)
{
int a;
supra_mask = mask+(mask<<8)+(mask<<16)+(mask<<24);
// The byte mask is duplicated to fill the other 3 bytes of 1 double word.

for (a = 0; a < n; a += 4)
// The bytes are processed in double words.

{
    *(int *)src ^= supra_mask;   src+=4;
}
for (a = (n & ~3); a < n; a++)
// The tail (if it exists) is processed.

{
    *src ^= mask;    src += 1;
}
}
```

This trick is applicable to more than byte encryption. It can be employed to optimize algorithms such as copying, initialization, comparison, searching, replacing — in other words, all uniform methods of data processing.

Data Alignment

Design limitations keep the burst cycle from starting with an arbitrary address. The cycle is aligned automatically by a boundary of 32 bytes, 64 bytes, or 128 bytes on K6, PII, and PIII; Athlon; or P4. (See *Mapping Physical DRAM Addresses to Logical Addresses.*)

What would happen if, on PIII, a double word was requested whose address is 30? Reading such a double word would require two burst cycles. During the first cycle, the cells belonging to the *[(30 % 32); (30 % 32) + 32)* interval, (i.e., the *[0; 32)* interval) will be loaded. This interval contains only part of the requested double word. Reading the other part of the requested double word requires another cycle: *[32; 64)*. As a result, the cell access time will at least double.

Don't rush to blame Pentium designers; most other processors forbid access to unaligned addresses. If any such attempt is made, they generate an exception. Even on Pentium processors, it is best to avoid such a situation.

Now, it is time to discuss a common fallacies related to data alignment.

Most manuals on optimization (as well as technical documentation provided by processor manufacturers) strongly recommend that you always align data independently from the addresses in which they reside. However, the alignment value doesn't play a role if the requested data fit within one packet cycle. Reading a word starting at the 0x40001 address will be accomplished without delays or penalties because it doesn't cross the burst cycle. Actually, *0x20 – (0x40001 % 0x20) = 0x1F*, and *0x1F > sizeof(WORD)*. This means that the distance to the right boundary of the burst cycle exceeds the size of the data to be read. Consequently, reading of a word can start from the 0x40001 address even though this address is not a multiple of four.

A detailed discussion of the alignment problem is provided in *Data Alignment Efficiency*, because it relates to cache more than to RAM. Here, I will only cover the influence of the starting address on the speed of processing of large memory blocks. (See Memory/align.c on the companion CD-ROM.)

During linear processing, the repetition factor of the alignment of the starting address plays a minor role. If the next portion of the requested data darts beyond the limits of the burst cycle, causing the processor to initiate another burst cycle, there is no need to be too upset; these data must be loaded anyway. Does it matter when this happens?

Timing does matter. When the processor reads data that crossed the boundary of the burst cycle, it is forced to spend at least one extra clock cycle to join the two parts of the data, which reduces the performance. This performance drop is insignificant: approximately 12% for PIII and 20% for Athlon (Fig. 2.33). This value usually can be ignored. Nevertheless, *if you want to achieve maximum performance, always align addresses* (Table 2.2).

Table 2.2. Recommended Address Alignment for Various Data Types

Data size	Boundary
1 byte (8 bits)	Arbitrary
2 bytes (16 bits)	Multiple of 2 bytes
4 bytes (32 bits)	Multiple of 4 bytes
8 bytes (64 bits or 1 word)	Multiple of 8 bytes
10 bytes (80 bits)	Multiple of 16 bytes
16 bytes (128 bits or 1 double word)	Multiple of 16 bytes

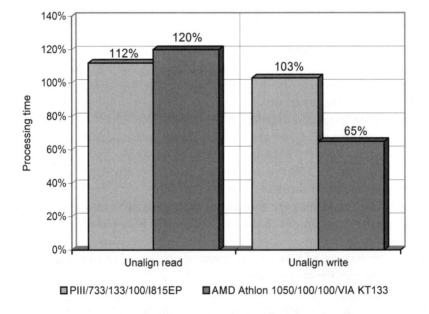

□ PIII/733/133/100/I815EP   ■ AMD Athlon 1050/100/100/VIA KT133

Fig. 2.33. Efficiency of aligning the starting address when processing a large data array (write operations do not require data to be aligned)

The situation is different for data writing. The write-delay mechanism implemented in Pentium and AMD Athlon processors prevents performance drops that otherwise would be caused by mismatched sizes of data being written to the boundaries of the burst cycles. On Pentium III, unaligned data are written only 3% slower; on AMD Athlon, they are written 35% *faster*. No, this is not a misprint! *Specific features of the Athlon processor and the North Bridge of the VIA KT 133 chipset cause data to be written more quickly when they are unaligned.*

This effect takes place only when data are written into RAM. Writing unaligned data into cache results in significant losses and overhead, reducing the performance multiple times. (See *Data Alignment Efficiency.*) Therefore, data alignment can be neglected only when processing vast blocks of memory (1 MB or higher) that exceed the amount of cache memory of all levels many times.

To conclude this discussion, consider how the choice of source and target addresses influences the performance when copying large memory blocks. (See Memory/align.memcpy.c on the companion CD-ROM.) As can be easily guessed, alignment of the target address is of little importance, and inadequate selection of the source address greatly reduces the performance (Fig. 2.34).

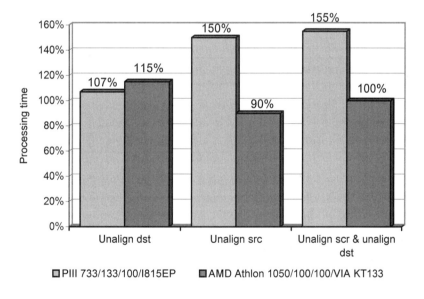

Fig. 2.34. Influence of the alignment of the source and target addresses on performance when copying memory blocks

Manual Data Alignment

Built-in alignment tools (see *Data Alignment Efficiency*) often prove to be insufficient. First, they are applicable only to structure elements. The compiler always aligns local and global variables in the manner it considers to be correct. Second, the maximum alignment level (in Microsoft Visual C++ and in Borland C++) is limited by multiples of 16 bytes. This means that you won't succeed if you try to align an array by the cache-line boundary (32 bytes for PIII, and 64 bytes for Athlon) using built-in tools. (Such alignment can be achieved using techniques discussed in *Data Alignment Efficiency.*) Some manuals recommend that you employ the assembly language in this situation. What should you do if you haven't mastered it yet?

You could use the built-in C functionality. Because 32-bit near pointers are actually 32-bit integers, all math functionality is available to the programmer. The solution to this problem is reduced to the following: Given some number (X), you can find another number (Y) that is the nearest to X and a multiple of N. The first formula that comes to mind is $Y = (X/N) \times N$. If N is a power of 2 (rather than any random integer), you can abandon the slow division operation. Instead, you can manually reset the respective binary digit using the logical *AND* operator. It also will be necessary to increment the *truncated* pointer by a value equal to the alignment power. This is necessary because during alignment the pointer is truncated and, as a result, intrudes upon the "alien" memory. Naturally, the amount of allocated memory must be increased by the rounding value. Thus, the final solution will look approximately as follows:

Listing 2.26. Manual Data Alignment Using Built-in Capabilities of C Language

```
char p;
p = (char*) malloc(need_size + (align_powr - 1));
p = (char *) (((int)p + align_power - 1) & ~(align_power - 1));
```

In Listing 2.26, `align_power` is the required alignment power, and `char*` is the pointer type. (This type need not be `char*`; for example, it could be `int*`.)

The same trick can be used to align arrays residing in the stack or data segment.

Listing 2.27. Manual Alignment of Arrays in the Stack or Data Segment

```
#define array_size 1024
#define align_power 64
int a[array_size + align_power -1];
int *p;
p = (int *) (((int)&a + align_power - 1) & ~(align_power-1));
```

The `p` pointer will point to the starting position of array aligned by 64-byte boundary. (This alignment method ensures the most efficient data processing.)

If necessary, you can use arrays to store various types of data by aligning them.

Listing 2.28. Using Arrays To Store Dissimilar Types of Aligned Data

```
char array[9];
#define a array[0]
#define b (int *array[sizeof(char)])[0]
#define c (int *array[sizeof(char)+sizeof(int)])[0]
#define d (int *array[sizeof(int)*3])[0]
```

This trick (although inelegant) allows you to store variables densely, without free, unallocated spaces between them, and to control the order of their locations in memory. Using this approach, you can distribute shared variables to different memory banks. This might be useful, because local variables appear in stack in the order preferred by the compiler, rather than in the order they were declared.

Aligning Data Flows

In contrast to the alignment of memory blocks returned by the `malloc` function, the alignment of addresses received by the function from outside is difficult. Suppose that you need to calculate the sum of the elements that compose an array. The simplest way of achieving this is as follows:

Listing 2.29. Nonoptimized Function Implementation (`*array` May Be Unaligned)

```
int sum(int *array, int n)
{
int a, x = 0;
for(a = 0; a < n; a++)
    x+=array[a];
return x;
}
```

The suggested implementation doesn't care about data alignment; it silently delegates this task to the code calling the function. This assumption is risky! A programmer might neglect a recommendation to use alignment in the function specification. In addition, it is not always possible to align the address passed to the function. (The programmer could receive the unaligned address from outside.)

Therefore, the called function must handle address alignment. Is it capable of doing this? At first, it might seem that the answer to this question is no. If `(x & 3) != 0`, then `((x + sizeof(int)*k) & 3) != 0`. But penalty clocks for accessing unaligned data are added only when unaligned data cross the boundaries of burst cycles. This circumstance can be used to your benefit.

Read the memory in double words until the current address satisfies the condition
`(((p % BRST_LEN) + sizeof(DWORD)) < BRST_LEN)` (i.e., until the double word that
crosses the boundary of the burst cycle has been reached). Pass this perilous section of
the route in tiny steps (1 byte in length), which will prevent penalty clock cycles. It
only remains to assemble these 4 bytes into a 1 double word. This can be easily accomplished using bitwise shift operations. Then, the previously described read cycle repeats (Fig. 2.35). This should continue until you reach the end of the memory block
that needs to be processed.

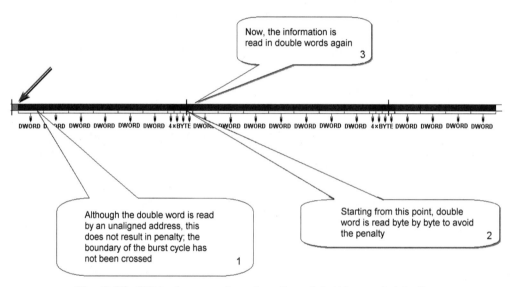

Fig. 2.35. Efficient processing of unaligned double-word data flow

One possible implementation of the suggested algorithm is in Listing 2.30. Note
that *there is no common solution to this problem.* The maximum number of double
words within a typical packet is eight. When working with unaligned addresses, this
value is even smaller! A loop of several interactions is rather slow. To avoid a performance drop, such a loop must be unrolled entirely. This is the main problem, because
the number of iterations depends on the value of the pointer offset in the packet-loop
cycle. Therefore, you need to create various loops according to the following formula:
`BRST_LEN - BRST_LEN/sizeof(DWORD)`. Each loop must process its own pointer
offset. For brevity, I only will provide one version; other versions likely will have similar implementations.

Listing 2.30. [Memory/align.dwstream.c] Efficient Processing of the Data Flow of Unaligned Double Words

```c
// -[Calculating the array sum]--------------------------------------------
//
//  ARG:
//      array  - Pointer to array
//      n      - Number of elements to be sorted
//
// README:
//      This function efficiently aligns unaligned arrays.
//      (However, it would be better if it didn't do this.)
//-------------------------------------------------------------------------
int sum_align(int *array, int n)
{
int a, x = 0;
char supra_bytes[4];

if (((int)array & 15)!=1)
    ERROR("-ERR: Invalid alignment\n");
    // Attention: This is a specific solution, when array & 15 == 1,
    // (i.e., when the pointer is shifted 1 byte to the right of
    // the address aligned by the 32-byte boundary).
    // A general solution to this problem without using loops,
    // which degrade performance, is impossible.
    // The only method requires the manual creation of a custom
    // "handler" for each situation, the total number of which
    // would equal 32 - 32/4 = 24. This is rather clumsy.

for(a = 0; a < n; a += 8)
{
    x += array[a + 0];
    x += array[a + 1];
    x += array[a + 2];
    x += array[a + 3];
    x += array[a + 4];
    x += array[a + 5];
    x += array[a + 6];
    // All double words that do not cross
    // the burst-cycle boundaries are copied.

    supra_bytes[0]=*((char *) array + (a+7)*sizeof(int) + 0);
    supra_bytes[1]=*((char *) array + (a+7)*sizeof(int) + 1);
```

```
    supra_bytes[2]=*((char *) array + (a+7)*sizeof(int) + 2);
    supra_bytes[3]=*((char *) array + (a+7)*sizeof(int) + 3);
    // The double word that crosses the burst-cycle boundary
    // is copied to the temporary buffer byte by byte.

    x += *(int *)supra_bytes;
    // The supra_bytes are retrieved and processed as double words.
  }

  return x;
}
```

At this point, you will encounter unexpected and unpleasant surprise: The optimized program runs *slower* than the initial nonoptimized version. On Pentium III 733/133/100/I815EP, the performance drops approximately 14%; on AMD Athlon 1050/100/100/VIA KT 133, it reaches the value of approximately 130%. Why does this happen? Preventing the crossing of the burst-cycle boundary was achieved at too high a price; it increased the number of memory-access attempts. This is the main factor responsible for performance drop.

Still, I don't want to abandon this algorithm. It can be improved.

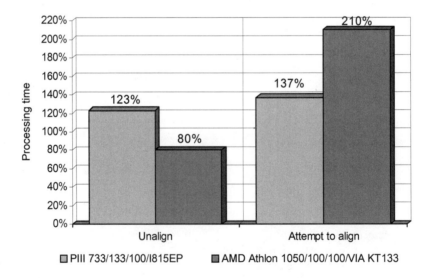

Fig. 2.36. Algorithm that "efficiently" processes unaligned double-word data flow actually decreases performance

Aligning Byte-Data Flows

Efficient processing of byte-data flows by double words (see *Memory Processing by Bytes, Double Words, and Quadruple Words*) is possible only when the starting address of the block is aligned by the 4-byte boundary. Unfortunately, this does not always occur. Byte streams do not need to be aligned by definition; therefore, the compiler (or programmer) can place them anywhere in the memory. Fortunately, it is not difficult to implement a function that would align such a flow.

Because the byte stream is *uniform*, you can start reading it from any position. Calculate the address of the nearest burst-cycle boundary. (In general, this equals `p + (BRST_LEN — ((int) p % BRST_LEN))`.) Starting from that position, process the byte stream in double words. (Do not forget that the block size is not always a multiple of `sizeof(DWORD)`). Wait! What about the initial `(BRST_LEN — ((int) p % BRST_LEN))` bytes? Just add an additional processing loop (Fig. 2.37).

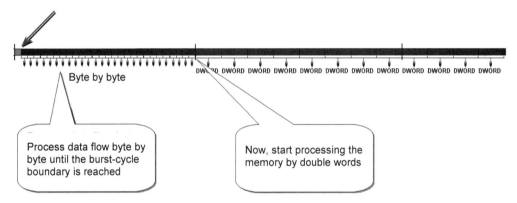

Fig. 2.37. Efficient technique of aligning byte-data flows

Now, return to the program that implements the simplest encryption algorithm (Listing 2.24). Let us improve this algorithm by making it align the processed data block. One of the possible implementations is provided below:

Listing 2.31. [Memory/align.bstream.c] Function That Aligns Byte Streams

```
// -[Simple byte-crypt]---------------------------------------------
//
//   ARG:
//      src    - Pointer to the encrypted block
//      mask   - Encryption mask (bytes)
//
```

```
//  DEPENCE:
//     unalign_crypt
//
//  README:
//     This function aligns the encrypted data on its own.
//----------------------------------------------------------------------
void align_crypt(char *src, int n, int mask)
{
int a;
char *x;
int n_ualign;

n_ualign= 32 - ((int) src & 15);
// The distance to the nearest burst-cycle boundary is calculated.
// It is necessary to shift the block by this value to align it.

unalign_crypt(src, n_ualign, mask);
// Encryption continues until the burst-cycle boundary is reached.

unalign_crypt(src+n_ualign, n-n_ualign, mask);
// The rest is encrypted because src+n_ualign
// is guaranteed to be an aligned pointer.
// (Do not forget to decrease the number of encrypted bytes.)
}
```

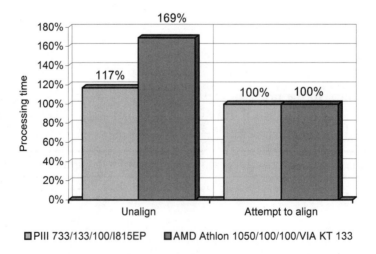

Fig. 2.38. Efficiency of the suggested technique for aligning byte streams of data

A test run of this program shows that the optimized version is equally efficient at processing aligned and unaligned data blocks. When the nonoptimized program processes unaligned data blocks, performance losses are approximately 17% on Pentium III 733/133/100/I815EP and 69% on AMD Athlon 1050/100/100/VIA KT 133.

You probably noticed that the `align_crypt` function is nothing more than the wrapping for the `unalign_crypt` (i.e., it can be modified to fit your needs). It is sufficient to replace the call to `unalign_crypt` with the call to your custom function.

Combining Calculations with Memory Access

In contemporary processors, accessing RAM no longer stops the executive pipeline. After the request is sent for loading the cell to the chipset, the processor temporarily pauses execution of the current machine instruction and proceeds with the next one. This circumstance allows the CPU to send the next query to the chipset before the previous request is accomplished. (See *Parallel Data Processing*.) However, the chipset's level of parallelism is not high. Therefore, when processing large amounts of data, the processor still must wait until the cells are loaded from RAM. Well, why don't you relieve the processor's boredom during idle clocks by making it do something useful (such as calculations)?

Suppose that you need to load N memory cells and calculate the cosine of the specific angles k times. It is preferable to accomplish these actions within a loop, rather than in series. By using a loop, the cosine will be calculated while cells are loaded from RAM, and the total time required to execute the task will be reduced.

A question arises almost immediately: What proportion will provide the best mix of calculations and memory access? Ideally, the time taken to execute calculations must equal the time taken to load cells from the memory; with such equality, the highest level of parallelism is achieved. The problem is that the relation of the memory-access speed to the time of machine-instruction execution varies widely on different systems. Therefore, this problem has no universal solution. (More details on this topic will be provided in *Chapter 3*.) However, it is not necessary to reach full parallelism. Full parallelism often cannot be achieved; for example, the number of calculation operations may not cover all delays caused by loading cells from the memory.

Try to evaluate the gain achieved by full and partial parallelism. The simple test program in Listing 2.32 investigates various "concentrations" of calculation operations per memory cell. For brevity, the listing shows only a fragment of this function. Note that the loop accessing memory should be unrolled in the optimized version; otherwise, you won't get any performance gain. Why? Rolled loops cannot be executed in parallel. In addition, loops with a small number of iterations are disadvantageous; the number of iterations in such loops always exceeds the required number by 1.

Note

This relates to the strategy of branch prediction. During the last iteration of the loop, the processor doesn't realize the loop has ended. Thus, the processor passes control to the first command of the loop. It later detects the error and performs a rollback, but this doesn't reduce execution time.

The necessity of unrolling loops results in enormous growth of the program size. Because the C language doesn't support cyclic macros, the entire code must be entered manually. This situation is a good example of a problem that cannot be solved elegantly using built-in C capabilities. (A macro assembler would solve this task easily and elegantly.)

Listing 2.32. [Memory/mem.mix.c] Combining Memory Access and Calculations

```
; /*-------------------------------------------------------------------
;  *                    Nonoptimized version
; ------------------------------------------------------------------*/
per=16;    // To load one calculation of the cosine, 16 bytes are needed.


for(a = 0; a < BLOCK_SIZE; a+=4)
   z += *(int*)((int)p1 + a);
// This loop for loading cells from memory is inefficient
// because the memory subsystem cannot keep pace with the processor.

for(a=0; a < (BLOCK_SIZE/per); a++)
x+=cos(x);
// Loop for calculating the sine


; /*-------------------------------------------------------------------
;  *                    Optimized version
; ------------------------------------------------------------------*/
for(a = 0; a < BLOCK_SIZE; a += per)
// Common loop that combines memory access with cosine calculations

{
   z += *(int*)((int)p1 + a);
   z += *(int*)((int)p1 + a + 4);
   z += *(int*)((int)p1 + a + 8);
   z += *(int*)((int)p1 + a + 12);
// Attention: The memory-access loop must be unrolled;
// otherwise, optimization will cause performance loss.
```

```
    x+=cos(x);
// The cosine calculation will take place while the previous cells
// are loaded, which will increase in performance.
}
```

A test run of this program on AMD Athlon 1050/100/100/VIA KT 133 (Fig. 2.39) established that the highest level of parallelism is achieved by performing a cosine calculation operation per 32 loaded bytes. On Pentium III/733/133/100/I815EP, the performance gain is more significant with a cosine calculation per 256 loaded bytes.

However, the program size becomes the payment for this gain. An unrolled loop comprising 64 data-loading commands looks odd. Any attempt to roll the loop will neutralize any performance gain. The rightmost point of the graph (Fig. 2.39), marked with the * character, illustrates this situation. It is easy to calculate that if the loop is rolled, the performance loss will be no less that 40%. As a result, the optimized version will run only 5% faster than the nonoptimized one. In most cases, however, the speed of operation is more important than the application size.

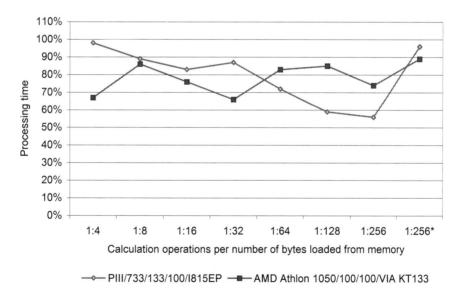

Fig. 2.39. Efficiency of combining calculation operations
with commands that access memory

Grouping Read and Write Operations

Some manuals dedicated to optimization declare that overlapping read and write bus transactions is undesirable. This statement is incorrect.

Contemporary chipsets are capable of processing queries out of turn; therefore, they determine the preferable strategy of physical exchange with the memory on their own. Because of this, *it is not necessary to avoid mixing read and write commands when processing vast amounts of data,* which exceed the capacity of cache memory of all levels many times. With smaller amounts of data, the performance drop caused by overlapping transactions will be rather large.

The code fragment in Listing 2.33 estimates the influence of overlapping read and write transactions when processing large data blocks.

Listing 2.33. [Memory/read.write.c] How Overlapping Read and Write Transactions Affect Program Performance

```
; /*-------------------------------------------------------------------
;  *                  No overlapping transactions
; -------------------------------------------------------------------*/
for (a = 0; a < BLOCK_SIZE; a += 4)
{
   *(int *)((int)p1 + a) = x;
}

for (a = 0; a < BLOCK_SIZE; a += 4)
{
   x += *(int *)((int)p1 + a);

}


; /*-------------------------------------------------------------------
;  *              Overlapping transactions constantly occur
; -------------------------------------------------------------------*/
for (a = 0; a < BLOCK_SIZE; a+= 32)
{
   x += *(int *)((int)p1 + a);
   *(int *)((int)p2 + a) =x;
}
```

Oops! Performance growth due to transaction overlapping was unexpected. However, even a superficial investigation shows that transaction overlapping plays a minor role here; loop unrolling actually is causing this performance growth. Combining two loops within a single loop is equivalent to unrolling a loop by two iterations.

To compensate for the side effect of loop unrolling, unroll two continuous loops by N iterations, and the "hybrid" loop by $N/2$ iterations. Note that N must be large enough to ensure that unrolling the loop by $N/2$ iterations is not much worse than unrolling it by N iterations. (Both the number of turns and length of straight sections influence the result. See *Loops*.) A sufficiently accurate result can be achieved when N equals 16; therefore, use this value as an example. (I won't provide the code fragment with the unrolled loop; you should know already how to perform this operation.)

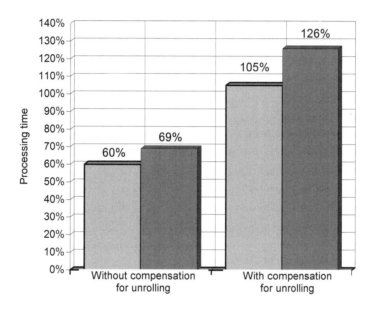

☐ PIII/733/133/100/I815EP ■ AMD Athlon 1050/100/100/VIA KT133

Fig. 2.40. Influence of overlapped read and write transactions on the processing time of large data blocks

This proves that overlapping transactions degrade the performance. This drop, however, is insignificant (about 5% on Pentium III 733/133/100/I815EP). In most cases, you can ignore this value. Even on AMD Athlon 1050/100/100/VIA KT 133, where the loss is about 26%, the drop is justified by the simplicity of the calculation algorithm.

Accessing the Memory
Only When Necessary

The most efficient method of optimizing memory access is... giving up memory usage. No, this is not a joke! Most applications use memory inefficiently, and expert algorithm development allows you to control their appetites.

Suppose that you have a graphical editor that, among other things, is capable of copying fragments of text or graphics into the clipboard and pasting them into other documents. Traditionally, this task is reduced to calling memmove (or memcpy) functions. However, there is a large variety of more elegant and efficient solutions. For example, why do you need the copied block to be duplicated? As long as the copied fragment was not modified, you can reference the original block. This is not a crucial matter for text editors; however, when processing graphic files with high resolution, this approach might keep you from making billions of memory-access attempts.

Even if the user wants to change the copied fragment, there is no need to duplicate the entire block. It is sufficient to isolate the modified part of the block and correct references to it as appropriate. This makes the algorithm more sophisticated and complicates application debugging, but the resulting gain is worth it.

This problem is related to algorithms more than to the memory subsystem, so I won't cover this topic in detail.

Optimizing Built-in C Functions
That Work with the Memory

Built-in libraries of the C language include a large number of functions that work with memory blocks: memcpy, memmove, memcmp, memset, and so on. These functions usually are implemented in assembly language and are well-optimized. Still, some performance reserves remain. Using tricks, it is possible to reduce drastically the time required for processing large memory blocks.

Optimizing memcpy

Most implementations of the memcpy function look approximately as follows: while (count--) *dst++ = *src++. There are at least three problems specific to this code: the *overlap of read/write transactions*, a *low level of cell processing parallelism*, and the *possibility of flow overlap within the same DRAM bank*.

Overlapping read/write transactions are eliminated by copying blocks of memory cells via the cache buffer. One loop will read several kilobytes of the source into cache, while other loop writes the contents of the buffer into the target. As a result, instead of the alternation of the read-write-read-write... transactions, you will get two separate series of transactions: read-read-read... and write-write-write.... Some transaction overlap will remain at the loop boundaries. However, if the buffer size is at least 1 KB, you can easily ignore this overhead.

Data loading parallelism can be intensified if you access the cells with a step equal to the size of the packet-read cycle. (See *Parallel Data Processing.*) For the sake of simplicity, you can settle on a step of 32 bytes. In performance-critical applications optimized for the newest generation of processors (AMD Athlon and Pentium 4) it is recommended that you determine this value automatically or specify it as an option.

The negative effect of overlapping data flows within the same DRAM bank will be eliminated automatically because data flows are processed sequentially, not in parallel.

In summary, three problems are eliminated in one motion: *Copying memory via the intermediate buffer eliminates all weak points of the algorithm of the built-in* memcpy *function, significantly improving its performance.*

Thus, the improved version of the memcpy function might look as follows:

Listing 2.34. [Memory/memcpy.optimize.c] Optimized Implementation of memcpy

```
for (a = 0; a < count; a += subBLOCK_SIZE)
{
for(b = 0; b < subBLOCK_SIZE; b += BRUST_LEN)
    tmp += *(int *)((int)src + a + b);

memcpy((int*)((int)dst + a ), (int*)((int)src + a), subBLOCK_SIZE);
}
```

On AMD Athlon 1050/100/100/VIA KT 133, the optimized version of memcpy runs approximately 31% faster. This is good!

Unfortunately, on Pentium III/733/133/100/I815EP, the performance growth is smaller. Eliminating one problem inevitably creates new ones.

The suggested method of optimizing the memcpy function has at least two serious drawbacks. First, increasing the number of loops from one to three involves significant overhead that no tricks can eliminate. Second, the loop that loads data from the RAM into cache nearly idles. By placing the received cells into an unused variable, the loop that writes data into the memory must access *repeatedly* the cells that already have been loaded. Apparently, the count and BRUST_LEN cells are copied twice. Unfortunately, the first loop cannot write the obtained cells directly into the memory; this would cause the bus transactions to overlap and would decrease performance.

Implementation of this algorithm using assembly language will improve its speed slightly. A much better result can be obtained by using prefetching. (See *Goals and Tasks of Cache Memory.*)

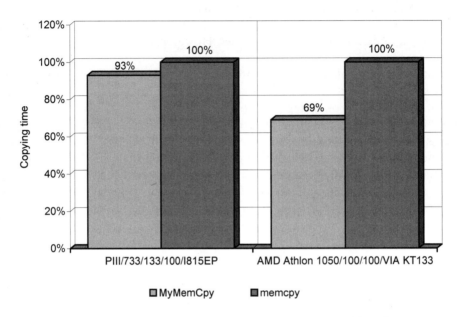

Fig. 2.41. Efficiency of parallel memory copying, with a clear performance gain (about 31%) on the Athlon processor

Optimizing memmove

The memmove function included in the standard built-in library of the C language has an advantage over its nearest relative, memcpy: The memmove function can copy overlapping memory blocks. At what cost is this achieved? If the target address is located to the left of the source (i.e., it resides in a lower address), the copy algorithm is implemented the same manner as the memcpy function. The memory cells are moved "backward" into the free, noninitialized area (Fig. 2.42).

The only limitation is that the number of memory cells moved per iteration must not exceed the difference of the source and target addresses. This means that if the target is located only 2 bytes from the source, it would be impossible to move memory blocks by double words.

The situation is more difficult when the target is located to the right of the source (i.e., it resides in higher addresses). An attempt to copy memory from left to right will result in a crash, because the cells moved to the "allocated" addresses will overwrite their contents. Strictly speaking, memcpy will work like memset. How can this situation be resolved? The source code of the memmove function can be analyzed. (In the standard Microsoft Visual C++ installation, the source code of this function is in the \Microsoft Visual Studio\VC98\CRT\SRC\memmove.c file.)

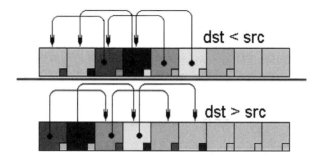

Fig. 2.42. Copying overlapping memory blocks: If the source is to the right of the target (*top*), memory can be moved without problems. If the source is to the left of the target (*bottom*), moving the memory cells "forward" will overwrite the source.

Listing 2.35. Implementation of the `memmove` Function in Microsoft Visual C++

```
; /*-------------------------------------------------------------------
;   *                      Overlapping Buffers
;   *          (copy from higher addresses to lower addresses)
; ---------------------------------------------------------------------*/
dst = (char *)dst + count - 1;
src = (char *)src + count - 1;

while (count--) {
 *(char *)dst = *(char *)src;
 dst = (char *)dst - 1;
 src = (char *)src - 1;
}
```

In this example, the memory is copied "back to front" (i.e., from right to the left). Cell overwriting is eliminated — at a price. As you already know, the memory subsystem is optimized for direct reading, and any attempt to perform this operation in the reverse order will decrease performance. How much? This question has no universally acceptable answer; this value depends on the specific features of the hardware.

On an Intel Pentium III processor with a Intel 815EP chipset, reverse memory copying is approximately 66% slower than direct copy. As for an AMD Athlon processor with a VIA KT 133 chipset, the difference is 2%, which certainly can be ignored. Because computers based on Athlon/KT 133 hold a much smaller segment of market than systems based on Intel Pentium, you should not rely on this configuration.

If you are using memmove intensely, the overall performance drop might be rather significant. No wonder the developer wishes to improve the speed of the program, at least slightly. To achieve this result, it is sufficient to copy the memory in blocks of a size equal to the difference between the source and target addresses, rather than by bytes or double words. If the block size is at least a couple of kilobytes, the memory will be copied forward, although "back to front." How can this be implemented? Consider the following example written in pure C, without using the assembly language. For simplicity, this example doesn't include auxiliary code that implements exception handling and alignment of the starting addresses with further movement of the "tail." (See *Data Alignment.*)

Listing 2.36. Forward, but "Back to Front," Memory-Block Copying

---

```
int __MyMemMoveX(char *dst, char *src, int size)
{
char *p1,*p2;
int a, x=1;
int delta;

delta = dst-src;
if ((delta<1)) return -1;

for(a = size; a > delta; a -= delta)
    memcpy(dst+a-delta, src+a-delta, delta);

return 0;
}
```

When compared to the built-in memmove function, this implementation runs approximately 20% faster (if the difference between the source and target addresses does not exceed the L1 cache size) and 30% faster (if memory blocks are moved a great distance) (Fig. 2.43). However, the limit has not been reached. If you rewrite the MyMemMoveX function using the assembly language, you will get a more dramatic performance increase. (See *Parallel Data Processing* and *Goals and Tasks of Cache Memory.*)

If the difference between the source and target addresses is small (less than 1 KB), you won't "deceive" the system, and memory will be copied in the reverse direction, rather than in the forward direction. In addition, overhead related to organizing the loop for block copying will degrade the performance considerably. Thus, your custom function will be slower that the built-in memmove function. Therefore, the custom MyMemMoveX function has a limited range of application.

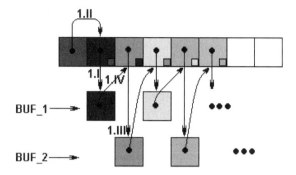

Fig. 2.43. "Four cycle" algorithm of direct memory movement
using two intermediate buffers

There also might be the situations in which you need to copy overlapped areas in the forward direction. You could have a data flow that doesn't support pointer positioning, or the entire block could be unavailable when copying begins. Consider a real-world situation that I experienced: When moving an image fragment in a graphical editor (Visual Studio), the technical specification required the image to be refreshed from the block start to the block end. (This enabled the user to work with the image without waiting until the block was moved entirely.) At the same time, references could not be used in data organization. (This is a project specification.) Does this lead to a dead end? Not at all! On the contrary, this is great opportunity of using your little gray cells.

The first solution that comes to mind is to move the memory via an intermediate buffer. The idea can be implemented by a simple code that might look as follows:

Listing 2.37. One Implementation for Moving Memory Via an Intermediate Buffer

```
MyMoveMem(char *dst, char *src, int size)
{
char *tmp;
tmp=malloc(BLOCK_SIZE);
memcpy(tmp, src, BLOCK_SIZE);
memcpy(dst, tmp, BLOCK_SIZE);
}
```

Is this good? Far from it. The suggested algorithm doubles the amount of required memory, which in some cases is unacceptable. It also doubles the time required for copying. Finally, it doesn't solve the task formulated in the project specification. You know that the image won't begin to refresh immediately; it will start only after a long time period used to fill the temporary buffer. Therefore, this algorithm isn't worth thinking about.

Wait! Do you need to copy into the temporary buffer the entire block that will be moved? It is sufficient to save only the part of the block that is overwritten by the tail, which protrudes to the left. This means that the maximum reasonable size of the buffer equals `dst - src`. Consider the simplified version of direct memory movement using two such buffers. You might name it *four-cycle streaming algorithm of memory copying*. The following explanation will clarify why the algorithm is called "four cycle:"

❑ *Cycle 1:* `memcpy(BUF_1, dst, dst - src)` — The source memory is saved because this fragment will be overwritten during the next cycle (Fig. 2.43).

❑ *Cycle 2:* `memcpy(dst, src, dst - src)` — The `dst - src` bytes are copied from the source to the target, disregarding the overwritten memory because it has been saved in the buffer.

❑ *Cycle 3:* `memcpy(BUF_2, dst + (dst - src), dst - src)` — The next portion of the source data is saved in the second intermediate buffer.

❑ *Cycle 4:* `memcpy(dst + (dst - src), BUF_1, dst - src)` — The contents of the buffer `BUF_1` are poured into the correct position (recently saved in `BUF_2`). That's all! The first buffer is free, and you can continue with Cycle 1. The "working cycle" of the "engine" has been completed.

As you can see, the copying takes place only in a forward direction, and the target memory is refreshed from start to end in small portions of `dst - src` bytes. (When you work in a graphical editor and drag the graphical fragments using the mouse, they cannot be moved far in one step.) By the way, Microsoft Paint, the built-in graphics editor supplied with Windows, uses the `memmove` function for moving the memory; therefore, it is very slow, even on PIII.

If the difference between the source and target addresses is between 4 KB and 8 KB, the suggested algorithm, despite moving the memory from buffer to buffer twice, is 1.1 times faster than `memmove` on PIII (Fig. 2.44). On Athlon, this algorithm is 1.7 times faster. However, this gain is proof of advanced features of the algorithm under consideration; rather, the gain is the result of features of the VIA KT 133 chipset.

Now, consider the following idea: Is it possible to decrease the number of buffers to one? This is possible. When Cycle 2 has been completed, the `[src[0]...src[dst-src]]` region (see Fig. 2.43) is free and can be used for temporary data storage.

However, there is one hidden danger: In contrast to custom temporary buffers, whose addresses can be chosen based on DRAM architecture and organization, the target address is passed from outside. You should be able to predict the conse-quences. When necessary, you can get by with a single buffer without seeing a significant decrease in performance. However, this will complicate an already complex algorithm. (See Listing 2.37.)

Listing 2.38. Four-Cycle Algorithm for Moving Memory Forward Using Two Intermediate Buffers

---

```
#define BUF_SIZE 256*K
int __MyMemMove(char *dst, char *src, int size)
{
char BUF_1[BUF_SIZE];
char BUF_2[BUF_SIZE];
char *p1, *p2;
int a, x = 1;
int delta;
delta = dst-src;
if ((delta>BUF_SIZE) || (delta<1)) return -1;
p1 = BUF_1;
p2 = src;

for(a = 0; a < size/delta; a++)
{
    memcpy(p1, dst, delta);
    memcpy(dst, p2, delta);
    if (x)
    {
        p1 = BUF_2; p2 = BUF_1;
        x = 0;
    }
    else
    {
        p1 = BUF_1; p2 = BUF_1;
        x = 1;
    }
    dst += delta;
}
return 0;
}
```

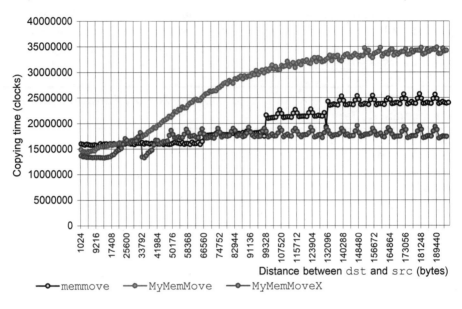

Fig. 2.44. Efficiency of different memory-moving algorithms

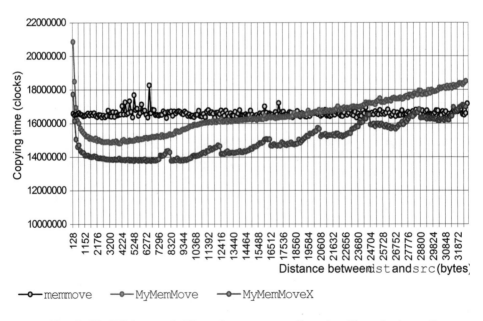

Fig. 2.45. Efficiency of different memory-moving algorithms (enlarged)

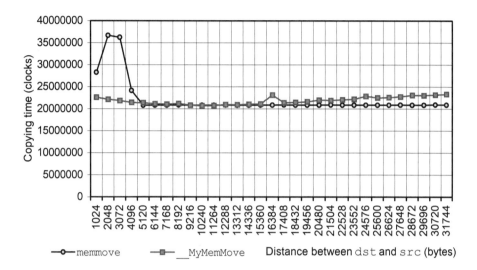

Fig. 2.46. Comparing the memmove and MyMemMove functions
on AMD Athlon 1050/100/100/VIA KT 133

Optimizing memcmp

The memcmp function is not the most popular one. (For example, the MSDN Library
mentions memcpy 500 times, while it only mentions memcmp 150 times and memmove 50
times.) This is no reason to neglect the quality of its implementation. Start with an
analysis of the built-in libraries of your compiler. In most cases, the comparison of
memory blocks is implemented as follows:

Listing 2.39. Another Implementation for memcmp in Microsoft Visual C++ 6.0

```
void * __cdecl _memccpy (void * dest, const void * src, int c, unsigned
count)
{
while ( count && (*((char *)(dest = (char *)dest + 1) — 1) =
*((char *)(src = (char *)src + 1) — 1)) != (char)c ) count--;

return(count ? dest : NULL);
}
```

Oops! This is a slow, bitwise comparison without any attempts at optimization. (Visual C++ includes the assembly implementation of the same function. You can find it in the \SRC\Intel directory.)

If both pointers are multiples of four, the comparison is performed by double words (which is considerably faster); otherwise, the comparison is done byte by byte. Is this good? Not quite. Repetition of the starting addresses is not a mandatory requirement for 32-bit comparison. (The 80x86 processors don't require you to perform alignment. Nevertheless, careless treatment of unaligned addresses can decrease performance. For more details, see *Data Alignment*.) If the three low-order bits of both pointers are equal, the function can align them on its own, by simply shifting one, two, or three bits "forward."

However, these considerations are pointless; in the speed optimization mode (using the /O2 command-line key), Microsoft Visual C++ abandons some library functions and replaces them with an intrinsic one. (See *pragma intrinsic* in companion documentation for your compiler.) The developers probably decided that it would be impractical to perform numerous checks and to "drag along" several versions of the function implementation. Therefore, they limited themselves to a universal solution: a trivial byte-by-byte comparison. No wonder that, after such "optimization," the memcmp performance has been degraded.

To prevent the compiler from making such decisions, use the pragma function preprocessor directive and specify the function name (#pragma function(memcmp), for example). On PIII, this will increase the execution speed approximately 36%. On Athlon, the difference in performance will be less impressive — about 10%. I should mention that Microsoft's implementation of memcmp is approximately 20% to 30% faster than that provided as a part of Borland C++ 5.5 compiler. However, this is not the limit!

With memcmp (as with most functions working with the memory), one of the most important problems is optimal interleaving of DRAM banks. (See *Strategy of Data Distribution over DRAM Banks*.) If the blocks that will be compared start from different pages of the same bank, the memory-access time increases dramatically. You must know how to track this situation so that you can increase one of the pointers by the length of DRAM page when necessary. This will accelerate the execution of the function approximately 40% on PIII and 60% to 70% on Athlon. However, there is one limitation: Memory must be processed by double words, rather than by bytes. If it is not, performance growth will be only 5% on PIII and about 28% on Athlon (Fig. 2.47).

What if the addresses of the blocks being compared are supplied from outside and cannot be corrected? There are two options: Resign yourself to low performance, or compare the block checksums, rather than blocks themselves. In theory, checksums of different blocks may coincide, but the probability of this situation is negligibly small.

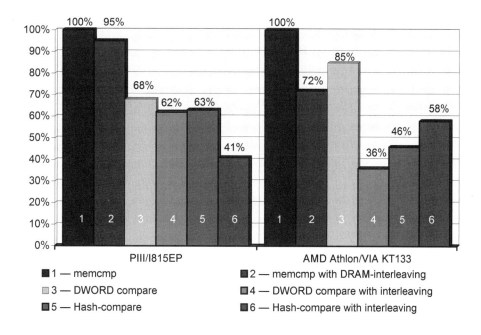

Fig. 2.47. Efficiency of different algorithms that compare memory blocks

Furthermore, it is not necessary to calculate the checksum of the entire block; it is sufficient to focus on a single DRAM page. You could use an even smaller value. The most important task is to limit switches between different pages of the same bank. After reducing the data flows processed in parallel from two to one, the hash algorithm works faster than the library function for comparing memory, leaving it behind by about 37% on PIII and about 54% on Athlon.

When memory bank interleaving is optimal, the hash algorithm is beaten by the function that compares memory in double words. In contrast to PIII, where the hash algorithm is only 1% slower, on AMD Athlon, this difference is 10%.

Thus, it is ill-advised to use the hash algorithm when DRAM bank interleaving is not optimal. Still, the rigidity of this statement is smoothed by one exception: If you reduce the length of the hashed block to the value of the burst cycle, on PIII, you will gain 61% in performance, surpassing the fastest double word algorithm by 22%.

Of course, you will have to pay for this; continuous switching of DRAM pages will become the price. Consequently, you will lose the ability to resist unfavorable interleaving of DRAM banks. Such growth of the execution speed is worth it! Unfortunately, this effect is characteristic only for Intel and can't be ported to AMD/VIA.

Nevertheless, Pentium processors hold more than 50% of the market. Thus, there are no reasons why you should abandon this trick. Even on AMD Athlon, the hash algorithm is considerably faster than the library function for comparing memory.

One of the possible implementations of this algorithm might look as follows:

Listing 2.40. Optimized Version of `memcmp` That Uses the Hash Algorithm

```
for(a = 0; a < BLOCK_SIZE; a += DRAM_PG_SIZE)
{
crc_1=0; crc_2=0;
for(b = 0; b < DRAM_PG_SIZE; b += sizeof(int))
    // Attention! This is a rather poor CRC calculation algorithm,
    // suitable for demonstration purposes only.
    crc_1 += *(int*)((int)p1+a+b);


for(b = 0; b < DRAM_PG_SIZE; b += sizeof(int))
    crc_2 += *(int*)((int)p2+a+b);

if (crc_1 != crc_2)
    break; // If the CRC sums do not match,
           // the memory blocks are different.
           // If necessary, it is possible to call
           // memcmp(p1+a, p2+a, BLOCK_SIZE-a)
           // to obtain a more precise result.
}
```

Notes about Win32 API Functions

Win32 API includes lots of functions intended for working with memory blocks, among which direct equivalents of the built-in C functions: CopyMemory (equivalent of memcpy), MoveMemory (equivalent of memmove), and FillMemory (equivalent of memset).

A question arises: Which functions are better to use — C library functions, or Win32 API functions? The answer to this question is straightforward: Microsoft has intentionally locked out the OS kernel-mode functions by including the following code in the winbase.h and winnt.h header files.

Listing 2.41. Fragment of the winbase.h File

```
#define MoveMemory RtlMoveMemory
#define CopyMemory RtlCopyMemory
#define FillMemory RtlFillMemory
#define ZeroMemory RtlZeroMemory
```

Listing 2.42. Fragment of the winnt.h File

```
#define RtlEqualMemory(Destination, Source,Length)
(!memcmp((Destination), (Source), (Length)))

#define RtlMoveMemory(Destination, Source,Length)
memmove((Destination), (Source), (Length))

#define RtlCopyMemory(Destination, Source,Length)
memcpy((Destination), (Source), (Length))

#define RtlFillMemory(Destination, Length, Fill)
memset((Destination), (Fill), (Length))

#define RtlZeroMemory(Destination, Length)
memset((Destination), 0, (Length))
```

A pretty business, this. Functions of the *xxx*Memory family are simply macro switches to the C library functions. This is not a corporate secret; it's a documented feature, implicitly confirmed by the Platform SDK documentation. A careful study of the description of the MoveMemory function will reveal the following information:

Listing 2.43. Fragment of the Description of the MoveMemory Function (Excerpt from Platform SDK Documentation)

```
Quick Info
Windows NT:   Requires version 3.1 or later.
Windows:   Requires Windows 95 or later.
Windows CE:   Unsupported.
Header:   Declared in winbase.h.
```

Well, what's peculiar here? It's simple: The "Import Library" string is missing! Consequently, the MoveMemory function is implemented in the winbase.h header file, and Microsoft is telling you this. However, this is not all; the story is just beginning.

Apply the dumbdin utility to view the list of functions exported by the kernel library of the operating system — the kernel32.dll file. Surprisingly, you will notice the following:

Listing 2.44. Fragment of the List of Exported Kernel Library Functions

---

```
598  255           RtlFillMemory (forwarded to NTDLL.RtlFillMemory)
599  256           RtlMoveMemory (forwarded to NTDLL.RtlMoveMemory)
600  257           RtlUnwind (forwarded to NTDLL.RtlUnwind)
601  258           RtlZeroMemory (forwarded to NTDLL.RtlZeroMemory)
```

Thus, functions such as `RtlMoveMemory`, `RtlFillMemory`, and `RtlZeroMemory` are still present in the OS kernel. These are not just stubs, whose entire body comprises a single return operator; they are worker functions. To check this statement, it is sufficient to call any of these functions directly, bypassing SDK.

One of the possible implementations of such code is in Listing 2.45. (Error handling is omitted for simplicity.)

Listing 2.45. Code Fragment of a Direct Call to `RtlMoveMemory`

```
HINSTANCE h;

#undef RtlMoveMemory
void  (__stdcall *RtlMoveMemory)(void *dst, void* src, int count);

h=LoadLibrary("KERNEL32.DLL");
RtlMoveMemory = (void (__stdcall *)(void *dst, void* src, int count))
    GetProcAddress(h, "RtlMoveMemory");
```

However, using `RtlMoveMemory` instead of `memmove` is not a good idea, and Microsoft did the right thing by stopping its call. The `RtlMoveMemory` function is not optimized. It does not align the addresses of moved memory blocks. In addition, when `src` < `dst`, it copies overlapping blocks byte by byte. This approach certainly can't be considered optimum.

On the Pentium III/733/133/100/I815EP platform, `RtlMoveMemory` is about 1.5 times slower that the `memmove` function supplied with Microsoft Visual C++ 6.0. On AMD Athlon 1050/100/100/VIA KT 133, however, the situation is reversed: The `memmove` function is about 30% slower than its competitor. (This gap is quite large.)

The situation is more stable with the `FillMemory` function. On all systems, it shows results that are no worse than those produced by the `memset` library function; therefore, either function can be used. A similar pattern exists for the `ZeroMemory` function, the relative of the `FillMemory` function. (The only difference between them is that `ZeroMemory` fills memory with zeroes, rather than with an arbitrary value.) However, `FillMemory` is three characters longer than `memset`; therefore, the latter function is preferable. Still, this opinion is subjective. Some aesthetes believe that `FillMemory` looks better and is more readable than `memset`. You are free to choose the one that you like.

At first, it might seem that, when initializing a large number of tiny memory blocks, `FillMemory` would incur significant performance overhead for multiple function calls. (In contrast to `FillMemory`, `memset` can be, and frequently is, used inline.) However, contemporary processors are so fast that the overhead caused by function calls can be ignored. The difference in the performance of `memset` and `FillMemory` is unlikely to exceed several percent, which won't influence the overall program speed.

You likely noticed that the list of Win32 API functions doesn't contain an analogue of `memcmp`. This is strange; the winnt.h file contains such a function:

Listing 2.46. Fragment of the winnt.h File with the Analogue of `memcmp`

```
#define RtlEqualMemory(Destination, Source, Length)
 (!memcmp((Destination), (Source), (Length)))
```

Among the functions exported by ntdll.dll is `RtlCompareMemory`. As you can guess from its name, this is the one you need. In contrast to `RtlMoveMemory`, the memory-comparison function is well-optimized. It even surpasses the `memcmp` library function

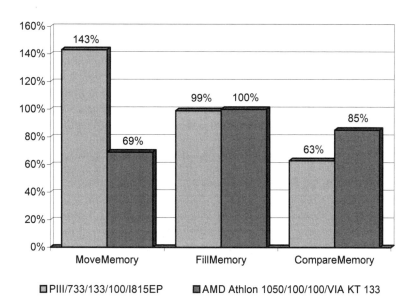

Fig. 2.48. Comparing the library functions supplied with Microsoft Visual C++ to their equivalent OS functions

of Microsoft Visual C++ 6.0 (Fig. 2.47). On Pentium III/733/133/I815EP, the performance gap is approximately 37%; on AMD Athlon 1050/100/100/VIA KT 133, it is approximately 15%.

Unfortunately, `RtlCompareMemory` is not implemented in Windows 9*x*; thus, any program that uses this function will run only under Windows NT/2000. It is possible to distribute the software product with the ntdll.dll library borrowed from the winnt\system directory. (You'll need to rename the file because Win9*x* has its own file named ntdll.dll.) However, implementing a custom `memcmp` function is a much better approach. (It is not a difficult task.) The main advantage of the `RtlCompareMemory` function over `memcmp` is it compares memory by double words, rather than by bytes. This is the true cause of its high performance.

The verdict is as follows: When developing performance-crucial applications, the best approach is to use custom implementations of functions that work with memory, optimized using the recommendations provided in this chapter. Generally, both library functions and OS API functions are nonoptimized.

Optimization Quality of Functions That Work with the Memory

The optimization quality of the library functions supplied with the compiler is an important topic; the performance of the compiled program is directly dependent on it.

Generally, programmers have no common opinion about library functions. Their opinions range from total unwillingness to use anything standard (out of the belief that standard things are rarely good) to unquestioning adoration. (Do not think that compiler developers are more foolish that programmers.)

Is one opinion right? What is the practical situation? Table 2.3 briefly outlines the state of affairs and describes key features of the base memory functions supplied with the most popular compilers and the Windows 2000 operating system. (The OS functions are listed for illustrative purposes; as previously explained, the usage of `RtlxxxMemory` functions is undesirable. See *Optimizing Built-in C Functions That Work with the Memory*.)

Table 2.3. Optimization Quality of C Library and OS Memory Functions

Function	Microsoft Visual C++ 6.0		Borland C++ 5.5	Watcom C++ 10	Windows 2000
	LIB	intrinsic			
`memcpy`/`CopyMemory`					
Copying	DWORD	DWORD	DWORD	DWORD	—
Aligning the source and/or target addresses	Aligns the target address by the 4-byte boundary	No alignment	No alignment	No alignment	—

continues

Table 2.3 Continued

Function		Microsoft Visual C++ 6.0		Borland C++ 5.5	Watcom C++ 10	Windows 2000
		LIB	intrinsic			
memmove/MoveMemory						
Copying nonoverlapping memory blocks		DWORD, forward direction	—	DWORD, forward direction	DWORD, forward direction	DWORD, forward direction
Copying overlapping memory blocks	src < dst	DWORD, backward direction	—	DWORD, backward direction	BYTE, backward direction	DWORD, backward direction
	src > dst	DWORD, forward direction	—	DWORD, forward direction	DWORD, forward direction	DWORD, forward direction
Aligning the source and/or target addresses		Aligns the target address by the 4-byte boundary	—	No alignment	No alignment	No alignment
memset/FillMemory/ZeroMemory						
Filling memory		DWORD, forward direction	DWORD, forward direction	DWORD, forward direction	DWORD, forward direction	DWORD, forward direction
Aligning the target address		Aligns the target address by the 4-byte boundary	No alignment	No alignment	No alignment	No alignment
memcmp/CompareMemory						
Comparing memory		BYTE, forward direction	BYTE, forward direction	BYTE, forward direction	BYTE, forward direction	DWORD, forward direction
Aligning the source and/or target addresses		No alignment	No alignment	No alignment	No alignment	No alignment

What is useful in this table? You should have noticed immediately the extremely careless optimization of library function in Borland and Watcom compilers. Memory functions of the C library supplied with the Microsoft Visual C++ compiler have better optimization. Their most distinguished feature is that they align the target address by the 4-byte boundary, which can improve performance significantly. (However, as shown in *Data Alignment*, it is better to align the source address than the target address.)

Nevertheless, Microsoft Visual C++ doesn't use any of the advanced optimization algorithms described in *Optimizing Built-in C Functions That Work with the Memory*, and memcmp functions are not optimized.

In other words, if the execution speed of the compiled application is your primary goal, you must use custom memory functions.

Optimizing C String Library Functions

I have already discussed the striking difference in execution speed when processing double words and bytes. (See *Processing Memory in Bytes, Double Words, and Quadruple Words*.) Now, it is time for you to apply this knowledge to the optimization of string functions.

The typical C string (Fig. 2.48) is a chain of single-byte characters terminated by a special character: the zero byte. (Do not confuse it with the 0 character.) Therefore, C strings are also known as ASCIIZ strings (The "Z" stands for "Zero.") This is an extremely nonoptimal data structure, especially when used on contemporary 32-bit processors.

The main drawback of C strings lies in the impossibility of quickly determining their length: You have to scan the entire string to find the terminating byte. In addition, the terminating character must be compared bytewise to each string character. As you know already, the performance of byte-memory reading is very low. You can try a trick: Load memory cells with double words, and then examine them through 4-bit masks. However, this approach is unlikely to improve the performance; it even may degrade it further.

The same problems prevent programmers from implementing efficient copying and concatenation of C strings. Indeed, how would you copy the string if you don't know its length?

Additionally, C strings can't contain the zero byte. (Such a byte would be mistaken for the string-termination character.) Thus, they are not suitable for processing binary data.

Pascal strings are free from these drawbacks; they explicitly store their lengths in a special field at the starting position of the string. To calculate the length of a Pascal string, one memory access operation is sufficient. (The length of a Pascal string can be calculated almost instantly.) By the way, when working with any data structures, particularly with lists, it is strongly recommended that you reserve a special field for storing the reference to the last element. This will help you avoid tracing the entire list when new items are added to its end.

How can you exploit this circumstance for optimizing the copying and concatenation of Pascal strings? One opportunity is shown in Listing 2.47.

Listing 2.47. Copy Functions for C Strings (*Left*) and Pascal Strings (*Right*)

```
char *c_strcpy(char *dst, char *src)      char *pascal_strcpy(char *dst, char *src)
{                                         {
char * cp = dst;                          int a;
while( *cp++ = *src++ );                   for(a = 0; a < ((*src+1) & ~3); a += 4)
// Copy the string by bytes,              *(int *)(dst+a)=*(int *)(src+a);
// simultaneously checking                // Copy the string by double words.
// each character to see if               // It is not necessary to check
// it is the zero byte.                    // for the zero byte;
                                          // the string length
                                          // is known beforehand.

                                          for(a=((*src+1) & ~3); a<(*src+1); a ++)
                                          *(char *)(dst+a)=*(char *)(src+a);
                                          // Copy the remainder of the string
                                          // tail (if present) by bytes.
                                          // This doesn't degrade the
                                          // performance because the maximum
                                          // tail length is 3 bytes.

return( dst );                            return( dst );
}                                         }
```

Listing 2.48. Concatenation Functions for C (*Left*) and Pascal (*Right*) Strings

```
char *c_strcat (char *dst, char *src)     char *pascal_strcat (char *dst, char *src)
{                                         {
char *cp = dst;                           int len;

while( *cp ) ++cp;                        len=*dst;
// Read the entire source string          // Use a single memory-access operation
// byte by byte to find the               // to determine the target-string length.
// string-termination character.
                                          *dst+=*src;
                                          // Correct the length of the target string.

while( *cp++ = *src++ );                   pascal_strcpy(dst+len, src);
// Write the source to the target end     // Copy the string using double words.
// byte by byte, until the
// zero byte is encountered.

return( dst );                            return( dst );
}                                         }
```

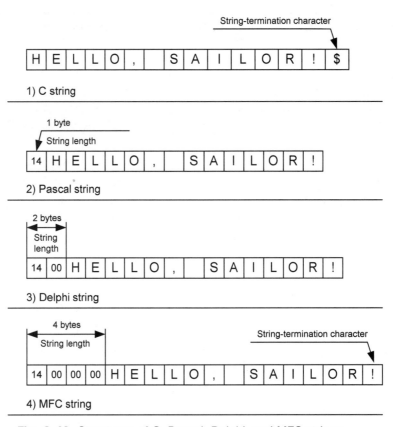

Fig. 2.49. Structures of C, Pascal, Delphi, and MFC strings

As you can see in Fig. 2.49, C strings are not limited in length. However, they cannot contain the zero byte; it would be interpreted erroneously as the string-termination character. Pascal strings store the string length in a special, single-byte field. This significantly improves the efficiency of string functions and allows any character to be stored within the strings. However, the string length is limited to 256 bytes. Delphi strings are a type of Pascal string. Their only difference from Pascal strings is the increased digit capacity of the string-length field. This allows strings to reach the lengths of 64 KB. MFC strings are a hybrid of C and Pascal strings with a 32-bit length field. This makes the maximum string length 4 GB.

Thus, in contrast to C strings, Pascal strings allow efficient block processing and, when necessary, can be copied by blocks of 128 bits. In addition, when concatenating Pascal strings, you do not need to scan the entire target string to find its end. This is because the string end is determined by the algebraic addition of the pointer to the starting position of the string. The first byte of the string contains its length.

Intense work with C strings can degrading the program performance considerably. Therefore, the best approach would be to abandon them. However, this presents a problem: You cannot "voluntarily" migrate to Pascal strings without changing all corresponding C libraries and API functions of the operating system. Functions such as fopen and LoadLibrary rely exclusively on ASCIIZ strings, and any attempt to "feed" them a Pascal string won't result in anything sensible. After failing to detect the string-termination character at the expected position, the function will intrude upon the memory that hasn't been allocated to it.

The only thing to do is to create "hybrid" strings (Pascal+ASCIIZ), explicitly storing the string length in a field reserved for this purpose and placing the terminating byte at the end. This approach is the one used by developers of the CString class of the MFC library (supplied along with the Microsoft Visual C++ compiler).

A simple test (see [Memory/MFC.str.c]) will help you to compare the efficiency of processing C and MFC strings in various operations, such as comparing and copying strings, and calculating their lengths. The greatest gap in performance is typical for the third operation.

Joining two MFC strings (if they have the same length) is almost twice as fast as concatenation of two similar C strings. This is not surprising; MFC strings access half the number of memory cells. If you need to add a small number of characters to the end of a long string, the performance gain from an MFC string will be approximately $\frac{strlen(dst)}{strlen(src)}$ times higher.

Comparison operations are equally efficient for C and MFC functions — or, to be precise, equally *inefficient*. Developers of the MFC library have given preference to byte-by-byte comparison (instead of double words), which has a negative effect on performance. Curiously, the strcmp library function supplied with Microsoft Visual C++ (which is not intrinsic) seems to be a single-string comparison function that processes strings by double words, rather than by bytes. On average, this function is executed two times faster. Thus, the most preferable MFC string comparison looks as follows:

Listing 2.49. [Memory/MFC.str.c] Efficient Comparison of MFC Strings

---

```
#include <String.h>

#pragma function(strcmp) // Turn out the intrinsic keyword.

if (strcmp(s0.GetBuffer(0), s1.GetBuffer(0)))
// Strings are not equal.
else
// Strings are equal.
```

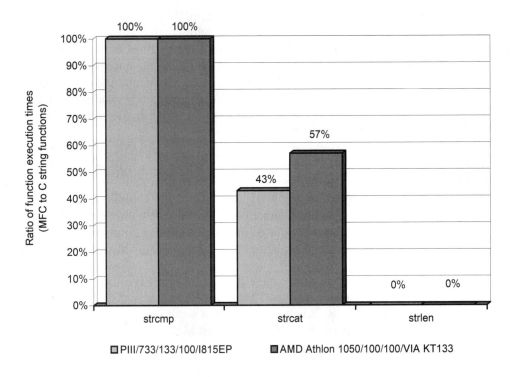

Fig. 2.50. Efficiency of MFC and C string functions
(MFC functions are significantly faster)

Optimization Quality of Functions That Work with Strings

Table 2.4 contain brief comparisons of the optimization quality of the C library functions and OS API functions intended for working with strings. Note that neither the operating system nor libraries supplied with common compilers are fully optimized. This means that a performance reserve remains.

Therefore, the best approach when writing performance-crucial applications is to *use custom implementations of string functions, optimized according to your requirements.* If you do not do this job yourself, no one will do it for you.

Table 2.4. Quality of C Library and OS API Functions That Work with Strings

Function	Microsoft Visual C++ 6.0		Borland C++ 5.5	Watcom C++ 10	Windows 2000
	LIB	intrinsic			
strlen/lstrlenA					
Calculating the string length	align / DWORD — unalign / BYTE	BYTE, forward direction	DWORD, forward direction	BYTE, forward direction	BYTE, forward direction
Aligning the source and/or target addresses	No alignment	No alignment	Aligns by the 4-byte boundary	No alignment	No alignment
Degree of loop unrolling (number of iterations)	1	1	1	1	1
strcpy/lstrcpyA					
Copying — Determining the source length	None	BYTE	BYTE	BYTE	BYTE
Copying — Wrapping strings	align / DWORD — unalign / BYTE	DWORD	DWORD	BYTE	DWORD
Aligning the source and/or target addresses	No alignment	No alignment	No alignment	No alignment	No alignment
Degree of loop unrolling (number of iterations)	1	1	1	2	1
strcat/lstrcatA					
Copying — Determining the source length	None	BYTE	BYTE	BYTE	BYTE
Copying — Finding the target length	align / DWORD — unalign / BYTE	BYTE	BYTE	–	BYTE
Copying — Wrapping strings	align / DWORD — unalign / BYTE	DWORD	DWORD	BYTE	DWORD, forward direction
Aligning the source and/or target addresses	No alignment	No alignment	No alignment	No alignment	No alignment
Degree of loop unrolling (number of iterations)	1	1	1	2	1

continues

Table 2.4 Continued

Function	Microsoft Visual C++ 6.0		Borland C++ 5.5	Watcom C++ 10	Windows 2000
	LIB	`intrinsic`			
`strcmp/lstrcmpA`					
Checking	BYTE, forward direction	BYTE	BYTE	DWORD, forward direction	BYTE, forward direction
Aligning the source and/or target addresses	No alignment	No alignment	No alignment	No alignment	No alignment
Degree of loop unrolling (number of iterations)	2	2	2	8	1
`strstr/---`					
Comparing	BYTE, forward direction	–	DWORD, forward direction	BYTE, forward direction	–
Aligning the source and/or target addresses	No alignment	–	No alignment	No alignment	–
Degree of loop unrolling (number of iterations)	1	–	1	1	–

Optimizing Block Algorithms

In contrast to streaming algorithms, the optimization of block algorithms is a complex job. Streaming-data processing assumes that the data are requested sequentially. Thus, it is not difficult to organize optimal translation (from the memory subsystem's point of view) of virtual addresses. Conversely, block algorithms can request randomly any memory cell within the limits of the allocated block.

Before the block size exceeds the notorious value of $(N — 1)\chi$ (i.e., about 4 KB), no problems arise, especially if the digit capacity of the data being processed is comparable to the value of the packet cycle of exchange with the memory. Otherwise, penalty delays will occur when you hit DRAM banks being recharged, and overhead will be produced by the prereading of data that are never accessed.

Ideally, you would reduce block size. Alas, this solution is not always possible. At that point, you would have to use the virtual addressing. Do not allow the term "virtual" to mislead you; it is not necessary to have the highest privileges and access to system tables. Virtual translation can be organized programmatically. One method was considered previously in this chapter, during the discussion of the optimization of streaming algorithms. Unfortunately, this topic is not directly related to the RAM subsystem, and cannot be covered in detail in this book.

Speculative Data Loading

The speculative data loading algorithm was introduced long ago, when computing dinosaurs dominated large computing halls, and horribly slow magnetic tape played the role of external memory. The first programs would load the data block from the tape, process the loaded data, then repeat these steps. When loading data, the reels with magnetic tape would rotate wildly. Then, they would stop while calculations took place. This show enchanted laymen. Nevertheless, *to achieve maximum performance, the tape device must work continuously.*

Unfortunately, history didn't preserve the name of the individual who had the brainstorm to combine data processing with the loading of the next block. The total execution time of a nonoptimized program generally is expressed by the following formula: $T = N \times (T_{type} + T_{dp})$, where T_{type} is the time required to load the data block from the tape, T_{dp} is the block-data processing time, and N is the total number of blocks. In contrast, the optimized algorithm takes the following time: $T_{optimize} = N \times (max(T_{type}, T_{dp}))$.

The maximum gain is achieved when the time required to load data from the tape is identical to the time taken by the calculations. This can be calculated easily as $T/T_{optimize} = N \times (T_{type} + T_{dp})/N \times T_{type} = 2$ (i.e., the processing time cut in half).

And, although reels with magnetic tape have passed out of use, they still can teach us all a good lesson. Consider how the vast majority of contemporary block algorithms work. When studying almost any program, you constantly will encounter the following scenario: load → process → repeat. The speed of RAM is much higher than that of the magnetic tape, but the clock speed of the processors even better!

You simply could mix the commands for loading the cell contents with the calculation instructions. (See *Combining Calculations with Memory Access.*) However, this doesn't ensure that they will be processed in parallel. After all, calculation instructions start execution only after the data to be processed has been loaded.

Now, recall the scenario of working with magnetic tape, and improve the data-loading strategy. In particular, access the next block to be processed long before it is required. Using this approach, you will eliminate the dependency between commands that load and process data, which will make it possible to execute them in parallel. If the data-processing time does not exceed the data-loading time (a common situation), data exchange with memory will take place continuously, closely approaching its maximum throughput. (See *Parallel Data Processing.*)

Consider the following example:

___

Listing 2.50. Typical Nonoptimized Data-Processing Algorithm

___

```
; /*------------------------------------------------------------
; *                     Nonoptimized Version
; -----------------------------------------------------------*/
for(a = 0; a < BLOCK_SIZE; a += 32)
{

// Loading cells
x += (*(int *)((int ) p + a));         // This command locks all the others.
x += (*(int *)((int ) p + a + 4));
x += (*(int *)((int ) p + a + 8));
x += (*(int *)((int ) p + a + 12));
x += (*(int *)((int ) p + a + 16));
x += (*(int *)((int ) p + a + 20));
x += (*(int *)((int ) p + a + 24));
x += (*(int *)((int ) p + a + 28));

// Performing some calculations
x += a/x/666;
}
```

___

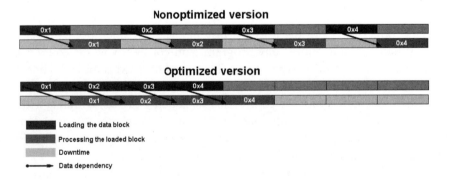

Fig. 2.51. Eliminating data dependency by prefetching
the block that will be processed next

The main drawback of this algorithm the calculation procedure `x += a/x/666` must wait until all preceding commands are completed. These commands, in turn, must wait until all the required data are loaded from the memory. This means that the first line of the loop `x+=*(int*)((int)p + a)` locks all the other ones.

Can this data dependency be eliminated? Yes, this is possible. It is sufficient to load the data at the offset of one or more iterations. (More details on this topic will be provided in *Goals and Tasks of Cache Memory.*) Figuratively, the data-loading command is shifted in relation to the instructions that perform the data processing (Fig. 2.51).

You will get code similar to the fragment in Listing 2.51. (Note that the program source code has undergone no major revisions.)

Listing 2.51. [Memory/Speculative.read.c] Efficiency of Speculative Data Loading

```
;  /*-------------------------------------------------------------------
;   *         Optimized version implementing speculative data loading
;   -----------------------------------------------------------------*/
// Loading the first portion of data
x += (*(int *)((int) p + a));
for(a = 0; a < BLOCK_SIZE; a += 32)
{

// Prefetching the next portion of data
y = (*(int *)((int) p + a + 32));      // ***

// Processing previously loaded cells
x += (*(int *)((int) p + a + 4));
x += (*(int *)((int) p + a + 8));
x += (*(int *)((int) p + a + 12));
x += (*(int *)((int) p + a + 16));
x += (*(int *)((int) p + a + 20));
x += (*(int *)((int) p + a + 24));
x += (*(int *)((int) p + a + 28));

// Performing some calculations
x += a/x/666;

// Requesting the prefetched data
x += y;
}
```

On Pentium III/133/100/I815EP, this simple trick decreases the execution time of this loop by approximately 25%.

Optimizing Sorting of Large Data Arrays

Donald A. Knuth wrote in *The Art of Programming, Volume 3: Sorting and Searching*: "According to assessments made by computer manufacturers, during the 1960s, about one-quarter of machine time was used for sorting. In most computer systems, it consumed more than half of the machine time."

About 40 years have passed. Processing power has grown fantastically during this time, but the situation with the searching has scarcely improved. For example, on AMD Athlon 1050, sorting 1 million numbers using one of the best sorting algorithms, the quick-sort algorithm, takes 3.6 seconds. When increased to 10 million numbers, sorting takes more than 5 minutes (Fig. 2.52). Sorting hundreds of millions of numbers requires astronomical time intervals. Despite this, sorting is one of the most common operations.

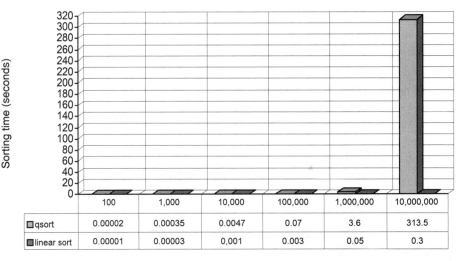

	100	1,000	10,000	100,000	1,000,000	10,000,000
☐ qsort	0.00002	0.00035	0.0047	0.07	3.6	313.5
☐ linear sort	0.00001	0.00003	0,001	0.003	0.05	0.3

Amount of sorted data

Fig. 2.52. Time required to sort different amounts of data using quick-sort and linear-sort algorithms

Of course, only scientists that model the movement of stars in galaxies or studying the human genome need to sort hundreds of millions of numbers. Nevertheless, in something as common as business applications, tables with hundreds of thousands of records are not rare. Furthermore, interactive applications have stringent requirements on performance. For example, it is highly desirable that table cells and user activities be refreshed in parallel.

The quick-sort algorithm requires $O(n \lg n)$ operations on average and $O(n^2)$ operations in the worst situation. This algorithm is very fast. Nevertheless, it needs to be improved! It reminds me of a quotation from a sci-fi novel by Arkady and Boris Strugatsky: "We are well aware that this task has no solution... We want to know how to solve it."

A simple and efficient sorting algorithm exists that, in the worst situation, requires $O(n)$ operations. No, this is not a joke! There is such an algorithm. On AMD Athlon 1050, it sorts 10 million numbers in approximately 0.3 seconds, *thousand times faster than quick sort.*

I discovered this algorithm time when I was participated in a computer-science contest. One of the problems required the participants to sort seven numbers using no more than three comparison operations. Seeing this problem as a perfect opportunity for showing off, I wrote a small program that sorted the numbers *without using any comparison operations.* Unfortunately, my solution was not considered superior. Only after a couple of years of carefully exploring the existing sorting algorithms could I evaluate the importance of the result.

The idea was based on the inequality $k + 1 > k > k - 1$, which is true for any k value. Each number k_x can be mapped to the corresponding point at the coordinate axis. The result, will be a naturally sorted series of points. Consider this idea on a specific example. Suppose that you have the following numbers: 9, 6, 3, and 7. Take the first number (9), shift it nine conventional units to the right from the origin on the coordinate axis, and mark this point. Then, take the next number (6), repeat the operation, and so on.

The result of these operations is shown in Fig. 2.53.

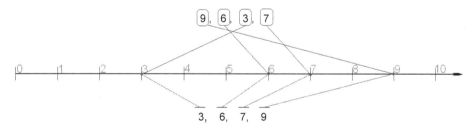

Fig. 2.53. Sorting using the mapping method

Now, move from left to right along the coordinate line, discarding all points that are not marked (or emphasize the marked points). You'll get a series of numbers sorted in ascending order. If you move along the coordinate line from right to left, you will sort the series in descending order.

Here comes the most interesting point: Regardless of the arrangement of the numbers, the number of operations required to sort them will always equal $N+VAL\_N$, where N is the number of data to be sorted, and VAL_N is the maximum number of values that they can take. Because *VAL_N* is a constant, it can be excluded from the formula that evaluates the algorithm's complexity. After that, this formula will look as follows: *O(N)*. Wow! Are you eager to implement the algorithm? This is not a difficult task. Replace the coordinate axis with a one-dimensional numeric array, and proceed:

Listing 2.52. Simplest Version the Linear-Sort Algorithm

```
#define DOT 1
#define NODOT 0
int a;
int src[N];
int coordinate_line[VAL_N];
memset(coordinate_line, NODOT, VAL_N*sizeof(int));

// Marking the required points on the coordinate axis
for (a = 0; a < N; a++)
 coordinate_line[src[a]]=DOT;

// Scanning the axis from left to the right to find the marked points,
// and copying all marked points into the source array
for(a = 0; a < N_VAL; a++)
 if (coordinate_line[a]) { *src = a; src++; }
```

Oops! Have you noticed the drawback in this implementation of the sorting algorithm? Indeed, it has a side effect: All duplicated numbers are eliminated. Consider the following series: 3, 9, 6, 6, 3, 2, 9. After you sort this series using the described method, you will get the following: 2, 3, 6, 9. Sometimes this side effect is beneficial; duplicate values are often unnecessary and degrade the application's performance.

What if the removal of duplicate values is not acceptable? It is sufficient to modify the algorithm slightly. To avoid removing the duplicate values, mark the numbers on the coordinate axis and count their number in appropriate cell of the array. The improved version of the algorithm might look as follows:

Listing 2.53. [Memory/sort.linear.c] Improved Linear-Sort Algorithm

```
int* linear_sort(int *p, int n)
{
int N;
int a, b;
int count = 0;
int *coordinate_line;          // Array for sorting

// Allocating memory
```

```
coordinate_line = malloc(VAL_MAX*sizeof(int));
if (!coordinate_line) /* insufficient memory */ return 0;

// init
memset(coordinate_line, 0, VAL_MAX*sizeof(int));

// Sorting
for(a = 0; a < n; a++)
    coordinate_line[p[a]]++;

// Formulating an answer
for(a = 0; a < VAL_MAX; a++)
    for(b = 0; b < coordinate_line[a]; b++)
        p[count++]=a;

// Releasing the memory
free(coordinate_line);

return p;
}
```

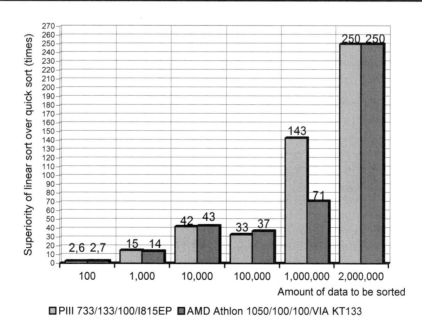

Fig. 2.54. Superiority of the linear-sort over the quick-sort algorithm. A linear search
of 2 million of numbers is executed 250 times faster on either processor

Now, compare this algorithm with the results of using the quick-sort algorithm and values of N to estimate efficiency. My experiments have shown that even the most primitive implementation of the linear-sort algorithm outperforms the quick-sort algorithm, for both a small and large number of the values (Fig. 2.54).

This result can be improved considerably if you use sparse arrays, rather than scan an entire `virtual_array`.

Having discussed the good news, I should mention the dark side of the linear-sort algorithm. Performance gain is achieved at the expense of RAM. The linear-sort algorithm has quite an appetite for memory consumption. Here are some evaluations.

The number of cells of the `coordinate_line` array is equal to the number of values that the sorted data can take. For 8-bit characters (`char`) this is 2 to the 8th power, or 256 cells. For 16-bit integers, it's 2 to the 16th power, or 65,536 cells. Finally, for 32-bit integers, it's 2 to the 32nd power, or 4,294,967,296 cells. Nevertheless, each cell of the `coordinate_line` array must accommodate the maximum number of duplicates, which, at worst, equals N. This means that in most situations, no less that 16 bits must be reserved for it (and 32 bits would be certainly better). Table 2.5 takes all these factors into account.

Table 2.5. Memory Consumed by the Linear-Sort Algorithm

Data type	Memory required for storing duplicates	Memory required without storing duplicates
`char`	1 KB	32 bytes
`char` (unsigned)	512 bytes	16 bytes
`_int16`	256 KB	8 KB
`_int16` (unsigned)	128 KB	4 KB
`_int32`	16 GB	1 GB
`_int32` (unsigned)	8 GB	256 KB

Quite impressive requirements: To sort 32-bit elements and store duplicate values, 8 GB of RAM would be required. Of course, 99.9% of memory cells will be vacant; swapping pages from the hard disk will hardly degrade performance, but still... The crux of this problem is that you won't have these 8 GB at your disposal. Windows 9x/NT operating systems limit the processor's address space by 4 GB, and more than 2 GB are used for internal purposes. Thus, the maximum heap size will be 1 to 1.5 GB.

You can split the `coordinate_line` array into eight equal parts and distribute it between eight processes. (Reading to and writing from an address space of another processor is possible; see descriptions of `ReadProcessMemory` and `WriteProcessMemory` in the Platform SDK document.) This is an ugly solution, but it is efficient. The linear-sort algorithm still will surpass the quick-sort algorithm 600 to 900 times, instead of 1,000 times, because of the overhead caused by the calls to API functions.

In addition, the data to be sorted do not always use the entire range of `_int32` values: from –2,147,483,648 to 2,147,483,647. This circumstance provides the possibility of significantly reducing memory requirements! Actually, the amount of required memory is `Cmem = N_VAL*sizeof(cell)`, where `N_VAL` is the number of allowed values, and `sizeof(cell)` is the size of cells that store *notches* or *projections* (i.e., duplicate values). In particular, sorting data belonging to the range of [0; 1,000,000] will require no more than 4 MB of memory, a rather insignificant amount.

Problems with RAM Testing

Memory overclocking is drastic method of improving performance. At the same time, it places stringent requirements on the memory modules. However, low-quality memory modules can malfunction without overclocking. The results of such malfunctions can vary from application crashes to distortion or loss of data.

Customers sometimes purchase defective memory, and users frequently encounter memory malfunctions. Curiously, most software developers ignore this problem and declare that any application has the right to expect defect-free hardware. Theoretically, this might be true. In reality, you must determine whether or not your hardware is operating properly.

Popular diagnostic utilities (such as CheckIt) are not suitable for this purpose. Unless the memory chip is defective, the test will run smoothly and won't find any signs of malfunction. However, when you start Microsoft Word or begin to play Quake, the system can freeze immediately. After you replace the memory module, the system will run smoothly. If the memory caused the problem, why didn't CheckIt detect it?

The reason for such behavior is not every fault in the memory chip results in immediate failure. The defect often manifests itself under certain conditions. A resource-consuming application that intensely uses memory is the most likely candidate for generating the required combination of circumstances that cause the failure. Popular diagnostic programs, on the contrary, test only a limited range of modes and do this under rather favorable conditions. Consequently, there is less probability of the malfunction being detected.

How can you overcome this problem? The only way out is to develop a custom test program. First, the probability of failure is closely related to the chip temperature. The higher the temperature, the more likely a failure. The temperature, in turn, depends on the intensity of the memory operation. During the linear reading of the cells, the chip, due to the packet exchange mode, has the time to cool, supporting a moderate temperature. When requesting a single cell, the entire DRAM page is read and then stored in internal buffers. No attempts are made to access the memory core until the next page of the same bank is requested.

Thus, before you start testing, it is necessary to heat the memory by reading it at a step equal to the length of the DRAM bank. This will cause the core of the memory bank work at the maximum intensity; read and recharge procedures will take place at each step. At the same time, avoid testing several banks simultaneously. Such testing will decrease the temperature of each bank, and the temperature gap within the chip increases the probability of detecting the failure. (The chip should be able operate under difficult testing conditions; otherwise, it should be dumped into the garbage can.)

Well, the memory module has heated; you can hardly touch it with your hand. Now is the best time to start real testing. Fill the DRAM page with a controlling series of numbers (a template), and switch the page to refresh memory cells. (Otherwise, the chip might return the contents of its buffers without accessing the memory array.) Switch the page back, and check what you have written. The code performing these operations might look as follows:

Listing 2.54. Simplified Implementation of the Memory-Testing Function

```
for (a=0; a < DRAM_BANK_SIZE; a += DRAM_PAGE_SIZE)
{
WriteTemplate(a);    // Writing the template

x = (DRAM_BANK_SIZE-a); // Switching the DRAM page

CompareTemplate(a);  // Checking what has been written
}
```

The template must satisfy stringent requirements. First, it must test each bit of the cell, for one and for zero, because defective cells of the memory array might provide either "always zero" or "always one." Second, it is highly desirable that adjacent bits in the entire eightfold word have opposite values. Such combinations create the highest noise level, provoking system for errors. Third, the template must ensure detection of the addressing errors. (Such errors occur when the chip returns the contents of the wrong row or column.)

Because these requirements are mutually exclusive, you will need several templates for testing. Do not forget perform "idle" reading from time to time to support the temperature of the memory chip at the maximum attainable level; otherwise, the testing efficiency will start to drop.

Now, it only remains to discuss the sequence of page enumeration. The first idea that comes to mind is a simple, sequential enumeration; next is random access to pages using a random template. Is this sufficient for detecting all types of errors? Unfortunately, no. Almost all contemporary memory controllers define the preferred order of processing requests on their own.

As an example, consider the Listing 2.54. The controller, having analyzed the request queue, sees that it can avoid double switching of pages. It avoids repetitive reading from the memory array and returns the buffer contents to the CPU!

Apparently, there is only one way to deceive the controller: Instead of checking the cells immediately after writing, wait for some time interval to elapse and perform the checking when internal buffers will until it is busy with other requests. This also will also enable you to detect recharging errors, in which the charge from the cell is lost before the cell is refreshed.

Chapter 3: Cache Subsystem

The cache subsystem typical of contemporary processors combines transparency with a capricious and rather egocentric character. In some ways, cache is similar to a young lady who makes everyone around her guess what is on her mind and how to please her. Although some consistency has started to appear (see *Cache Management in the New Generation of x86 Processors*), as a whole, the cache subsystem remains a giant heap of wonders and surprises. Cache is hard to understand. Unfortunately, official documentation is an inadequate guide; its incomplete information will mystify you (and sometimes even will include incorrect or unreliable data).

The description of the cache subsystem in this chapter doesn't reveal one-hundredth of these mysteries. However, it should give you the necessary basic and most important information.

Principles of SRAM Operation

To acquire expert knowledge of cache operation, it is not necessary to cover all technical details of Static Random Access Memory (SRAM). It is invisible to the programmer, and details of its design and implementation are completely hidden by the cache controller. However, using a hardware device without knowing what is "under the hood" and how it operates is not the way for a true professional.

A small amount of "must know" information never hurt any programmer. I won't reveal all the secrets of SRAM, but will explain what it is, how it operates, and why it operates in this manner.

Historical Overview

The history of static memory has deep roots. The memory installed on the first computers was static by nature, and it didn't undergo major changes for a long time. Only the component base evolved: Relays gradually were replaced by vacuum valves, which were replaced by transistors, and then TTL and CMOS chips. Nevertheless, the basic concept of static memory has remained the same.

Dynamic Random Access Memory (DRAM) was invented much later than SRAM. Even now, dynamic memory can't compete with the operating speed of static memory.

At the Core

The core of SRAM is a set of *triggers*, logical devices with two stable states that correspond to logical 0 and logical 1. In other words, each trigger stores one bit of information — the same amount as a dynamic memory cell. (See the *In the Core* subsection of *Chapter 2.*)

Still, the trigger beats the capacitor in at least two areas. First, trigger states are stable: If the power supply is uninterrupted, they can be preserved for infinite intervals. (Capacitors need to be recharged periodically.) In addition, triggers do not suffer from inertia and can work without problems at frequencies up to several gigahertz. (Capacitors fail between 75 MHz and 100 MHz.)

However, triggers have drawbacks; the most important among these are high price and low density of information storage. In contrast to a DRAM cell, which only requires one capacitor and one transistor, a typical SRAM cell comprises no less than four, and usually from six to eight, transistors. Therefore, 1 MB of static memory is usually several times more expensive than the same amount of dynamic memory.

Trigger Design

All triggers are based on a circuit composed of two logical NOT elements (inverters) connected as a "gate" (Fig. 3.1). Consider the principles of its operation: If you supply a signal that corresponds to 1 to the line Q, the signal will pass through the D.D1 element, then turn to 0. However, after it is supplied to the input of the next element,

D.D2, this 0 will return to 1. Because the output of D.D2 is connected to the input of D.D1, it will support itself even when there is no signal on line Q (i.e., the trigger will become stable). In this respect, the trigger is analogous to a dragon biting its own tail.

Naturally, if a signal that corresponds to 0 is supplied to the line Q, the opposite situation will take place, and the trigger again will become stable.

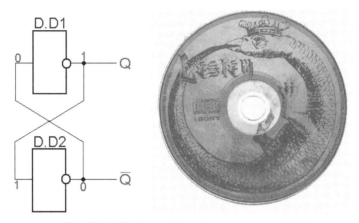

Fig. 3.1. Design of the simplest trigger (*left*), analogous to a dragon biting its own tail (*right*)

Design of the Logical NOT Element (Inverter)

How does the NOT element work? This question has an ambiguous answer. Depending on the available element base, the final implementation might vary widely. I have provided a diagram of the simplest inverter, comprising two complementary *p*- and *n*-type CMOS transistors connected in series (Fig. 3.2).

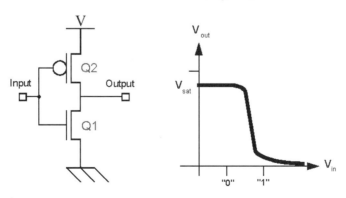

Fig. 3.2. Design of the NOT element (inverter)

If a zero-level signal is supplied to the gates, the *p*-channel is connected, and the *n*-channel remains disconnected. As a result, the supply voltage is at the output (i.e., a high level). On the contrary, if a high-level signal is supplied to the gates, the *p*-channel is disconnected, and the *n*-channel is connected. Output is short-circuited to the mass (ground), and zero voltage is established on it (i.e., a low level).

Design of the SRAM Array

Like the cells of dynamic memory (see *RAM Design and Working Principles*), triggers are joined into a uniform array comprising *rows* and *columns*. (The latter also are known as *bits*.)

In contrast to a dynamic memory cell, which can be managed by a single transistor, a static memory cell is controlled by two or more transistors. This isn't surprising when you recall that the trigger, in contrast to capacitor, has different inputs for logical ones and zeroes. Thus, each SRAM cell comprises at least six transistors: Four are required for the trigger, and the remaining two are required for the gates (Fig. 3.3).

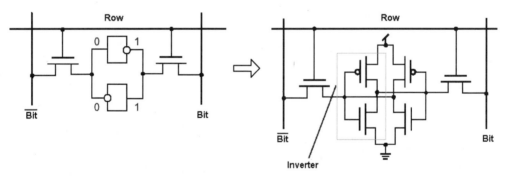

Fig. 3.3. Design of a six-transistor cell of SRAM
(the *right* diagram is a detailed version of the *left* diagram)

Six transistors are not a limit: There are much more sophisticated constructions. The main drawback of a six-transistor cell is that only one row of the memory array can be processed at a time. Parallel reading of the cells residing in different rows of the same memory bank is impossible, as is reading one cell in parallel with writing another one. Only *multiport memory* is free from this limitation. Each cell of such memory contains one trigger but has several sets of controlling transistors, each of which is connected to its own row and bit lines. This allows different cells of the memory matrix to be processed independently. This approach is more advanced than dividing memory into banks. In the latter case, parallelism is achieved only when the cells that belong to different banks are accessed, which isn't always an option. However, multiport memory allows *any* cells to be processed simultaneously, freeing the programmer from the necessity of understanding all the details of the hardware architecture. The most common type of multiport memory is two-port (Fig. 3.4).

⚠ *Attention*

To create a single cell of two-port memory, at least eight transistors are required. If cache memory is 32 KB, a single core would require more than 2 million transistors! This memory is different from the type used in L1 cache of Intel Pentium microprocessors.

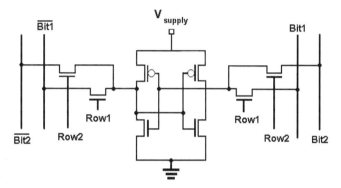

Fig. 3.4. Design of a single eight-transistor cell of two-port SRAM

Fig. 3.5. DRAM cell

Fig. 3.6. DRAM cell implemented on a chip

Design of the Interface Wrapping

By its design, the interface wrapping of the static memory array is similar to the wrapping of the dynamic memory array. (See *Conventional DRAM (Page Mode DRAM).*) Therefore, I will cover this topic briefly, without concentrating on technical details.

The only difference between static and dynamic RAM interfaces is that static memory chips have a smaller capacity (and, consequently, a smaller number of address lines). Because SRAM chips are located much closer to the processor, they can afford to operate without multiplexing. Thus, to achieve maximum performance, row and column numbers most frequently are transmitted simultaneously.

If static memory is implemented as a standalone chip (rather than integrated with the processor), its input lines often are combined with its output lines. In this arrangement, it is necessary to determine the operation mode by the state of the Write Enable (WE) output. A high level at the WE output prepares the chip to read data; a low level prepares it to write data. Static memory integrated with the processor usually doesn't use multiplexing. In this case, the contents of one cell can be read as another cell is written. (The input and output lines are separate.)

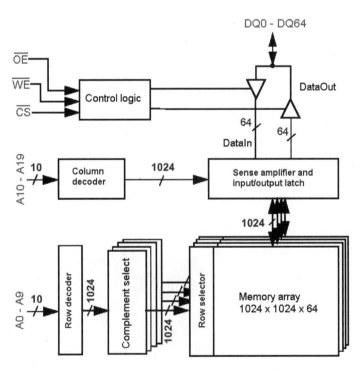

Fig. 3.7. Design of a typical SRAM chip

Row and column numbers are sent to row and column decoders (Fig. 3.7). After decoding, a decoded row number is supplied to the auxiliary decoder, which calculates the respective array. Then, the signal is supplied to the row selector, which opens the gate of the required page. Depending on the chosen mode of operation, the sense amplifier connected to the bit lines of the array either reads the state of the triggers for the appropriate row line, or resets them according to the information being written.

Read and Write Timing Diagrams

The read and write timing diagrams for static memory are practically identical to those for dynamic memory. This is not surprising; the interface wrappings for both types of memory are similar.

Read Cycle

The read cycle starts by dropping the Chip Select (CS) signal to a low state. This informs the chip that it is selected for work.

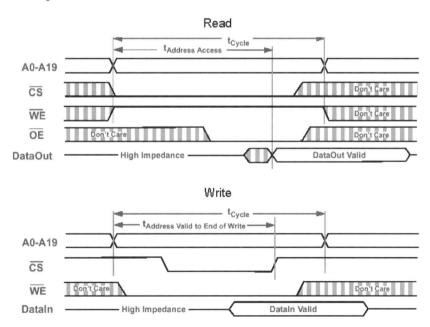

Fig. 3.8. Timing diagrams for reading and writing asynchronous static memory

By the time the signal stabilizes, a ready-to-use cell address (i.e., a row number and a column number) must be present on each address line. The WE signal must be switched to a high level (corresponding to the operation of reading the cell). The level of the Output Enable (OE) signal doesn't play a role; for the moment, there is no information at the output (to be more precise, output lines are in the so-called high-impedance state).

After a time interval ($t_{Address\ Access}$), determined by the control logic speed and the speed of transient processes in the inverters, the long-awaited data appear at the output lines. This data can be read directly until the work-cycle interval (t_{Cycle}) elapses. Normally, access time for the static memory cell doesn't exceed 2 nanoseconds, and it often is even smaller!

Write Cycle

The write cycle is executed in reverse order. First, the address of the cell to be written is sent to the bus. Simultaneously, the WE signal is reset to the low state. After the address is decoded, amplified, and supplied to appropriate bit lines, the CS is reset to the low level, which instructs the chip to supply the high-level signal to the required row line. The gate holding the trigger will open, and, depending on the state of the bit line, the trigger will be switched to the required state.

Types of Static Memory

There are at least three types of static memory: *asynchronous* (just considered), *synchronous*, and *pipelined*. All these memory types resemble their respective types of dynamic memory. (See *RAM Design and Working Principles*.) Therefore, I'll provide only brief descriptions of them.

Asynchronous Static Memory

Asynchronous static memory and the memory controller operate independently. The controller cannot be sure that the end of the data-exchange cycle coincides with the start of the next clock pulse. As a result, each exchange cycle becomes longer by at least one clock cycle, decreasing performance. Because of this, asynchronous memory has fallen out of use. (The last PC model to use this memory for *Level 2* (L2) cache was based on the Intel 80386 processor.)

Synchronous Static Memory

Synchronous static memory performs all operations synchronously with the memory bus clock. Thus, cell access time requires a single clock cycle. Synchronous static memory is used to implement *Level 1* (L1) cache in contemporary processors.

Pipelined Static Memory

Pipelined static memory is synchronous static memory equipped with special gates that hold data lines. This allows you to read (or write) one cell while you transmit the address of another cell. Besides this, pipelined memory can process several adjacent cells during one working cycle. To achieve this, it is sufficient to pass the address of the first cell of the *packet*. The chip will calculate the addresses of the other cells automatically; you only need to supply (or read) the data!

Sophisticated hardware implementation has increased cell access time in the pipelined memory to one clock cycle. However, this doesn't negatively influence the performance, because all subsequent cells of the packet are processed without delays.

Pipelined static memory is used in L2 cache implementation of the Pentium II microprocessor family. (See *RAM Design and Working Principles*.) Its timing looks as follows: 2-1-1-1.

Working Principles of Cache

This brief description of the cache subsystem architecture is meant to help novice programmers master the common features of cache memory design. Experienced professionals also will find this material useful; it will allow them to refresh their knowledge, answer some questions, and understand some aspects that were not described properly in the documentation.

The information provided here is more than sufficient for understanding how to work with cache memory. Nevertheless, I recommend that programmers carefully read the technical documentation supplied by processor manufacturers; it contains interesting facts that were not included in this book.

Origins

Dynamic memory is relatively inexpensive, but with today's requirements, it doesn't give adequate performance. Static memory on all frequencies has an access time equal to one clock cycle, but it is rather expensive; therefore, it cannot be used as the main memory of contemporary PCs.

Can at least a part of the memory be based on SRAM? This is a sound idea. After all, what is RAM? It is temporary storage for the data loaded from external storage (the hard disk). Disks are too slow, and intense work with them does not allow high performance. By placing frequently accessed data in RAM, you can significantly reduce the time required to access and process such data.

At first, it may seem that performance gain is achieved only when loaded data are used many times. This is not correct. Suppose that you need to re-encode the contents of a specific file. Because each byte of this file is accessed only once, does it need to be loaded into RAM? The disk drive, due to features of its design, doesn't "want" to read a single byte; it must process an entire sector. Because of this, the read sector must be stored somewhere. Furthermore, you can speed up data exchange considerably if you process more than one sector per operation. In this case, the disk drive will not have to spend time positioning the read/write head when it accesses each sector. Finally, storing data in RAM will allow you to delay data write until it is most suitable for the disk drive.

Thus, *it is not necessary to implement all of the main memory using expensive SRAM chips.* Even a small percentage of SRAM greatly increases system performance.

If this small amount of "fast" memory were addressed directly (i.e., were available like other computer resources to the programmer), programming would become extremely complicated. Worse, portability would be lost. Such tactics "bind" the programmer to the features of a specific hardware platform. Designers came up with a solution: They made cache memory invisible to the programmer. This approach gave birth to cache memory.

Goals and Tasks of Cache Memory

Cache memory is a very fast storage device with a small capacity, intended for temporary data storage. It is much faster than the main memory, but it is neither addressed nor directly visible to the programmer.

The goals of cache memory include the following:

☐ Ensuring quick access to frequently used data
☐ Interfacing the processor and memory controller
☐ Preloading data from the main memory
☐ Implementing delayed data writes

Ensuring Quick Access to Frequently Used Data

Architecturally, cache memory resides between the processor and the main memory (Fig. 3.9) and covers all address space (although occasionally, it covers only a part of it). By intercepting requests to the main memory, the cache controller checks if the valid copy of the requested data is in cache memory. If such a copy is available, the data are retrieved from cache memory. This situation is known as a *cache hit*. Otherwise, a *cache miss* takes place, in which the request is redirected to the main memory.

To achieve maximum performance, it is necessary to ensure that cache misses occur as rarely as possible. (Ideally, they don't occur.) Because the cache size is much smaller than the RAM size, this isn't a trivial task! The main duty of the cache controller is to accumulate the necessary, frequently used data, and to quickly remove garbage (data that are no longer needed). Because the cache controller doesn't know the aim of the data being processed, powerful artificial intelligence is needed to solve this problem adequately. Unfortunately, the cache controllers of contemporary PCs have no intelligence (whether artificial or not); therefore, they blindly rely on templates known as caching strategies.

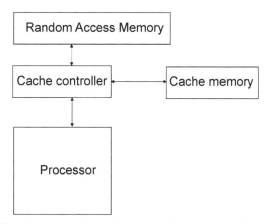

Fig. 3.9. Location of cache in the memory hierarchy

The strategy of *placing data into cache memory* is an algorithm that determines whether a copy of requested data should be included in cache memory. On processors of the Intel Pentium class (and compatible AMD processors), all data requested at least once are stored in cache.

The entire RAM contents cannot be placed into cache; sooner or later, cache will be full. (Using this particular strategy, it will happen quite soon.) Eventually, you'll need to free some space in cache to save a new portion of important data.

The search for the least required data is known as the *replacement strategy*. A decision could be based on the number of attempts required to access each portion of data (a frequency analysis). Another approach could be based on the time of the last access by selecting the data that were *Least Recently Used* (the LRU algorithm), or on when a specific portion of data was loaded from the main memory, by preempting the data loaded early (the *First In, First Out*, or FIFO, algorithm). Finally, the data to be preempted could be chosen randomly (the *randomize* algorithm). The latter strategy is used in AMD-K5 processors.

In contemporary processors of the x86 family, only the FIFO and LRU strategies are used. Frequency analysis is not used in x86 processors because of the complexity of its implementation.

Interfacing the Processor and Memory Controller

Contemporary processors usually consider memory cells as bytes or double words. However, the minimum portion of data used in exchange with physical memory is a packet, containing at least four 64-bit cells.

An analogy can be drawn with a package of goods. For example, if you want a pencil, you must buy the entire box. Naturally, until you need these pencils, you must store them somewhere. Taking one pencil from the pack and discarding the remaining ones is impractical. This is more unreasonable with loaded packets of data, which have a suitable storage place: cache memory. After a data packet is loaded from the main memory, cache enables the CPU to process it in portions of any length. This explains the choice of data-loading strategy. (See *Data Alignment Efficiency*.) The cache controller must place into cache all accessed cells; it would be impractical to discard them.

Prefetching Data

There are several strategies for loading data from the main memory into cache. The simplest algorithm, known as *loading on demand*, accesses the main memory only after the data requested by the processor are found to be missing from cache (in other words, when a cache miss occurs). As a result, cache will contain only the required data. However, when the cell is accessed for the first time, the processor will have to wait approximately 20 FSB clocks, and sometimes longer!

Conversely, the strategy of *speculative loading* places data into cache before they are accessed. How does the cache controller know which memory cells will be needed next by the processor? It can't know, but it can guess.

Guessing algorithms. Guessing algorithms are classified into two groups: *intellectual algorithms* and *nonintellectual algorithms*. An example of a nonintellectual algorithm is the *preloading* strategy. Assuming that data from the RAM are processed sequentially, in the ascending order of their addresses, the controller intercepts the request for reading the first cell and loads some cells directly after the requested one. If data processing really is sequential, the next requests of the CPU will be processed almost instantly because the requested cells already will be in cache! The preloading strategy is derived from the necessity of coordinating the digit capacity of RAM and the CPU.

The most serious drawback of preloading (or of any other nonintellectual guessing algorithm) is that the data-processing algorithm doesn't necessarily match the data-loading algorithm. Memory cells often are requested by the processor in an order different from the one used by the cache controller when it loads them from the main memory. Some of the loaded data are never used, and a serious performance drop can result.

An intellectual cache controller doesn't base prediction on the address of the cell that should be loaded next on dumb templates. Rather, this prediction is based on an analysis of previous access operations. By investigating the sequence of cache misses, the controller attempts to discover the dependence between its elements. If it succeeds, it predicts the next members. If memory access occurs according to a regular template, the intellectual strategy of *speculative loading* can eliminate delays caused by waiting for the data to be loaded from the main memory.

Until recently, intellectual cache controllers were used only in supercomputers or high-performance workstations. Currently, they also are implemented in Intel Pentium 4 and AMD Athlon XP processors. (See *Cache Management in the New Generation of x86 Processors.*)

Data search strategies. Depending on the chosen strategy, data from the main memory might start loading after a cache miss is reported (the *look-through* strategy), or while cache is checked for specific data copy. If a cache hit occurs, data loading is interrupted (the *look-aside* strategy). The latter reduces overhead produced by cache misses, and reduces data-loading latency, but it increases energy consumption, which may be an oversized payment for an insignificant performance gain.

Delaying the Writing of Data

The presence of temporary data storage allows the data that will be written to be accumulated, and then, when the system bus becomes free, to be flushed into RAM in one operation. This eliminates unnecessary delays and increases the performance of the memory subsystem. (See *Cache Organization.*)

The delayed write mechanism is implemented in x86 processors starting with Pentium and AMD-K6. Earlier models had to write each modified cell directly into RAM, which limited their operating speed considerably. Fortunately, such processors are rarely used, and programmers generally can forget about this problem.

Cache Organization

To simplify communication with RAM, the cache controller manipulates data blocks, rather than operating with bytes. Programmatically, cache memory is a set of fixed-size data blocks, known as *cache lines*, whose size is based on that of the burst-read or burst-write cycle. (See *Interaction between the Memory and the Processor.*)

Each cache line is filled or downloaded entirely during one burst-read cycle. If the processor accesses even 1 byte of memory, the cache controller initiates the whole memory-access cycle and requests the entire block. The address of the first byte of the cache line is always a multiple of the size of the burst cycle. The start of the cache line always coincides with the start of the burst cycle.

Since the cache size is much smaller than the RAM size, more than one set of memory cells always maps to each cache line. Consequently, it is necessary to store both the contents of the cached cell and its address. For this purpose, each cache line has special field, known as the *tag*. It stores the linear address and/or the physical address of the first byte of the cache line. This means that cache memory is *associative memory* by nature.

In some processors (for example, in early models of Pentium), only one set of tags stores physical addresses. This makes the processor less expensive; however, at least one extra clock cycle is required to convert the physical address into the linear address, which decreases performance.

Other processors (for example, AMD-K5) have two sets of tags to store physical and linear addresses. The processor accesses physical tags only in two situations. The addressing method used in x86 processors allows the same cell to have more than one linear address; therefore, mismatched linear addresses are not evidence of a cache miss. The processor uses the physical tag to determine whether a cache miss actually occurred. In addition, it accesses the physical tag when an external device (including another processor in a multiprocessor system) asks the processor whether a specified cell is in cache. In all other cases, linear tags are used exclusively, which eliminates constant address translation.

In contrast to the familiar addressable memory accessed by the cell number, associative memory is accessed by the cell contents. This type of memory sometimes is referred to as *content-addressed memory*. Cache lines, unlike RAM cells, have no addresses and can be numbered in an arbitrary order. Expressions such as "cache controller has accessed cache line No. 69" don't make sense; it would be correct to say "Cache controller has accessed cache line 999," where 999 is the *content* of the related tag.

The effective capacity of cache memory is always smaller than its physical capacity, because some cells are used to create tags. The set of tags is called *tag memory*; other cells form *cache-line memory*. Manufacturers always specify the *effective* cache amount, rather than its physical capacity; therefore, the programmer needn't worry about the cache memory consumed by tags.

Blocking and Non-Blocking Cache Memory

There are two main types of cache memory: *blocking* and *non-blocking*. Strangely, these terms are not clarified in most popular publications. (I first encountered them in technical documentation on the AMD-K5 processor.) Therefore, this issue deserves consideration here.

Blocking cache memory, as its name implies, blocks access to cache after each cache miss. Whether or not the requested data are in cache, no other requests will be processed until the cache line that caused the miss is loaded (or unloaded) completely. Blocking cache memory is used rarely because its performance can be inefficient when cache misses occur frequently.

Non-blocking cache memory allows cache to work while cache lines are loaded (or unloaded). Cache misses do not prevent cache hits from occurring. Although non-blocking cache memory is more complicated (and, consequently, more expensive), it is widely used in the newer models of x86 processors (as well as in most other contemporary processors).

Associative Cache Concepts

Consider how cache works, step by step. Suppose that the processor accesses the memory cell whose address is *xyz*. The cache controller intercepts this request and attempts to find out if the requested data are in cache. At this point, interesting events start to take place: This check is reduced to *searching* for the respective address range in tag memory.

Depending on the architecture of the cache controller, tags can be viewed in parallel or in sequence. Parallel searching is fast but hard to implement (and, therefore, rather expensive). Sequential searching is inefficient with a large number of tags. By the way, how many tags are in cache? Their number equals the number of cache lines. For example, 32 KB cache will contain more than *a thousand* cache lines and, consequently, more than *a thousand* tags. How long will it take to view a thousand tags? Even if several tags were viewed in each clock, the search would take hundreds of clock cycles, which would neutralize the performance gain. Although DRAM is slow, accessing it would take less clocks than cache scanning.

Nevertheless, cache works! Parallel and sequential search aren't the only search algorithms available, nor are they the most advanced ones. There are other, more elegant solutions. Consider the two most popular ones: *direct-mapped cache* and *N-way set associative cache.*

In the first solution, each memory cell is mapped directly to a strictly defined cache line. Each cache line has a set of corresponding memory cells, which, in turn, are strictly defined, rather than arbitrarily selected.

If cache comprises four lines, then the first packet of the cached memory corresponds to the first cache line, the second packet relates to the second line, the third packet is mapped to the third line, and the fourth packet is linked to the fourth line. The fifth packet is mapped to the first cache line, the sixth packet to the second line, and so on (Fig. 3.10). When direct-mapped cache is used, cell addresses are related to the number of cache lines in the following relationship:

$$N = \frac{ADDR}{CACHE.LINE.SIZE} mod \frac{CACHE.SIZE}{CACHE.LINE.SIZE}$$

In this relationship, N is the number of the cache line, $ADDR$ is the address of the cell in the cached memory, $CACHE.LINE.SIZE$ is the length of the cache line (in bytes), $CACHE.SIZE$ is the size of cache memory (in bytes), and *mod* takes the remainder after the integer division of the left term by the right term.

To find out if the requested cell is in cache, it is sufficient to view a single tag of the respective cache line. To calculate the number of that cache line, three arithmetic operations are necessary. (Because the lengths of the cache lines and the size of cache memory are powers of 2, operations such as division and calculation of the remainder can be implemented efficiently at the hardware level.) Thus, the necessity of scanning all tags is eliminated naturally.

However, another problem arises. What would happen if the processor attempted to access sequentially the second, sixth, and tenth cells of the cached memory? There would be plenty of free lines in cache. Nevertheless, each new cell would preempt the previous one, because all of them are mapped to the second cache line. As a result, cache would become inefficient. (This is known as *thrashing*.)

A programmer who takes care of program optimization must organize data structures to eliminate frequent read operations of the cells whose addresses are multiples of the cache size. Naturally, this requirement can't always be observed, and the performance of direct-mapped cache is far from optimal. It generally has been replaced by N-way set associative cache.

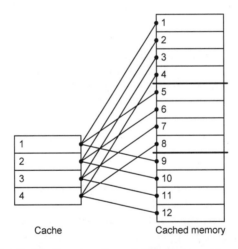

Fig. 3.10. Construction of direct-mapped cache

N-way set associative cache comprises several independent banks, each of which represents a standalone, direct-mapped cache. Look at the illustration presented in Fig. 3.11. Each cell of cached memory can be stored in *one* of two cache lines. Suppose that the processor reads the sixth and tenth cells of the cached memory. The sixth cell goes to the second line of the first bank, and the tenth cell goes to the second line of the next bank (because the first bank is busy).

The number of banks in cache is known as its *associative property*, or *way*. Cache efficiency grows as this number is increased. (For rare exceptions to this rule, see *Influence of the Size of Processed Data on Performance*.)

Ideally, at the highest level of splitting, each bank would contain only one line. Under this condition, each cell of the cached memory can be saved in any cache line. Such cache is known as *fully associative cache* or simply *associative cache*.

Contemporary PCs employ 2-way to 8-way cache. Most frequently, such computers use 4-way cache.

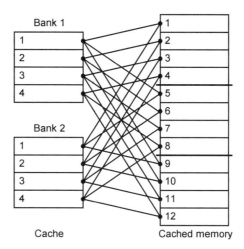

Fig. 3.11. Construction of N-way set associative cache

Write Policies and Coherence Support

If all memory cells were available only for reading, their cached copy always would be identical to the original. (Can any program do without write capabilities?) Ensuring write capabilities generates two problems. The cache controller must trace modification of the cache memory cells by flushing into the main memory all modified cells before they are replaced. It also must trace all attempts to access the main memory made by peripheral devices (including other processors in multiprocessor systems). Otherwise, something read from the data could be different from what was written!

The cache controller must ensure the *coherence* of cache memory with RAM. Suppose that a peripheral device (or another processor) accesses a memory cell that has been modified in cache, but has not been written into the main memory. In this case, the cache controller must update the main memory immediately; otherwise, "old" data would be read from RAM. Similarly, if a peripheral device (or another processor) modifies the main memory (for example, via Direct Memory Access), the cache controller must find out if the modified cells were loaded into cache; if this occurred, it must modify them.

Coherence support is a serious task. The simplest (but not the best) solution is to cache the main memory cells as read-only, then to perform write operations directly to the main memory, bypassing cache. This approach is the *write-through* policy. This policy can be easily implemented at the hardware level, but it will be inefficient.

Buffering partially compensates for memory-access delays. The data written at the first stage are placed into a special *store/write buffer*, which holds about 32 bytes of data. This buffer accumulates data until it is filled or until the bus is released; then, the entire contents of this buffer are written into the memory during a single write operation.

This mode, known as the *write-combining* policy, improves performance, but it doesn't solve all problems. Much processor time is required to flush the buffer contents into the main memory. This is frustrating, particularly because most computers have one processor, and it is the processor, not peripheral devices, that works intensely with the memory. Therefore, coherence support is expensive. A more sophisticated (and more efficient) algorithm is implemented by the *write-back* policy, which minimizes access to the memory. Each cell of cache memory has a *state flag*, which is useful when modifications are traced.

If the cached cell was modified, the cache controller sets its associated flag to the *dirty* state. When a peripheral device accesses the memory, the cache controller checks for the respective address in cache memory. If the address is present, the cache controller checks the state flag. Dirty cells are flushed to the main memory, and the cache controller clears their flags.

When replacing old cache lines with newer ones, the cache controller can remove the clear lines from cache instantly, without writing into the main memory. When all the lines are dirty, the cache controller chooses the least useful one (based on the data-replacement policy) and flushes it to the main memory, freeing space for the new "clear" line.

MESI Protocol

The mysterious acronym *MESI*, frequently encountered in publications, stands for the four possible states of the cache line: Modified, Exclusive, Shared, and Invalid.

What is the meaning of each status? The following explanations (and Table 3.1) should help answer this question:

Modified	This status is assigned automatically to cache lines when they are modified. A line with this attribute simply cannot be discarded from cache. When such a line is preempted, its contents must be flushed to a second level of cache or to the main memory.

Exclusive   This status is assigned automatically to cache lines when they are loaded from a second level of cache or from the main memory. Modification of a line with the exclusive attribute automatically changes this attribute to modified.
Depending on the system architecture, when an exclusive line is removed from cache, it is discarded (inclusive cache), or its contents are exchanged with those of a second level of cache (exclusive cache).

Shared   This status is assigned to cache lines potentially present in the cache memory of other processors (in multiprocessor systems). Besides this, the shared attribute indicates that the line is coherent with the contents of its respective cells of the main memory.

Invalid   This status means that the line is missing from cache and must be loaded from a higher level of cache or from RAM.

 Note

In AMD Athlon, a new status has been added: Owner. The protocol name has been changed to *MOESI*.

Table 3.1. Practical Descriptions of the MESI Protocol

Status	Modified	Exclusive	Shared	Invalid
Is this a valid cache line?	Yes	Yes	Yes	No
Is the cache-line copy stored in the memory valid?	No	Yes	Yes	This cache line has no corresponding memory
Do other processors have copies of this line?	No	No	Maybe	Maybe
How is writing performed?	To this line only, without accessing the bus	To this line only, without accessing the bus	Into the memory, using the write-through policy and invalidating this line in the cache memory of other processors	Directly via the bus

L1 and L2 data cache of the Pentium, AMD-K6, and AMD Athlon processors support all four status types. The code cache supports only two of them: Shared and Invalid. Other types are not supported because the code cache doesn't support line modification.

Some readers may be surprised and ask: How does self-modifying code work in this case? (I'd answer: Who told you that it works at all?) Whether or not the modified cell is in the code cache, the write instruction cannot change its contents directly. Therefore, the cell is placed into L1 cache, L2 cache, or RAM. Although the processor traces these situations and refreshes the respective lines of the code cache, you should avoid self-modifying code whenever possible. This recommendation is given for the following reasons: When you refresh the lines, all previously decoded information is lost, and the processor has to clear the whole pipeline and refill it from scratch.

At the same time, contemporary systems interpret as "self-modifying" not only truly self-modifying code (according to its canonical definition): Any attempt to write into the memory area that resides in the code cache will be considered "self-modifying" code as well. This means that any mix of code and data, frequently encountered in "manually written" assembly programs, will be no faster than an asphalt roller, although formally it doesn't modify the machine code. (The CPU doesn't know anything about it.)

Two-Level Cache Organization

The maximum capacity of cache memory is limited not only by its price, but also by electromagnetic interference. (See *RAM Design and Working Principles.*) This imposes stringent requirements on the maximum number of address lines and, consequently, on the amount of addressable memory. You could implement output multiplexing or sequential address transmission (as the developers of Rambus DRAM did). However, this inevitably will decrease performance, and access to the cache memory cells unfortunately will require more than one clock.

Two-port static memory is very expensive, but single-port memory is unable to ensure parallel processing of multiple cells, which results in frustrating delays.

The natural approach involves creating a multilevel cache hierarchy (Fig. 3.12). Most contemporary systems have at least two levels of cache memory. The first, and the closest to the processor, is known as Level 1 (L1) cache. L1 cache is usually implemented by fast, two-port synchronous static memory that operates at the same clock frequency as the processor's core. The size of L1 cache is usually small and rarely exceeds 32 KB. Because of this, it must store only the most frequently used data. As a result, it only requires one clock to process two full-sized cells.

Attention

The x86 processor is equipped with static memory that is not truly two-port memory! It has a two-port interface, but the core of its memory comprises several banks (usually eight) implemented on single-port arrays. Thus, parallel access is possible only to cells that belong to different banks. (See *Data Distribution over Cache Banks*.)

Between L1 cache and the main memory lies Level 2 (L2) cache. It is implemented on the basis of single-port pipelined static memory, known as Burst Static Random Access Memory (BSRAM). It often operates at a reduced clock frequency. Because single-port memory is much less expensive, L2 cache is usually hundreds of kilobytes, and sometimes even reaches several megabytes! Nevertheless, the access speed of L2 cache is relatively slow (although it exceeds the access speed of the main memory).

Note that the minimum unit of data used in exchange between L1 and L2 cache is the entire cache line, not 1 byte. The average time required for reading the cache line is five clocks of the L2 cache clock frequency. (Recall that the BSRAM timing is 2-1-1-1.) If L2 cache operates at half the clock frequency of the CPU, then accessing one cell will require ten clocks of the processor. Naturally, this value can be reduced. In servers and high-performance workstations, L2 cache usually operates at the full clock frequency of the processor's core, and it often has four times the bit capacity of the data bus. This approach accomplishes the packet-exchange cycle in one clock. However, such systems are expensive.

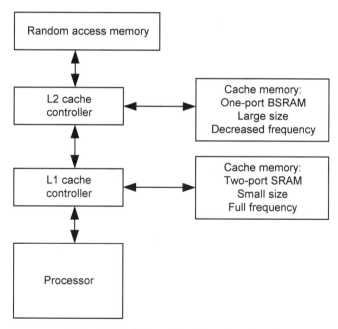

Fig. 3.12. Hierarchy of two-level cache

Inclusive architecture. L2 cache implemented via inclusive architecture always duplicates the contents of L1 cache; therefore, the effective capacity of cache memory is equal to the L2 cache size: $L2.CACHE.SIZE - L1.CACHE.SIZE + L1.CACHE.SIZE = = L2.CACHE.SIZE$.

Suppose L2 cache is filled, and the CPU attempts to load one more cell. L2 cache will detect that all cache lines are filled, then it will try to get rid of the least useful one by finding the line that wasn't modified. (Any other method would require it to flush data into RAM, which would take additional clocks.)

After data are read from the main memory, L2 cache passes these to L1 cache. If L1 cache is full, it also will need to get rid of unnecessary data using the same method.

Thus, the loaded data fragment is in both L1 and L2 cache memory, which isn't good. Nevertheless, practically all contemporary processors (K6, PII, PIII) are based on inclusive architecture.

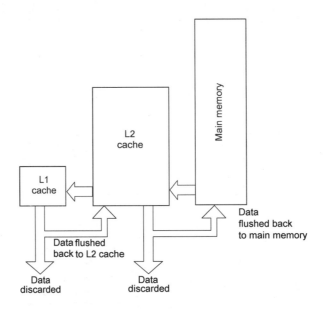

Fig. 3.13. Inclusive architecture

Exclusive architecture. A cache subsystem based on exclusive architecture never stores redundant data copies. In this case, the effective capacity of cache memory is determined by the *sum* of the sizes of cache memory at all levels.

L1 cache never discards cache lines when memory space is insufficient. Even if the line wasn't modified, the data are moved into L2 cache and settled where the cache line passed to L1 cache was located. Thus, L1 and L2 cache memory exchange their lines, and cache memory is used efficiently.

The exclusive cache subsystem is implemented only in newer models of AMD Athlon processors. (See *Influence of the Size of Processed Data on Performance.*)

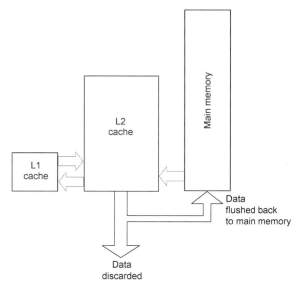

Fig. 3.14. Exclusive architecture

Write Buffers

To prevent delays caused by cache misses when data are written, contemporary processors actively use various methods of buffering. Instead of immediately sending the data to be written to their destination, the processor temporarily stores them in a special buffer, from which the data is flushed into L1 cache, L2 cache, or RAM when the cache controller or bus is released.

This technique is useful when the number of read operations significantly exceeds the number of write operations. If the frequency of cache misses during write operations doesn't exceed the rate of buffer flushing, there are no penalties, and the total effective speed of write operations is one clock.

A common belief states that increasing the number of buffers in the processor increases the frequency of cache misses it can withstand during write operations (without significant performance degradation). However, the *maximum frequency of cache misses is determined not by the number of buffers, but by their flushing speed and the write policy.*

In particular, AMD-K6 and Athlon processors always flush the contents of the buffers into L1 cache, which gives them a high flushing speed. (Under favorable conditions, each 32/64-byte buffer is flushed during one clock cycle.) In these processors, flushed data are available for reading immediately and remain so until they are removed from L1 cache!

Pentium 4 processors and those based on the P6 core direct the contents of buffers to L2 cache, rather than to L1 cache (unless the data to be written are in L1 cache). The efficiency of this strategy is disputable. On one hand, the processor tolerates a much lower cache-miss intensity during write operations; on the other hand, flushing the data to be written into L2 cache doesn't fill L1 cache, increasing the latter's effective capacity.

An important consequence of this buffer unloading policy is *distortion of the cache-write policy*. Although L1 cache formally is based on the write-back policy, it operates according to the write-through policy because a cache miss during a write operation directly updates the higher level of cache memory without loading modified data into L1 cache. Curiously, Intel first mentioned this in documentation on the Pentium 4 processor, where the "L1 cache write policy" column referred to " write through," rather than " write back," used in documentation on earlier processors.

Increasing the number of write buffers doesn't compensate for the slow speed of flushing their contents into the memory. The only benefit provided by a large buffer is that it tolerates *local* overloading, when several misses occur simultaneously (or sequentially with minimum time gaps), and are followed by "silence."

Read after write. In contrast to their name, write buffers are available for writing and for reading. Reading data from the write buffers is faster than reading data from L1 cache by at least one clock. (More details on this topic and on using this for program optimization are in *Write Buffering Specifics*.)

Nevertheless, reading of the buffer contents (especially on the processors of the Pentium family) must be performed with care. The data written into the buffer can travel to L2 cache at any moment. This will increase their access time considerably. Buffers are flushed automatically at the bus idle time, and they are flushed *immediately* in the following situations:

❏ Executing an instruction with the bus-exclusive locking prefix (LOCK)
❏ Performing serialization instruction (such as CPUID)
❏ Executing the SFNCE buffer flushing instruction (Pentium III and higher)
❏ Executing the MFENCE buffer flushing instruction (Pentium 4)
❏ Handling an exception or calling an interrupt
❏ Reading to or writing from an input/output port
❏ Executing the BINIT instruction

Write ordering. In addition to other functions, buffers must perform *write ordering*. Later processor models of the x86 family split machine instructions into micro-operations and execute them in the order preferred by the processor core of a Reduced Instruction Set Computer (RISC). However, breaking the order of read or write operations into RAM or cache memory can disturb normal operation of a program!

Consider the following code fragment: `a = *p; *p = b;`. If the data read block was busy processing the previous instruction, the `a = *p` command would need to wait in the queue, but the `*p = b` command would be fetched for execution by the idle write block.

It is possible to stall the write block until the read operation is accomplished. However, such a measure won't improve the performance. Is there a way out? Yes, the data to be written can be stored temporarily in some intermediate buffer, rather than in cache or the main memory. To avoid complicating the microkernel architecture with an extra buffer, its designers decided to delegate this task to write buffers. The policy of flushing data from the buffer guarantees that the data placed into the buffer will not leave before all preceding instructions are completed. No conflicts arise, because the data leaving the write buffers are in order.

At the same time, write buffering reduces the number of memory-access operations. If a cell was written several times, only the last result will be written into the main memory (or into cache).

Implementation and characteristics of write buffers. Early models of the Pentium family had only two write buffers: one for each U- or V-pipe. Pentium with MMX technology has four buffers, but Pentium II has 12 buffers! Starting with Pentium II, write buffers were renamed *store* buffers (although to avoid confusion, I will continue to use the older term, write buffers). The size of each buffer is 32 bytes; therefore, in Pentium II, up to 384 bytes (96 double words) can be stored for each operation without causing cache misses. However, attempts to write into noncached memory when buffers are full would result in uncorrectable cache misses and, consequently, in delays.

Therefore, it is expedient to alternate write operations with calculations, giving buffers time to unload their contents.

Cache Subsystem of Contemporary Processors

The cache subsystem of contemporary processors (such as PII, PIII, P4, and Athlon) has a hierarchy that comprises the following components: the Memory Order Buffer (MOB), L1 cache, write buffers, the Memory Interface Unit (MIU), the Bus Interface Unit (BIU), and L2 cache (with the Dual Independent Bus (DIB), its local bus) (Fig. 3.15).

Memory Order Buffer. The data leaving the executive pipeline are redirected to the MOB, where they accumulate and wait to be moved into the main memory. The MOB plays the same role as the lounge in an airport: Passengers arrive in a random order, and depart according to the time specified on their tickets, if the weather is fine and the plane is ready to take off.

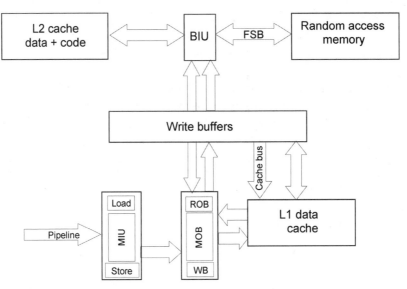

Fig. 3.15. Cache subsystem of contemporary processors

The data stored in the MOB always are available to the processor, even if they are not flushed to the main memory. However, the MOB is small (40 entries in P6), and the executive pipeline stops when it overflows. Therefore, the MOB contents should be flushed immediately. This can be accomplished in one of at least three ways:

1. If the modified cell is already in L1 cache, it goes directly to the cache line that corresponds to it. This requires only one clock, during which one cell, or even two nonadjacent cells, can be written into cache. (The maximum number of cells that can be written into cache simultaneously is defined by the cache subsystem architecture of the specific processor, as explained in *Influence of the Size of Processed Data on Performance.*)

2. If the modified cell is missing from L1 cache, it goes to any free write buffer. This also takes only one clock, and the number of simultaneously written cells is determined by the number of ports available to the write buffers. (For example, AMD-K5 and Athlon processors have one such port.)

3. If the modified cell is missing from L1 cache, and there are no free write buffers, the processor loads the respective data copy into L1 cache, then proceeds as described in Option 1. Depending on the circumstances, data loading might take dozens to thousands of processor clocks; therefore, this situation should be avoided whenever possible.

L1 cache. L1 cache is located directly on the chip. It is implemented on the basis of two-port static memory. It drains two independent banks of cache memory, each controlled by a dedicated cache controller. One bank caches machine instructions; the other bank caches the processed data. In the technical specification of the processor, the developers usually specify the total size of L1 cache. This leads to an ambiguity, because the sizes of the code cache and the data cache are not necessarily equal. (In the latest processor models, they are not equal.) In addition, a portion of L1 cache is reserved for internal use.

Near L1 cache are the associative translation buffers, also known as the Translation Look-aside Buffers (TLB), of the data pages and code pages. The TLB occupy fixed cache lines, and the space allocated to them is excluded from the "official" cache size: If the specification declares that the processor has an 8 KB data cache, all 8 KB are available directly for data caching. Therefore, the actual cache size must exceed 8 KB.

Write buffers. The location of write buffers in the cache hierarchy is uncertain. In block charts provided in documentation for Intel Pentium and AMD Athlon, write buffers are missing. Intel's system programming manual, in the *Memory Cache Control* chapter, has a diagram titled "Internal Caches, TLBs, and Buffers" that displays write buffers connected to only the BIU.

After analyzing documented information related to buffers and conducting my own experiments, I concluded that write buffers are connected to at least the Reorder Buffer (ROB) and Write Buffer (WB) of the MOB, the MIU, and the BIU. On K5, K6, and Athlon, write buffers must be connected to L1 cache as well.

Regardless, write buffers delay writes to cache or to the main memory by performing this operation as the cache controller, internal bus, or system bus become free. This preempts lengthy delays and increases the processor's performance.

Memory Interface Unit. The MIU is one of the processor's executive devices. At the functional level, it comprises two components: the *memory-read device* (load) and the *memory-write device* (store).

The read device is connected to the write buffers and to L1 cache via the MOB. If the requested memory cell is present in at least one of these devices, only one processor clock will be needed to read it.

Regardless of the type of data being processed, the entire cache line must be loaded. Although both Intel and AMD don't mention this detail, it can be detected through experimentation. Intel Pentium and AMD Athlon only have one MIU. Nevertheless, they manage to process several memory-reading instructions per clock cycle, if the data are aligned by the 4-byte boundary and reside in the same cache line. Therefore, the bus connecting the MIU and L1 cache must have at least a 256-bit width, which can be implemented easily (especially considering the proximity of the processor core and L1 cache).

The MIU is connected to the ROB and WB of the MOB.

Bus Interface Unit. The BIU is the only link connecting the processor to the outside world. It drains all information moved from the write buffers and L1 cache. It also accepts requests for loading data from the data cache and machine commands from the code cache.

From "outside," the BIU is contacted by L2 cache and the main memory. Clearly, overall system performance depends on the operating speed of the BIU.

L2 cache. Because of features of each processor's design, L2 cache can be integrated with the processor chip (on-die), or it can reside on a standalone chip outside the processor.

On-die implementation is distinguished by practically unlimited operation speed. The length of the conductors connecting L2 cache to the BIU is relatively small, and cache operates at the full processor-core frequency. In addition, the width of its bus in newer processors, such as PIII and P4, reaches 256 bits. However, on-die implementation significantly increases the chip area, and, consequently, its cost. (The percentage of chips discarded because of manufacturing defects grows exponentially with an increase of the chip area.) Nevertheless, advanced manufacturing technologies (and competition between leading manufacturers) have produced integrated L2 cache in most contemporary processors.

Dual Independent Bus. To increase overall system performance, L2 cache communicates with the BIU via its own *local* bus, which reduces the Front Side Bus (FSB) workload considerably.

Because of the proximity of L2 cache to the processor's core, the length of the local bus is relatively small. Therefore, it can operate on much higher frequencies than the system bus. For a long time, the digit capacity of the local bus remained the same as that of the system bus (64 bits). This tradition was broken with the release of Pentium III "Coppermine," equipped with a 256-bit local bus, which allowed the entire 32-byte cache line to load within a single clock! This made L1 and L2 cache practically equal. (See *Influence of the Size of Processed Data on Performance.*) Unfortunately, AMD Athlon doesn't have a wide bus.

As previously mentioned, the DIB architecture reduces the workload of the FSB because most memory requests are processed locally. The workload factor of the system bus in single-processor workstations is about 10% of its maximum throughput; the remaining 90% of requests are processed by the local bus. Even in a four-processor server, the workload on the system bus doesn't exceed 60%, creating a false impression that the system bus is not the bottleneck that limits overall system performance.

However, interpretation of these percentages doesn't correspond to reality. Low workload on the system bus is explained by the high latency of the main memory, which the system bus spends at least half of its time waiting for, rather than transmitting requests. Fortunately, newer processor models have implemented prefetching commands that can prevent latency, allowing the bus to operate at its full speed. (See *Practical Uses of Prefetching*.)

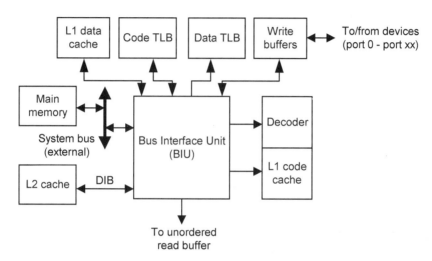

Fig. 3.16. Flow chart of the cache subsystem implemented in processors based on the Intel Pentium 6 core

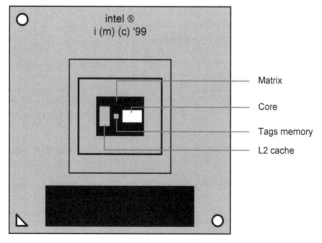

Fig. 3.17. Physical implementation of cache memory (Intel Pentium III "Coppermine" processor)

Architecture and Characteristics of Contemporary Microprocessors

Providing detailed listings of cache characteristics for all contemporary microprocessors is a thankless but necessary task. This is especially true because code optimal for one processor might prove to be extremely inefficient for another one.

The most important parameter is the L1 cache size. The structures of the most frequently used data must be organized to fit entirely within L1 cache. When large data arrays are processed, these should fit within L2 cache and be moved into the main memory only in extreme cases. (For more details, see *Influence of the Size of Processed Data on Performance.*)

The cache size differs widely in various processor models, and it is difficult to choose which model should be relied upon. If possible, you should optimize your program for the minimum cache size, then test the program with such a cache on the processor. Alternatively, it makes sense to orient your program toward the most popular processor models. (In this case, you'll have to predict, or find out, which model will be most popular when you release your program.)

The next important characteristics are the associative number and the bank size of cache memory. If the associative number is smaller than necessary, cache memory will be thrashing, sometimes reducing the performance ten times or more. To avoid such situations, you must make sure that intensely used data do not reside at addresses that are multiples of the cache-bank size. Note that it is difficult to meet this requirement because bank sizes vary greatly. To ensure that collisions are eliminated, you must test the program on all types of processors and correct the placement of the data structures when necessary. (See *Working with a Limited Associative Number of Cache.*)

The fourth important characteristic is the write policy. The write policy influences the efficiency of memory-write operations. All caches of contemporary processors support the write-through policy and the write-back policy. However, the number of buffers isn't constant and varies with the processor model — from two 64-bit buffers in early models of Intel Pentium, to 12 buffers in Pentium III. (See *Write Buffering Specifics.*)

The fifth important feature is the cache-line size. In the latest Intel and AMD processors, this has been extended to 64 bytes. However, more isn't necessarily better. Prefetching is most efficient for sequential data processing; otherwise, cache would be thrashing.

There are many factors in addition to the ones detailed here. Clearly, *simultaneous code optimization for all microprocessors is a difficult task.*

Table 3.2 lists the key cache characteristics of the most popular processors.

Table 3.2. Key Characteristics of L1 and L2 Caches of Contemporary Processors

Processor parameter			Pentium II Celeron	Pentium III Celeron	Pentium 4	AMD Athlon
L1		Total size (KB)	32	32	**	128
		Type	Separate	Separate	Separate	Separate
	C O D E	Size (KB)	16	16	12 ops	64
		Protocol	SI	SI	**	SI
		Associative number (way)	4	4	4*	2
		Line size (bytes)	32	32	6 ops	64
		Banks in line	1	1	**	**
		Bank size (KB)	4	4	**	32
		Number of ports	1	1	1*	1*
		Replacement algorithm	LRU	LRU	**	LRU
		Blocking	No*	No*	No*	No*
		Frequency-to-core ratio	1:1	1:1	1:1	1:1
		Access time (clocks)	Normal	1	1	1
		Line-split	6–12	6–12	**	1
		Size (KB) 16	16	8	64	**
	D A T A	Protocol	MESI	MESI	MESI	MOESI
		Associative number (way)	4	4	4	2
		Line size (bytes)	32	32	64	64
		Banks in line	8	8	8*	8*
		Bank size (KB)	4	4	2	32
		Number of ports	2	2	2	2
		Replacement algorithm	LRU	LRU	LRU	LRU
		Write policy	Back	Back	Through	Back
		Blocking	No	No	No	No
		Frequency-to-core ratio	1:1	1:1	1:1	1:1

continues

Table 3.2 Continued

	Processor parameter	Pentium II Celeron	Pentium III Celeron	Pentium 4	AMD Athlon
L2	Placement	Unified/ On-die	Unified/ On-die	On-die	**
	Size (KB)	128/256/ 512 >	128/256/ 512 >	128/256/ 512 >	512/1024/ 2048
	Type	Inclusive	Inclusive	Exclusive	Inclusive/ Exclusive
	Protocol	MESI	MESI	MESI	MESI
	Associative number (way)	4	4/8	4/8	2/16
	Line size (bytes)	32	32	64×2	64*
	Bank size (KB)	32/64/128	32/64/128	32/64/128	32/64/128
	Number of ports	1*	1*	1*	1*
	Replacement algorithm	LRU	LRU	LRU	LRU
	Write policy	Back	Back	Back	Back
	Blocking	No	No	No	No
	Frequency-to-core ratio	0.5:1/1:1	0.5:1/1:1	1:1	1:1
	Access time (clocks)	10*	4*	2*	8*
	Timing	2-1-1-1	1-1-1-1	1-1-1-1	1-1-1-1
Reorder buffer, inputs		40	40	**	**
Reservation station, outputs		20	20	**	**
Read buffer (bytes)		4×32*	4×32*	**	**
Write buffer (bytes)		32*	32*	6×64	**
System bus frequency (MHz)		66/100	66/100/133	100×4/ 133×4	100×2
Bus width	L2 ←→ L1	64	256	256	64
	L2 ←→ DRAM	64	64	64/128*	64

* presumably

** data unavailable

Optimizing Cache and Memory Access

Influence of the Size of Processed Data on Performance

Without doubt, the smaller the data array, the faster it is processed. To achieve maximum performance, it is necessary to design the algorithm of the program so that all intensely processed data fit within L1, or at least within L2, cache. Otherwise, intensive exchange with the main memory will consume all processor time.

However, at this stage, another question arises: How does the data size influence performance, and vice versa? For example, it would be interesting to know the drop in program speed if the processed data block exceeds the limits of L1 or L2 cache by 1 KB. There is an additional question: Is all cache memory available, or must part of it be reserved for the storage of stack variables, arguments, and the function's return address? Popular manuals usually stay silent on this topic, mainly offering the following strict rule: If your data doesn't fit in cache, you have only yourself to blame.

Even such an indisputable authority as Agner Fog only approximates the number of clocks required to load a cell from different levels of the memory hierarchy. (See his manual, *How To Optimize for the Pentium Microprocessors.*) As useful as this information might be, it doesn't provide a general impression of the existing pattern. As previously explained (see *Calculating the Full Access Time*), "access time" is an abstract concept, closely related to pipelining and parallelism. Therefore, it is time to ensconce yourself in front of the computer and attempt to answer these questions.

Write a small test program that processes blocks of increasing size within a loop, then display the results as a graph. You will investigate four main combinations of data processing: sequential reading, sequential writing, reading a memory cell with subsequent modification, and writing a memory cell with subsequent reading. The investigation of parallel processing also is desirable. (See *Parallel Data Processing.*) However, this task is too lengthy to be included in this book.

Listing 3.1. [Cache/cache.size.c] Dependence of Processing Time on the Data Size and Processing Mode

```
#define BLOCK_SIZE (715*K)    // Size of the data block being processed
#define STEP_FACTOR  (1*K)    // Block increment step
#define X       1             // :'b' (to subtract the linear component)
                              // :'1' (to display the graph as is)
```

```
// Memory allocation
p = malloc(BLOCK_SIZE);

// Header
printf("---\t");
for (b = 1*K; b < BLOCK_SIZE; b += STEP_FACTOR)
 printf("%d\t", b/K); printf("\n");



/*-------------------------------------------------------------------------
 *
 *          SEQUENTIAL READING
 *
 --------------------------------------------------------------------- */
printf("R\t"); for (b = 1*K; b < BLOCK_SIZE; b += STEP_FACTOR)
{
 PRINT_PROGRESS(25*b/BLOCK_SIZE); VVV;
 A_BEGIN(0)
    for (c = 0; c <= b; c += sizeof(int))
       tmp += *(int*)((int)p + c);
 A_END(0)
 printf("%d\t", 100*Ax_GET(0)/X);
}
printf("\n");



/*-------------------------------------------------------------------------
 *
 *          SEQUENTIAL WRITING
 *
 --------------------------------------------------------------------- */
printf("W\t"); for (b = 1*K; b < BLOCK_SIZE; b += STEP_FACTOR)
{
 PRINT_PROGRESS(25+25*b/BLOCK_SIZE); VVV;
 A_BEGIN(1)
    for (c = 0; c <= b; c += sizeof(int))
       *(int*)((int)p + c) = tmp;
 A_END(1)
 printf("%d\t", 100*Ax_GET(1)/X);
}
printf("\n");
```

```
/*-------------------------------------------------------------------
 *
 *      SEQUENTIAL READING followed by WRITING
 *
 -------------------------------------------------------------------- */
printf("RW\t"); for (b = 1*K; b < BLOCK_SIZE; b += STEP_FACTOR)
{
PRINT_PROGRESS(50+25*b/BLOCK_SIZE); VVV;
A_BEGIN(2)
for (c = 0; c <= b; c += sizeof(int))
{
    tmp += *(int*)((int)p + c);
    *(int*)((int)p + c) = tmp;
}
A_END(2)
printf("%d\t", 100*Ax_GET(2)/X);
}
printf("\n");


/*-------------------------------------------------------------------
 *
 *      SEQUENTIAL WRITING followed by READING
 *
 -------------------------------------------------------------------- */
printf("WR\t"); for (b = 1*K; b < BLOCK_SIZE; b += STEP_FACTOR)
{
PRINT_PROGRESS(75+25*b/BLOCK_SIZE); VVV;
A_BEGIN(3)
for (c = 0; c <= b; c += sizeof(int))
{
    *(int*)((int)p + c) = tmp;
    tmp += *(int*)((int)p + c);
}
A_END(3)
printf("%d\t", 100*Ax_GET(3)/X);
}
printf("\n");
```

The resulting graph can vary depending on the architecture of the processor used for the test. It should resemble Fig. 3.18. The curve that shows the rate at which reading occurs looks like a gently sloping hill, smoothed by erosion. The other curves look like newly erected mountains, constantly changing the steepness of their slopes.

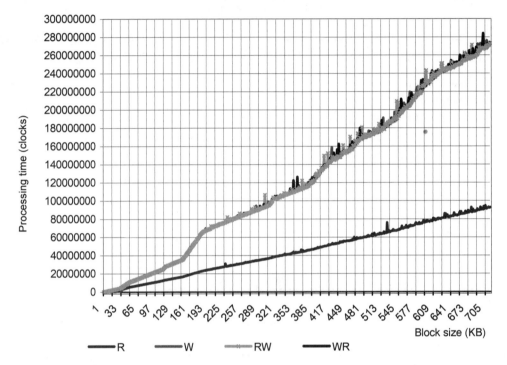

Fig. 3.18. Dependence of the processing time on the block size,
without subtracting the linear component (AMD-K6)

If you scrutinize these curves, you'll notice that the first rise is around the 32 km mark (sorry, I mean KB). This is the size of L1 cache of the AMD-K6 microprocessor (quite a good one, by the way).

After it passes the cache size, the read curve starts to rise linearly, with a constant proportion close to 1. In other words, within the section *L1.CACHE.SIZE; L2.CACHE.SIZE*, the block processing time (depending on the block size) changes as follows:

$$\frac{T(size(BLOCK1))}{T(size(BLOCK2))} = \frac{size(BLOCK1)}{size(BLOCK2)}$$

Here, *T* is the processing time. After the data leave the boundary equal to the L1 cache size, the program execution speed drops considerably. It is much harder to hike uphill than to walk along a flat path without any luggage (and L1 cache represents the flat path).

The read curve climbs steeply. At first, its proportionality factor seems close to 1.5 or even 2. However, this is only an illusion. The formula of dependence between processing time and block size is identical to the reading formula. If you don't believe me, check! Press a ruler to the monitor: Processing the 89 KB block took 200,000 processor clocks, and the 177 KB block took 400,000 clocks. Therefore, *89 : 177* is approximately *200,000 : 400,000 = 0.5.*

Alas, Fig. 3.18 is not illustrative because it comprises two components: the linear growth of time (the increasing number of memory-access operations) and a superimposed nonlinear component (the changing access speed for different types of memory).

In this case, *memory-access speed* is more informative than the total processing time of the data block. Therefore, you must eliminate the linear component. If you don't need precise calculations, it is sufficient to divide the results of each measurement by the number of loop iterations (Fig. 3.19).

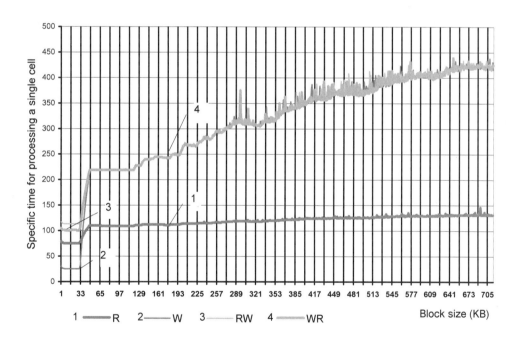

Fig. 3.19. Dependence of the processing time on the block size (AMD-K6)

In L1 Cache

As long as the size of the processed block doesn't exceed the size of L1 cache (32 KB for AMD-K6), all four curves are nearly horizontal, which means the processing speed remains practically constant. This becomes evident in Fig 3.19, after the linear component has been eliminated; you don't need to calculate the coefficient.

Notice the small "drift" at the beginning of all four curves. How would you interpret it? The block processing time doesn't decrease with the increase of the block size; rather, the decrease is caused by the overhead that results from measuring the time of the loop execution.

Fig. 3.19 easily allows you to discover that the cell write operation is initially three times faster than the read operation, and four times faster than the read-after-write operation. This is due to the overhead produced by organizing the loop. The Microsoft Visual C++ 6.0 compiler, which was used to compile and build this test program, was able to recognize the write loop and replaced it with a single machine command: REP STOSD. The read loop required several machine commands.

Depending on the processor's microarchitecture, accessing cache memory can take one to three clocks. The maximum number of simultaneously processed cells varies from two to four. The parameters for the most popular processors are provided in Table 3.3.

Table 3.3. Main Parameters of Cache Memory for Popular Processor Models

Processor	Operation	Latency (clocks)	Throughput (clocks)	Max. operations
AMD-K5	Read	1	2	R+R/R+W
	Write	1	1	
AMD-K6	Read	2	1	R+W
	Write	1	1	
AMD Athlon	Read	–	2	R+R+W+W
	Write	–	2	
Pentium II/ Pentium III	Read	3	1	R+W
	Write	1	1	
Pentium 4	Read	2	1	R+W
	Write	2	1	

How can you calculate the *actual access time* of the cell? Consider an example that uses the AMD-K6 processor. First, define the actual access time. The latency column specifies the number of clocks that elapse from the instant the cell is accessed until the read (or write) operation is completed. The cell read operation is accomplished in two stages: calculating the effective address and data loading. For AMD-K6, each stage is accomplished during one clock; therefore, the full access time of the cell is two clocks.

However, if there are no data dependencies, the processor can start loading the next cell without waiting for the previous operation to finish. This can occur after one clock, rather than after two clocks, because the effective address calculation unit will be free and ready to use. Thus, N independent cells can be read during $N \times Throughput + Latency$ clocks. When N is large, the value of latency can be ignored. Thus, the actual access time is one clock on K6. On Athlon, it is 0.5 clock. (Athlon is capable of loading two 32-bit cells per clock.)

However, there is a problem: Parallel commands are executed if the commands are available. In a rolled loop with a form such as `for(a=0; a < BLOCK_SIZE; a++)` `x+=p[a];`, memory is accessed only once during each iteration (if the variables `a` and `x` are located in the registers). Because of this, the execution time of this loop will be much longer than $N \times Throughput + Latency$. To solve this problem, it is necessary to unroll at least two iterations of the loop. (This problem was covered in detail in *Unrolling Loops*.) However, another aspect is more important here: How would the performance change if the data-block size is larger than the L1 cache size?

Exceeding the Limits of L1 Cache

When the limits of L1 cache are exceeded, all four curves in Fig. 3.19 rise sharply and stop only when the size of the processed block is approximately 1.5 times the size of L1 cache. Why 1.5 times, and not 2 or 3 times? The *gradual* change of the processing speed is remarkable because it seems its gradient must be stepwise.

Consider the filled cache and imagine what would happen if you tried to load another cache line. To free some space, the Least Recently Used (LRU) strategy would preempt the oldest cache line. During sequential processing of the memory block, this would be the first line — the starting line for processing the next iteration of the loop!

Because of this, when the next iteration begins, the first cache line would be missing from cache. The cache controller would be forced to access L2 cache and, once again, replace the oldest (the second) cache line, because there would be no free lines in cache. Consequently, when the next memory cell is accessed, the cache controller again would enter the state of thrashing; it would be forced to reload all cache lines one by one. Because a cache miss accompanies each memory-access operation, the size of the processed block is no longer critical. It doesn't matter whether it exceeds the cache size by one, two, or ten cache lines; just one extra cache line guarantees that there will be no cache hits. This is the worst possible result!

However, the gradient of the curve isn't stepwise; it's smooth. Is this caused by measurement errors or by errors in the reasoning? The error is in the argumentation: Due to the limited association number of cache, the cells of the cached memory relate to strictly defined cache lines, rather than random ones.

This concept is easier to understand on an example that illustrates direct-mapped cache. Suppose such cache is filled. When the next cell is accessed, the cache controller will load it into the cache line with the number `(cache_size+1) % cache_size == 1`. At the next iteration of the loop, the first cell will go *to the same line* (because `1 % cache_size == 1`), rather than to the oldest cache line, No. 2. Line No. 1 will be thrashing, but it won't influence all other lines. Accordingly, if the size of the processed block exceeds the cache size by two lines, there will be two thrashing cache lines. Finally, when a data block is processed whose size is twice that of cache, the entire cache will be thrashing.

In N-way set associative cache, saturation occurs even earlier. This is not surprising, since each cell of the cached memory can pretend to be one of several possible cache lines.

Cache is composed of two banks. When there is no free space, each new cell goes to the first cache line of the first bank (because this line was least recently used). At the next iteration, the cell that was processed first will be missing from cache. It will have to be reloaded at the expense of preempting the first cache line of the *second* bank.

As a result, two cache lines, instead of one, will be thrashing. If the size of the processed block exceeds the cache size by 1.5 times, the entire cache will idle. Accordingly, 4-way associative cache will become saturated when the processed block exceeds the cache memory size by 1.25 times, and 8-way associative cache will show a worse result of 1.125 times. Thus, a high associative number has advantages *and* drawbacks. The maximum attainable size of the cached data is equal (in kilobytes) to the following formula:

$$CACHE.SIZE + \frac{CACHE.SIZE}{WAY}$$

Note

This rule has exceptions. (See *Influence of the Size of Processed Data on Performance*.)

Return to Fig. 3.19. Cache saturation occurs when a 48 KB data block is processed (i.e., when the size of cache memory is exceeded by 16 KB). This coincides with the size of one cache bank (i.e., it is within the measurement's margin of error): 2-way associative cache of the K6 processor contains two 16 KB banks.

Consider another example (Fig. 3.20). Here, 4-way associative cache of the Celeron 300A processor reaches saturation at 20 KB. This corresponds to the previous formula

$$16 + \frac{16}{4} = 16 + 4 = 20$$

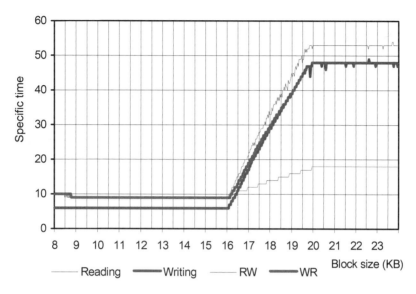

Fig. 3.20. Dependence of the processing time on the block size (Celeron 300A)

In L2 Cache

For each 32-bit cell, loading data from L2 cache takes approximately the following processor clocks:

$$\frac{F.CPU}{F.L2.CACHE \times \frac{N.BUS}{32}}$$

Here, *F.L2.CACHE* is the operating frequency of L2 cache, *F.CPU* is the core frequency, and *N.BUS* is the width of the local cache bus. This formula doesn't account for factors such as cache controller latency and BIU latency; these are negligible during pipelined data processing.

Thus, on an AMD Athlon processor, a data block that exceeds the L1 cache size but fits within L2 cache would be read approximately 2.5 times slower (Fig 3.21). The actual performance gap will be smaller (especially when processing loops that were not unrolled) because the processor can execute other commands while it loads data from L2 cache. This parallelism partially compensates for the drop in operation speed. Data are loaded from L2 cache approximately 1.5 times slower than from L1 cache.

The situation is quite different for data write operations. If the lines loaded into cache memory were not modified, the cache controller simply replaces them with new lines. If they were modified, it is forced to unload them into the cached memory, which approximately doubles the cell access time. Nevertheless, this delay can be reduced — for example, by introducing a special buffer between L1 cache and the BIU.

The K6 processor, however, has no such buffer; therefore, the time (in processor clocks) required to write data into L2 cache can be calculated as follows:

$$2 \times \frac{F.CPU}{F.L2.CACHE \times \frac{N\_BUS}{32}}.$$

Exceeding the Limits of L2 Cache

According to the general argumentation on the nature of cache, the way in which the operating speed changes as the processed block grows is used to determine the cache size. Immediately noticeable in the speed curve of the data write is a sharp, stepwise rise around the 128 KB mark.

The read curve changes synchronously with the write curve; although this step is less pronounced, it still appears. Does this mean that the L2 cache size equals 128 KB? That assumption doesn't correspond to the BIOS (Basic Input/Output System) assessment. (BIOS evaluates the L2 cache size as 512 KB, four times 128 KB.) Were you duped? Or is cache misbehaving?

You may think that cache could comprise several SRAM chips with different access times. However, do not rush to return the motherboard to the vendor! It is in working condition, and it fully corresponds to the declared parameters and characteristics. The described result is obtained because the cells of the cached memory can correspond to strictly defined cache lines, rather than any given line. The processed block ignores the free space in cache as it grows in size, and it starts to claim cache lines occupied by other data objects or even by code, the stack, or intensely used variables (although in this example, the main loop fits within L1 cache).

The sample program used in Listing 3.1 (see the DoCPU.h file on the companion CD-ROM) intensely uses the stack. It calls the DoCPU_A1 and DoCPU_A2 functions to measure the time intervals of loop execution and saves the result in the local variable DoCPU_buff. About 6 KB is required for the printf function, and more space is needed to accommodate the input/output of the operating system and switching between tasks. If the size of the processed block exceeds the size of L1 cache memory, then contents of the stack, along with local variables, inevitably will be moved into L2 cache. In this program, the stack, local variables, and processed data are mapped to the same cache lines, and are replaced constantly.

Thus, it is not sufficient to fit within L2 cache! In addition, free space must be distributed efficiently between the processed data, stack, and code. This is one of the most difficult optimization problems, and it does not have a general solution. Without analyzing the code of the operating system and all running applications, it is impossible to determine the intensity with which specific cache lines are used; consequently, it is impossible to plan an optimal strategy of data placement. *The effective size of*

L2 cache coincides with its physical size only in rare situations. The lower the cache associative number, the higher the probability of conflicts.

To determine the change to the processing speed when the L2 cache size is exceeded, use the formula for the change that takes place when the L1 cache size is exceeded. This means that from *L2.CACHE.SIZE* to *L2.CACHE.SIZE + L2.CACHE.SIZE × WAY*, the read line rises in proportion with the following formula:

$$\frac{F.L2.CACHE \times N.CACHE.BUS}{F.MEM \times N.MEM.BUS}$$

Here, *F.L2.CACHE* is the cache operating frequency, *F.MEM* is the memory operating frequency, *N.CACHE.BUS* is the width of the L2 cache bus, and *N.MEM.BUS* is the width of the memory bus.

From this formula, it is clear that *processors whose L2 cache is not integrated rarely react to its overflow.* However, cache located at the motherboard operates at the system bus frequency according to the timing 2-1-1-1. This is comparable to the operating speed of synchronous dynamic memory, which operates at the same frequency with a timing of 3-1-1-1, or even 2-1-1-1.

Processors equipped with on-die L2 cache behave differently. The operating frequency of integrated cache (even if it is not implemented on-die, but is mounted on a separate cartridge) is at least two to four times higher than the system bus frequency. Another important factor is the cache controller has significantly lower latency than the memory controller. Because of this, newer processors of the x86 family are oversensitive to the exceeding the limits of L2 cache; they react to this situation by decreasing performance by a factor of approximately three.

Features of the Cache Subsystem in AMD Athlon

In general, AMD Athlon behaves similarly to its predecessor, AMD-K6; nevertheless, the internal architecture of its cache subsystem has undergone significant changes. For the first time in the history of the x86 family of processors, AMD developers have implemented exclusive L2 cache, whose effective size has been declared equal to the sum of the cache memory of both levels (in this case, 64 + 256 = 320 KB). Trust is a good thing! However, you should check this fact yourself (Fig. 3.21).

Where are the promised 320 KB? The step near the 257 KB mark is caused by the conflict between the stack and the processed data. However, the total performance degradation starts around 273 KB, significantly less than expected value, as declared by the developers!

Between 273 KB and 320 KB, the growth of access time is not linear. Rather, access time grows according to the formula *1/x*, which means the exclusive architecture alleviates the performance drop when exceeding the size limit of L2 cache. The effective size of L2 cache proved to be larger than its physical size. L2 cache of the same size on PIII reaches saturation at 194 KB (Fig. 3.22).

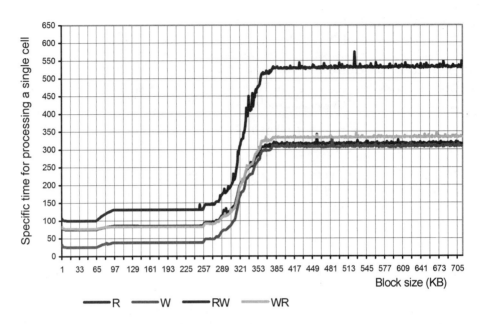

Fig. 3.21. Dependence of the processing time on the block size (AMD Athlon)

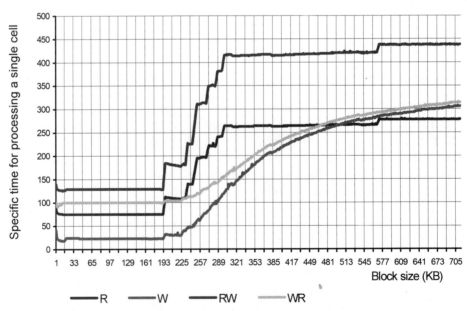

Fig. 3.22. Dependence of the processing time on the block size (PIII)

Features of the Cache Subsystem in Pentium II and Pentium III

Despite their inclusive architecture, which is far from advanced, the cache subsystems of the Intel Pentium II and, especially, Pentium III processors have much higher performance than AMD Athlon. Thanks to its 256-bit bus, PIII can load a 32-byte data packet from L2 cache within one clock. Compare this parameter to the same characteristic of Athlon (nine clocks, because, with a 64-bit bus and a cache-line length of 64 bytes, L2 cache operates according to the following timing: 2-1-1-1-1-1-1-1). Consider Fig. 3.21, where the read curve remains ideally horizontal and has no step between the marks equal to the sizes of L1 and L2 cache. *The effective size of L1 cache of the PIII processor is equal to the L2 cache size, which makes it 256 KB.* The situation with memory write is somewhat worse, and performance drops outside the boundaries of L1 cache. However, this drop is so small that it can be ignored.

Another interesting aspect: When the write curve goes outside the limits of L2 cache on PII and PIII processors, it becomes nonlinear. Instead of the stepwise performance drop that occurs on K6 and Athlon, the write performance for PII and PIII decreases slowly and reaches saturation at 1 MB. (This value is almost four times the size of L2 cache.) What is the cost of this gain? Unfortunately, official documentation doesn't provide a direct answer to this question. Many third-party manuals don't answer it either; they bypass detailed discussion of this topic and use references such as "specific features of buffering." I will try to explain these features here.

When Intel processors write memory cells, their corresponding cache lines are loaded into L2 cache as exclusive. Other processors (particularly, Athlon and K6) mark these lines as modified.

What happens when a cell missing from L1 cache is written to the memory? If there are no free write buffers available (such as when memory writes are intense), the processor has to load the modified cell into L1 cache. It sends the request to L2 cache, which reads a 32-byte data block into one of its lines, assigns it the `exclusive` attribute, and passes its copy to L1 cache. This action is repeated until the size of the processed data block exceeds the L1 cache size. After that, the processor has to remove the least needed line to free space for the new one. Because all cache lines are modified, the processor chooses the oldest one and transfers it to L2 cache. However, L2 cache already contains its copy; therefore, it simply refreshes the contents of appropriate line and changes its attribute from exclusive to modified.

What happens when L2 cache is filled, and the processor attempts to write another cell? L1 cache simultaneously sends two requests to L2 cache: Load a new data block, and refresh the contents of the preempted cache line. This task is difficult for L2 cache because it has no free space. L2 cache tries to discard the least needed information — the exclusive lines. These discarded lines don't need to be moved into the main memory; therefore, this is the "cheapest" option. Moreover, while L2 cache loads the new portion of data from RAM, the line moved from L1 cache resides in a special buffer.

Later, it is written into the main memory, bypassing L2 cache. With this approach, each newly loaded portion of data receives the exclusive attribute, which automatically makes it a primary candidate for preemption. This means that *when you go beyond the limits of L2 cache, the written data will always replace the same cache line, leaving previously written lines intact.* This is a distinguishing feature of PII and PIII processors. It also is their main advantage over K6 and Athlon. In those AMD processors, if a data block is processed that doesn't fit within the limits of L2 cache, *all* its lines are replaced sequentially.

Suppose that the size of data to be written is twice the size of L2 cache. In this situation, the cache memory of K6 and Athlon will be almost thrashing. On PII and PIII, only half of all access operations will result in cache misses; the remainder will be preserved in cache. (To tell the truth, this is not quite right. The limited associative number of cache causes the whole bank, not a single line, to be reloaded constantly.)

Under these conditions, when the size of the processed block exceeds the boundaries of L2 cache, the line's behavior becomes clear. Preserving some part of the cached memory delays saturation, smoothing the sharp angles of the write line. Furthermore, saturation is never reached because the stored lines increase the performance of any block size. Separately, as the following relationship increases, the efficiency of this strategy goes to zero:

$$\frac{BLOCK.SIZE}{L2.CACHE.SIZE}$$

When the size of the processed block is more than four times the cache size, it can be disregarded.

Write before read, and read before write. The operation of writing before reading a cell is executed as quickly as a single write operation. This isn't surprising; when a L1 cache miss occurs, the data are stored in a temporary buffer from which they always can be retrieved within the write clock. Reading before writing is another matter: When a miss occurs, it is necessary to wait until the data are read from L2 cache. As a result, each operation takes at least four additional clocks.

Influence of the Size of Executable Code on Performance

Generally, the code cache is organized the same way as the data cache. Actually, the code cache is simpler because machine commands, in contrast to data commands, don't require the support of write operations. (A modification of executable code directly refreshes the cached memory and reloads the corresponding line of the code cache. Thus, to avoid a performance drop, it is imperative to avoid using self-modifying code in deeply nested loops.)

Without diving into details, it is possible to say that the influence of the size of executable code on performance is regulated by the same rules that exist for the size of the read (but not modified) data block.

Trace how the execution speed of the block of code changes as its size increases. This task is not a trivial one! In contrast to data processing, you cannot change the size of the executable block as desired without using self-modifying code. Nevertheless, this problem has an elegant solution. It is sufficient to stop using high-level programming languages and turn to the Macro-assembler, whose advanced preprocessor will enable you to generate blocks of executable code of any size.

To prevent possible side effects, formulate each block of code as a separate program, and use a batch file to avoid specifying translation parameters manually.

As a result, you will obtain the following:

Listing 3.2. [Cache/ code.cache.size.xm] Assembly Program That Generates an Arbitrary Number of NOP Machine Operations

```
; CODE_SIZE EQU    ?   ; // The CODE_SIZE macro is generated automatically
                       ; // by the batch file.
; /*----------------------------------------------------------------
; *
; *       MACRO THAT GENERATES N NOP MACHINE COMMANDS
; *
; *              (The NOP mnemonics means "no operation"
; *               and takes 1 byte; that is, N NOP commands
; *               produce N bytes of executable code)
; *
; ---------------------------------------------------------------*/
NOPING MACRO N        ; // MACRO START //
 _N = N         ; _N := N (gets the argument passed to the macro)
 _A = 0         ; _A (the loop counter)

WHILE _A NE _N        ; while( _A <= _N){
    NOP    ; Inserts NOP into the source code
    _A = _A + 1   ; _A++;
 ENDM         ; }
 ENDM              ; // MACRO END //


; /*----------------------------------------------------------------
; *
; *   CALLING THE MACRO THAT CREATES THE CODE_SIZE KB BLOCK OF NOP COMMANDS
; *
; ---------------------------------------------------------------*/
NOPING CODE_SIZE*1024
```

Listing 3.3. [Cache/code.cache.size.c] Consequences of Exceeding the Limits of L1 (L2) Cache

```
#include "code.cache.size.h"    ; This file is created by
                                 ; the batch translator.
                                 ; If contains the CODE_SIZE definition.
#include <DoCPU.h>

main()
{
int a;
A_BEGIN(1);                      ; The measurement of execution time is started.
   DoCPU(&a);                    ; The block of CODE_SIZE NOP commands
                                 ; are executed.
   A_END(1);                     ; The measurement of execution time is stopped.

// The measurement results are displayed.
printf("%03d\t %d\n", CODE_SIZE, Ax_GET(1));
}
```

Listing 3.4. [Cache/code.cache.size.make.bat] Batch File That Translates the Test Program

```
@ECHO OFF
IF #%1#==#MAKE_FOR# GOTO make_it


REM MAKE ALL
ECHO = = = ASSEMBLING THE EXAMPLE DEFINING THE CODE-CACHE SIZE = = =
ECHO Utility for the book \"Code Optimization: Effective Memory Usage"
ECHO @ECHO OFF                               > CODE.CACHE.SIZE.RUN.BAT
ECHO ECHO = = demonstrating the definition of the cache size = =    >>_
CODE.CACHE.SIZE.RUN.BAT
ECHO ECHO Utility for \"Code Optimization: Effective Memory Usage" >>_
CODE.CACHE.SIZE.RUN.BAT
ECHO ECHO N NOP     ...CLOCK...                >> CODE.CACHE.SIZE.RUN.BAT
ECHO ECHO ------------------------------------- >> CODE.CACHE.SIZE.RUN.BAT


FOR %%A IN (2,4,8,16,32,64,128,256,512,1024,2048) DO CALL  %0 MAKE_FOR %%A
ECHO DEL %%0                                  >> CODE.CACHE.SIZE.RUN.BAT
```

```
GOTO end

:make_it
ECHO /%0/%1/%2 *
SHIFT
ECHO CODE_SIZE EQU %1                    >  CODE.CACHE.SIZE.MOD
ECHO #define CODE_SIZE %1                 >  CODE.CACHE.SIZE.H
TYPE CODE.CACHE.SIZE.XM                   >> CODE.CACHE.SIZE.MOD
CALL CLOCK.MAKE.BAT   CODE.CACHE.SIZE.C > NUL
DEL  CODE.CACHE.SIZE.MOD
DEL  CODE.CACHE.SIZE.H
IF   NOT EXIST CODE.CACHE.SIZE.EXE  GOTO err
IF   EXIST CODE.CACHE.SIZE.%1.EXE   DEL CODE.CACHE.SIZE.%1.EXE
REN  CODE.CACHE.SIZE.EXE CODE.CACHE.SIZE.%1.EXE
ECHO CODE.CACHE.SIZE.%1.EXE               >> CODE.CACHE.SIZE.RUN.BAT
ECHO DEL CODE.CACHE.SIZE.%1.EXE           >> CODE.CACHE.SIZE.RUN.BAT
GOTO end

:err
ECHO -ERR compilation error! For more details see  CODE.CACHE.SIZE.ERR
TYPE CODE.CACHE.SIZE.ERR
EXIT
:end
```

Exceeding the Size of L1 Cache

The test of the resulting program shows that exceeding the limits of the L1 code cache degrades performance more significantly than exceeding limits during data processing. This happens because the multistage pipelines of contemporary processors are over-sensitive to even short interruptions in the timing of the data flow.

In particular, on AMD Athlon 1050, the code command-execution time increases at least 200% when the cache limits are exceeded. (Recall that data-access time in a similar situation increases only 10%, as shown in Fig. 3.23.)

A wide bus on Pentium III limits the performance drop. It still consumes 25% of the processor time. Nevertheless, the size of the code cache is 32 KB, in contrast to 64 KB on AMD Athlon. Now, decide which processor is preferred.

Exceeding the Size of L2 Cache

Remember that L2 cache stores both code and data. As previously shown in this chapter, the effective size of L2 cache doesn't always coincide with the physical size, because both executable code and processed data can claim the same cache lines. As a result, performance will start to drop long before the sum of the sizes of frequently executed code and intensely accessed data exceeds the size of L2 cache.

At this point, the performance drop will be staggering — about thirty times on Athlon, and about six times on PIII. Even the fastest processor would be unable to withstand this! However, executable code rarely exceeds the limits of L2 cache. Even if this happens, the code almost always can be split into several smaller loops processed sequentially.

Thus, *when developing a program, try to design it so that all frequently executed loops fit within L1 or at least L2 cache.*

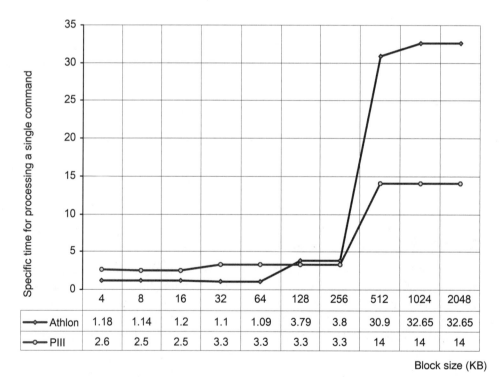

	4	8	16	32	64	128	256	512	1024	2048
Athlon	1.18	1.14	1.2	1.1	1.09	3.79	3.8	30.9	32.65	32.65
PIII	2.6	2.5	2.5	3.3	3.3	3.3	3.3	14	14	14

Block size (KB)

Fig. 3.23. Change of the command-execution time, depending on the size of the executable code

Data Alignment Efficiency

In the preceding chapter, I covered the problem of data alignment and large data blocks that greatly exceed the size of cache memory. Here, I will consider the efficiency of aligning data that fit within L1 (or L2) cache memory. As you'll soon notice, these are quite different things!

One common fallacy states that it always takes more time to access unaligned data than to access aligned data. Although this was true for Pentium with MMX technology and earlier models, this is not applicable to contemporary processors based on the P6 core. For example, starting from an address such as 0x40001, a double word can be read on contemporary processors without any penalty, because such a double word will not cross the cache line. The distance from the end of the cell being read to the beginning of the next cache line is 27 bytes, as shown by the following formula: $SET.ADDRESS + CACHE.LINE.SIZE - sizeof(cell) - ADDRESS = ((0x40000 + 0x20) - 4 - 0x40001) = 27$. Consequently, the requested data fit within a single cache line, and they do not need to be aligned.

This alignment strategy will not work on early models of Pentium or on Pentium with MMX technology. However, the number of early models in operation is decreasing practically every day. Because of this, the following information relates only to processors based on K5, P6, or newer cores.

Processing Line-Split Data

Processors of the P6 family perform the data-read operation in one clock when the data block being read has a size of 1 byte, word, or double word and fits within a single line of L1 cache. If the data block crosses the boundary of the 32-, 64-, or 128-byte cache line, its trailing portion goes to the next cache line (Fig. 3.24). In this case, the data-read operation will take 6 to 12 clocks. Such data blocks are known as *line-split* data.

This happens because the processor is unable to read two cache lines simultaneously during one clock cycle. Although cache memory is two-port and supports parallel processing of two cache lines, the *Load Unit* can load only one cell per clock. The complete load time takes at least three clocks. However, under favorable conditions, the pipeline passes one cell per clock, eliminating the three-clock latency.

When line-split data block the pipeline, trailing cells are processed after the header part. Hence, the minimum loading time (in clocks) for line-split data is as follows: $2 \times Load.Unit.Latency = 2 \times 3 = 6$. In addition, when processing line-split data, the cache controller is forced to perform additional calculations to evaluate how the two parts must be joined in the block. This adds to the overhead.

Athlon handles line-split data better; it usually loses only one clock per read operation, and it sometimes manages to accomplish such an operation without any losses. Although the latter statement conflicts with official documentation, it has been confirmed by experiments. Athlon has two queues that handle requests to load data from L1 cache; therefore, it can read both cache lines simultaneously. When writing line-split data, Athlon shows results significantly worse that its reading results because it only has one write queue. Nevertheless, the efficient and expertly designed write buffering mechanism limits delays; they are approximately 1.5 times smaller than on PII or PIII.

On both AMD and Pentium processors, a write operation of line-split data blocks the *store forwarding* capabilities, which often results in an alarming performance drop. (See *Write Buffering Specifics*.)

! *Attention*

Some machine instructions (MOVAPS, in particular) require alignment of all their operands. Any attempt to pass unaligned data (regardless of whether or not they pass the cache-line boundary) causes an exception to be thrown. Any requirement for aligned operands should be mentioned in the description of the machine instruction. As an example, consider a description of the MOVAPS instruction: "When the source or destination operand is a memory operand, the operand must be aligned on a 16-byte boundary, or a general-protection exception (#GP) is generated."

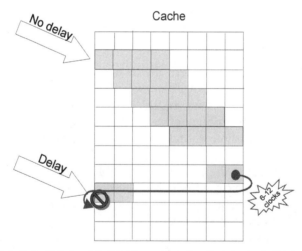

Fig. 3.24. If the data to be read start in one cache line and continue in another line, such data are processed with a delay

Natural Data Alignment

Data whose size is 1 byte never cross the cache-line boundary; therefore, they don't need to be aligned. Data of the 1-word size that start from *even addresses* also fit within one cache line. Finally, double words that start from addresses *divisible by four* never cross the boundaries of cache lines (Fig. 3.25).

Summarizing this information produces Table 3.4.

Table 3.4. Preferred Alignment for Various Data Bytes

Data size	Alignment		
	PPlain, PMMX	PPro, PII, PIII	Athlon
1 byte	Arbitrary	Arbitrary	Arbitrary
2 bytes	Multiple of 2 bytes	Multiple of 2 bytes	Multiple of 2 bytes
4 bytes	Multiple of 4 bytes	Multiple of 4 bytes	Multiple of 4 bytes
6 bytes	Multiple of 4 bytes	Multiple of 8 bytes	Multiple of 8 bytes
8 bytes (1 word)	Multiple of 8 bytes	Multiple of 8 bytes	Multiple of 8 bytes
10 bytes	Multiple of 16 bytes	Multiple of 16 bytes	Multiple of 16 bytes
16 bytes (1 double word)	Multiple of 16 bytes	Multiple of 16 bytes	Multiple of 16 bytes

Natural data alignment is also known as *overcautious alignment* because it is based on the worst-case assumption (that the data to be aligned cross both cache lines) without taking into account the real situation.

Overcautious alignment increases the amount of memory required for the application to run, which can decrease performance considerably.

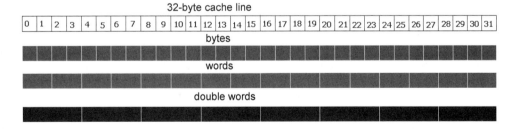

Fig. 3.25. Natural data alignment

How Compilers Align Data

Most compilers handle all aspects of data alignment; the application programmer doesn't need to think about such problems. However, the strategies used by compilers are not always efficient. Thus, some situations require you to use your little gray cells!

An alignment strategy depends on the variable type: Both the Microsoft Visual C++ and Borland C++ compilers align *static* and *global* variables according to their sizes. They ignore the alignment repetition factor, specified by the `pack` pragma or the appropriate command-line option of the compiler.

In addition, these compilers (and most others) don't care about optimal organization of variables. Instead, they place variables into the memory using the order in which they were declared in the program. What are the results of this approach? Consider the following example:

```
// ...
static int a;
static char b;
static int c;
static char d;
// ...
```

The compiler aligns the `c` variable by the address that is a multiple of four, and leaves out 3 bytes that follow the `b` variable, creating an unoccupied "hole." This hole is almost useless, but it still increases the amount of consumed memory.

Now, consider what would happen if the variables were declared as follows:

```
// ...
static int a;
static int c;
static char b;
static char d;
// ...
```

In this case, the compiler would place the variables one against another, without leaving any holes. Add this trick to your arsenal; you will use it! (However, bear in mind that a loop such as `for(;;) b = d` will run inefficiently because the `b` and `d` variables will be placed in the same bank, which makes synchronous processing of these variables impossible. See *Data Distribution over Cache Banks* for more details.)

Automatic variables. Also known as local variables, these are aligned by addresses that are multiples of four, regardless of their size. Most compilers adopt this policy because machine commands that push and pop data to and from the stack only operate with one data type — 4-byte double words. Consequently, `char` variables in stack take the same space as `int`. It is impossible to eliminate the holes, even if you regroup variable declarations in the program.

Local arrays also are extended to sizes that are multiples of four. Thus, `char a[11]` and `char b[12]` take the same space in the memory. (This statement is not true for `int` arrays because the size of each array element equals 4 bytes; therefore, the array size will always be a multiple of four.)

Another subtlety is found in each local variable: It is given an address in relation to the top of the stack. Therefore, its exact address is unknown at compile time. This address will be determined much later: at run time. This address depends on the operating system, the requirements for stack usage of all previously called functions, and many other factors. How can alignment be accomplished in this situation?

The Borland C++ compiler simply takes the four least significant bits of the register pointer to the top of the stack and resets them to zero, pointing to the stack top and rounding to the address divisible by 16.

The Microsoft Visual C++ compiler forcibly rounds the sizes of all local variables to multiples of four. The initial value of the stack pointer also must be a multiple of four. (This is ensured by the operating system.) This means the value of the stack pointer at any point in the program will be a multiple of four. Therefore, it doesn't require additional alignment.

Dynamic variables. Such variables are placed in the *heap*, a memory region allocated by a special function similar to `malloc`. The alignment factor (if it exists) is function-specific. For example, `malloc` aligns memory regions by addresses divisible by 16.

Structures. By default, each element of a structure is aligned by the value that equals its size (i.e., `char` isn't aligned, `short int` is aligned by even addresses, `int` and `float` are aligned by addresses that are multiples of four, and `double c __int64` is aligned by addresses that are multiples of eight). As previously mentioned, this is not the best strategy. This alignment is intolerable for structures that work with network protocols, hardware, or typified files. How can you prevent the compiler from basing the alignment of a structure on the size of its element? Unfortunately, there is no universal solution. Alignment management has no standards; therefore, it can be different for each compiler.

Microsoft Visual C++ and Borland C++ support the `pack` pragma, which can be used to specify any alignment level. For example, `#pragma pack(1)` forces the compiler to align the elements of all subsequent structures by addresses that are multiples of one (i.e., it disables alignment). Command-line options, such as `/Zn?` (Microsoft Visual C++) and `-a?` (Borland C++), play a similar role. (The `?` character is the alignment factor.)

However, it would be unwise to abandon structure alignment. If the internal representation of the structure is not important, aligning its members can increase the speed of the program considerably. Fortunately, the effect of the `pack` pragma is local, in contrast to the command-line options that correspond to it. This means that the `pack` pragma can be encountered multiple times with different arguments in the code of a program. Furthermore, the `pack` pragma can save the previous packing value, then restore it (using `pack(push)` to save and `pack(pop)` to restore the alignment factor from the internal stack of the compiler). The calls to `push/pop` can be nested.

The following example illustrates the usage of the `pack` pragma:

```
#pragma pack(push)
#pragma pack(1)
struct IP_HEADER{
// ...
}
#pragma pack(pop)
```

If you don't plan to use the program on processors prior to PII, it is sufficient to align the starting address of the structure by the address that represents a multiple of 32. If the structure size doesn't exceed 32 bytes, you needn't worry about aligning each structure member.

Optimal Alignment

Normally, a program only accesses the line-split data occasionally, and the overhead can be ignored. Significant gain won't result from the alignment of such variables.

Frequently used variables. Loop counters and other frequently used variables are another matter. If these variables are not aligned, the performance loss probably will be significant. Therefore, it is inadvisable to let the things run their course. To illustrate this, run Listing 3.5, which uses a 32-bit variable as the loop counter. This variable is offset 62 bytes from the starting position, which guarantees that it will be line-split on Intel Pentium II and Pentium III, and on AMD Athlon.

Listing 3.5. [Cache/align.for.c] Consequences of Using a Line-Split Loop Counter

---

```
#define N_ITER1000                   // Number of loop iterations
#define _MAX_CACHE_LINE_SIZE   64 // Maximum possible number of cache lines

#define UN_FOX(*(int*)((int)fox + _MAX_CACHE_LINE_SIZE - sizeof(int)/2))
#define FOX    (*fox)                 // Defining aligned (FOX) and
                                      // unaligned (UN_FOX) counters
fox = (int *) _malloc32(MAX_CACHE_LINE_SIZE*2); // Allocating memory


/*-----------------------------------------------------------------------
 *
 *          OPTIMIZED VERSION
 *     (Loop counter doesn't split the cache line)
 *
 -----------------------------------------------------------------------*/
```

```
for(FOX = 0; FOX < N_ITER; FOX+=1) c++;

/*-----------------------------------------------------------------
 *
 *        PESSIMIZED VERSION
 *     (Loop counter splits the cache line)
 *
---------------------------------------------------------------*/
for(UN_FOX = 0; UN_FOX < N_ITER; UN_FOX+=1) c++;
```

The test run of this program on Pentium III 733 shows that the line-split loop counter decreases the performance almost 500% (Fig. 3.26). On AMD Athlon, the performance drops about 200%, confirming the assumption that Athlon is insensitive to alignment. If Athlon were the dominating processor, alignment would be unnecessary. (Of course, I'm joking.)

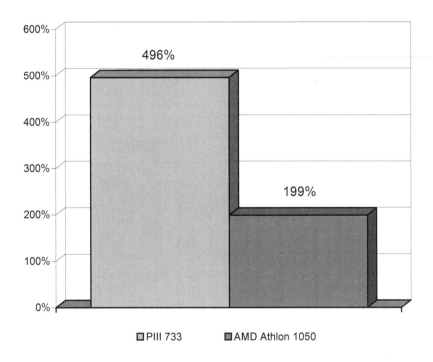

Fig. 3.26. Performance drop when processing line-split data

Array processing. The situation is different with the sequential processing of data arrays. This topic already was covered in this book. However, that discussion focused on interaction with the main memory, and the time required to load a cell from the main memory greatly exceeds the delay caused by a cache-line conflict. For this reason, it doesn't make sense to align streaming data.

However, if the data fits within L1 or L2 cache, the negative effect of cache conflicts becomes significant (for loops that were not unrolled). A slightly modified version of the Memory.align.c program can be used to study this problem in more detail. Decrease the block size to between 8 KB and 16 KB, then start the program.

On the rolled read loop (Fig. 3.27), PIII showed a performance drop of 7%. This is the expected result. During the cache-line conflict, the processor isn't idle; rather, it is processing commands that make up the loop body. Thus, the delay is almost masked.

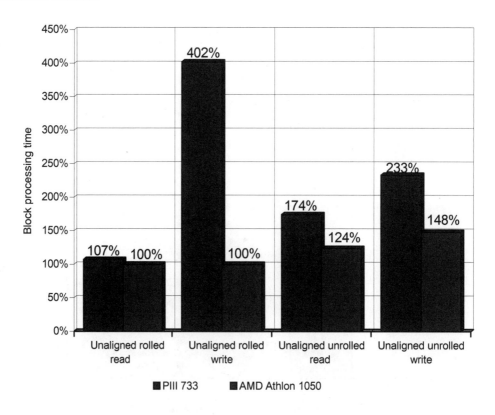

Fig. 3.27. Influence of data alignment on performance
(aligned data processing is taken for 100%)

On the unrolled write loop, the program slowed more than 300%! What has caused this result? The Microsoft Visual C++ compiler replaced the rolled write loop with a single machine command: `REP STOSD`. This minimized the overhead produced by organizing the loop. Furthermore, because the length of the write buffers equals the length of the cache line, matching the write starting address with the starting address of the cache line ensures efficient address translation. This allows the processor to unload the entire 32-byte buffer within one clock.

In comparison, the rolled results shown by Athlon look rather impressive. After Athlon unrolls the loop, the program begins to degrade: The unaligned version is slower by 24% at data read, and by 48% at data write. However, PIII is weaker, slowing by 74% and 133%, respectively.

Data Distribution over Cache Banks

Data alignment is related to a problem overlooked by the authors of manuals on optimizing for Pentium and AMD processors: data distribution over cache banks. Therefore, this aspect is practically unknown to the programming community.

Intel Architecture Optimization Manual for Pentium MMX–Pentium II contains the following scant information: "The data cache consists of eight banks interleaved on four-byte boundaries. On Pentium processors with MMX technology, the data cache can be accessed simultaneously from both pipes, as long as the references are to different cache banks. On the P6 family of processors, the data cache can be accessed simultaneously by a load instruction and a store instruction, as long as the references are to different cache banks... If both instructions access the same data-cache memory bank, then the second request (V-pipe) must wait for the first request to complete. A bank conflict occurs when bits 2 through 4 are the same in the two physical addresses. A bank conflict incurs a one clock penalty on the V-pipe instruction."

The second part of this quotation has disappeared from the manual on optimization for Pentium III. The *Intel Pentium 4 Processor Optimization Reference Manual* doesn't say a word about cache banks. The *AMD Athlon Processor x86 Code Optimization Guide* gives just two sentences on this topic: "The data cache and instruction cache are both 2-way set associative and 64-Kbytes in size. It is divided into 8 banks where each bank is 8 bytes wide." The latter phrase is understandable only by individuals who have sound knowledge of the layered memory architecture, a general idea of how cache works, and an idea of how cache is implemented at the hardware level. There is also an annoying confusion in terminology: There are at least two types of cache banks.

Associative cache is divided into independent areas known as banks. The number of banks defines the way of association. At the physical level, these banks comprise several arrays of static memory, which are also designated by the term "banks." Memory layering was covered in detail in *RAM Design and Working Principles*.

The explanations provided there should help you determine which bank is referred to in the manuals. Nevertheless, if you are just beginning to study computer science, you may have a tough time.

Sometimes, AMD can be distinguished by the high quality of its documentation. One example is the excellent *AMD-K5 Processor Technical Reference Manual*, which I often read before going to sleep. It's more than a manual on an outdated and obsolete processor; it presents a definitive and comprehensive description of the architecture, which has yet to be updated by anything revolutionary. Even the new Hammer processor is based on the same principles and a similar core.

In particular, organization, goals, and working principles of cache banks are explained as follows: "The data cache overcomes load/store bottlenecks by supporting simultaneous accesses to two lines in a single clock, if the lines are in separate banks. Each of the four cache banks contains eight bytes, or one-fourth of a 32-byte cache line. They are interleaved on a four-byte boundary. One instruction can be accessing bank 0 (bytes 0–3 and 16–19), while another instruction is accessing bank 1, 2, or 3 (bytes 4–7 and 20–23, 8–11 and 24–27, and 12–15 and 28–31, respectively)."

Now things should be clearer. Only one question remains: What is the purpose of these complications? The answer is simple: The implementation of a two-port static memory array is expensive because it requires eight CMOS transistors, not six. Therefore, the designers have split static memory into several independent banks and connected a dual-port interface to it. On 64 KB cache, it is possible to save about a million transistors. Sometimes, however, this savings is costly elsewhere; a two-port memory core can process any two requests simultaneously, but cache with a two-port interface can process only requests directed to different banks in parallel.

Thus, to achieve the highest data-processing speed, you must observe a set of rules and plan a data flow that avoids delays caused by coupled requests to the same cache banks.

The cache line is not an isotropic entity; rather, it comprises four or eight independent banks with a size of 32 bits, 64 bits, or 128 bits (Fig. 3.28). Their independence allows parallel read/write operations to occur in each bank within one clock. The level of parallelism depends on the number of functional devices connected to executive pipelines of the microprocessor and the number of ports of cache. In particular, PII microprocessors can execute one write and one read operation of two different banks per clock.

If two 32-bit variables are in separate banks, then the value of one variable can be assigned to another variable within one clock. Conversely, if variables cross the boundaries of banks (Fig. 3.29), a delay occurs; the processor can't write into the banks processing the read request. The value of this delay can vary with the processor model. (On PII, it is five clocks.)

Returning to the optimal strategy of data alignment, *it is best to place all data (including 1-byte variables) by addresses that are multiples of four*, which allows parallel processing. If you observe this requirement, each variable will have exclusive access to its corresponding bank. In addition to the alignment, you'll need to make sure that cells processed in parallel have unequal bits responsible for the data offset in cache lines. If the bits are equal, even cells located in different cache lines inevitably hit the same SRAM array.

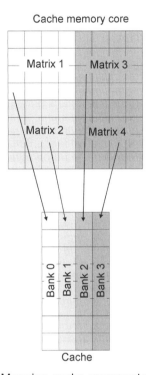

Fig. 3.28. Mapping cache memory to cache lines

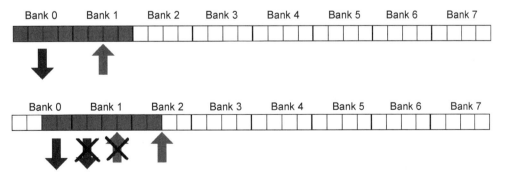

Fig. 3.29. Cells located in different cache banks (i.e., in different static memory arrays) are read or written in one clock. If they were not, each variable would be processed sequentially, which would require twice as many clocks

Note

This limitation is not applicable to a read operation that directly follows a write operation. In such a situation, the data being written are directed to the write buffer. Cache memory is accessed only once, and even this happens only when the data to be read are missing from the buffer. (See *Cache Organization*.)

Note that such alignment loosens the data packing and requires a large amount of memory. As a result, the data may not fit into L1 cache or even into L2 cache. Instead of the expected increase of the operation speed, you risk neutralizing the gain obtained by parallel processing!

How important are the consequences of cache-bank conflicts? To clear up this question, write a test program under the following circumstances:

❒ On PIII, cache-bank conflicts only decrease performance when read operations are combined with write operations. (PIII has one read unit; it is impossible to load two cells per clock even when they reside in different banks.)

❒ At least four iterations of the memory-processing loop must be unrolled; otherwise, write buffering will wait during delays caused by cache-bank conflicts. It will not unload data until a "better time," and a single write instruction will have nothing to couple with.

Listing 3.6. [Cache/banks.c] Consequences of Cache-Bank Conflicts

```
//============================================================================
//            NO CONFLICTS
//----------------------------------------------------------------------------
// Distribution of variables over cache banks on PIII
// =================================================
// !<bank0>!<bank1>!<bank2>!<bank3>!<bank4>!<bank5>!<bank6>!<bank7>!
// !0 1 2 3!4 5 6 7!8 9 0 1!2 3 4 5!6 7 8 9!0 1 2 3!4 5 6 7!8 9 0 1!<- offset
// !-!-!-!-!-!-!-!-!-!-!-!-!-!-!-!-!-!-!-!-!-!-!-!-!-!-!-!-!-!-!-!-!
// !*-*-*-*!       !       !       !       ! <<-- ((int)_p32+a+0);
// !       !*-*-*-*!       !       !       ! <<-- ((int)_p32+a+4);
// !       !       !       !*-*-*-*!       ! <<-- ((int)_p32+a+12);
// !       !       !       !       !*-*-*-*! <<-- ((int)_p32+a+16);
//============================================================================
//
```

```
// Distribution of variables over cache banks on Athlon
// ======================================================
// !<--  bank 0 -->!<--  bank 1 -->!<--  bank 2 -->!<--  bank 3 -->!...
// !0 1 2 3 4 5 6 7 8 9 0 1 2 3 4 5 6 7 8 9 0 1 2 3 4 5 6 7 8 9 0 1 ...
// !-!-!-!-!-!-!-!-!-!-!-!-!-!-!-!-!-!-!-!-!-!-!-!-!-!-!-!-!-!-!-!-!...
// !*-*-*-*         !               !               ! <<-- ((int)_p32+a+2);
// !       *-*-*-*! !               !               ! <<-- ((int)_p32+a+6);
// !               !       *-*-*-*! !               ! <<-- ((int)_p32+a+12);
// !               !               !*-*-*-*         ! <<-- ((int)_p32+a+16);
//=============================================================================
optimize(int *_p32)
{
 int a;
 int _tmp32 = 0;

 for(a = 0; a < BLOCK_SIZE; a += 32)
 {
    _tmp32  += *(int *)((int)_p32+a+0);   // bank 0 [Athlon: bank 0]
    *(int *)((int)_p32+a+12) = _tmp32;    // bank 3 [Athlon: bank 1]

    _tmp32  += *(int *)((int)_p32+a+4);   // bank 1 [Athlon: bank 0]
    *(int *)((int)_p32+a+16) = _tmp32;    // bank 4 [Athlon: bank 2]
 }
}


//=============================================================================
//          DEMONSTRATION OF CACHE-BANK CONFLICTS
//-----------------------------------------------------------------------------
// Distribution of variables over cache banks on PIII
// ====================================================
// !<bank0>!<bank1>!<bank2>!<bank3>!<bank4>!<bank5>!<bank6>!<bank7>!
// !0 1 2 3!4 5 6 7!8 9 0 1!2 3 4 5!6 7 8 9!0 1 2 3!4 5 6 7! 8 9 0 1 <- offset
// !-+-+-+-+-!-+-+-+-+-+-+-!-+-+-+-+-+-+-!-+-+-+-+-+-+-!-+-+-+-+-+-+-
// !     *-*-*-*   !       !       !       !       ! <<-- ((int)_p32+a+2);
// !      !^    *-*-*-*   !       !       !       ! <<-- ((int)_p32+a+6);
// !      !|     !^    !*-*-*-*!   !       !       ! <<-- ((int)_p32+a+12);
// !      !|     !|    !       !*-*-*-*!   !       ! <<-- ((int)_p32+a+16);
//        |      |
//        +-------+--- <- CONFLICT
//=============================================================================
//
```

```
// Distribution of variables over cache banks on Athlon
// ================================================
// !<-- bank 0 -->!<-- bank 1 -->!<-- bank 2 -->!<-- bank 3 -->!
// !0 1 2 3 4 5 6 7 8 9 0 1 2 3 4 5 6 7 8 9 0 1 2 3 4 5 6 7 8 9 0 1
// !-+-+-+-+-+-+-+-!-+-+-+-+-+-+-+-!-+-+-+-+-+-+-+-!-+-+-+-+-+-+-+-+
// !    *-*-*-*    !               !               ! <<-- ((int)_p32+a+2);
// !        *-*-*-*!               !               ! <<-- ((int)_p32+a+6);
// !            ^     *-*-*-*!      !               ! <<-- ((int)_p32+a+12);
// !            |          !*-*-*-*  !               ! <<-- ((int)_p32+a+16);
// !         CONFLICT      !        !               !
//
//================================================
conflict(int * _p32)
{
int a;
int _tmp32 = 0;

for(a = 0; a < BLOCK_SIZE; a += 32)
{
                                        // BANK CONFLICTS ARE IN BOLD:
    _tmp32  += *(int *)((int)_p32+a+2);  // bank 0 + 1 [Athlon: bank 0]
    *(int *)((int)_p32+a+12) = _tmp32;   // bank 3      [Athlon: bank 1]
    _tmp32  += *(int *)((int)_p32+a+6);  // bank 1 + 2
                                        // [Athlon: bank 0 + 1]
    *(int *)((int)_p32+a+16) = _tmp32;   // bank 4      [Athlon: bank 2]

}
}
```

On PIII, an impressive conflict appeared (Fig. 3.30). Reading two adjacent 32-bit cells, offset from the starting position of the first bank by 16 bits, caused the performance to drop 320%. Reading two cells required two or more penalty clocks, rather than the expected two clocks.

The value of the penalty increased the number of clocks to five; therefore, the loss is close to the experimental percentage:

$$100 \times \frac{2+5}{2} = 350\%$$

(This occurs because overhead produced by factors such as writing and organizing the loop was not included.)

On Athlon, the consequences of cache-bank conflicts are less dramatic; the performance dropped only 109%. This advantage over PIII occurs because of a twofold superiority in the width of cache banks. (Only two of them overlapped.) In contrast to PIII, which had a blocked cache, Athlon produced a small jam that quickly dispersed.

This doesn't mean it is impossible to block Athlon. To achieve this, overlap several banks. This would require a program inapplicable for testing PIII. Nevertheless, spontaneous conflicts of cache banks on Athlon are less probable.

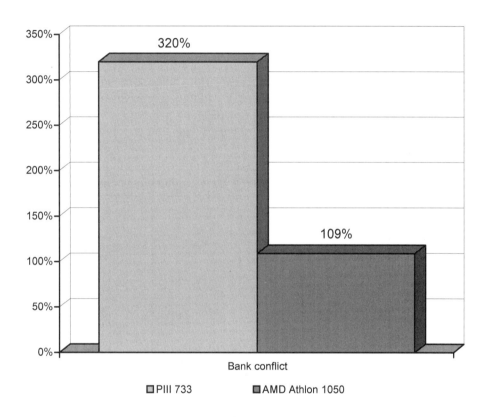

Fig. 3.30. Performance drop caused by a cache-bank conflict

Working with a Limited Associative Number of Cache

Optimizing data organization will remain the task of programmers until the arrival of processors equipped with fully associative cache. The *Cache Organization* section showed that each cell of the cached memory can't claim each cache line; rather, each cell is mapped to a limited number of cache lines, which determines the associative number, or way, of cache.

Because the associative number of L1 cache memory is usually small (PII or PIII have 4-way, and AMD Athlon has 2-way), poor data organization can reduce the size of cache memory ten times or more.

If the set bits of cached cells are equal, they are mapped to the same cache line. It is necessary to avoid such situations. How are the set addresses calculated? The following formula can be used: *set.address = my.address & ((mask.bank – 1) & ~(mask.line – 1))*. (The *mask.line* is $2^{mask.line} = CACHE.LINE.SIZE$, and the *mask.bank* is $2^{mask.bank} = BANK.SIZE$.) In particular, 16 KB, 4-way associative cache on the PII or PIII processor reserves 4 bits to 11 bits of the linear memory address for set addresses.

Thus, processing memory cells with a step equal to or a multiple of the cache-bank size is inefficient and should be avoided at all costs. Many processors have a cache-bank size equal to or a multiple of 4 KB. This value is not a tenet, but it will do as a working basis.

Is the following optimal code?

Listing 3.7. Cache-Line Conflict Caused by a Limited Associative Number

---

```
for(a = 0; a < googol; a++)
{
// ...
   a1 += bar[4096*1];
   a2 += bar[4096*2];
   a3 += bar[4096*3];
   a4 += bar[4096*4];
   a5 += bar[4096*5];
// ...
}
```

Alas, it is not optimal. When this program is run on PII or PIII, the `bar[4096]` cell is not in L1 cache at the first iteration of the `for` loop. A delay of two to four clocks is required to load the data from L2 cache (or from the main memory, in the worst case).

The set address of the cell equals zero. (Although it is not critical, assume that the `bar` array is aligned by the 4 KB boundary.) Therefore, the cache controller places 32 bytes of read data into the 0 cache line of the first (or, to be more precise, *conventional* first) cache bank. The set address of the `bar[4096*2]` cell also equals zero; therefore, the next portion of data also claims the 0 cache line. Because the 0 line of the first cache bank is occupied, the cache controller uses the second bank, and so on.

However, the number of cache banks is limited. When the fifth cell — `bar[4096*5]` — is read, the 0 lines of all four cache banks are occupied. Because the fifth cell also claims the 0 cache line, the cache controller is forced to preempt the "oldest" line (the 0 line of the first cache bank), then write up-to-date information into this line.

Consequently, at the next iteration of the `for` loop, the `bar[4096]` cell once again is missing from L1 cache, and another delay is needed to load it. The cache controller detects no free banks and preempts the 0 line of the second bank, which stored the `bar[4096*2]` cell, and so on. Do you catch what's happening? Cache will not run because it has no cache hits, only cache misses. This occurs even when only five cells are being processed.

To avoid a performance drop, the processed data should be reorganized until the cells to be read go to different cache lines. If this is impossible, then these cells should be processed in several sequential loops, as shown in Listing 3.8.

Listing 3.8. Optimized Version That Accounts for N-Way Set Associative Cache

```
for(a = 0; a < googol; a++)
{
// ...
   a1=bar[4096];
   a2=bar[4096*2];
   a3=bar[4096*3];
// ...
}

for(a = 0; a < googol; a++)
{
// ...
   a4=bar[4096*4];
   a5=bar[4096*5];
// ...
}
```

Now, consider how the following code will be executed on the AMD Athlon processor. At first glance, everything will occur as described in the previous scenario, except 2-way associative cache of the Athlon processor will appear to "sink" at the third iteration. However, it will only appear to do so.

Listing 3.9. Code That, Against Common Sense, Is Optimal for AMD Athlon

```
for(a = 0; a < googol; a++)
{
// ...
   a1 += bar[4096];
```

```
a2 += bar[4096*2];
a3 += bar[4096*3];
a4 += bar[4096*4];
a5 += bar[4096*5];
// ...
}
```

The first reaction is surprise and praise: Great! Good for Athlon! After that fit of enthusiasm, the second reaction is, why? How is it implemented? If you read the Athlon manual on optimization from cover to cover, you'll find the answer between the lines of *Appendix A*. In AMD Athlon processors, the read/write queue contains 12 positions that temporarily store the data read from L1 cache. Cache-line conflicts still arise, but they are masked by the data-buffering system.

Does this discovery mean that, when optimizing programs exclusively for Athlon, you need not worry about the small associative number of cache? Alas, the situation is not so cheerful. In Listing 3.9, there was no performance drop only because there were less than 12 simultaneously processed cells.

You must be especially careful when you choose to use the read step to process block algorithms. If this step happens to be a multiple of the cache-bank size, a noticeable performance drop cannot be avoided.

Consider the following example:

Listing 3.10. [Cache/L1.overassoc] Incipient Cache-Line Conflicts and Their Influence on Performance

```
#define N_ITER        466           // Number of iterations

                                     // In theory, LINE_SIZE*N_ITER bytes
                                     // of cache memory will be allocated.
                                     // In this case, 466 × 64 = ~30 KB,
#define CACHE_BANK_SIZE (4*K   )     // the size of the cache bank.

#define LINE_SIZE      64            // Maximum cache-line size

#define BLOCK_SIZE        ((CACHE_BANK_SIZE+LINE_SIZE)*N_ITER) // Block size

/*-----------------------------------------------------------------------
 *
 *        VERSION ILLUSTRATING CACHE-LINE CONFLICTS
 *
 -----------------------------------------------------------------------*/
int over_assoc(int *p)
{
```

```
int a;
volatile int x=0;

// Attention: The top-level loop has been skipped
// because the profiler would run it ten times.

for(a=0; a < N_ITER; a++)
// Memory is read with the step of 4 KB. As a result,
// saturation is reached quickly
// on PII, PIII, P4, and Athlon.
// Because more than 12 cells are processed,
// read buffering implemented on Athlon
// cannot save the situation.

    x+=*(int *)((int)p + a*CACHE_BANK_SIZE);

return x;
}
```

At the read step equal to 4 KB, this program will "skid" on all processors because cache memory will be unable to store a single cell. (I seem to hear a voice saying: "Why not a single cell? There must be four cells on PII or PIII, and two on Athlon, as indicated by their association numbers." Alas, at the next iteration, the last stored cells will be removed from cache.)

How can cache conflicts be prevented? The processed array must be restructured so that the set address of each loaded cell is different. One way of solving this problem is to increase the step value by the size of the cache line. (To achieve this, it is also necessary to change the array; otherwise, the program will read *other* data.)

The optimized code might look as follows:

Listing 3.11. [Cache/L1.overassoc.c] Optimized Code That Eliminates Cache-Line Conflicts

```
/*-----------------------------------------------------------------
 *
 *          VERSION THAT ELIMINATES CONFLICTS
 *
 -----------------------------------------------------------------*/
int optimize(int   *p)
{
int a=0;
volatile int x=0;

// Attention: The top-level loop has been skipped
```

```
// because the profiler would run it ten times.

for(a=0; a < N_ITER; a++)
{
// Memory is read with the step of CACHE_BANK_SIZE+LINE_SIZE
// (in this case, 4,096 + 64 = 4,160 bytes).
// The set address of each cell is different.
// Therefore, there are no conflicts, and
// 100% of cache memory is used.

    x+=*(int *)((int)p + a*(CACHE_BANK_SIZE+LINE_SIZE));
}
return x;
}
```

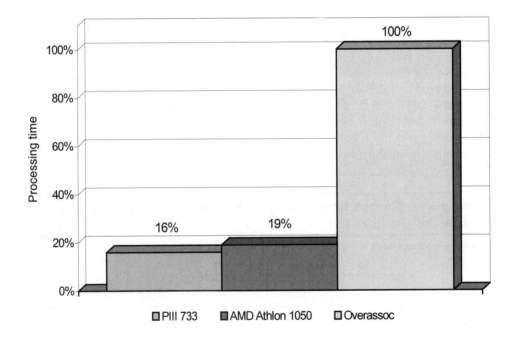

Fig. 3.31. Cache-line conflicts cause performance to decrease when
the loaded data hit the same cache line

The test run of this program shows that, as a result of optimization, the execution speed increased more than six times on Pentium III 733 and more than five times on AMD Athlon 1050. This is good performance gain, even if the conflicting cells were only read, not modified. Write conflicts are about 1.5 times more "expensive."

Therefore, if your program executes extremely slowly with a small amount of processed data, check it for cache-line conflicts.

Processing Two-Dimensional Arrays

Parallel data processing (covered in detail in *Chapter 2*) is a rather efficient method — for ruining your program. The memory subsystem is not as simple as it may seem; a single imprudent step can destroy all optimization.

Suppose that you have a vast two-dimensional array, and you need to calculate the sum of its cells. Take the 512×512 matrix composed of int variables. Bidimensionality of the array produces the problem of choosing how to perform the calculation: by rows or by columns.

Calculation by rows merely reads data sequentially from the memory. This is not the best method of data processing. Reading the array by columns looks more attractive. If the width of the array exceeds the length of the burst-read cycle, requests to the memory are generated at *each* cache miss. (See *Parallel Data Processing*.) The only limitation is that the product of the columns and the cache-line size must not exceed the L1 cache size.

See if this condition has been satisfied. At first glance, it may appear to be: On PIII, the cache-line size is 32 bytes, the L1 cache size is 16 KB, and $512 \times 32 = 16,384$. AMD Athlon has a 64 KB cache and a cache-line size of 64 bytes. Multiply 512 by 64 bytes. You'll get 32 KB, which should fit easily within cache. Will it really fit? Start the following program:

Listing 3.12. [Cache/column.big.c] Peculiarities of Processing Large, Two-Dimensional Arrays

```
#define N_ROW    (512)
#define N_COL    (512)     // The row number is nonoptimal
                           // because it is a multiple of the
                           // cache-bank size. Consequently,
                           // cache is not used completely.

/*-------------------------------------------------------------------
 *
 *      SEQUENTIAL PROCESSING OF AN ARRAY BY COLUMNS
 *
```

```
------------------------------------------------------------------------*/
int FOR_COL(int (*foo)[N_COL])
{
int x, y;
int z = 0;
for (x = 0; x < N_ROW; x++)
{
    for (y = 0; y < N_COL; y++)
        z += foo[x][y];
}
return z;
}


/*------------------------------------------------------------------------
 *
 *        SEQUENTIAL PROCESSING OF AN ARRAY BY ROWS
 *
------------------------------------------------------------------------*/
int FOR_ROW(int (*foo)[N_COL])
{
int x, y;
int z = 0;
for (x = 0; x < N_COL; x++)
{
    // If the matrix height is a multiple of the cache-bank size,
    // the limited associative number of cache will cause its effective
    // size to be reduced considerably. This will lead to a shortage of
    // cache memory, which will result in cache misses.
    for (y = 0; y < N_ROW; y++)
        z += foo[y][x];
}
return z;
}
```

Strange as it may seem, the data doesn't fit within cache! The associative number of cache must be accounted for. Because addresses of the cells to be read are multiples of 4,096, only 4 cells can be placed in cache simultaneously, not 1,024 cells. Even L2 cache is not sufficient. Suppose that you have 4-way associative L2 cache whose size equals 128 KB. Each of its banks is capable of storing 8 such cells ($CACHE.SIZE/WAY/STEP.SIZE = 131,072/4/4096 = 8$). Consequently, four banks will hold 128 cells ($8 \times 4 = 32$). And you have 1,024 cells!

In this situation, cache memory will be thrashing. Cache misses will reach 800% on PII or PIII; they'll reach 1,600% on Athlon. Using the burst mode, the cache lines will be filled, but only a small part of the data will be claimed. As a result, this code will run very slowly.

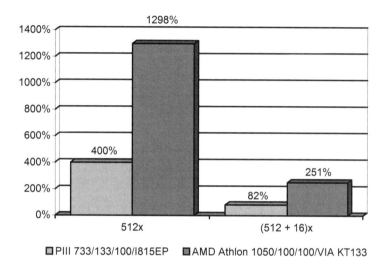

Fig. 3.32. Time required to process two-dimensional arrays, dependent on the read step

The data exchange between cache and the main memory is performed in packets whose lengths are 32 bytes to 128 bytes. Therefore, the cell access time will be very different when sequential cell processing is used. Delays will occur only when the first cell of the packet is read; the remaining cells of the packet will be processed almost instantly.

In conclusion, it is more profitable to process large, multidimensional arrays that do not fit within L1 cache (and, especially, within L2 cache) by rows, rather than by columns. You can process arrays that fit within cache as you wish.

Write Buffering Specifics

Store-Forwarding Pitfalls

Starting with the K5 processor, x86 processors began to use transparent write buffering. (See *Cache Organization.*) Write buffers are available not only for writing, but also for reading. This means that the result of command execution becomes available immediately after it is placed into the buffer. There is no need to wait until it is unloaded into cache memory! Such a trick, known as store forwarding, greatly reduces the time required to access the data.

Consider this approach in the following example. Suppose that the loop is similar to the following:

```
for(a = 0; a < BLOCK_SIZE; a += sizeof(tmp32))
{
    p[a] += tmp_1;
    tmp_2 -= p[a];
}
```

Instead of pumping the data through the "systemic circulatory system" (execution unit → write unit → cache → write unit → execution unit), the AMD Athlon processor pumps the data through the "pulmonary circulatory system" (execution unit → write buffer → execution unit). The latter is much shorter! Pentium processors appear to behave in a similar manner, although their documentation doesn't provide intelligible information on this topic.

Write buffering is characterized by certain limitations; it is efficient only when the *same* data are read that were written. Otherwise, the processor penalizes your program, and its execution speed drops considerably.

As an illustration of this statement, consider the following example and the left portion of Fig. 3.33:

```
*(int *)((int)p) = x;        // Data is written into the buffer.
y = *(int *)((int)p + 2);    // The buffer is missing [p+2; p+4] bytes.
```

Generally, you write into the buffer cells with the numbers 0, 1, 2, and 3, then request cells with the numbers 2, 3, 4, and 5. Cells with the numbers 4 and 5 are missing from the buffer; to load them, the processor must access cache. Cache, however, does not contain even cells 2 and 3 because they have not left the buffer yet!

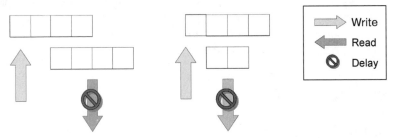

Fig. 3.33. Delays caused by overlapped read and write areas

How the processor will handle this situation is unclear. It may read part of the cells from the buffer and another part from cache, then join both parts of the data.

In my opinion, the processor probably flushes the buffer contents into cache and retrieves the requested data from there without any tricks.

Regardless, these steps require additional clocks, which leads to a performance drop. (On PIII, the penalty is six clocks; on Athlon, it is ten.)

If all requested data are within the buffer, but the addresses of the read and written cells do not match, the delay still occurs. The processor has to perform conversions by truncating "extra" bits from the written result (Fig. 3.33, *right*).

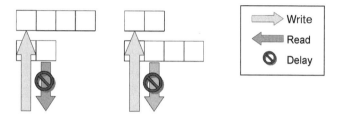

Fig. 3.34. Delays caused by mismatched bit capacity of the data

Finally, if the cell addresses match, but the cells have different sizes, delays are inevitable. If the size of the written cell is smaller than the size of the read cell (Fig. 3.34, *right*), only part of the requested data goes to the buffer. The remainder is in cache, and the situation reverts to the one previously considered.

The delay that occurs when writing a cell of a higher bit capacity (Fig. 3.34, *left*) is harder to understand. Although the data are retrieved directly from the buffer (bypassing cache), the truncation of extra bits takes additional time (at least one clock).

The same is true for several short write operations followed by a long read operation. Consider the following example:

```
*(char *)((int)p + 0) = 'B';
*(char *)((int)p + 1) = 'O';
*(char *)((int)p + 2) = 'F';
*(char *)((int)p + 3) = 'H';
BOFH = *(int *)((int)p + 0);      // Delay! The data being read are not
                                  // the same as those just written.
```

At first, it seems that everything is OK here. After all, the requested data fit within the write buffer. However, a six-clock delay occurs because the written cells and the read cells have different sizes. The data that are loaded simply are not the same as the data just written! The write buffer is addressed quite differently from cache memory, and the processor cannot determine instantly whether or not the bytes to be written are located in adjacent cells.

Hence, the following rule: *A data-read operation following a data-write operation must have the same starting address and a bit capacity that does not exceed (preferably, is the same as) that of the written data.* Because of this, you should avoid working with mixed data types (such as bytes and double words). In general, try to reduce all data to the unified data type of the maximum size.

If you need to read a small portion of the data that were just written, you could use bitwise operations and the recommendations of Intel in *Intel Architecture Optimization Reference Manual*: "If it is necessary to extract a nonaligned portion of stored data, read out the smallest aligned portion that completely contains the data, and shift/mask the data as necessary. The penalty for not doing this is much higher than the cost of the shifts."

Suppose that the nonoptimized example looked as follows:

```
// Nonoptimized code
for(a = 0; a < BLOCK_SIZE; a += sizeof(int))
{
    *(int *)((int)p + a) += x;
    y += *(char *)((int)p + a + 2));
}
```

The processor "dislikes" the code line in bold; it becomes the program's bottleneck. Suppose that you try to correct the problem as follows:

```
// Optimized code
for(a = 0; a < BLOCK_SIZE; a += sizeof(int))
{
    *(int *)((int)p + a)+= x;
    tmp = *(int *)((int)p + a);      // The same data is read
                                     // into the temporary variable.
    x += ((tmp & 0x00FF0000) >> 0x10); // The required cell is cut "manually."
}
```

In contrast to Intel's recommendation, on PIII, the optimized version will run even *slower* than the initial one! Perhaps on P4 the situation will improve, and manual bitwise operations will prevail over a nonoptimized version. Regardless, because your program is designed to run not only on P4, but on earlier models of the x86 family as well, do not place bets on Intel's tip.

So far, this discussion has focused on reading and writing the same data. However, when the processor checks for the requested data in the buffer, it doesn't analyze all address bits; *it only analyzes the address bits "responsible" for selecting a specific cache line in L1 cache.* These bits are the set addresses.

If the addresses of the cells to be read or written are multiples of the cache-bank size (calculated by dividing the cache size by its associative number), the processor will be disorganized. It will be unable to detect which portion of data it must retrieve. As a result, a forced delay will last until cells of the same "name" are moved from the buffer into L1 cache, which requires six (PIII) or ten (Athlon) processor clocks.

Consider the following example:

```
*(int *)((int)p) = x;
*(int *)((int)p + L1_CACHE_SIZE/L1_CACHE_WAY_ASSOCIATIVE) = y;
z = *(int *)((int)p);          // Delay
```

Because the data to be written have identical set addresses, the processor cannot perform store-forwarding from the buffer. It must wait until both cells go to cache. With the smallest cache-bank size (2 KB on P4), all intensely and frequently used variables will be within the limits of 1 KB.

Note that this section does not relate to the write operation that follows a read operation. Code that looks approximately as follows will run efficiently:

```
for(a = sizeof(int); a < BLOCK_SIZE; a += sizeof(int))
{
x += *(char *)((int)p + a - (sizeof(int)/2));
*(int *)((int)p + a) += y;

}
```

To conclude this discussion, conduct an experiment that would allow an numerical evaluation of the performance drop caused by inefficient data access. To make this example more illustrative, sequentially test all six combinations (see Listing 3.13) mentioned in Intel's optimization manual. (The AMD *Athlon Processor x86 Code Optimization Guide* covers this problem rather superficially; therefore, even if you are an enthusiastic fan of AMD, don't be fastidious about this and refer to Intel's manual. Both processors will behave the same way.)

Listing 3.13. [Cache/mem.stall.c] Memory Delays from Reading/Writing Data of Different Sizes

```
// Allocating memory
p = (int*)_malloc32(BLOCK_SIZE);


/*-------------------------------------------------------------------
 *
 *          OPTIMIZED VERSION
 *          Long Write/Long Read (same address)
 *
------------------------------------------------------------------- */
for(a = 0; a < BLOCK_SIZE; a += sizeof(tmp32))
{
```

```
   *(int *)((int)p + a) = tmp32;
   tmp32 += *(int *)((int)p + a);
}

/*--------------------------------------------------------------------
 *
 *            NONOPTIMIZED VERSION
 *            Short Write/Long Read (same address)
 *
 -------------------------------------------------------------------- */
for(a = 0; a < BLOCK_SIZE; a += sizeof(tmp32))
{
   *(char *)((int)p + a) = tmp8;
   tmp32 += *(int *)((int)p + a);
}

/*--------------------------------------------------------------------
 *
 *            NONOPTIMIZED VERSION
 *            Short Write/Long Read (overlap space)
 *
 -------------------------------------------------------------------- */
for(a = sizeof(tmp32); a < BLOCK_SIZE; a += sizeof(tmp32))
{
   *(char *)((int)p + a + (sizeof(tmp32)/2)) = tmp8;
   tmp32 += *(int *)((int)p + a);
}

/*--------------------------------------------------------------------
 *
 *            NONOPTIMIZED VERSION
 *            Long Write/Short Read (same address)
 *
 -------------------------------------------------------------------- */
for(a = 0; a < BLOCK_SIZE; a += sizeof(tmp32))
{
   *(int *)((int)p + a) = tmp32;
   tmp8 += *(char *)((int)p + a);
}

/*--------------------------------------------------------------------
 *
 *            NONOPTIMIZED VERSION
 *            Long Write/Short Read (overlap space)
 *
 -------------------------------------------------------------------- */
```

```
for(a = sizeof(tmp32); a < BLOCK_SIZE; a += sizeof(tmp32))
{
   *(int *)((int)p + a) = tmp32;
   tmp8 += *(char *)((int)p + a + (sizeof(tmp32)/2));
}

/*-------------------------------------------------------------------
 *
 *         NONOPTIMIZED VERSION
 *         Long Write/Long Read (overlap space)
 *
--------------------------------------------------------------------- */
for(a = sizeof(tmp32); a < BLOCK_SIZE; a += sizeof(tmp32))
{
   *(int *)((int)p + a) = tmp32;
   tmp32 += *(int *)((int)p + a - (sizeof(tmp32)/2));
}
```

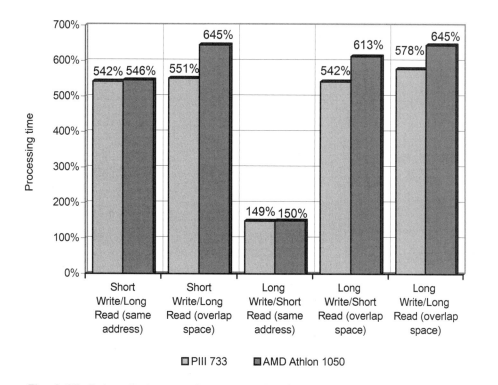

Fig. 3.35. Delays that occur when processing data of different lengths (in L1 or L2 cache), when processing without delay is 100%

The results of running this program on AMD Athlon 1050 and Intel Pentium III 733 processors are in Fig. 3.35. If the block being processed doesn't exceed the size of L1 (or L2) cache, an attempt to read the data missing from the buffer results in a fivefold, or even sixfold, performance drop.

On P4, the penalty is greater. *Intel Pentium and Intel Xenon Processor Optimization Reference Manual* says: "The performance penalty from violating store-forwarding restrictions was present in the Pentium II and Pentium III processors, but the penalty is larger on the Pentium 4 processor."

Reading a small portion of data after writing a large data block is a pleasant exception. If the addresses of the data blocks coincide, the cell-access time only increases 1.5 times.

Outside the cache. When the processed data exceeds the limits of L2 cache, the pattern changes significantly. The penalty decreases to between 1.5 times and 3 times, and a short read after a long write on PIII (and, presumably, on PII and P4) executes without any delays. Nevertheless, AMD Athlon will penalize you with a twofold performance drop.

Converting data to the unified type by extending them to the greatest bit capacity will produce more significant losses. The specific cell-access time grows rapidly as the size of the processed block is increased.

Thus, there is no universal strategy for working with data of different types. It is up to you to decide what it best in each case: penalty delays or increased memory requirements.

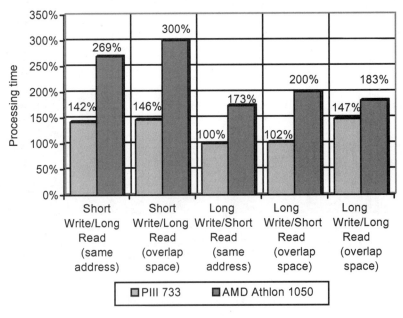

Fig. 3.36. Delays that occur when processing data of different lengths (in the main memory); 100% is processing without delay

More Store-Forwarding Pitfalls

You already know that when you attempt to write a cell missing from L1 cache, the processor temporarily will store the data to be written in a free buffer (if one is free). After that, it will unload this data into L1 or L2 cache whenever possible.

Reading data from the buffer is at least one clock faster than accessing L1 cache. Besides this, buffers have more ports than cache, and they are capable of processing more than two requests simultaneously. (An exception is write buffers of the AMD-K5 processor, which have only one port.) How can you use these facts?

On P6 and K6, the following code will execute as quickly as possible, whether or not the *p cell is present in cache memory:

```
*p = a;
b = p*;
```

However, using write buffers conceals a dangerous pitfall. Consider the following example, which may seem to produce the same result as the previous example:

```
*p = a;
f = (sin(x) + cos(y)) / z;
b = p*;
```

The read and write commands are no longer adjacent. They are separated by an "alien" instruction. Suppose that the compiler has generated the ugliest code, storing the results of all four calculations in temporary variables. In addition, all four variables (including f) are missing from cache and claim different write buffers. Only five buffers are filled between the operations that write the *p cell and read its contents. Presumably, *p remains in the buffer.

These suppositions are wrong! Write buffers, in contrast to cache memory, tend to flush by *moving* (not copying) their contents into L1 and/or L2 cache. The previous code fragment is unstable because its execution speed depends on whether the processor has flushed its buffers or not. The performance of such code depends on the processor's "mood," and different runs might show different results.

In K6, the buffer contents are unloaded into L1 cache, from which the data can be read within a single clock. On P6, the same situation results in a cache miss. The processor, therefore, has to access L2 cache, which will cost many clocks.

You could eliminate the problem by regrouping the commands: Move the calculation operation one line up or down, then couple the read/write commands, which guarantees that the buffers are not flushed prematurely. However, this solution isn't always attainable; the commands might have a data dependency or even reside in different functions or threads. Depending on the state of specific page attributes, write caching may or may not be allowed. For example, in video memory areas, it is not allowed. If it was, the display wouldn't refresh when writing occurred; it would refresh only after an indefinite time interval, when the data are removed from L1 cache. This would be far from satisfactory. Hence, I would offer the following advice: Make sure that the memory area being processed allows caching.

You also must consider buffering. On PPro, PII, or PIII, a write miss *doesn't* load the cache line. (The only exception is writing line-split data.) On K6 or Athlon, a write miss *doesn't immediately* load the cache line. However, because the contents of buffers are passed to L1 cache, such loading still takes place.

For this reason, the recommendations for Pentium and Pentium with MMX technology are applicable to contemporary processors. As a practical implementation, consider the following:

```
volatile trash;

trash = *p;

*p = a;

f = (sin(x) + con(y)) / z;

b = *p;
```

What has changed? Pay special attention to the line in bold, which loads the cell contents into an unused variable. This trick doesn't decrease the performance. (P6 and K6 processors can wait while the cell is loaded from the main memory in parallel with its writing.) However, it guarantees that the buffer contents won't be moved further than L1 cache when they are accessed. L1 cache is always available, and reading it doesn't take a long time.

As usual, this aspect has its subtleties. When data are loaded into an unused variable, the optimizing compiler can ignore the assignment (which is useless from its point of view). In this case, the trick won't work. One of the methods that allows the programmer to prevent the compiler from such initiatives is the declaration that a variable is volatile.

Experimental confirmation of automatic buffer unloading. After discussing the theoretical aspects, it makes sense to investigate the "live" process of buffer unloading. The following questions should be answered: How much time does data to be written spend in buffers? In what order and at what speed are data moved from there?

However, write buffers are not visible, and you have no means of controlling them. The buffer is like a "black box" and only reveals its input and output. How can you find out what's inside it? You cannot solve this problem directly, but you can send requests and measure the time of their execution. After that, it will only remain to compare several facts and draw conclusions. If the data are read instantly, they almost certainly are still in the buffer. A slight delay signifies that the data are no longer in the buffer and should be moved into L1 cache. Finally, a sharp increase in the access time means the data are unloaded directly into L2 cache.

How shall you proceed? By sequentially writing an increasing number of cells that subsequently access the first cell, you eventually will encounter a sharp drop in performance. This will mean that the cell whose content you are trying to read has left the buffer. Proceeding further, you will be able to discover the buffer unloading strategy: whether data are unloaded in the background mode, or whether unloading only occurs after buffer overflow.

Generally, it is possible to write the test program in pure C. However, this likely will produce many difficulties: C doesn't support repeat macros and, consequently, doesn't allow duplicate write commands for a specified number of iterations. Write operations within the loop will lose measurement precision immediately. First, overhead produced by organizing the loop is comparable to the time required to load data from L1 cache. Second, the code generated by the compiler may contain redundant memory-access operations. Finally, buffers can be unloaded as branches are processed.

Forgive me, application programmers; in this case, I would choose the assembly language. The following listings are well-commented, and it shouldn't be difficult for you to understand them.

Listing 3.14. [Cache/store_buf.xm] Some Write Buffers Are Unloaded While Others Are Filled

```
; N_ITER EQU   ?            ; Auto generation
; /*-----------------------------------------------------------------
;   *
;   *        Macro that automatically duplicates its body N times
;   *
; -------------------------------------------------------------------*/
STORE_BUFF MACRO N
 _N = N
 _A = 0
WHILE _A NE _N
    MOV [EBX+32*_A], ECX;   *(int *)((int)p + 32 * _A) = x;
    _A = _A + 1
 ENDM
ENDM


; /*-----------------------------------------------------------------
;   *
;   *        UNLOADING BUFFERS WHEN THE BUS IS BUSY
;   *
; -------------------------------------------------------------------*/
```

```
STORE_BUFF N_ITER      ;  *p+00 = a;
              ; *p+32 = a;
              ; *p+64 = a;
              ; This fills the write buffers
              ; by writing each new cell to a new buffer. Buffers are unloaded
              ; and written in parallel. To prove this,...


MOV EDX, [EBX]        ; b = *p;
              ; the first written buffer is accessed. If that buffer
              ; has not been unloaded yet, its contents will be read
              ; as quickly as possible; otherwise, a jam will occur.

ADD EBX, 32*N_ITER    ; Moving the pointer to the next buffer
```

Listing 3.15. [Cache/store_buf_nop.xm] Kernel of the Program Demonstrating How a Buffer Is Unloaded When the Bus Is Idle

```
; N_ITER EQU  ?   ; Auto generation
; /*----------------------------------------------------------------------
;  *
;  *            Macro that duplicates its body N times
;  *
;  ----------------------------------------------------------------------*/
STORE_BUFF MACRO N
 _N = N
 _A = 0
WHILE _A NE _N
    NOP          ;    MACRO BODY
    _A = _A + 1
 ENDM
ENDM


; /*----------------------------------------------------------------------
;  *
;  *        UNLOADING A BUFFER WHEN THE BUS IS IDLE
;  *
;  ----------------------------------------------------------------------*/
MOV [EBX], ECX ; *p = a;
        ; Some value is written into *p. The value just written
        ; falls into to the write buffer (store buffer) first.

STORE_BUFF N_ITER
        ; One or more NOP commands are used.
```

```
                    ; In parallel to their execution, buffers contents are flushed
                    ; into L1 cache (AMD) or L2 cache (Intel).

MOV EDX, [EBX]; b = *p;
                    ; The contents of the *p cell are read. If the corresponding
                    ; buffer has not been flushed yet, the cell will be read
                    ; as quickly as possible; otherwise, a delay will occur.

ADD EBX, 32    ; (int)p+32;
                    ; The pointer is moved to the next buffer.
```

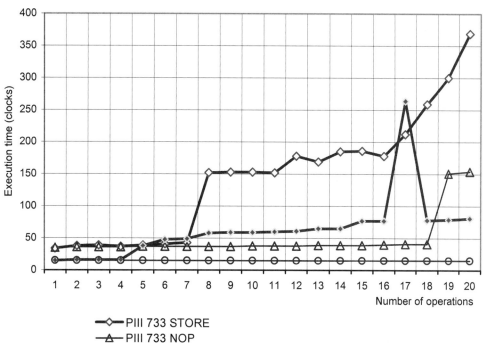

Fig. 3.37. Unloading write buffers

The results of running this program on Pentium III and AMD Athlon are in Fig. 3.37. Start with the line that represents the dependence of the loading time on the number of write commands (Pentium III 733 Store). After seven write commands, the data-load time, without an apparent reason, increased from approximately 35 to 150 clocks (i.e., more than four times). Therefore, the first cell had already left the buffer and moved into L2 cache. This happened despite the availablility of buffers! This proves that buffers may be unloaded spontaneously, even if there are free buffers. Assuming that write operation took one clock, the unload time for the contents of the first buffer was 7±1 clocks.

The next three measurements show similar run times. Then, the line rises slightly and forms a kind of step. What does this mean? Apparently, the second buffer accomplished its unloading at this moment, and, because the bus was busy, there was a delay in the reading of cells from L2 cache.

The next step occurs at the 14th write operation. This isn't surprising; from this moment, the system lacked free buffers. (PII and PIII processors have only 12 buffers; adding the 2 just-flushed buffers, this equals 14.) Each subsequent write operation took approximately seven clocks to unload the contents of at least one buffer. No wonder the performance decreased rapidly.

Now, start the second version of the program (Pentium III 733 NOP). It executes a single write operation, then pauses to feed the processor with some NOP commands. After this, the program checks for the presence of the written data in the buffer. Buffer flushing also occurred, approximately in the same time interval as the previous program. (PII and PIII processors can execute up to three NOP commands per clock; therefore, the clocking results must be divided by three.)

On PIII, it only takes two clocks to write data to L2 cache. This can lead to an interesting conclusion: Buffer contents are unloaded according to the internal timer, rather than at the first opportunity (when the bus is free). The time the data "lives" in write buffers may not be identical on all processors. Nevertheless, magnitude of this value has been determined. This time is visibly shorter than the execution time of most arithmetic commands; therefore, the assumption that separating read and write commands is undesirable has been confirmed.

Consider the implementation of the write buffering mechanism on Athlon (the AMD Athlon 1858 Store line). You should notice that Athlon doesn't experience a sharp drop in performance because it unloads the buffer contents into L1 cache. (PII and PIII processors unload buffer contents into L2 cache.) Therefore, the buffer unloading time on Athlon has been reduced. Apparently, the processor also doesn't unload buffers until necessary.

There is a peak in the line that reflects a considerable increase in the access time at the 17th write operation. Processing the 16th and 18th write operations doesn't cause any problems; these operations easily fit the smooth line. Additional investigation would be required to explain this occurrence.

Combining Write and Calculation Operations

Write buffering allows you to delay the physical flushing of data into cache or the main memory until this operation is most convenient for the processor. As long as at least one buffer is available, this trick greatly improves the performance. If there are no free buffers, the processor is forced to idle until the buffer contents are flushed. When this happens, write with buffering behaves in the same way as a normal write operation.

Another important function of write buffers is write ordering. The data supplied to the buffers are out of order; they are sent there as micro-operations called *micro-ops* are completed. Here, the data are sorted, and they leave the buffers in an order that corresponds to the program's sequence of original machine commands.

Hence, buffer overflow automatically blocks cache memory until the system unloads the data that caused a cache miss. All other attempts to write into the memory (whether or not they result in a cache hit) will be blocked temporarily. This isn't a cheerful prospect — or is it?

This situation can be avoided if you plan data processing so that the speed at which buffers fill doesn't exceed the speed at which their contents unload into cache or to the main memory. PII and PIII processors contain twelve 256-bit buffers, each of which can correspond to any 32-byte memory region, aligned by the 32-byte boundary. In other words, write buffers stand for 384-byte fully associative cache, comprising 12 cache lines of 32 bytes each.

P4 processors have up to 24 write buffers, each of which, apparently, can contain up to 512 data bits.

Athlon, like PII and PIII, has 12 write buffers integrated with read buffers. Documentation doesn't provide clear information about their length; however, you can assume that the length of each buffer is 64 bytes. The AMD processor has half the number of write buffers on P4. Nevertheless, Athlon always unloads buffer contents into L1 cache, whereas P4 processors (and processors based on the P6 core) unload data into L2 cache if they are missing from L1 cache.

It is difficult to say which policy is better. Suppose I said that, when writing large amounts of data unlikely to be accessed soon, Intel processors provide performance gain because they doesn't stuff L1 cache with unnecessary data. Someone else could argue that AMD Athlon unloads buffers faster, decreasing the probability of jams. I could counter this argument by saying the 256-bit bus connecting L1 cache to L2 cache on PIII and P4 neutralizes the differences in performances; as a result, buffers are unloaded even faster than on Athlon. My opponent could respond that Athlon can unload the contents of L1 cache as it writes new data into it; therefore, Athlon doesn't "suffer" from such a situation. The pros and cons of the architecture of each processor are never-ending.

Regardless, when optimizing the program, you must expect the worst configuration (in this scenario, twelve 32-byte write buffers).

Consider the following example. Do you think it is optimal?

Listing 3.16. [Cache/write_sin.c] Candidate for Optimization That Combines Read Commands with Arithmetic Command Execution

```
/*---------------------------------------------------------------
 *
 *              NONOPTIMIZED VERSION
 *
-------------------------------------------------------------*/
for(a = 0; a < 192; a += 8)
// The 192 DWORD cells give 776 bytes of memory, more than
// twice the capacity of the write buffers on PII or PIII.
// A jam will occur during execution. Subsequent
// write operations will execute slowly
// because they will have to wait each time for the buffers
// to be unloaded.

{
    // To eliminate overhead, the loop needs to be unrolled.
    // Otherwise, its splitting will decrease the performance.
  p[a + 0] = (a + 0);
    p[a + 1] = (a + 1);
    p[a + 2] = (a + 2);
    p[a + 3] = (a + 3);
    p[a + 4] = (a + 4);
    p[a + 5] = (a + 5);
    p[a + 6] = (a + 6);
    p[a + 7] = (a + 7);
}

for(b = 0; b < 66; b++)
x += x/cos(x);
// Some arithmetic commands are executed.
```

The execution of the `for` loop on PII or PIII is far from optimal. Even if all the buffers are clear initially (which is not guaranteed), there will be no free buffers until more than 50% of the loop has been executed. The program will stall because all subsequent write operations will be forced to wait until the buffers are unloaded. The bus is continuously busy; therefore, the program will have a lengthy wait. In addition, the bus will be idle during the calculation loop. How impractical!

You can reorganize the loop by splitting it into several loops, each of which fills no more that 12 to 14 buffers. In Listing 3.16, only two loops would be required (*192/96 = 2*). Between these memory-write loops, you can place the loop that performs calculations. Plan this loop so that the buffers can be unloaded while the arithmetic loop executes. Note that if the calculation time exceeds the time required to unload the buffers, such regrouping makes no sense; the performance would be determined by the CPU-core clock speed, rather than by writing to memory.

It is expedient to split the arithmetic loop into two loops. Place the first part before the first memory-write loop, and place the second part after it. This will ensure that all buffers are free when the write loop starts its execution.

Listing 3.17. [Cache/write_sin.c] Optimized Version That Combines Memory-Write Operations with Arithmetic Operations

```
/*-------------------------------------------------------------------
 *
 *          OPTIMIZED VERSION
 *
-------------------------------------------------------------------*/
// Part of the planned calculations will be executed
// to provide enough time for buffers to unload
// their current contents; they may not be empty
// when the loop starts execution.
for(b = 0; b < 33; b++)
   x += x/cos(x);

// Next, 96 write operations are executed, in the DWORD cells
// which corresponds to the write buffers' capacity
// when the loop ends. Practically all buffers will be filled.
// I wrote "practically" because some part of the buffers
// will have time to unload.
for(a = 0; a < 96; a += 8)

{
   p[a + 0] = (a + 0);
   p[a + 1] = (a + 1);
   p[a + 2] = (a + 2);
   p[a + 3] = (a + 3);
   p[a + 4] = (a + 4);
   p[a + 5] = (a + 5);
   p[a + 6] = (a + 6);
   p[a + 7] = (a + 7);
}

// The remaining part of the calculations will be
// performed. This will work if all buffers
```

```
// have had time to unload. In this case,
// full parallelism is achieved!
for(b = 0; b < 33; b++)
   x += x/cos(x);

// The remaining 96 write operations will be performed.
// Because the buffers will have had time to unload, the
// write operations will be completed as quickly as possible.
for(a = 96; a < 192; a += 8)

{
   p[a + 0] = (a+0);
   p[a + 1] = (a+1);
   p[a + 2] = (a+2);
   p[a + 3] = (a+3);
   p[a + 4] = (a+4);
   p[a + 5] = (a+5);
   p[a + 6] = (a+6);
   p[a + 7] = (a+7);
}
```

The results of running the optimized version of this program are neither wonderful nor horrible (Fig. 3.38). PIII and Athlon showed approximately twofold performance growth, whether or not the written memory cells are in L1 cache.

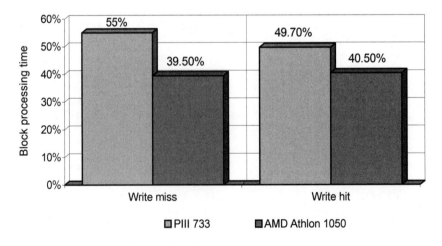

Fig. 3.38. Efficiency of combining memory-write operations with calculations
(non-optimized version gives 100%)

Finally, two pairs of split loops can be joined into one super-loop without any performance loss. This is necessary when the memory-write loop is split into more than two loops.

Listing 3.18. Combining Two Split Loops into One Loop

```
/*-----------------------------------------------------------------------
 *
 *           OPTIMIZED, COLLAPSED VERSION
 *
 ------------------------------------------------------------------*/
for(d = 0; d<192; d += 96)
{
for(b = 0; b < 33; b++)
    x += x/cos(x);

for(a = d; a < d+96; a += 8)
{
    p[a + 0] = (a + 0);
    p[a + 1] = (a + 1);
    p[a + 2] = (a + 2);
    p[a + 3] = (a + 3);
    p[a + 4] = (a + 4);
    p[a + 5] = (a + 5);
    p[a + 6] = (a + 6);
    p[a + 7] = (a + 7);
}
}
```

What if the algorithm only makes provisions for write operations, and there are no calculations? Should you artificially introduce a command that causes a delay? No! If you have planned the execution carefully, the code will execute during the same time at the same speed.

Cache Management in the New Generation of x86 Processors

Programmatic cache management simply has been unlucky. The concept of "invisible" cache, actively promoted by Intel, has distracted programmers from the hardware implementation of the cache controller. As a result, tools have not been provided for controlling it. Designers had to leave a loophole for system programmers that allowed them to stop the caching of memory pages that belong to peripheral devices.

Before most applications were grinding compact data structures processed multiple times, the strategy of loading cache lines on demand was effective. It became less useful with the arrival of multimedia applications. The dramatically increased volume of the processed data, along with the arrival of streaming algorithms that accessed each cell only once, resulted in continuous cache overloads. The overall system performance was limited by RAM throughput, rather than by the operating speed of the processor.

AMD, the first manufacturer to address this problem, included the `prefetch` instruction in its 3DNow! command set. This instruction enabled programmers to load in advance the cells required first. Data was loaded without the intervention of, and without stopping, the executive pipeline. This approach killed two birds with one stone: First, "manual" management of the cache controller allowed programmers to choose the optimal strategy of prefetching, which significantly reduced the number of cache misses. Second, prefetching made it possible to load the next portion of data while the previous one was being processed, masking the RAM latency.

After AMD-K6, an improved version of prefetching appeared in Pentium III, along with an entire set of commands for "manual" cache management. Intel certainly didn't want to be left in the dust by its competitors!

Memory management continued to improve with the arrival of Pentium 4. In addition to a large number of new commands, this processor implemented a new mechanism: *hardware prefetching with an intellectual preloading algorithm.* (This mechanism later appeared in Athlon XP.) In this area, the processor used a method similar to branch prediction: By analyzing the order in which the application requested data from the main memory, the processor tried to predict the address of the next cell to be processed. Then, the processor could load the speculated address into cache before it was requested. Although hardware prefetching is automatic, data structures needed to be organized to reduce (ideally, to eliminate) errors in the processor's predictions.

If cache management commands are used properly, they (as well as hardware prefetching) can increase the speed of basic memory operations at least *three to five times.* Unfortunately, caching optimization cannot be delegated to the compiler. It is performed at the level of data structures and processing algorithms, and compilers are unable to optimize algorithms. (It is unlikely that they will be able to do so soon.) Therefore, programmers must take on this job.

Software Prefetching on AMD-K6+ and Pentium III+ Processors

Software prefetching is supported on the AMD-K6 processor, the VIA C3 microprocessor compatible with it, Pentium III, and Pentium 4. However, K6 and C3 preload data using different techniques than those used by PIII and P4. Therefore, these processors are incompatible. This has reduced the popularity of prefetching; programmers are forced to implement functions in two versions, or to limit the user's choice by specifying a processor. Both approaches involve considerable overhead, and the performance gain rarely compensates for this.

The release of the AMD Athlon processor, supporting a "dual" set of prefetching commands, improved the situation, although a lot of unresolved problems remains.

K6 is no longer manufactured and soon will be wiped off the market. Therefore, in this section, I will cover prefetching commands from the 3DNow! set briefly. The main discussion will focus on prefetching commands included in the set of MMX commands, supported by most contemporary processors.

Note that prefetching is expedient only when the required operating speed can't be achieved with other approaches.

Software Prefetching on AMD-K6, AMD Athlon, and VIA C3

On AMD-K6, AMD Athlon, and VIA C3, software prefetching is accomplished using one of two instructions: `prefetch` or `prefetchw`. The suffix at the end of the latter command informs the processor that the data to be loaded will be modified. Data loaded using the `prefetch` command also can be modified; however, the processor will be forced to run an extra cycle to change the attributes of the appropriate cache line from exclusive to modified. There are two key differences between these cache lines:

❐ Exclusive (or nonmodified) cache lines are discarded into the bit bucket (also known as "the black hole" or `/dev/null`) when they are taken from cache.
❐ Modified cache lines are moved into the main memory (or into a higher level of cache), whether or not they have been modified. This requires extra processor clocks. (For more details, see *Cache Organization.*)

The `prefetch` instruction initiates the request to the memory cell, just like any other command that accesses memory. Unlike these other commands, the `prefetch` instruction does not place the loaded data into a register. Furthermore, it doesn't wait until this data is loaded; it immediately returns control. Untimely completion of the request initiator doesn't relieve the cache controller from the necessity of accomplishing this request. However, if the requested cells are already in L1 cache, nothing happens; the `prefetch` instruction behaves like the `NOP` command (no operation).

If the requested cells are not in L1 cache, the cache controller accesses L2 cache. If the requested cells are not found there, the cache controller sends its request to the main memory (third-level cache) and fills the cache lines of all caches of lower levels. Because the cache controller and the processor's execution pipeline operate independently, prefetching allows the next portion of data to load while the previous one is processed. If the time required to load data doesn't exceed the processing time, the processor never idles, the executive pipeline doesn't stop, and the memory-access time is masked.

The `prefetchw` instruction works like `prefetch`, but it automatically assigns the modified status to the loaded line. If you plan to modify this line, `prefetchw` allows you to save 15 to 25 clocks of processor time. Conversely, if you are not sure whether the line will be modified, loading the line as exclusive would be better; unloading a line that is marked "modified" but that wasn't changed will cost more clocks.

Although AMD describes its prefetching commands as hardware-independent (such as in its optimization manual for Athlon), the number of bytes loaded by the `prefetch` and `prefetchw` instructions is determined by the size of the processor's cache lines. Different processors have different cache-line lengths: 32 bytes on K6/C3, and 64 bytes on Athlon/Duron. Accordingly, the optimum step and minimum prefetching distance differ. (For more details, see *Practical Uses of Prefetching*.)

In addition, AMD's prefetching instructions are not supported on Pentium processors. Therefore, AMD's implementation has no advantages over Intel's implementation.

Programmatic Prefetching on Pentium III and Pentium 4

On Pentium III and Pentium 4 processors, programmatic prefetching is accomplished by the following instructions: `prefetchnta`, `prefetcht0`, `prefetcht1`, and `prefetcht2`. The suffix specifies the type of the data to be loaded and defines the level of cache into which the data will be placed. The `nta` suffix refers to nontemporary data, which you plan to use once, and `t0`, `t1`, and `t2` designate temporary data, which you plan to use multiple times.

Regardless of the command used for prefetching, cache lines loaded from the main memory are always assigned the exclusive status. When lines are prefetched from L2 cache, they retain their previous status. Pentium processors do not implement the capability of loading a cache line and automatically assigning it the modified status. However, becaust of the multistage system of write buffering, the cache-line attributes are changed in the *primary* exchange cycle, not in the *secondary* one, as with K6/Athlon. Therefore, on Pentium processors, this operation doesn't produce overhead.

In contrast to the K6/Athlon prefetching instructions, the Pentium instructions *recommend* that the processor performs prefetching. The processor declines this recommendation and doesn't perform prefetching if one of the following conditions is true:

❐ The requested data already are in cache or in the level nearest to the processor.
❐ Information on the page to which the requested data belongs is missing from the Translation Look-aside Buffer (TLB).

❏ The processor's memory subsystem is busy moving data between L1 and L2 cache.

❏ The requested data belong to noncached memory (a page with uncacheable (UC) or uncacheable, speculative write combining (USWC) attributes).

❏ The data cannot be loaded because of an access error. (No exception is thrown.)

❏ The prefetching instruction is preceded by the LOCK prefix. (The "invalid opcode" exception is generated.)

If none of these conditions are true, the processor preloads data. The prefetching algorithm is hardware-dependent and varies from processor to processor. Therefore, prefetching commands on PIII and P4 should be considered separately.

Pentium III. The `prefetchnta` instruction loads data into L1 cache, bypassing L2 cache. It is expedient to place data that will not be accessed repeatedly into the cache level closest to the processor. It is undesirable to write over the contents of other cells; these contents still might be needed, and data that are used once won't be requested from L2 cache after they are removed from L1 cache.

The `prefetcht0` instruction loads data into both levels of cache memory. The data that will be accessed several times will be useful after they have been moved from L1 cache and loaded into L2 cache.

Like the `prefetchnta` instruction, the `prefetcht1` and `prefetcht2` instructions load data only into L2 cache, without placing them into L1 cache. Therefore, it is inexpedient to preload the appropriate cache lines into L1 cache. The `prefetcht1` and `prefetcht2` instructions will be needed in L2 cache!

The size of the data loaded into each cache line equals the size of the cache line: 32 bytes.

Pentium 4. None of the Pentium 4 prefetching commands allow data to be loaded into L1 cache. All data — temporary or not — are placed into L2 cache. The efficiency of such a strategy is disputable; nevertheless, the access time of L2 cache is much shorter than that of RAM. Therefore, this prefetching method is better than nothing.

A question arises: If *all* prefetching commands load data into L2 cache, how do they differ? There is no difference between `prefetcht0`, `prefetcht1`, and `prefetcht2`. The `prefetchnta` command loads data only into the first bank of L2 cache, rather than into any available bank. (The 8-way associative L2 cache of the P4 processor has eight such banks.) Because of this, `prefetchnta` never takes more than 1/8 of the total L2 cache space. As previously mentioned, data used once should not preempt data used several times from higher levels of cache. However, on P4, such preemption occurs. Unfortunately, it cannot be prevented. The least recently used cells are not preempted; rather, cache lines of the fixed bank, which may be used intensely by the application processing them, are preempted. In other words, the design of programmatic prefetching on P4 is rather lame.

The size of the data loaded into each cache line of L2 cache equals the size of the cache line: 128 bytes.

The differences in prefetching implementation on PIII and P4 complicate the optimization of applications. Each processor requires an individual approach; either PIII will be horribly slow, or P4 won't show its real potential. For maximum efficiency, you should implement all crucial procedures in four versions: for PIII, P4, K6, and Athlon. Quite a serious headache for programmers, don't you think? This doesn't mean you should abandon prefetching; sometimes, it is required.

Table 3.5 should simplify the behavior of prefetching instructions on different processor models.

Table 3.5. Prefetching Instructions on Different Processors

Instruction	Description			
	AMD-K6/C3 VIA	**AMD Athlon**	**Pentium III**	**Pentium 4**
prefetch	Loads 32 bytes into all levels of cache memory and assigns the exclusive attribute to the line	Loads 64 bytes into all levels of cache memory and assigns the exclusive attribute to the line	Not supported	
prefetchw	Loads 32 bytes into all levels of cache memory and assigns the modified attribute to the line	Loads 64 bytes into all levels of cache memory and assigns the modified attribute to the line		
prefetchnta	Not supported	Loads 64 bytes into L1 cache	Loads 32 bytes into L1 cache	Loads 128 bytes into L2 cache
prefetcht0		Loads 64 bytes into L1 and L2 cache	Loads 32 bytes into L1 and L2 cache	Loads 128 bytes into L2 cache
prefetcht1		Loads 64 bytes into L2 cache	Loads 32 bytes into L2 cache	
prefetcht2		Loads 64 bytes into L3 cache (if available)		

Hardware Prefetching on Pentium 4

To say that AMD is ahead of Intel in the implementation of programmatic prefetching support is to tell a half-truth. Prefetching is not an invention of AMD; it is widely used in other computers. Because direct cache management cannot be accomplished without knowledge of the characteristics of the memory subsystem and architecture of the processor, cache management is always hardware-dependent. In the world of "large" computers, which have fairly predictable configurations, programs often are optimized for specific hardware.

PCs are another matter. An optimal prefetching strategy depends on the type of RAM, the RAM access time and latency, chipset characteristics, width and clock frequency of the system bus, the processor core architecture, the CPU clock frequency, the caching policy, the length of cache lines, the bit capacity and frequency of internal bus, the latency of cache memory, and so on. Because of the variety of PC configurations, software prefetching causes more problems than it solves.

Pentium 4 developers took an important step by implementing *hardware prefetching*, or an *improved read-ahead strategy*. Previously, cache controllers of general-purpose microprocessors only started to load cache lines after they were explicitly requested. They lacked the intelligence to predict which line would be requested next!

P4 is capable not only of preloading the next 256 bytes (two cache lines) into L2 cache, but also of tracing regular patterns of data access. This allows the cache controller to predict the next cache line that will be accessed.

The prediction algorithm is undocumented; nevertheless, it is not too difficult to guess its general features. Suppose that the processor registers a sequence of cache misses when it accesses the cache lines numbered *N*, *N+3*, *N+6*, *N+9*, and so on. You don't need to be a prophet to predict that the line numbered *N+12* will be next. This means that P4 can recognize the arithmetic progression and calculate its members. As for recognizing the geometric progression, the documentation is silent. To check if P4 can do this, you must have the processor at your disposal.

Determining the step of arithmetic progression if you have several of its elements is a simple task. However, detecting a progression within an arbitrary sequence of numbers is difficult. Is Pentium 4 capable of solving this task? Its designers honestly admit in *Intel Pentium and Intel Xenon Processor Optimization Reference Manual* that it is not: P4 "follows only one stream per 4K page (load or store)." This means that within a single page, data processed within a loop must be accessed using a regular pattern; otherwise, the prediction mechanism will be "confused," and there will be no hardware prefetching. To facilitate this, you should split the data being processed into no more than eight blocks and place the blocks in different 4 KB regions. Why eight blocks? Because P4 cannot trace simultaneously more than eight regular patterns (in the developer's terminology: *data streams*). In addition, preloading is performed only within a single 4 KB region of memory. When you go beyond the limits of such a memory block, the prediction mechanism is disabled, and tracing of the access pattern is restarted. This means that the processor again waits until several cache misses have occurred, then it determines the step of the progression and starts the next prefetching session. Consequently, the memory cells read at a larger step (about 1 KB) can never be prefetched and are processed inefficiently.

Thus, hardware prefetching is more visible to the programmer than Intel would have you believe. In contrast to software prefetching, hardware prefetching speeds up applications, even those unaware of its existence. Maximum efficiency, however, can be achieved when the structure of the processed data is organized. However, such restructuring is not always possible. Therefore, despite the power of hardware prefetching, software prefetching doesn't lose its position; even on P4, it remains one of the most efficient tools for optimizing applications.

Prefetching Efficiency in Multitasking Systems

Processes running in multitasking systems do not monopolize cache memory. On the contrary, they must share it. Does this reduce prefetching efficiency? It has no effect on the efficiency of prefetching into L1 cache. The time interval between switching from task to task represents an eternity for the processor, which corresponds to millions of clocks. Whether the contents of L1 cache are discarded or not, prefetching allows pipeline data to be loaded from the main memory, preventing performance drops.

The situation isn't so clear with L2 cache. If the algorithm being optimized allows data to be loaded and processed in parallel, the state of L2 cache doesn't play a role. The operating speed of the program is limited by the calculation speed, rather than the memory subsystem throughput. (See *Practical Uses of Prefetching*.) However, if the data-processing time is shorter than the time required to load data from the main memory, it is impossible to avoid a decrease in performance. Prefetching will improve the performance of your program, but this improvement will be insignificant.

Simultaneous execution of two or more applications intensely exchanging data with the memory is rare for workstations (although this situation is normal for servers). Many times, the PC user works with one application while other programs run in background mode and consume minimal memory. (Sometimes they are "sleeping," never touch L2 cache, and have little effect on the prefetching efficiency.)

Practical Uses of Prefetching

If the code-grinding algorithm allows the address of the next cell to be predicted with a sufficiently high probability, this algorithm is a good candidate for optimization. The more precisely the address of the next cell is predicted, the more significant the gain obtained by prefetching. This relates to loops with a constant step, geometric transforms in 2D or 3D graphics, memory copying and initialization, string operations, etc. It makes less sense to process lists and binary trees using optimization. You do not know the order of their elements beforehand; this can be determined only by examining the list (or tree). In general, it is impossible to determine the address of the next element. However, you often can *guess* this address. For example, you can assume that the starting position of the next element directly follows the end position of the preceding one. If the list (or binary tree) isn't too fragmented, the number of hits will exceed the number of misses, and prefetching will have a positive effect.

Consider the following code:

Listing 3.19. Candidate for Optimization Using Prefetching

```
#define STEP_SIZE L1_CACHE_LINE_SIZE
for(a=0; a<BLOCK_SIZE; a+=STEP_SIZE)
{
_jn(c, b);
// Any calculation is performed.

b+=p[c];
// The next cell is read.
}
```

If the block being processed is missing from both L1 and L2 cache, and if the loop step is equal to or greater than the cache-line size, each attempt to access the memory will cause a delay of 10 to 12 clocks of the system bus. This is required to transfer the requested cells from the slow RAM into cache. On Pentium III 733, it will take more than 50 processor clocks! As a result, the time required to execute Listing 3.19 depends on the operating speed of the memory subsystem, rather than on the processor's clock frequency.

However, because the address of the cell to be processed next is known beforehand, it is possible to load data into cache while the calculations are made. The code optimized for PIII might look as follows:

Listing 3.20. Optimized Version Using Prefetching (on Pentium III)

```
#define STEP_SIZE L1_CACHE_LINE_SIZE
for(c=0; c<BLOCK_SIZE; c+=STEP_SIZE)
{

// The command for prefetching the next 32-byte line
// into L1 cache will be executed. Loading will take place while
// the _jn function is executed. When the required cell is requested,
// it already will be in L1 cache, and the processor
// will be able to retrieve it without any delays.
   _prefetchnta(p+c+STEP_SIZE);
```

```
// The cell to be processed during the next iteration of the loop,
// rather than the one processed during the current iteration,
// will be loaded into cache. During execution of the _jn function,
// the requested cache line simply cannot be loaded in time!
// (See Practical Uses of Prefetching.)
   _jn(c, b);

// Some calculations will be performed.

// The next cell will be read. During all iterations
// of the loop, except the first iteration, the cell
// is guaranteed to be present in L1 cache. As a result,
// the time required to read it will be reduced to one CPU clock.
   b += p[c];
}
```

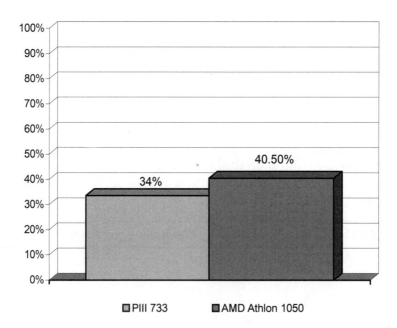

Fig. 3.39. Efficiency of software prefetching after optimization (Listing 3.20)

On PIII 733/133/100, the optimized version will execute 34% faster. On AMD Athlon 1050/100/100, the performance gain will be about 40% (Fig. 3.39). Note that this loop accesses memory once per iteration. The more attempts to access memory, the more significant the gain from optimization.

Maximum performance growth is achieved in the following cases: *data are pre-fetched into the cache level that corresponds to their purpose, the requested data are loaded exactly when they are requested*, and *only needed data are prefetched*. (Although the prefetching instructions aren't blockable and can avoid reloading the data already in cache, it will cost processing time. Additional calls decrease the performance.)

On P4, Listing 3.19 doesn't need to be optimized because the processor detects the sequence of data-access operations and loads the needed data beforehand. The software prefetching instruction would produce unneeded (but insignificant) overhead.

To transfer Listing 3.19 to K6 or C3, replace the `prefetchnta` instruction with its closest analogue: `prefetch`.

Determining the Preferred Cache Hierarchy

The closer the data are to the processor in the cache hierarchy, the more quickly they can be retrieved. This means that if you decide to use prefetching, the best approach is to load the data into L1 cache. (Exceptions to this rule will be considered later in this chapter.)

On Pentium III, if the data will be used many times, it is best to prefetch them into all levels of cache memory. Then, if the data are discarded from L1 cache, they can be loaded from L2 cache with minimum delay, and the processor won't need to access slow RAM. It is inexpedient to load into L2 cache data that will be used only once (or data that never will be discarded from L1 cache). This is especially true if L2 cache stores something useful.

All of the above-mentioned is true for PIII, but it is not quite applicable to Pentium 4. P4 never loads data into L1 cache. This processor places them into the first bank of L2 cache, and programmers have no freedom of choice. The only difference between the `prefetchnta` command and one of the other Pentium prefetching commands is `prefetchnta` cannot discard more than 1/8 of the total cache amount. (Proponents of Murphy's law should not be surprised that the most needed data will be discarded.)

On AMD-K6 or VIA C3, you will have no problem determining the preferred cache hierarchy — there is no possibility of choosing it. The data are always loaded into all cache levels, and the contents of L2 cache are preempted even more intensely than on P4! For this reason, the developers that need to optimize their programs for K6 or C3 won't find anything interesting in this section.

In Listing 3.20 and the graph it produces (Fig. 3.40), it doesn't matter whether the `prefetchnta` or `prefetcht0` command is used: Each cell is accessed once, and no valuable data, which you'd regret discarding, are stored in L2 cache. (Bear in mind that in multitasking operating systems, cache is shared by several applications; therefore, it is unwise to overwrite its contents without a good reason.)

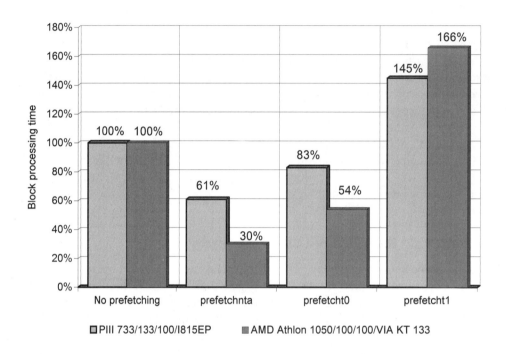

Fig. 3.40. Comparison of the efficiency of different prefetching methods

Consider another example: Suppose that you have an algorithm that processes two blocks within a loop. One of these blocks, BLOCK1, fits within L2 cache; the other one, BLOCK2, exceeds the size of L2 cache considerably. (See Listing 3.21.) Both blocks can't fit within L2 cache; however, there at least must be room for the smaller one! Alas, the processor, trying to cache all the cells being processed, will constantly remove the data contained in BLOCK1 from cache and replacing them with the data from BLOCK2. At the next iteration of the loop, cache won't contain BLOCK1 or BLOCK2 data, and you will have to wait again for this data to be loaded from slow RAM.

Listing 3.21. Candidate for Optimization by Prefetching Nontemporary Data

---

```
for(...) // Loop that executes several times
for(c=0; c<BLOCK2_SIZE; c+=STEP_SIZE)

{
   b+=p1[d]; if ((d+=32) > BLOCK1_SIZE) d=0;
// The BLOCK1 block is processed. Because this block
// is processed within the for(...) loop, it is desirable
// to prevent it from being discarded from L2 cache.
```

```
   b+=b % (c+1);
// Some calculations are performed.

  b+=p2[c];
// The BLOCK2 block is processed. This block
// exceeds the size of L2 cache considerably;
// therefore, it does not need to be cached.
// In addition, during subsequent iterations of the loop,
// the required data will be missing from cache.
// Furthermore, cache already contains BLOCK1,
// which should not be discarded. Alas,
// the processor takes the initiative and places
// the data from BLOCK2 into L2 cache,
// using the least optimal caching strategy.
}
```

Is it possible to decrease the number of cache misses (thus improving the performance) without significantly complicating the algorithm? Of course, it is possible. (Again, the exception is K6 or C3.) Just use the command for prefetching nontemporary data. By using prefetching, you will not need to wait while the cells of the BLOCK2 block are loaded. In addition, you will be able to load BLOCK2 directly into L1 cache (on P4, into the first bank of L2 cache), without overwriting the contents of BLOCK1 stored in L2 cache. (On P4, BLOCK1 will be partially overwritten.)

To summarize, the prefetchnta instruction is the most profitable option because it doesn't overwrite L2 cache on most processors, and on P4, it only overwrites minimal data in L2 cache.

Listing 3.22. Optimized Version That Prefetches Nontemporary Data

```
for(...)
for(c=0; c<BLOCK2_SIZE; c+=STEP_SIZE)
{

    b+=p1[d]; if ((d+=32) > BLOCK1_SIZE) d=0;
    // The BLOCK1 block (present in L2 cache) is processed.
    // It does not need to be prefetched into L1 cache.
    // Prefetching won't improve the performance because,
    // on PIII, it takes little time to access L2 cache.
    // On P4, prefetching simply doesn't allow you
    // to load data into L1 cache.

    _prefetchnta(p2+c+STEP_SIZE);
    // Before proceeding with the calculations, the command
    // is issued that prefetches data from BLOCK2 into L1 cache
    // (into L2 cache on P4). This avoids the wait for data
```

```
    // to be loaded from slow RAM, and prevents BLOCK1
    // from being discarded from L2 cache.

    b+=b % (c+1);
    // Note that only data that will be accessed
    // during the next iteration are loaded.
    // Why? The loading time exceeds the time
    // required to calculate b+=b % (c+1). In addition,
    // loading the data for the next iteration will load
    // only the first iteration of the loop,
    // rather than each next nearest iteration.
    // This technique is valid and ensures
    // maximum growth of the execution speed.

    b+=p2[c];
    // Data are loaded from L1 cache (from L2 cache on P4).
}
```

On PIII, using the `prefetchnta` command improves performance by 49%, and `prefetcht0` improves it by 32% (Fig. 3.41).

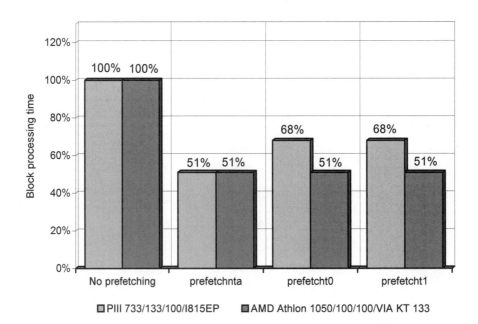

Fig. 3.41. Influence of different prefetching types on application performance

Planning the Prefetching Distance

Because RAM is slow, cache lines take a long time to load. Consequently, prefetching must be done beforehand and in such a way that when the data to be processed are needed, they already have been loaded into cache.

With linear data processing, this can be achieved easily. Loops are another matter. What if the time required to load the data exceeds the time of an iteration? The problem presented in Listing 3.21 was solved in Listing 3.22 by prefetching data that would be processed during the next iteration of the loop. Pay attention: The data for the *next* iteration was preloaded, not the data for the *next nearest* iteration. Because of this, loop execution was inefficient only during the first iteration; all subsequent iterations ran extremely efficiently.

If there is enough time to load the required data during the execution of the preceding iteration, the loading interval doesn't exceed the time of an iteration. If this is true, then why is a shift necessary? After all, there must be time for the data to load during the current loop iteration.

The answer to this question can be found in the interaction between the processor core and the memory subsystem. This topic was covered in detail in *Chapter 2*. (See *Interaction between the Memory and the Processor*.) Here, I'll remind you of the most common aspects. Of interest is the behavior of the CPU when it reads a memory cell missing from both L1 and L2 cache.

The CPU spends one clock ensuring that neither L1 nor L2 cache contain the requested cell. Then, the processor decides to retrieve the missing data from the main memory. The processor spits the cell address into the address bus, then takes several extra clocks to pass it to the memory controller. Next, the chipset calculates the column number and the row number, and checks if the respective memory page is open. If the page is open, the chipset sets the Column Address Strobe (CAS) signal. Two to three clocks later (depending on the CAS latency, which is determined by the quality of the memory chip), the long-awaited data appear on the bus.

(If the requested row is closed but the maximum number of the rows that can be opened simultaneously has not been reached, the chipset sends the Row Address Strobe (RAS) signal and the row address to the memory chip. The chip takes two or three clocks to understand it. Then, the CAS signal is sent again, and the wait again occurs for the data to appear on the bus. If the CAS signal is not sent, several more clocks will be lost while one of the pages closes.)

The memory controller swallows the first portion of data during one clock. At the beginning of the next clock, it passes the data to the waiting processor while it pulls the second portion of data from the memory chip. The number of data portions loaded per bus-exchange cycle varies from processor to processor; it is determined by the size of the L2 cache lines. PII and K6, which have 32-byte cache lines, can be filled with four 64-bit portions of data. Full memory access requires 10 to 12 system bus clocks, but only 4 of these clocks are needed to transfer the data. During the other clocks, the bus remains idle.

However, if the address of the next cell to be processed is known beforehand, the processor can send the next request to the controller without waiting for the previous one to be fulfilled. Pipelining masks the memory latency by decreasing the access time from between 10 and 12 clocks to 4 clocks (Fig. 3.42). Although it will still take 10 to 12 clocks to read the first cell, this delay can be ignored if the data processing is cyclic. This provides an answer to the question of why a shift of one iteration is required for efficient data prefetching. This shift compensates for the latency time (T_l), which exceeds the effective data-transfer time (T_b).

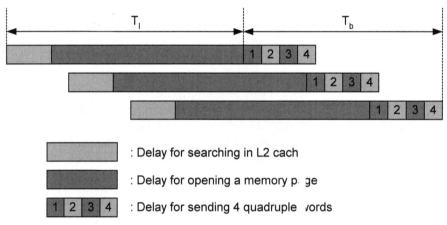

: Delay for searching in L2 cach

: Delay for opening a memory p ge

| 1 | 2 | 3 | 4 | : Delay for sending 4 quadruple ords

Fig. 3.42. Demonstration of the memory-exchange pipeline

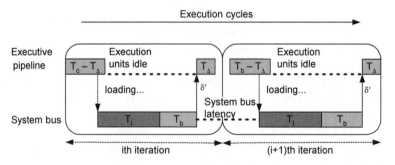

Fig. 3.43. Executing a loop without prefetching ($T_\Delta = T_c - (T_i + T_b)$)

Loop-execution time without prefetching. If prefetching is not used, the loop-execution time is the sum of the time required to execute the calculating instructions of the loop (T_c), the latency time (T_l), and the time needed to load data (T_b). During calculations, the system bus is idle; while data is loading, the executive pipeline is idle and the bus is operating. At this connection, the memory-access time is determined by the latency of the memory subsystem, rather than by the bus throughput. The bus operates at 15% to 20% of its workload capacity, even in an ideal scenario (Fig. 3.43).

Loop-execution time when $T_c >= T_l + T_b$. If the time required to execute the calculating instructions of the loop is greater than or equal to the sum of the memory-latency time and the data-loading time, prefetching allows the system bus to operate and the pipeline to execute simultaneously (Fig. 3.44).

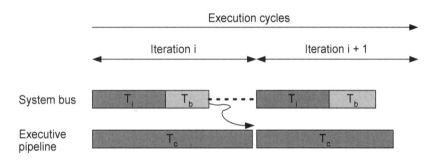

Fig. 3.44. Executing a loop $(T_c >= T_l + T_b)$ with a prefetching distance of one iteration (the arrow indicates data dependence)

Memory-access delays are masked, and the loop-execution time is determined exclusively by the calculations. In addition, the performance is improved according to the following formula:

$$1 + \frac{T_l + T_b}{T_c}$$

In the best scenario (when $T_c = T_l + T_c$), the loop-execution time is cut in half.

The minimum prefetching distance equals one iteration. However, if the program runs on a fast computer with slow memory (a typical office or home computer), there won't be enough time to load the requested memory cells during the execution of the previous iteration. This will jam the bus, causing the processor to idle. Consequently, the program will run inefficiently.

The best way to resolve this situation is to increase the prefetching distance to two or three iterations. Several loop iterations will be lost; however, two or three iterations are only a drop in the ocean.

Loop-execution time when $T_l + T_b > T_c > T_b$. Suppose that the full memory-access time (i.e., the sum of the latency time and the data-loading time) exceeds the calculation time (T_c). If the calculation time exceeds the data-loading time, efficient parallel operations are still possible! It is only necessary to request the next portion of data before the previous portion is received. This is achieved by increasing the prefetching distance by several iterations. The minimum number of iterations can be determined using the following formula:

$$psd = \frac{T_l + T_b}{T_c}$$

Here, *psd* stands for *prefetch scheduling distance*, measured in iterations. To be on the safe side, it is best to choose a larger prefetching distance.

In the worst case, performance is doubled; on average, performance is quadrupled or quintupled. The typical memory latency is about ten clocks, and the data-loading time is four clocks. If $T_c = T_b$, then the following formula is true:

$$1 + \frac{10 + 4}{4} = 4.5$$

The workload of the system bus reaches 80% to 90% (or, ideally, 100%). Great result, isn't it?

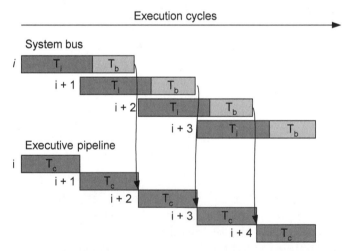

Fig. 3.45. Executing a loop ($T_l + T_b > T_c > T_b$) with a prefetching distance of two iterations (arrows indicate data dependence)

Loop-execution time when $T_b > T_c$. Finally, if the data-loading time (T_b) exceeds the calculation time, full parallelism becomes impossible. Because the data-loading time exceeds the duration of an iteration, the executive pipeline inevitably idles, which preloading cannot help. Still, it will help mask the memory latency, which provides two- or threefold performance growth. This isn't insignificant.

The optimal prefetching distance can be determined using the following formula:

$$psd = 1 + \frac{T_l}{T_b}$$

Because the loop-execution time often is determined exclusively by the data-loading speed (actually, by the system bus frequency, whose workload capacity reaches 100%), it doesn't make sense to be zealous about code optimization. Such exclusive determination can occur if you are copying or comparing memory blocks. (Copying optimization deserves special discussion. See *Secrets of Copying Memory, or New Commands of Pentium III and Pentium 4.*)

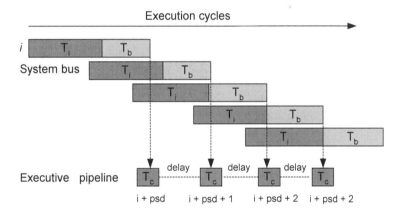

Fig. 3.46. Executing a loop ($T_b > T_c$) with a prefetching distance of three iterations (arrows indicate data dependence)

Practical planning of prefetching. To calculate the optimal prefetching distance, you need to know the memory-latency period (T_l), the data-loading time (T_b), and the duration of a loop iteration (T_c). Because all three arguments are hard-ware-dependent, you must determine their values *dynamically* during run time or calculate the lower limit of the prefetching distance *statically*. Consider each algorithm in detail.

Dynamic calculation of the prefetching distance provides the greatest performance growth and is implemented easily. Several algorithms are possible. By measuring the time required to execute the first iteration of the loop (for example, by using the RDTSC instruction), you will find the result of $T_c + T_l + T_b$. By repeating the iteration, you will find the value of T_c. (Because the data are already in cache, little time is required to access them.) The difference between these two values will give you the result of $T_l + T_b$, which, with the pure T_c value, is sufficient for calculating $\dfrac{T_l + T_b}{T_c}$.

Determining the pure T_b time is rather difficult. Therefore, I would advise using the fork algorithm: By testing various prefetching distances and comparing the lengths of the corresponding loop iterations, you will find the optimal value within the nearest iterations. This value will be optimal because the best prefetching distances usually change during loop execution. This is especially true of branching loops that process heterogeneous data.

Besides this, the dynamic algorithm for determining the prefetching distance automatically adapts to new processor models. In programs intended for long-term usage, static calculation of the prefetching distance is inexpedient. No one knows how processors will change in the coming years, and even their current characteristics are subject to dispersion. In Celeron 800, the ratio of the system bus frequency to the core frequency is 1:8; in Pentium 4 1300, the ratio of the same parameter is not quite 1:3. Consequently, the result of $\dfrac{T_l + T_b}{T_c}$ will differ greatly on different processors. The prefetching distance optimal for Celeron would be too small for P4, which would idle and wait for the next portion of data to be loaded. As a result, migration from Celeron to P4 barely increases the performance of such a program.

For this reason, you should plan the prefetching distance with a reserve (at least three iterations more than the required minimum). A simplified formula for calculating the minimum prefetching distance, and descriptions of its elements, is as follows:

$$psd = \left| \frac{N_{lockup} + N_{xfer} * (N_{pref} + N_{st})}{CPI * N_{inst}} \right|$$

- ❏ psd — Prefetch scheduling distance (in loop iterations)
- ❏ N_{lockup} — Memory latency (in clocks)
- ❏ N_{xfer} — Time required to load cache lines (in clocks)
- ❏ N_{pref} and N_{st} — Number of prefetched and discarded cache lines
- ❏ CPI — Time required to execute one instruction (in clocks)
- ❏ N_{inst} — Number of instructions per loop iteration

Practically all members of this formula are unknown. Memory latency varies greatly because it is determined by the type of the memory (SDRAM, DDR SDRAM, Rambus DRAM), the quality of the memory chips (RAS and CAS latency), the level of the chipset's features, and the relation of the system bus frequency to the processor's core frequency. The time required to load cache lines is proportional to the length of these lines (currently 32 bytes, 64 bytes, or 128 bytes, depending on the CPU model). Manufacturers constantly increase the length of cache lines.

The average time required to execute a single instruction is an abstract value, analogous to the average income of the citizens of a specific state. In addition to very fast commands, which can be executed within a single clock, there are other commands that require dozens or even hundreds of clocks to execute! (For example, integer division, a common operation, requires 50 to 70 clocks.)

Thus, static planning of the prefetching distance is similar to fortune-telling. Nevertheless, you can make some guesses.

In the *Intel Pentium 4 Optimization,* Intel provides the following formula, explicitly mentioning its limitations:

$$psd = \left| \frac{60 + 25 * (N_{pref} + N_{st})}{1.5 * N_{inst}} \right|$$

Calculating the number of instructions within the loop (N_{inst}) is an interesting task: Even if you use the assembly language to implement crucial loops, the translator may include unsolicited instructions (for example, NOP instructions for alignment).

The exact number of the instructions can be determined only if they are calculated manually in the assembly code. Although most compilers can generate such listings, this is a tedious job, and you'll have to do it each time you introduce changes into the source code of the program. If an external function is called from the loop (for example, an API function of the operating system), you'll have to either retrieve the source code of the OS or disassemble the function. These source codes are rarely available, and not every programmer knows how to use a disassembler. After such efforts, the result that you will have obtained may be incorrect.

Fortunately, the range of the optimal prefetching distance is rather wide. Even increasing the minimal value ten times rarely decreases performance by more than about 15%. (For loops repeated multiple times, it decreases even less.) Therefore, if the execution speed of the code is not crucial, dynamic calculation of the prefetching distance can be replaced by static planning, with a subsequent increase of the result.

Providing the user with the option of specifying the prefetching distance is a good idea. To avoid cluttering the interface and confusing beginners, you can place these settings in the registry.

Improving Prefetching Efficiency

Preventing slacking. If prefetching is shifted several iterations, it will result in *slacking*—inefficient execution of the first *psd* loop iterations. The requested data will be missing from cache, and the processor will be forced to wait for the data to be loaded from the slow RAM. If the loop is executed many times (a hundred or even a hundred thousand times), the overhead will be so small that it is unlikely you would even think of accounting for it. If the loop is executed several dozen times, its execution time will have little influence on system performance and can be ignored. However, if such a loop is called multiple times (for example, from within another loop), the losses caused by the idle time might be large.

Consider the following example:

Listing 3.23. Prefetching Slack Time

```
for (a = 0; a < N; a++)
{
 for (b = 0; b < BLOCK_SIZE; b+=STEP_SIZE)
 {
     _prefetchnta (p[a][b+STEP_SIZE]);
     // To apply this example to K6 or Athlon, replace
     // the prefetchnta instruction with prefetch.

     computation (a[a][b]);
 }
}
```

Because the prefetching distance of the b loop equals one loop iteration, the first iteration of the loop always will be inefficient. This is idling. When the BLOCK_SIZE parameter has a small value and N is large, it is hard to be resigned to this situation. When the prefetching distance is comparable to the number of the iterations of the b loop, its efficiency goes to zero. In particular, the hardware preloading mechanism of P4 cannot deal with nested loops.

How can you improve the performance of the algorithm without complicating it? Simply preload the next cell to be processed at the last iteration of the b loop. In Listing 3.23, this would be the p[a+1][0] cell.

The optimized version of the code might look as follows:

Listing 3.24. Eliminating the Prefetching Slack Time (Preliminary Version)

```
for (a = 0; a < N; a++)
{
 for (b = 0; b < BLOCK_SIZE; b+=STEP_SIZE)
 {
     if (b == (BLOCK_SIZE - STEP_SIZE))
         _prefetchnta (p[a+1][0]);
     else
         _prefetchnta (p[a][b+STEP_SIZE]);

     computation (p[a][b]);
 }
}
```

Note that the use of branches in the loop body will have a negative effect on the loop's performance. Therefore, it is best to discard the conditional jump by rewriting the code as follows:

Listing 3.25. Eliminating the Prefetching Slack Time (Final Version)

```
for (a = 0; a < N; a++)
{
for (b = 0; b < (BLOCK_SIZE-STEP_SIZE); b+=STEP_SIZE)
{
   _prefetchnta (p[a][b+STEP_SIZE]);
   computation (p[a][b]);
}
_prefetchnta (p[a+1][0]);
computation (p[a][b]);
}
```

After this program was rewritten, only one slack iteration remained. It occurred during the first run of the b loop. (To be more precise, there will be *psd* idle runs.) Even if N is small, the slack iteration would have little influence on performance.

Reducing the number of prefetching instructions. All previous considerations were based on the assumption that the loop step equals the cache-line size. This is not always true. An illustrative example follows:

Listing 3.26. Misuse of Prefetching

```
int p[N];
#define computation (x) zzz+=(x)*0x666; zzz+=p[x];
for (a = 0; a < N; a+=sizeof(int))
{
 _prefetchnta (p[a + 32*3]);
 computation (a);
}
```

Each element of the p array takes only 4 bytes. The cache-line size, depending on the processor model, is 32 bytes to 128 bytes. Therefore, during most iterations of the loop, the prefetching command will slack; the requested data will be in cache already, and there will be no need to load them from the slow RAM. In this situation, the prefetching command behaves similar to the NOP instruction except the former produces overhead. Prefetching misuse (or overprefetching) makes the loop to execute even slower. Listing 3.26 will run faster without prefetching (Fig. 3.47). (You also should account for the overhead produced by passing arguments to the prefetching function.)

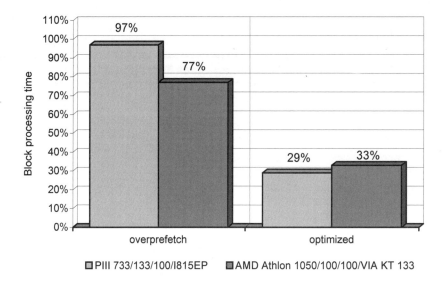

Fig. 3.47. Effect of overprefetching on performance (assuming that the time required to copy memory using the built-in `memcpy` function equals 100%)

The solution to this problem is to unroll the loop, then adjust the loop step until it matches the cache-line size. This will decrease the overhead produced by loop execution and remove the unneeded prefetching operation. As a result, the execution speed of the code will increase considerably.

Listing 3.27. [cache_prefetch_unroll] Unrolling the Loop to Eliminate Extra Prefetching Requests

```
for (a = 0; a < N; a+=32)
{
    _prefetchnta (p[a + 32*3]);
    computation (a+0);
    computation (a+4);
    computation (a+8);
    computation (a+12);
    computation (a+16);
    computation (a+20);
    computation (a+24);
    computation (a+28);
}
```

This technique has drawbacks. Multiple duplication of the loop body greatly increases the amount of executable code. Consequently, you risk exceeding the cache limits. In addition, the step size (and, consequently, the cache-line size) can only be selected at the stage of software development, and it is almost impossible to change this size at the run-time stage. What's wrong with hard encoding? If the program executes on the processor using different cache-line lengths, it will run inefficiently. Orienting the cache-line length to 32 bytes means you will be clinging to processors whose days are numbered. But optimizing your code to a length of 128 bytes makes no sense. Workstations based on P4 may take several years to drive PIII off the market; at that time, most processors may still have 32- or 64-byte cache lines. It seems that the only answer is to implement all performance-crucial functions in several versions, then choose an appropriate version at run time.

Some programmers might suggest inserting a simple conditional operator into the loop, such as `if ((a % PREFETCH_CACHE_LINE_SIZE) == 0) prefetch(a+psd)`. However, division is an extremely slow operation; the performance would drop so far that you'd need a winch to pull it up. Even if you replaced division with bitwise operations (or introduced an additional counter into the loop), overhead would remain. It would be much better to choose 32-byte cache lines and give up optimization for P4 and newer processors, which are fast enough without it.

Mixing prefetching with other instructions. The preceding prefetching examples had one cache line per loop iteration. If several memory blocks are processed simultaneously, one prefetching instruction will be insufficient. The best approach is to reorganize the data structure, placing the shared data blocks as close together as possible (ideally, within the same cache line). Unfortunately, this is not always feasible. When you cannot decrease the number of prefetching instructions, you should at least improve the efficiency of their execution.

Consider the following example:

Listing 3.28. Nonoptimized Processing of Four Memory Cells in One Iteration

---

```
for (a = 0; a < N; a+=32)
{
    computation1 (p1[a]);
    computation2 (p2[a]);
    computation3 (p3[a]);
    computation4 (p4[a]);
}
```

If memory blocks `p1`, `p2`, `p3`, and `p4` are far apart, at least four prefetching instructions are required per iteration. Hence, you will have to make the following decision:

Should you place these instructions at the start of the loop body, or is it better to mix them with other loop instructions?

Each technique has strong and weak points, and the best choice depends on the situation. A large number of sequential prefetching requests overloads both the system bus and the internal bus, jamming the load and fill buffers. As a result, the execution of instructions that access the data slackens — even if those data are in L1 cache. Prefetching instructions should be alternated with the calculations; then, they can be executed in parallel without overloading the bus. However, this statement is only true for calculating instructions, not for write commands. To achieve the best system performance, I strongly recommend that you use a minimal number of transactions between data reads and writes.

As you can see, the optimal placement of prefetching commands can be complicated. If the loop body exclusively consists of calculating instructions that do not write anything into the memory, then it is better to mix prefetching instructions with the other instructions that make up the loop body. If write commands are present in the loop body, it is best to combine the code in a way that prevents read and write transactions from overlapping.

This means that between prefetching instructions and write commands, there must be at least 30 CPU clocks. What if this is impossible? It would be better to group all prefetching operations than to allow them to mix with write operations. Optimal layering can be chosen experimentally, but remember that it is system-dependent.

Optimizing Data Structures for Hardware Prefetching

Expert usage of software prefetching allows the programmer to forget about hardware prefetching. This approach has been preferred because only Pentium 4 and the latest versions of AMD Athlon implement hardware prefetching. In addition, it's unclear whether hardware prefetching will be developed further in processors yet to be released. However, as previously demonstrated, it sometimes is impossible to achieve maximum application efficiency without optimizing for a specific processor model. This means that versions of the same code fragment must be implemented separately for K6 (VIA C3), Athlon, PII, PIII, and P4.

Because software prefetching produces overhead, it makes sense to abandon it any time hardware prefetching shows good results. These situations include loops repeated many times based on regular templates. Note that there must be no more than one flow per page, and the total number of flows must not exceed eight. Consider the following code:

Listing 3.29. Code Optimized Efficiently by Hardware Prefetching, with One Regular Template on a Page

---

```
int x[BIGNUM];
for(a = 0; a < BIGNUM, a++)
 sum+=x[a];
```

Now, consider a minor modification to Listing 3.29. In the following code fragment, two arrays are added within the loop body:

Listing 3.30. Code That "Blinds" Hardware Prefetching, with Two Regular Templates on the Page

---

```
int x[256];
int y[256];
for(a = 0; a < 256, a++)
{
    sum1+=x[a];
    sum2+=y[a];
}
```

Because both arrays are within the same page, the hardware prefetching mechanism is blinded, and data are not prefetched. Performance can be improved by splitting the loop in two. Each small loop can process its own array. Alternatively, the x and y arrays can be separated by a memory region of at least 4 KB.

> ### ▶ Note
>
> Loop splitting cannot be achieved simply by separating the x and y arrays with one more array. The order in which arrays are placed in memory is a task of the compiler; it will not necessarily coincide with the order in which they were declared in the program.

Finally, performance can be improved by converting two arrays into an array of elements within a single structure:

Listing 3.31. Code Optimized Correctly by Hardware Prefetching

---

```
struct ZZZ{int x; int x;} zzz[1024];
for(a = 0; a < 1024, a++)
{
    sum1+=zzz.x[a];
    sum2+=zzz.y[a];
}
```

At first, it may be difficult to see what was achieved by the conversion; there are still two regular templates per page. However, both templates are combined within *one common template*. The previous code accessed memory cells numbered *N*, *N+1024*, *N+4*, *N+1028*, *N+8*, *N+1032*, and so on. Listing 3.31 accessed cells numbered *N*, *N+4*, *N+8*, *N+12*, and so on.

Remember that the template is not determined by the addresses of the accessed cells; rather, it is determined by the addresses of the cells that caused a cache miss. Within any 128-byte memory block already in L2 cache, it is possible to use an irregular template; only the 128-byte block itself must be requested regularly.

Is it possible to execute the following code efficiently on P4?

Listing 3.32. Code That "Blinds" Hardware Prefetching, with Read and Write Operations on One Page

```
struct ZZZ{int x; int x; int sum;} zzz[BIGNUM];
for(a = 0; a < BIGNUM; a++)
{
    zzz.sum[a] = zzz.x[a] + zzz.y[a];
}
```

This code will run inefficiently! Within one page, both read and write operations are executed, and hardware prefetching doesn't take place. What should you do? If the zzz array contains no more than 1,024 elements, you can ensure that the read and write operations don't occur within the same page by dividing the zzz structure into three independent arrays as follows:

Listing 3.33. Correctly Optimized Code, with Read and Write Operations on Different Pages

```
int x[BIGNUM]; int x[BIGNUM]; int sum[BIGNUM];
for(a = 0; a < BIGNUM, a++)
{
    sum[a] = x[a] + y[a];
}
```

Note that this technique considerably reduces the efficiency of code execution on other processors. Why? You know that placing the data within the same DRAM page drastically reduces its latency. When accessing a cell, it is sufficient to transfer its column number, because its row number would be the same as the number used during the previous operation.

However, alternating access to data in different DRAM pages requires you to pass the full cell address, which takes at least two clocks of the system bus. In P4, you can compensate for the latency with hardware prefetching; other processors have nothing you can use as compensation. This is just confirmation of the statement that code optimal for P4 isn't necessarily optimal for other processors, and vice versa.

Secrets of Copying Memory, or New Commands of Pentium III and Pentium 4

Processing strings, structures, arrays, and objects; passing arguments to functions; playing sound; or displaying images on the screen represent a long, but far from complete, list of the areas to which memory-copying functions can be applied. Compiler developers put great effort into making the built-in memory-copying function fly as fast as possible. (In C language, this is the memcpy function.) However, optimization problems have no general solutions; an algorithm optimal for one situation often proves inefficient in another situation.

Copying memory is not as trivial as it might seem. It has peculiarities and secrets. This section is dedicated to these problems. (Additional information can be found in *Optimizing Built-in C Functions That Work with the Memory*.)

Optimizing Memory Copying

The built-in memcpy function included with the standard C library is used most often to copy memory. This is a fast function; most implementations of it are based on the cyclic REP MOVSD move command, which copies 4 bytes of data per iteration. In some situations, however (such as when working with large blocks) the performance of memcpy drops dramatically, and most programmers have an irrepressible desire to optimize it, at least slightly.

Trying to rewrite memcpy in assembly language is wasted labor. Even if you remove all wrapping code that would ensure data is copied in blocks whose sizes are not multiples of four, you will see little performance gain. However, choosing the correct starting address for the block to be copied will improve the result. This statement is confirmed by Fig. 3.48, which illustrates how the speed at which memory blocks are copied depends on the size of the offset from the starting point of the block, allocated by the malloc function. (In this example, the address it returned is a multiple of 0x10.)

Large memory blocks (which significantly exceed the size of L2 cache) whose starting addresses are multiples of four will be processed almost 1.5 times faster than blocks that start from other addresses. Medium-sized blocks (which fit in L2 cache) will be processed almost three times faster than blocks starting from addresses that are not multiples of four.

This is not surprising; due to a lack of alignment, each octet of copied double words inevitably will contain 1 double word that starts in one cache line and continues in another line. Pentium processors can't stand such double words, and this leads to delays.

Therefore, when you copy many strings, structures, objects, or arrays, it is highly desirable to make sure that they are placed in the memory at addresses that are multiples of four. (See *Data Alignment Efficiency*.)

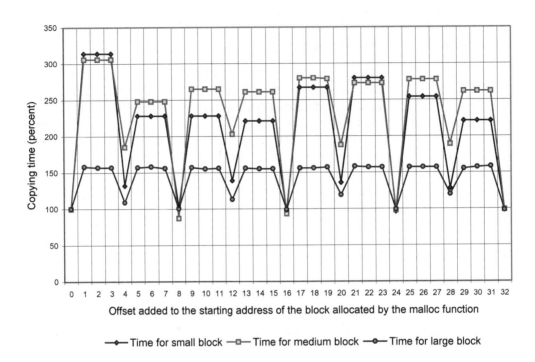

Fig. 3.48. Dependence of the copying time on the starting address of the copied block on the Pentium III 733/133/100 processor (in which the time required to copy memory blocks whose starting addresses are multiples of 0x10 equals 100%)

However, it sometimes may appear that aligning data will be impossible. This happens when the address of the object to be copied is passed from the outside. Such an address might be returned by the operating system. You shouldn't be upset by this; you can increase the starting address to a value that is a multiple of four and avoid the performance drop. The omitted tail can be copied separately. Even if this causes a delay, the time lost will be negligible because the maximum length of such a tail never exceeds 3 bytes.

Another trick works when you are copying large memory blocks. If you are copying memory from left to right (i.e., increasing the addresses), and the copied block is processed as usual, from the end to the beginning, then extra clocks would be spent waiting until the starting positions of the block are loaded into cache. If you copy memory from right to left instead (i.e., from larger addresses to smaller ones), when the copies have been made, the starting positions of the block will be in cache and available almost instantly.

However, don't hurry to criticize the STD or REP MOVSD instruction, which copies double words in the reverse direction. The memory subsystem of the IBM PC is optimized for direct copying. Copying in the reverse direction will cause performance to drop as much as 15%. You would have to process the entire block from right to left by copying each portion of it from left to right. This can be achieved as follows:

Listing 3.34. Optimizing Memory Copying by Placing the Start of the Copied Block into Cache (Applicable to All Processors)

```
my_memcpy(char *dst, char *src, int len)
{
int a=STEP_SIZE;          // Size of the copied fragments

while(len)                // The entire block must be copied.
{
    if (len < a) a=len;   // If the tail is smaller than
                          // the size of the copied fragment,
                          // the latter is corrected.

    dst-=a; src-=a;       // The pointers are reduced
                          // by the required value.

    memcpy(dst, src, a);  // The next fragment is copied.

    len-=a;               // The remaining block is shortened.
 }
}
```

The only problem that remains is to choose the correct size of the copied fragments. The larger the copied portions, the better; this reduces the overhead produced by the framing code. However, if the block is too large, it can exceed the size of L1 cache (which on P4 is only 8 KB).

Cache contains both the block being copied and the block previously copied. Therefore, the size of the copied fragments must not exceed half of the size of the smallest cache (i.e., 4 KB). However, this strategy would be far from optimal on PIII. On Celeron, the overhead produced by executing the framing code would outweigh the performance gained from cache hits.

In my opinion, the most beneficial strategy is to copy the memory in 64 KB to 128 KB fragments. On average, this produces a 10% to 15% gain in speed over the built-in memcpy function. In some situations, the gain might be much larger. It is not difficult to specify the optimal fragment size. This can be achieved via the user-configurable settings file (or by determining the processor type and its parameters automatically).

These probably are familiar methods of optimizing memory copying on early models of the Pentium processors. There are more popular methods of pessimizing memory copying. First, however, I'd like to draw your attention to a common fallacy that relates to the MOVSQ machine instruction. This MMX command operates with a 64-bit (8-byte) operands, which makes it rather popular among programmers who naively assume that the larger the size of the operand, the faster the copy operation. In practice, this is not so. When processing large memory blocks (whose sizes significantly exceed the size of L2 cache) on fast processors (such as PIII), you will get the same (or no worse) performance. On PII, the speed of execution will be reduced approximately 1.3 to 1.5 times! The performance of the MOVSD command depends on the memory-access time, rather than on the processor's clock rate. Therefore, because of the wrapping code, large memory blocks copied using MOVSQ won't be faster.

Medium-sized memory blocks (that fit in L2 cache) have better performance if they are processed using the MOVSQ command, rather than the MOVSD command. (On PII, performance improves 10%; on PIII, it is increased 40%.) However, a further decrease in the sizes of the blocks being copied produces the opposite effect. The blocks that do not exceed the size of L1 cache are copied 40% to 80% slower on PII when the MOVSQ command is used (because of the overhead produced by the wrapping code). On PIII, the performance gained by using MOVSQ is only several percent more than copying that uses MOVSD (Fig. 3.49).

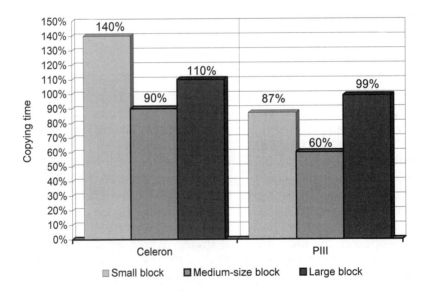

Fig. 3.49. Results of testing the function that copies memory by quadruple words, using different-sized blocks on Celeron 300A/66/66 (from the Pentium II family) and Pentium III 733/133/100 (in which performance of the built-in memcpy function equals 100%)

Thus, it is inexpedient to use the copying function based on the MOVSQ command as the main memory-moving function. Its usage is justified only when it is necessary to process repeatedly 0x40 KB to 0x80 KB blocks already in cache. Otherwise, it would be much better to use the built-in memcpy function. (Besides this, you should bear in mind that early models of Pentium processors without MMX extensions have no MOVSQ command. Such processors are still in use; therefore, you should not discard a large number of potential users of your program for minor improvement in performance.)

Another fallacy is that MOVSD doesn't limit performance, and the programmer can create manually an optimized loop that executes faster than this command.

Actually, the cache lines of L1 cache comprise eight independent banks that can be processed in parallel. (PII processors are capable of processing two such banks per clock.) In a correctly organized loop, it is theoretically possible to copy 8 bytes in two clocks. The REP MOVSD instruction copies only 4 bytes during the same time.

In practice, you won't achieve twofold performance gain; the lion's share of the performance increase will be neutralized by the wrapping code. I didn't succeed in creating a loop that would show improvement of at least couple of dozen percent over the REP MOVSD instruction on all processor models. At best, the code executed as well as, and usually two or three times slower than, the built-in memcpy function.

Perhaps you should address the Direct Memory Access (DMA) controller? (I will keep silent about the lack of DMA-controller access given to application software by contemporary operating systems.) The myth about the possibility of using DMA to copy memory is groundless. *Memory-to-memory* transfers are not implemented in the original IBM AT nor in its contemporary clones. As an example, take *Intel 82801 (ICH) and Intel 82801AB (ICH0). I/O Controller Hub Datasheet* and find the description of transfer modes. There, among other valuable information, you'll see the following:

Bit	Description
3:2	**DMA Transfer Type**. *These bits represent the direction of the DMA transfer. When the channel is programmed for cascade mode, (bits[7:6] = "11") the transfer type is irrelevant.* 00 = Verify-No I/O or memory strobes generated 01 = Write-Data transferred from the I/O devices to memory 10 = Read-Data transferred from memory to the I/O device **11 = Illegal**

Nothing is said about the impossibility of using the DMA to copy the memory directly. However, it is not difficult to guess that the illegal "11" combination is the error message that will appear if you attempt to perform a memory-to-memory transfer.

Optimizing memory copying in new Pentium processors. The commands for managing caching, introduced with the PIII processor, are excellent tools for quadrupling the copying speed of compact memory blocks. The copying speed of moderate and large blocks can be at least tripled.

Strange as it might seem, this excellent result is achieved using only two commands: the `prefetchnta` instruction for prefetching the data into L1 cache (into L2 cache on P4), and the `movntps` instruction for noncached writing of eightfold words, which unloads 128-bit operands from the `SIMD` register into the memory.

▌ *Attention*

The data being copied must be aligned by the 16-bit boundary; otherwise, the processor will generate an exception.

Because `prefetchnta` is a non-blockable instruction (i.e., it returns control long before it is completed), the processor can load the next portion of data from the source buffer while it moves the previous portion into the target buffer. Such a copying technique doesn't dirty L2 cache; it leaves previously cached data intact and instantly available, which is rather important for most algorithms.

Despite all their advantages, these commands have a major drawback: They are supported only on PIII+. Earlier processor models (including AMD Athlon) generate the "invalid opcode" exception.

Because computers based on PII and PMMX are still used, it is necessary to do one of the following:

❑ Create separate versions of your programs for newer and older processors. (This will increase difficulties with their testing and maintainance.)
❑ Handle the invalid-opcode exception and emulate the missing commands programmatically. (This will decrease the program's operation speed considerably.)
❑ Automatically detect the processor model when the program starts and, based on the results of this detection, use the appropriate copying function. (Placing different versions of this function into different DLLs is a good idea; it allows you to remove branches within the function.)

The latter approach seems preferred, although it is not free from drawbacks.

New commands are useful. Compilers that support them are available (such as Intel's compilers). You also can use fragments written in assembly language in your favorite compiler.

However, it would be a mistake to think that support of the new commands by the compiler will increase the application's performance automatically, and all optimization will be reduced to recompiling. New commands suggest new programming concepts, which require the developer to revise all the program's algorithms. For now, only humans can solve algorithmic problems; these are too tough for compilers.

Writing programs in assembly language also is not the best approach. Intel has suggested a compromise: It has introduced *intrinsic operators*, functional equivalents of the processor commands that have a high-level user-friendly interface. For example, void _mm_prefetch(char *a, int sel) is not a function; rather, it represents a covert call to the prefetchx command. After encountering it in the source code of the program, the compiler won't call a function — it will insert the respective construction directly into the code, minimizing the overhead. (Some operators are replaced by one machine command; others are replaced by an entire group of shared machine commands. This doesn't change the issue seriously.)

Detailed descriptions of intrinsic operators and their respective machine instructions can be found in Intel's *Instruction Set Reference* and in the manual supplied with the compiler, *Intel C/C++ Compiler User's Guide with Support for the Streaming SIMD Extensions 2*. The illustrative examples provided in the *Intel Architecture Optimization Reference Manual* are written mostly in C with intrinsic operators. To understand these examples, you need to know which intrinsic operator corresponds to which CPU command. (Their mnemonics are often mismatched.) Therefore, regardless of the programming language you choose (a "naked" assembly language, or a high-level language such as C or FORTRAN), you'll have to consult the reference table.

Intel has provided a usable solution, but what advice can be given to the users of other compilers? Should you abandon your chosen development tools for the sake of progress? (Note that Intel supplies compilers for only two languages, C/C++ and FORTRAN, and these compilers are not freeware.)

The way out lies in using fragments written in machine code, because it is unlikely that your compiler would be able to understand mnemonics invented after its release. In MASM and TASM assemblers, code usually is entered manually via the DB directive. Microsoft Visual C++ and Borland C++ compilers use the emit directive for the same purpose. Unfortunately, the syntax of this directive is compiler-specific, which results in portability problems.

In the Microsoft Visual C++ compiler, emit is preceded by a _ character and must be placed within the assembly block.

Listing 3.35. Creating the INT 0x66 Instruction "Manually" for Visual C++

```
main()
{
__asm
{
_emit  0xCD
```

```
_emit  0x66
; Creation of the INT 0x66 instruction (opcode CD 66)


    }
}
```

The Borland C++ compiler recommends that you enclose `emit` in `__` characters. It expects `__emit__` to appear outside the assembly block.

Listing 3.36. Creating the `INT 0x66` Instruction "Manually" for Borland C++

```
main()
{
__emit__(0xCD, 0x66);
; Creation of the INT 0x66 instruction (opcode CD 66)
}
```

Manual entry of machine codes and commands is a tedious job that requires a certain level of skill. Intel's *Instruction Set Reference* contains the basic opcodes of instructions, but it does not provide a list of all addressing modes. For example, the opcode of the `prefetchnta` instruction is `0F 18 /0`. If you try to specify it as `__emit__(0xF, 0x18, 0x0)`, you won't succeed. (This error frequently is made by beginning programmers.)

After all, `prefetchnta` expects to accept an operand that represents the pointer to the memory address whose contents must be preloaded. Where is it? It's there: The last byte of the instruction's opcode is preceded by the `/` character, which means that not all contents of the byte are present; rather, only the bits that store the instruction's opcode are shown. The remaining ones define the addressing type by telling the processor where to look for the instruction's operand(s). (The first eight pages of Intel's *Instruction Set Reference* cover this topic in detail.)

Listing 3.37 demonstrates the implementation of the two commands necessary for memory-copying optimization.

Listing 3.37. Assembly Implementation of the PIII+ Processor Command for Visual C++

```
__forceinline void __fastcall __prefetchnta(char *x)
// This function prefetches a 32-byte line into L1 cache (PIII),
// or a 128-byte line into L2 cache (P4). It is an analogue of
// _mm_prefetch((char*)mem, _MM_HINT_NTA).
```

```
{
__asm
{
    mov eax, [x]

    _emit   0xF
    _emit   0x18
    _emit   0x0
    ; prefetchnta [eax]
}
}


void __forceinline __fastcall __stream_cpy(char *dst, char *src)
// This function copies 128 bits (16 bytes) from src to dst.
// Both pointers must be aligned by the 16-byte boundary.
// This function is an analogue of
// _mm_stream_ps((float*)dst,_mm_load_ps((float*)&src)).

{
__asm
{
    mov     eax, [src]
    mov     edx, [dst]

    _emit   0xF
    _emit   0x28
    _emit   0x0
    ; movaps xmm0, oword ptr [eax]

    _emit   0xF
    _emit   0x2B
    _emit   0x2
    ; movntps oword ptr [edx], xmm0
}
}
```

It may seem that calling manual commands would be simple. Instead, you'll encounter a conglomeration of traps, difficulties, and problems. Here, I will give a brief description of these.

Arranging single processor commands as `cdecl` or `stdcall` functions is inefficient. (Although, to give PIII and P4 their due, their operating speeds allow you to ignore the overhead produced by function calls.) Instead, the `__forceinline` qualifier can be used. This qualifier instructs the compiler to place the called function into the body of the calling function.

Note that there are several situations in which function inlining cannot be used. For example, you cannot inline *naked* functions (i.e., functions that do not have a prolog and epilog, often used by programmers that do not rely on the optimizer to eliminate redundant code). Further limitations can be found in the description of the `inline` qualifier in the documentation supplied with your compiler.

By the way, Microsoft's calling convention (the `__fastcall` keyword) directs the compiler to pass the first function argument via the ECX register, and the second via the EDX register. If this is so, why are the contents of the first register passed via EAX in Listing 3.37, where ECX can be access easily? Alas, the optimizer doesn't allow this. The optimizer detected no explicit references to the function arguments (and forgot about the registers). Therefore, the optimizer saw no need to pass these unused arguments. As a result, the registers contain noninitialized garbage, and the function does not work! Unfortunately, any attempt to access the arguments from the assembly block automatically creates a frame addressed via the EBP register (i.e., the function arguments are passed via local stack variables, rather than via registers).

It is impossible to avoid overhead when proceeding in such a way. Nevertheless, this overhead is minor and can be ignored, albeit grudgingly.

The optimized copying algorithm also doesn't provide any reason for unclouded happiness. The *Intel Architecture Optimization Reference Manual* for PII and PIII provides an implementation example. However, I would recommend investigating the algorithm yourself, rather than simply copying the program code into the clipboard and compiling it.

First, a prefetching loop must instruct the processor to load the data from the main memory into L1 cache. (For P4, this must be L2 cache.) The data loaded into cache can be read within one clock and placed into the SIMD register, which, like a relay baton, is passed to the noncached write instruction that unloads it into the memory. (The intermediate register is required because, as previously explained, memory-to-memory addressing is not possible in Intel 80x86 processors.)

It only remains to find an optimal prefetching and writing strategy. The first solution that comes to mind — alternating the data-movement and data-prefetching instructions — is incorrect. It is impossible to explain why this solution is incorrect without diving into the details of bus transaction. A general explanation is as follows: The processor only has one system bus, but requests for reading and writing the memory are divided into several phases that might overlap. In such a system, it is impossible to achieve full parallelism, and the unordered processing of requests produces overhead. Decreasing the number of transactions between data reads and writes significantly increases the memory-access rate, which, in turn, significantly improves overall system performance.

Consequently, it is more expedient to perform prefetching in one loop and to copy memory in another one. What length is required for the memory fragments to be copied? Experimentation demonstrates that the best performance is achieved when 4 KB blocks (i.e., one page) are preloaded. Performance tends to drop dramatically when the block size is increased.

Now, you must solve some technical problems. Suppose that you are copying a memory block whose size is not a multiple of the page size. The remaining tail of the last page must be moved separately. In addition, the noncached write command requires (and the read command recommends) that the data be aligned by a 16-byte boundary to avoid generating an exception. This requirement for alignment could be mentioned in the function specification. However, it would be better if the function automatically aligned the pointers passed to it and remembered to copy the remainder using the ordinary method.

In Listing 3.38, the implementation of the turbo-copying function, optimized for two processors, uses two definitions: _PREFETCH_SIZE, which equals 32 bytes for PIII and 128 bytes for P4, and _PAGE_SIZE, which equals 4 KB on both processors. The source and target addresses must be aligned by the 16-byte boundary. The size of the block being copied must be a multiple of the page size. (These limitations were introduced to simplify the example.)

Listing 3.38. [Cache/_turbo_memcpy.size.c] Memory Turbo-Copying Function That Uses the New Commands for Managing Caching on PIII+

```
_turbo_memcpy(char *dst, char *src, int len)
{
int a, b, temp;
for (a = 0; a < len; a += _PAGE_SIZE)
{
    temp = *(int *)((int) src + a + _page_size);
    for (b = a; b < a + _PAGE_SIZE; a += _PREFETCH_SIZE)
        __prefetchnta(src+b);
    // Prefetching

    for (b = a; b < a + _PAGE_SIZE; b += 16 * 8)
    {
        __stream_cpy(dst + b + 16*0, src + b + 16*0);
        __stream_cpy(dst + b + 16*1, src + b + 16*1);
        __stream_cpy(dst + b + 16*2, src + b + 16*2);
        __stream_cpy(dst + b + 16*3, src + b + 16*3);
```

```
    __stream_cpy(dst + b + 16*4, src + b + 16*4);
    __stream_cpy(dst + b + 16*5, src + b + 16*5);
    __stream_cpy(dst + b + 16*6, src + b + 16*6);
    __stream_cpy(dst + b + 16*7, src + b + 16*7);
  }
}
return temp;
}
```

The results of testing the turbo-copying function on memory blocks of different sizes are shown in Fig. 3.50. They are rather impressive (especially because the copy function is implemented in pure C). However, this isn't the limit!

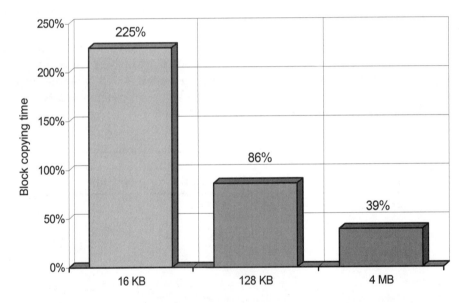

Fig. 3.50. Results of testing the turbo-copying function on different-sized memory blocks on Pentium III 733/133/100 (in which the performance of the built-in memcpy function equals 100%)

By writing the code in the assembly language, you can improve its performance by several percent and achieve at least fivefold performance growth over the built-in memcpy function when copying small data blocks.

It is rather interesting to consider particular optimization situations. If the data being copied are already in cache (a common situation when processing small data blocks), the prefetching loop can be eliminated. (This is especially true for programs executing on P4, where the prefetching command loads data into L2 cache, rather than into L1 cache.) If you are copying larger blocks processed from the beginning, it is advisable to use an additional prefetching loop that loads the copied data into cache.

The optimal copying strategy depends on the situation. There are no universal solutions; each program requires individual approach. Therefore, I won't provide a solution and will give you the freedom to work creatively.

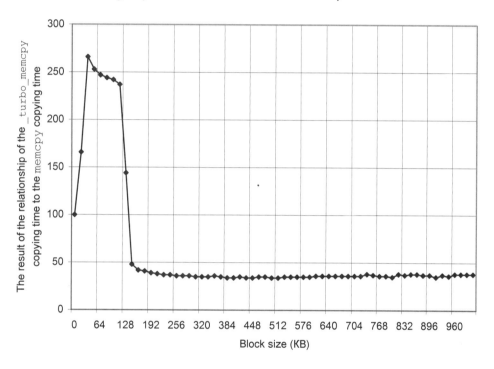

Fig. 3.51. Dependence of the performance of the turbo-copying function on the size of the preloaded block (Pentium III 733/133/100)

Optimizing Memory Initialization

The techniques used to optimize memory copying generally are applicable to memory initialization, which fills the memory block with a specific value (typically 0). Usually, this operation is accomplished by the standard memset C function or by the FillMemory Win32 function. (Both versions represent the same function: The winnt.h header file defines the FillMemory macro as RtlFillMemory, and on the x86 platform, RtlFillMemory is defined as memset.)

Most `memset` implementations use the cyclic memory-write instruction `REP STOSD`, which initializes 1 double word per iteration. It requires a different alignment than the `REP MOVSD` instruction.

When the initial address is aligned by the 8-byte boundary, the unexpected effect of initializing memory cells already in L1 cache (and, on PIII+, in L2 cache) is a considerable improvement in performance. On PII and PIII, 42 iterations of writing double words are executed in 32 loops. Alignment by the 4-byte boundary, recommended by official documentation, produces a much worse result: Only 12 iterations are executed during 32 clocks.

This occurs because no time is spent aligning internal buffers and cache lines. Data flush occurs as buffers are filled; therefore, data flush doesn't interfere with the alignment operations. Because the bit capacity of the bus (and of the buffer) is 64 bits (8 bytes), an initial address that is not a multiple of eight forms a 4-byte hole. Thus, before the data is flushed, it is necessary to align the buffer to cache and fill in the missing 4 bytes, which takes time.

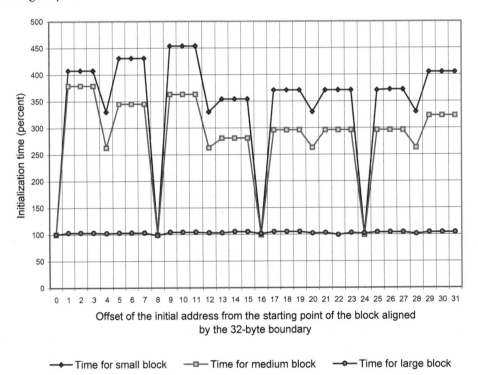

Fig. 3.52. Dependence of the initialization time of different-sized memory blocks on the alignment of the initial address (Pentium III 733/133/100)

This is true not only for the REP STOS instruction, but also for any cyclic write, whether you are initializing words, double words, or even bytes. Thus, it is recommended that you align data structures initialized multiple times and already in cache by addresses that are multiples of eight.

Cyclic write into a memory area missing from cache is another matter. Alignment of the starting address by the 8-byte boundary isn't preferable to alignment by the 4-byte boundary. On PIII, the starting address can remain unaligned because the performance would only increase a fraction of a percent. However, on PII, starting a write cycle from an address that is not a multiple of four slows the performance considerably. Such a large performance loss cannot be ignored, even with the decreasing use of PII-based computers.

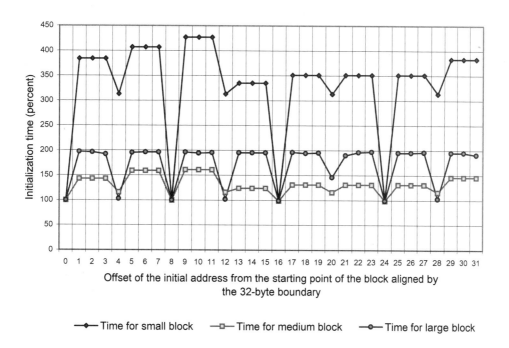

Fig. 3.53. Dependence of the initialization time of different-sized memory blocks on the alignment of the initial address (Celeron 300A/66/66)

These concepts are illustrated in Figs. 3.52 and 3.53. These graphs show how the initialization speed of different-sized memory blocks depends on the alignment of the initial address for the Pentium III (Fig. 3.52) and the Celeron (Fig 3.53) processors. (See the memstore_direct program on the companion CD-ROM.)

The speed at which memory cells missing from cache are written is rather inconsistent. It depends on the state of the processor's internal buffers. The initialization time of small (4 KB to 8 KB) data blocks might differ greatly, especially if consecutive write operations do not pause to flush the buffers. A lack of pauses during the initialization of many memory blocks results in jams: L2 cache overflows, and, as a result, the system slows considerably. Although the average dispersion of the write speed decreases, high peaks and deep holes appear on the graph, with the peaks typically preceding the holes. The generation of these is related to task switching in a multitasking operating system: If other tasks do not overload the bus, at least some buffers have time to unload the data and prepare to receive efficiently the next portion of the data to be written (Fig. 3.54).

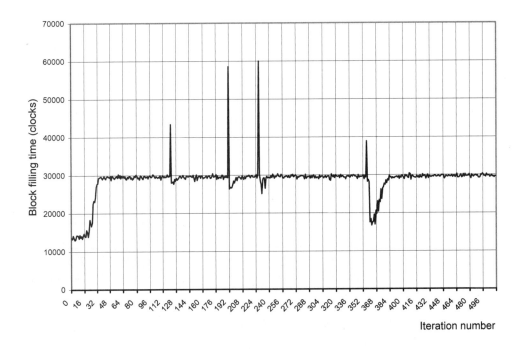

Fig. 3.54. Inconstancy of the speed at which memory cells missing from cache are written (during sequential processing of 512 memory blocks of 4 KB each)

Write-speed inconstancy creates problems during application profiling, because different sections of the program must execute under different conditions. A slowdown in one section occurs if the preceding code filled all the buffers. As a result, initialization became extremely inefficient.

Serious problems exist during optimization of the memory initialization function, because the dispersion of the execution speed complicates any evaluation of the optimization efficiency. You will need to run many tests to calculate the average execution time.

In contrast to copying, memory initialization is always more efficient when it is performed in the forward direction, regardless of the direction used to process the initialized block. This is because writing a cell that is missing from cache doesn't load this cell into L1 cache; the data go to the buffers, from which they are unloaded into L2 cache. For this reason, on blocks that do not exceed the size of L2 cache, no gain will be obtained. Blocks several times the size of L2 cache will be processed faster if they are initialized in the reverse direction. However, this gain is small, usually 5% to 10%, and it is masked by the inconstancy of the initialization speed (Fig. 3.55).

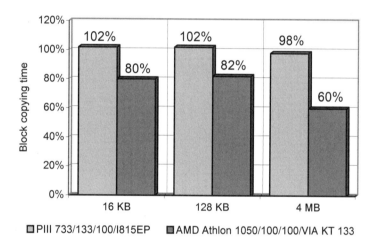

Fig. 3.55. Time of initialization, with subsequent processing for different-sized memory blocks, if the initialization time for the built-in `memset` function equals 100% and time is required for forward initialization of small blocks processed from their ends to their beginnings (see the `memstore_direct` program on the companion CD-ROM)

Optimizing memory initialization in the latest processors. The previously considered instruction for the noncached writing of eightfold words, `movntps`, approximately triples the speed of memory initialization but leaves L2 cache intact. This is ideal for the initialization of large data arrays that do not fit within cache. The initialization of small data structures that are subsequently processed is another matter. With compact blocks, the built-in `memset` function works approximately 150% to 200% faster than `movntps` (Fig. 3.56). With moderate-sized blocks, `movntps` retains its leadership, although its gain is only 25% to 30%. Therefore, the need for this instruction is doubtable; after all, there is no such command on PII and earlier processors.

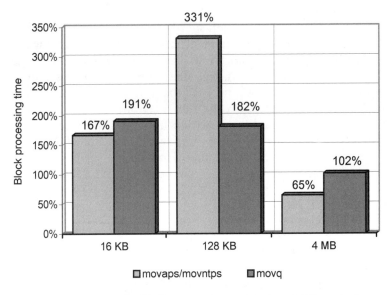

Fig. 3.56. Initialization time of memory blocks of different sizes, if the initialization time of the built-in `memset` function equals 100%

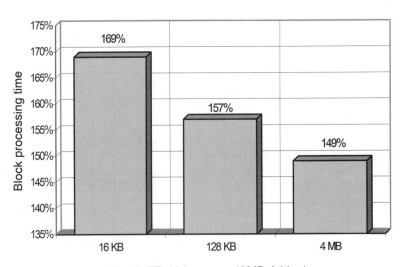

Fig. 3.57. Using `movq` (AMD Athlon)

Chapter 4: Machine Optimization

Comparative Analysis of C/C++ Optimizing Compilers

An enormous number of C/C++ compilers are available. Which criteria deserve the most attention when you are choosing a compiler?

The cost? For professional developers, the price factor plays a minor role; the expenses of purchasing the right compiler are returned after a couple of good programs are written. Besides, many amateur developers don't purchase licensed products.

The level of correspondence to the ANSI C/C++ standards? Most developers have only a superfluous acquaintance with these standards. Few developers can say honestly that they have never used nonstandard extensions or compiler-specific libraries.

Quality of code optimization? Most programmers understand the importance of this criterion. Some even believe that a really cool compiler can improve code that is lame by design. This is partially true, because optimization can eliminate most programming bugs and blunders. However, there is one question that arises: Which bugs and blunders will be corrected?

Optimization techniques remain a mystery. Not every software developer knows *what will be optimized* by a favored compiler or *what features distinguish it* from its competitors. The companion documentation usually stays silent on this topic, content with promotional slogans that don't provide useful information. As far as I know, no popular literature covers these aspects of code optimization; machine code generated by the compiler remains the only source of information on the topic.

Investigation of assembly listings and my experience developing C/C++ optimizing compilers provide a base for this chapter. I intentionally avoided promotional slogans and ideas collected in conversations with my colleagues and fellow programmers. This should reduce errors, omissions, and fallacies significantly.

Unfortunately, providing a detailed description of the optimizing principles is a thankless job. Therefore, I will only describe what should be optimized.

While testing, I used the three most popular compilers: *Microsoft Visual C++ 6.0*, *Borland C++ 5.0*, and *Watcom C 10.0*. The results of testing are presented in Table 4.1 and are described in this chapter.

**Table 4.1. Support of the Main Optimization Techniques
(Unsupported Functional Capabilities Are in Gray)**

Desired compiler action	Microsoft Visual C++ 6.0	Borland C++ 5.0	Watcom C 10.0
Spawns constants	Yes	No	Yes
Wraps constants	Yes	No	Yes
Calculates constant expressions	Yes	Yes	Yes
Wraps functions	No	No	No
Deletes unused variables	Deletes implicitly unused variables; traces genetic relations	Deletes explicitly unused variables; does not trace genetic relations	Deletes implicitly unused variables; traces genetic relations
Deletes unused assignments	Yes	Yes	Yes
Deletes variable copies	Yes	No	Yes
Deletes redundant assignments	Yes	No	Yes
Deletes redundant function calls	No	No	No
Simplifies algebraic operations	Partially	No	No
Optimizes subexpressions	Calculates identical expressions and accounts for regrouping only once	Partially optimizes, without accounting for regrouping	Calculates identical expressions and accounts for regrouping only once
Replaces division with shifts	Yes	Yes	Yes

continues

Table 4.1 Continued

Desired compiler action	Microsoft Visual C++ 6.0	Borland C++ 5.0	Watcom C 10.0
Replaces division with multiplication	Yes	No	No
Replaces modulo operators with bitwise operations	Yes	Yes	Yes
Quickly calculates remainders	No	No	No
Replaces multiplication with shifts	Yes	Yes	Yes
Replaces multiplication with addition	Yes	Yes	No
Uses LEA for quick addition (multiplication, division)	Yes	Yes	Yes
Replaces conditional jumps with arithmetic operations	No	No	No
Removes redundant conditions	Yes	No	No
Removes false conditions	Partially	No	No
Balances case trees	Yes	Yes	No
Creates jump tables	Yes	Yes	Partially
Unrolls loops	No	No	No
Merges loops	No	No	No
Moves invariant code outside the loop	Yes	No	Yes
Substitutes loops with the precondition for loops with the postcondition	Yes	Yes	Yes
Replaces ascending loops with descending loops	Yes	No	No
Removes branches from loops	Yes	No	No
Accounts for usage frequency when placing variables into a register	Yes	Yes	Yes

continues

Table 4.1 Continued

Desired compiler action	Microsoft Visual C++ 6.0	Borland C++ 5.0	Watcom C 10.0
Passes arguments via registers by default	No	No	Yes
Number of registers for passing function arguments	2	3	4
Addresses local variables via ESP	Yes	Yes	Yes
Optimizes the initialization of constant strings	Yes	No	No
Removes dead code	Yes	No	Partially
Optimizes constant conditions	Yes	No	Yes

Constant Expressions

The "war" between constants and variables is ongoing. Some individuals advise replacing variables with constants whenever possible; others recommend the opposite approach: using variables instead of constant values.

Machine instructions can accept either registers or constant values as their operands. The operands, in turn, can contain either the final value or a pointer to the memory cell from which this value should be retrieved. Due to architectural limitations, only one operand of the instruction can access the memory. Hence, it is impossible to assign the value of one variable directly to another variable.

To achieve the desired result, the contents of the first variable must be loaded into a general-purpose register, then that register must be assigned to another variable. The cost of this solution is an increase in the code size, a decrease in its operating speed, and one register spent. You should use registers sparingly; there are only seven registers on the Intel 80x86 platform.

By replacing the variable with its actual value, you can eliminate the intermediate assignment and make the code more compact. However, if this variable is accessed multiple times, placing it into a register is more beneficial. In 32-bit mode, this helps you save an average of 4 bytes per access operation and increases the execution rate of the instruction from two CPU clocks to one.

Thus, the optimal strategy is as follows: Place the most frequently used variables into the registers. If there are no free registers, then replace the variables with their actual values.

Replacing Variables with Constant Values (Spawning Constants)

In the jargon of the developers of optimizing compilers, replacing variables with their actual values is known as *spawning constants*. The following example should help you to find the underlying idea:

```
int a=0x666;
if (b > a) b = a;
```

Because direct comparison (and direct assignment) of two variables is impossible, the preferred approach is to replace the a variable with its actual value. (This saves one assignment operation, among other benefits.)

```
int a=0x666;
if (b > 0x666) b = 0x666;
```

Constant spawning isn't difficult; even compilers that aren't characterized as optimizing are capable of doing it. However, few compilers spawn constants correctly. As previously shown, the optimal strategy uses registers and actual values.

The Microsoft Visual C++ and Watcom compilers replace variables with their actual values whenever possible, even when it is more expedient to place them into registers. The Borland C++ compiler is unable to spawn constants.

Calculating the Values of Variables at Compile Time (Wrapping Constants)

Compiler developers have used the term *wrapping constants* to designate a process similar to *spawning constants*. However, wrapping is applied to the entire set of constant expressions, rather than to a single constant expression.

It is logical that if all the members of some expression (or subexpression) are constant variables, the value of such an expression also is a constant.

For example:

```
int a=0x666;
int b=0x777;
int c=b-a;
printf("%x\n", c);
c = a + b;
printf("%x\n", c);
```

The value of the c variable is invariant to the input data of the program. It can be calculated at compile time by eliminating the a and b variables and replacing c with its actual value. As a result of all conversions, the optimized code of this program will look as follows:

```
printf("%x\n", 0x111);
printf("%x\n", 0xDDD);
```

That's great, isn't it? Wrapping constants does more than compact the code; it eliminates the necessity of loading variables from the slow RAM, saves registers, and significantly improves the operating speed of the program by relieving the processor of the need to perform part of the calculations. Performance gain is impressive particularly when you wrap operations such as division, multiplication, calculation of the remainder, and processing of floating-point values.

The Microsoft Visual C++ and Watcom compilers always wrap constants; the Borland C++ compiler cannot do this.

Calculating Function Values at Compile Time (Wrapping Functions)

Theoretically, if all arguments of a function are constant values, its return value can be calculated at compile time. Consider the following example:

```
func(int a, int b)
{
 return a+b;
}

main()
{
 printf("%x\n", func(0x666, 0x777));
}
```

This example is simple, but none of the compilers under consideration are able to calculate the func value beforehand!

The reason: On most contemporary compilers, the *function* represents the smallest translation unit. The compiler analyzes its syntax and generates the target code, which remains invariant to other functions of the program. *Inline functions* are the exceptions, but this topic deserves to be considered separately.

Thus, Microsoft C++, Borland C++, and Watcom are unable to perform pass-through optimization or wrap functions.

Algebraic Expressions

Removing Unused Variables

Programmers often declare variables that are not used in their programs. This problem is significant in the C programming language, which, in contrast to its "big brother" C++, doesn't support the declaration of variables at the place they are used. To avoid running constantly from one part of the program to another, experienced developers declare variables beforehand. This provides a reserve. When it turns out that a smaller number of variables can be used, many developers forget to delete the extra variables. Optimizing compilers, trying to save memory, automatically discard unused variables. This procedure often is accompanied by warning messages, because an unused variable might be the consequence of errors or misprints. Such warning messages rarely present problems; still, it is best to eliminate them by correcting the code. Note that initializing a variable or assigning it a value (such as the result of an arithmetic calculation or a function) do not employ the variable. To be employed, its value must be used within the program at least once.

Consider the following example:

```
int a=0;
int b;
b = a;
```

Although the value assigned to the a variable is passed to the b variable, the a variable is still considered by the compiler to be unused: The result of its assignment to b is not used in the program.

Microsoft Visual C++ and Watcom do an excellent job of removing unused variables. In this example, both compilers will discard the a and b variables. The Borland C++ compiler can't trace genetic relationships between variables; therefore, it is unable to discard implicitly unused variables. In this example, it will remove the b variable because the value assigned to it is never used. However, Borland C++ will preserve the a variable because its value is copied to b.

Removing Copies of Variables

If two or more variables have the same value, it is possible to preserve one variable and discard the other variables by removing unnecessary assignments. Consider the following example:

```
int a=b;
printf("%x %x \n", a, b);
```

The program can operate without the a variable if its code is rewritten as follows:

```
int a=b;
printf("%x %x \n", b, b);
```

Microsoft Visual C++ and Watcom successfully delete variable copies. Borland C++ can't do this.

Deleting Unused Assignments

It doesn't make sense to execute the assignment if the value assigned to a variable is never used within the program.

Suppose that an accurate programmer, willing to follow recommendations provided in popular manuals, has explicitly initialized all variables when they are declared. Look at the result:

```
int *p=0;
int a=sizeof(int);
p = malloc(a*1024)
```

The initialization of variables (especially pointers) at declaration clearly is a good programming style. If the software developer forgets about the call to malloc, when the zero pointer is accessed for the first time, it will throw an exception and reveal the error. Conversely, uninitialized pointers generate a "roaming" error that is hard to detect: The program might work, but it might be unstable and corrupt the data of other functions (which likely would be different each time the program is run). Just try to find that bug!

The cost of reliability is an increase in code size and a decrease in performance. Therefore, optimizing compilers will detect that the p variable has been assigned the 0 value, which is never used in the program. Then, they will discard this unused assignment.

```
int *p=0;
int a=sizeof(int);
p=malloc(a*1024)
```

Microsoft Visual C++, Borland C++, and Watcom successfully accomplish this task.

Removing Unnecessary Assignments

The operation that assigns the value of one variable to another variable (i.e., a=b) is meaningless; you can always remove the assignment by replacing the copy of the variable with its original. Suppose that the nonoptimized code is as follows:

```
int a=b;
printf("%x %x \n", a, b);
```

```
a = a + 1;
printf("%x %x \n", a, b);
```

The a variable isn't the copy of b; therefore, it cannot be removed. However, you can easily get rid of the a=b assignment.

```
int a, b;
printf("%x %x \n", b, b);
a = b + 1;
printf("%x %x \n", a, b);
```

Microsoft Visual C++ and Watcom always remove unnecessary assignments. Borland C++ cannot do this.

Removing Unnecessary Expressions

If the result of the calculation of a specific expression is not used in the program, there is no need to perform that calculation. How can such meaningless code appear in the program? This usually happens because of the negligence of the programmer who thinks about the code created only after the completion of programming.

Consider the following example:

```
c = a/b;
c = a*b;
printf("%x\n", c);
```

Because the result of calculating the value of the a/b expression isn't used in the program, the division and assignment operations can be discarded.

```
c = a/b;
c = a*b;
printf("%x\n", c);
```

All three compilers eliminate unnecessary expressions rather well.

Removing Unnecessary Function Calls

The removal of unnecessary expressions should not be extended to the removal of functions. (Such an action should be done only using tricks that go beyond the scope of this book.)

Consider the following example:

```
c=func_1(0x666, 0x777);
c=func_2(0);
printf("%x\n", c);
```

At first, it seems that the call to the func_1 function can be eliminated; the value that it returns is never used, and the c variable immediately accepts the result returned by the `func_2` function, which is displayed on the screen. However, what would happen if the `func_1` function has another job besides returning a value? It could write the arguments passed to it into a file. In this case, removing this function will disturb normal operation of the entire program!

For this reason, the optimizing compiler must not reduce function calls. However, it must avoid assigning the return value if this value is never used in the program. (See *Removing Unnecessary Assignments*.)

None of the compilers under consideration remove "extra" function calls.

Performing Algebraic Conversions

The process of calculating multiple algebraic expressions can be simplified significantly: At compile time, perform all possible algebraic transforms to reduce the expression. The following example from the built-in Help system of the Microsoft Visual C++ compiler is very illustrative. (See the description of the `PreCreateWindows` function in the Help system.)

```
cs.y = ((cs.cy * 3) - cs.cy)/2;
cs.x = ((cs.cx * 3) - cs.cx)/2;
```

If you open the parentheses (an elementary mathematical operation), you will see the following :

```
cs.y = cs.cy;
cs.x = cs.cx;
```

Both assignments are meaningless. (See *Removing Unnecessary Assignments*.) Therefore, they can be reduced. This eliminates two multiplications, two divisions, two subtractions, and two assignments. Not bad.

Unfortunately, algebraic transforms are not a strength of most optimizers, even the newest ones. Thus, none of compilers considered here can reduce the previous example.

Although the redundancy is obvious, Microsoft Visual C++, Borland C++, and Watcom cannot remove the division and multiplication in the following expression:

```
a=2*b/2.
```

Even Microsoft Visual C++, the most advanced compiler in this respect, reduces only the simplest expressions, such as `a=3*b-b` or `a=b-b`. Borland C++ and Watcom have only one feature in this area that they can be proud of: They automatically calculate the result of multiplication or division by 1 or 0 (for example, after optimization, `a=b*0; c=d/1` will be `a=0; c=d`).

Therefore, I strongly recommend that you *always* complete algebraic reductions yourself. The compiler is not going to do this for you.

Note that these limitations do not apply to constant expressions, such as `2*3+4/2`. These can be reduced by all three compilers.

Optimizing Subexpressions

If the expression contains two or more identical subexpressions, it is sufficient to calculate the subexpression once.

Consider the following example:

```
if ((a*b)>0x666 && (a*b)<0xDDD) ...
```

After you assign the result of calculating `(a*b)` to an intermediate variable, you can remove one multiplication operation.

```
tmp=a*b;
if (tmp>0x666 && tmp<0xDDD) ...
```

All three compilers under consideration can optimize expressions. However, not all of them can detect identical expressions after regrouping. For example:

```
if ((a*b)>0x666 && (b*a)<0xDDD) ...
```

The product doesn't depend on the order of multipliers; `(a*b)` equals `(b*a)`. Microsoft Visual C++ and Watcom only calculate the value of `(a*b)` once, but Borland C++ considers `(a*b)` and `(b*a)` to be different expressions (with all the consequences).

Arithmetic Operations

Addition and Subtraction

The higher models of Intel Pentium microprocessors can accomplish up to two operations of integer addition (or subtraction) per clock. At first, it might seem that everything is optimized. However, the limit is far from being reached. The LEA instruction can calculate the sum of two registers and one constant per clock, then place the result into any register. (In contrast, the ADD command stores the result in one of the operands.)

The LEA command allows you to complete the following calculation within one clock: (int c=a+b+0x666; int d=e+f+0x777). This can be achieved only if a, b, c, d, e, and f are register variables. Officially, the LEA instruction is intended for calculating the effective cell offset, and is applicable only to near pointers. However, specific architectural features of Intel 80x86 microprocessors cause the internal representation of near pointers to equal their actual values. The result equals the algebraic sum of its operands. Thus, LEA can be used instead of ADD.

Microsoft Visual C++, Borland C++, and Watcom know this trick and actively use it when necessary.

Division

Division is an expensive operation; it takes 40 or more CPU clocks, even on the newest Pentium processors. This is horrible! Fortunately, the division process can be optimized.

If the divider is equal to a power of 2, the division instruction can be replaced by a faster bitwise-shift instruction, which takes one clock. However, this is an uncommon case; therefore, you often need to replace division with multiplication. Multiplication executes more quickly, taking about four clocks on average (at least ten times the speed of division). Many formulas are suitable for such transformations. The most popular one is as follows:

$$\frac{a}{b} = \frac{2^N}{b} * \frac{a}{2^N}$$

Here, N is the length of the number (in bits). If you divide by a constant, division takes only five clocks: 2 raised to a power of N is a constant expression calculated at compile time, multiplication takes four clocks, and the following expression is calculated by a bitwise shift within one clock:

$$\frac{a}{2^N}$$

Unfortunately, Borland C++ and Watcom do not replace division with multiplication. Only Microsoft Visual C++ can do this. Therefore, the Microsoft compiler is the most advanced in this respect. (Certainly, this is a feature to be proud of.) All three compilers actively use bitwise shifts.

Calculating the Remainder

Calculation of the remainder is no faster than division. (At the machine level, this operation is executed using division). It would be wonderful if this process could be speed up. Suppose that the divider equals a power of 2 (for example, $2N = b$). If the number being divided is unsigned, then the remainder will equal N least significant bits of the number being divided. If the number being divided is signed, then to retain the sign, it is necessary to set all bits, except the first N ones, equal to the sign bit. If the first N bits are set to 0, all bits of the result must be reset, regardless of the value of the sign bit.

Thus, if the number being divided is unsigned, then the expression $a\%2^N$ is translated into the construction AND a, $2^N - 1$. If the number is not unsigned, the translation becomes ambiguous. The compiler might insert an explicit check for equality to 0, or it may use sophisticated mathematical algorithms. The most popular algorithm is DEC x\ OR x, -N\ INC x.

If the first N bits of the x number equal 0, then all bits of the result (except the high-order sign bit) will equal 1. However, OR x, -N will set the high-order bit to 1.

Therefore, the value will equal –1, and INC –1 will produce 0. Conversely, if at least one of the *N* low-order bits equals 1, nothing is "borrowed" from the high-order bits. In this situation, INC x returns the initial value.

Theoretically, it is possible to calculate the remainder by using multiplication and bitwise shifts. To do so, the divider must represent a multiple of $k * 2^t$, where *k* and *t* are integer numbers. If these conditions are met, the remainder can be calculated by the following formula:

$$a\%b = a\%k * 2^t = a - ((\frac{2^N}{k} * \frac{a}{2^N}) \& -2^t) * k$$

Unfortunately, the three compilers under consideration do not use this trick for code optimization. However, if the divider equals a power of 2, each of these compilers can use it to search quickly for the remainder (a trivial task).

Multiplication

Multiplication is a fast operation; there is no need to optimize it. However, most compilers struggle for each CPU clock!

If one of the multipliers equals a power of 2, bitwise shifts are used.

By the way, some rules for quickly multiplying a number by 3, 5, 6, 7, 9, 10, etc., aren't widely known. Addition proves to be helpful in these situations; *a**3 can be written as *(a<<1)+a*. This can be executed within one clock. (The LEA command can add registers or multiply a register by 2, 4, or 8.)

Microsoft Visual C++ and Borland C++ expertly replace multiplication with bitwise shifts, combining this operation with addition when necessary. Watcom prefers to do without LEA. For this reason, it is always one clock behind its competitors. (If you account for coupling, Watcom lags by 1.5 clocks.)

Branches

Replacing Conditional Jumps with Arithmetic Operations

Super-pipelined processors, such as the latest members of the Intel 80x86 series, are oversensitive to branching. During normal execution of a program, as the current code is processed, the prefetching block has time to read and decode the next portion of instructions without allowing the memory bus to idle. If branches are encountered, they immediately negate this work by clearing the pipeline. The latest Pentium microprocessors have long pipelines, which cannot be filled quickly; this might take dozens of CPU clocks. During this time, the processor would idle. Therefore, a performance-crucial program must contain the minimum number of branches.

This is easier said than done. For example, how would you eliminate branches in if (a>b) a=b? It is impossible to eliminate the branch directly. An attempt to rewrite the code as a=((a>b)?b:a) will not produce the desired result; from the compiler's point of view, the ? operator represents a branch, as does the if operator. However, by dropping to the level of assembly code, you can find a solution:

```
SUB b, a
; The a variable is subtracted from the b variable. The result is written into b.
; If a > b, the processor will set the carry flag to 1.


SBB c, c
; The c variable is subtracted from c, and the carry flag is accounted for.
; The result is written back to c (a temporary variable).
; If a <= b, the carry flag is off, and c will equal 0.
; If a > b, the carry flag is on, and c will equal -1.


AND c, b
; A quick bitwise operation, (c & b), is performed. The result is written into c.
; If a <= b, the carry flag is 0, and c equals 0.
; This means that c = (c & b) == 0; otherwise, c == b - a.


ADD a, c
; The contents of a are added to the contents of c.
; The result is written into a.
; If a <= b, then c = 0 and a = a.
; If a > b, then c = b - a, and a = a + (b-a) == b.
```

This code finds the smallest of two numbers without branches. Similar tasks can be solved using this method. Newer Intel 80x86 processors provide a range of commands for this purpose; they simplify programming, without using branches, and reduce the number of mathematical transforms.

Unfortunately, none of the compilers under consideration can reduce branches. Therefore, you must reduce branches manually if you want to write performance-crucial code.

Removing Redundant Conditions

The simplification of logical conditions is similar to algebraic transforms. Consider the following example:

```
if (a>0 && a<0x666 && a!=0) ...
```

The a!=0 check is redundant; if a is greater than 0, it cannot equal 0. Microsoft Visual C++ recognizes such situations and eliminates redundant checks. Borland C++ and Watcom are unable to do this.

Removing Conditions Guaranteed To Be False

Sometimes programmers may err by creating conditions that are guaranteed to be false. For example:

```
if (a!=0 && a==0) ...
```

Clearly, since a does not equal 0, it can never equal 0. In such a situation, Microsoft Visual C++ doesn't generate any code for it. It dismisses the entire IF-THEN branch. Surprisingly, it does not issue warnings. This isn't good, because the problem originated with the programmer's error. Borland C++ and Watcom do not optimize such code; they interpret it "as is."

Microsoft Visual C++ also cannot always detect conditions guaranteed to be false. For example, it won't optimize the following code:

```
if (a<0 && a>0x666) ...
```

The switch Operator

Balancing a Logical Tree

The switch operator is popular with programmers. (This is especially true for software developers writing Windows applications.) It can have numerous branches. Linear processing of these branches is extremely inefficient.

In rare code, switch operators can contain thousands of value sets. If you try to solve this problem directly, the logical tree will be scraping the sky. Tracing such a tree will take a significant amount of time. This will have a negative effect on performance.

Think over the problem: What is the job of the switch operator? The common description is as follows: The switch operator provides a special way of choosing a variant, which checks if the value of the given expression matches one of the specified constants in a specific branch. However, it is possible to say that switch is the operator that allows you to search for a specific value. Thus, the linear switch tree represents a trivial algorithm of a sequential search — the most inefficient of such algorithms.

Suppose that the source code of the program looks as follows:

```
switch (a)
{
   case 98 : ...;
   case 4  : ...;
   case 3  : ...;
   case 9  : ...;
   case 22 : ...;
   case 0  : ...;
```

```
    case 11 : ...;
    case 666: ...;
    case 096: ...;
    case 777: ...;
    case 7  : ...;
}
```

The corresponding nonoptimized logical tree will be 11 nodes tall (Fig. 4.1, left). The left branch of the root node will contain 10 children; the right branch will not have a single child node (except the corresponding `case` handler).

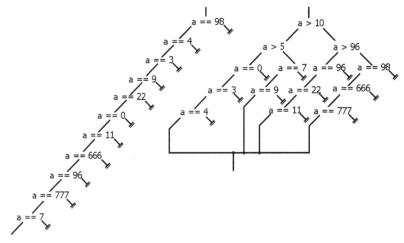

Fig. 4.1. Logical tree before (*left*) and after (*right*) optimization

To correct this disbalance, it is possible to divide one branch in two and graft the halves to the new node. This node contains the condition that specifies the branch that should be searched for the variable being compared. For example, the left might contain nodes with even values, while the right one — the nodes with odd values. However, this approach is not the best one. Trees rarely contain equal numbers of even and odd values (i.e., an equal number of nodes with even values on the left branch and nodes with odd values on the right branch). Therefore, this criterion isn't a good one; a disbalance will occur again. The following approach is better: Take the smallest value and throw it into the A heap, then take the largest value and throw it into the B heap. Continue in this manner until all available values are sorted.

The `switch` operator implies that each value should be unique; each number may occur only once in the set (or range) of values. Therefore, the heaps should contain an equal number of values. (In the worst situation, the number of values is one heap will be greater by one as compared to the number of values in another heap.) In addition, all numbers in the A heap will be smaller than the smallest number in the B heap. Consequently, it is sufficient that one comparison can determine the heap, which should be searched for the value to be compared.

The height of the new tree will equal the following:

$$\left[\frac{N+1}{2}\right]+1$$

Here, N is the number of nodes of the initial tree. Actually, the branch is divided by two and a new node is added. This produces the following:

$$\left[\frac{N}{2}\right] \text{ and } +1$$

Then, $N + 1$ is required to round the result up to the next integer. For example, if the height of the nonoptimized tree is 100 nodes, this operation reduces it to 51 nodes. What? You say that 51 is still a large amount? You can use the same approach to divide each branch in two. This will reduce the tree's height to 27 nodes. Further compaction will produce the following: 16 → 12 → 11 → 9 → 8. The tree cannot be packed more densely. (If you don't understand why, build the tree.) Nevertheless, 8 nodes is significantly fewer than 100! Tracing the optimized tree will require less than nine comparison operations.

Of the three compilers under consideration, only Watcom cannot compact `switch` operators. Visual C++ and Borland C++ do a good job of it.

Creating a Jump Table

If the values of the chosen branches represent an arithmetic progression, it is possible to form a *jump table,* an array indexed by `case` values and containing pointers to respective `case` handlers. Regardless of the number of branches in the `switch` operator — one or a million — this operator is executed within a single iteration. Great!

All compilers under consideration can create jump tables. Each of them will optimize the following example successfully:

```
switch (a)
{
    case 1  : ...;
    case 2  : ...;
    case 3  : ...;
    case 4  : ...;
    case 5  : ...;
    case 6  : ...;
    case 7  : ...;
    case 8  : ...;
    case 9  : ...;
    case 10 : ...;
    case 11 : ...;
}
```

However, Watcom isn't equal to the task when it comes to reordered progression; it can't handle several independent progressions. Microsoft Visual C++ and Borland C++ successfully optimize the next example, but Watcom creates an unbalanced logical tree. In the worst situation, Watcom's tree is executed within 11 iterations. (This result is approximately ten times worse than the results of its competitors.)

Loops

Unrolling Loops

Branches serve as a basis for loops, and, as shown in the *Optimizing Branches* section, branches have a negative effect on performance. Therefore, you should remove them, even if doing so increases the size of the program. Short loops of three to five iterations should be unrolled into linear code that repeats the loop body a specified number of times. Consider the following example:

```
for(a=0; a<3; a++)
 printf("%x\n", a);
```

To eliminate branches, this code should be rewritten as follows:

```
printf("%x\n", 0);
printf("%x\n", 1);
printf("%x\n", 2);
```

This trick is not guaranteed to improve the performance. An increase in code size can produce a situation in which the program ceases to fit within the available RAM. As a result, the operating system would be forced to use the slow hard disk. L1 cache also has a size limit, and situations may occur in which an unrolled loop won't fit within it. Finally, Intel Pentium microprocessors only start to couple instructions from the second pass; therefore, unrolling a loop reduces the speed of code execution by a factor of nearly two.

Thus, only experiments can help you choose the optimal strategy for each situation. Experiment is the developer's prerogative. Therefore, the three compilers under consideration do not unroll loops.

Merging Loops

If two loops have identical headers, it is possible to combine them within the common loop. Consider the following source code:

```
for(b = 0; b < 10; b++)
   x[b] = b;

for(b = 0; b < 10; b++)
   y[b] = b;
```

You can improve the application's performance and reduce the code size, without losing functionality, by rewriting this code as follows:

```
for(b = 0; b < 10; b++)
{
    x[b] = b;
    y[b] = b;
}
```

Unfortunately, none of the compilers under consideration can merge loops.

Moving Invariant Code outside the Loop

Invariant code doesn't change during execution of the loop. Therefore, this code does not need to be executed at each iteration. It would be better to move this code outside the loop.

Consider the following example:

```
for(a=0; a<(b*2); a++)
    printf("%x\n", a*(b/2));
```

The expressions (b*2) and (b/2) are invariants. Therefore, the optimized code will look as follows:

```
tmp_1 = b*2;
tmp_2 = b/2;
for(a=0; a<tmp_1; a++)
    printf("%x\n", tmp_2+=tmp_2);
```

This saves one division operation and two multiplication operations per iteration, which is rather good.

Microsoft Visual C++ and Watcom successfully recognize invariant code and move it outside the loop. Borland C++, unfortunately, isn't capable of doing this.

Substituting a Loop with the Precondition
for a Loop with the Postcondition

There are three basic types of loops: *a loop with the precondition, a loop with the postcondition,* and *a loop with the condition in the middle of the loop body* (Fig. 4.2). Combined loops can have several conditions located anywhere within the loop. The loop with the postcondition only contains a branch; all other types of loops contain a branch and a jump.

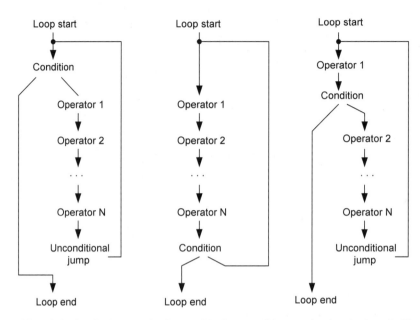

Fig. 4.2. Logical tree of a loop with the condition at the beginning (*left*), at the end (*center*), and in the middle (*right*)

The three compilers under consideration always substitute a loop with the precondition for a loop with the postcondition. Such a replacement can be achieved only if the loop body is corrected. This is not a trivial task. Unfortunately, detailed consideration of this technology goes beyond the scope of this book.

Replacing a Loop Increment with a Decrement

Because decrement machine instructions reset the zero flag when they reach zero, there is no need to compare the decreased variable to zero; the processor does this for you. Hence, the loop for (a=10; a>0; a--) is translated into shorter and faster code than the loop for (a=0; a<10; a++).

If the loop argument is not used within the loop body, the Microsoft Visual C++ compiler will always translate it into a loop with a decrement. Consider the following source code:

```
for(a=0; a<10; a++)
 printf("Hello, Sailor!\n");
```

Because the a variable is not used within the loop body, the loop header can be rewritten as follows:

```
for(a=10; a>0; a--)
```

Of the three compilers under consideration, only Microsoft Visual C++ is capable of using this trick. Borland C++ and Watcom never use it.

Removing Branches

Branches within a loop are always undesirable, especially on newer Intel microprocessors. (Note that most C compilers for the Convex platform refuse to compile programs that place branches within loops.)

The capability of removing some types of branches within loops is a unique feature of the Microsoft Visual C++ compiler. The algorithm of this optimization is complicated, and can't be described in detail within the scope of this chapter. Therefore, the example here will simply give the code before and after optimization.

Consider the following example, which has a condition in the middle of the loop body:

```
do
{
printf("1st operator\n");
if (--a<0) break;
printf("2nd operator\n");
} while(1);
```

Microsoft Visual C++, without hesitation, translates this into a loop with a post-condition, removing the break operator.

```
printf("1st operator\n");
a--;
if (a>=0)
{
   a++;
   do
   {

        printf("1st operator\n");
        printf("2nd operator\n");
   } while(--a<0);
}
```

The desired performance acceleration comes with an undesired increase in program size: the loop operators that precede the break branch now occur twice.

Again, note that only Microsoft Visual C++ is capable of removing branches within a loop. Borland C++ and Watcom cannot do this.

Function Calls

Optimizing the Passing of Arguments

Calling conventions for standard types of functions and for passing arguments (such as cdecl, stdcall, or PASCAL) to these functions are declared strictly; the compiler can't take any initiative here. The standard requires it to pass arguments via the stack (i.e., via slow RAM). Thus, the more arguments passed to the function, the more significant the overhead.

If the function type is not specified explicitly, the compiler can pass arguments as it wishes. The most efficient way of passing arguments is to use registers, because reading or writing to the registers takes only one CPU clock. (Memory access might require dozens of CPU clocks, depending on a variety of factors: the operating rate of the memory chips and memory controller, the bus frequency, the presence or lack of requested cells in the cache, and so on.) The main problem is that even the newer Pentium microprocessors only have seven general-purpose registers. These must be shared among arguments, return values, register variables, and temporary variables. Because the variables containing arguments to be passed should be placed in RAM, allocating all general-purpose registers for arguments would neutralize the entire performance gain.

Microsoft Visual C++ allocates two registers for passing arguments, Borland C++ reserves three, and Watcom assigns four. The best strategy remains disputable; there is no commonly accepted opinion on this topic. I consider two registers to be the best solution. (The Microsoft C 7.0 compiler, the ancestor of Microsoft Visual C++, used three registers to pass arguments. However, after a series of experiments, discussions, and disputes, Microsoft's developers concluded that the use of two registers ensures better performance.)

Another important aspect is the default type of function call. The Microsoft Visual C++ and Borland C++ compilers pass variables via registers only when the function is preceded by the __fastcall qualifier. (The only exception is the this implicit argument; by default, this is passed via a register.) Watcom passes variables via registers by default. Therefore, if you are using Microsoft Visual C++ or Borland C++, insert the __fastcall qualifier manually.

Optimizing the Function Prolog/Epilog

Early C compilers used the base stack pointer, known as the BP register (EBP in 32-bit mode), to address local variables by placing special code known as the *prolog* at the beginning of each function. The prolog placed the contents of the BP register into the stack and copied the pointer to the stack top, stored in the SP (ESP) register.

Then, by decreasing the value of the SP register, the early compilers allocated memory for local variables of the function. (The stack grows from bottom to top.)

After the function was completed, the *epilog* code moved the stack pointer "down," releasing the memory occupied by local variables. The epilog then restored the value of the BP register.

Why was the BP register necessary? It stored the pointer of the *stack frame*, the memory region allocated for local variables.

Microsoft Visual C++, Borland C++, and Watcom use a different method of addressing local variables — directly via the ESP register. This significantly complicates the compiler implementation, because the pointer to the stack top changes during the program run time, and addressing becomes "floating." Nevertheless, this technique releases one more register for register variables and removes two memory-access operations (saving/restoring EBP), which significantly improves the performance.

Variable Distribution

In C/C++ languages, the register keyword allows programmers to force variables to be stored in registers. Nevertheless, most compilers ignore the programmer's directions and store variables in whatever way they consider to be optimal. Compiler developers argue that the compiler knows how to build the most efficient code. Usually, they say: "Don't try to help the compiler." This reminds me of the passenger who says: "I need to go to the airport," and the taxi driver who ignores this instruction and heads to another place, the one he considers "the most convenient."

Working with the compiler must not turn into struggling with it! The compiler's refusal to place the variable into the register is understandable, but the compiler should stop the compilation process with an error message that recommends removing the register qualifier, or issue a warning.

That's enough digression. Another topic deserves attention: the strategy of distributing variables used by each compiler.

When available registers are scarce, Borland C++ and Watcom save registers for the most intensely used variables and store other variables in the slow RAM. Microsoft Visual C++ doesn't account for the frequency of variable usage; it stores variables in registers in the order they were declared in the program.

String Initialization

Microsoft Visual C++ is distinguished favorably from its competitors in that it initializes constant strings by double words, rather than by bytes. Furthermore, only Microsoft Visual C++ can store short strings in registers.

Because of this, I recommend that you use Microsoft Visual C++ to compile programs that intensely manipulate strings.

Dead Code

Code that never takes control is known as *dead code*. Consider a common situation: The programmer declares a function, but never uses it. Why should the dead code vainly consume the memory space? Alas, none of the compilers under consideration remove such a function. This job is delegated to the linker. Intellectual linkers remove functions that are never referenced. (It would be better if this work was done beforehand by the compiler.)

Now, suppose that the program contains the following code, which displays the debug message on the screen (provided that the DEBUG macro is declared as TRUE):

```
if (DEBUG) printf("some debug message");
```

When the final release is complied, the DEBUG macro is declared as FALSE, and debug code never runs. Therefore, it makes sense to delete this code. Microsoft Visual C++ deletes the condition check and the body of conditional operator (in this case, the call to the printf function); however, it forgets to clear the constant string. Still, hope remains that the advanced linker will delete it after the linker detects no references to it.

Watcom entirely deletes dead code, including the condition check, the body of the conditional operator, and the constant string. Borland C++ never deletes dead code and dutifully checks the FALSE constant for equality to TRUE.

Constant Conditions

Constant conditions are encountered frequently in many programs. For example, an endless loop (or a loop with the condition in the middle of its body) is declared as follows by most programmers:

```
while(1)
{
// Loop body
}
```

A check such as 1 == 1 is pointless and can be omitted. Microsoft Visual C++ and Watcom do just that, but Borland C++ dutifully checks that 1 equals 1. (What if this wasn't true?)

Determining the Winner

Well, which compiler is the best? Microsoft Visual C++ deserves the title and trophy. After a significant lag, Watcom takes the second position. Borland C++ is the outsider, showing a surprisingly low result. (Why is it called an "optimizing compiler"?)

You may have noticed that there are no numeric tests in this chapter. I didn't provide them because the gain produced by the optimizer strongly depends on the type of code being optimized. The gain can vary more than ten times, depending on the program being compiled.

Mortal Combat:
Assembler vs. Compiler

Some programmers worship machine code generation; others tend to do everything manually. Such individuals sometimes implement their programs in naked assembly language. Of course, everyone has the right to make a choice; however, the choice should be intelligent, rather than blind.

Meanwhile, each party spreads unfeasible rumors. Individuals loyal to compilers assure their fellow programmers that humans are unable to account for all the specific features of the architecture of contemporary processors; therefore, only the optimizer is capable this job. Their opponents usually provide an assembly implementation of the canonic "Hello, World!" program as their rebuttal. This program is *300 times* smaller that the most optimal code generated by any compiler.

How can you decide whom to believe? This uncertainty often irritates beginner programmers trying to decide if they should study assembly language, or if it simply would be a waste of time.

Machine optimization will *always* be second to optimization done manually. The reason is simple: Machine optimization always acts according to the strict predefined template, whereas human beings can derive radical new solutions. To those who emphasize the overwhelming architectural features of contemporary processors, I would object: Compilers are developed by humans, too. Optimal planning of the command flow is not beyond the capabilities of programmers that have sufficient background. Furthermore, optimizing techniques for the latest generation of processors are significantly easier than for those released five years ago.

Nevertheless, assembly language is not a magic wand, and it is unable to work wonders. Implementing a polynomial algorithm in assembly language has never turned an algorithm into a logarithmic one. Except for special cases, qualitative gain is out of question; only quantitative gain is possible. (The example of the "Hello, World!" program is an exception. It will be considered in detail further on.) Furthermore, manual optimization will become a laughing-stock if it is used unskillfully (or if knowledge gained from 10-year-old optimization manuals is applied).

Brief Historical Overview, or Assembly Language Brings Eternal Spring

Until the mid-1990s, the struggle between assembly language and compilers showed no clear winner. With the arrival of newer, faster microprocessors, interest in assembly language decreased. It seemed that high-level programming languages could solve most problems, and the need to fight the code for each clock had been eliminated forever. This euphoria didn't last long. With the increase in processor rate, the task delegated to processors became more challenging. The functional capabilities of high-level languages again became insufficient, and interest in assembly code was renewed.

Few successful or even noticeable projects of that time could do without assembly language. Assembly code was present in MS-DOS, Windows, Quake, Microsoft Office, and many other products. In other words, an inefficient compiler will remain inefficient even on a fast processor; therefore, it can take only a limited segment of the market.

Competition between compiler developers turned out to favor consumers (primarily programmers), because it resulted in the development of efficient algorithms of machine optimization. By the late 1990s, the quality of optimizing compilers almost had reached its theoretical limit. When solving *routine problems*, the quality of machine optimization became comparable to the quality of manual optimization achieved by a programmer with the average level of professional skills.

Today, programmers that can do without visual development tools are quite rare, and "pure" high-level languages are out of fashion. Assembly language looks archaic, on par with the punch-card machine or a "dinosaur" computer. Nevertheless, the rumors of its pending death are exaggerated.

Assembly language is still alive! The best confirmation of this statement is that Microsoft has declared assembly language, rather than C/C++ or PASCAL, as the main driver-development language. Without assembly language (or specialized compilers), it is impossible to use the advantages of new multimedia commands for parallel data processing. Assembly language remains indispensable for creating high-performance mathematical and graphical libraries. (Look into the CRT\SRC\Intel directory of the Microsoft Visual C++ distribution kit. Assembly code is present, and practically all functions for handling strings are implemented using this language.)

Generally, inlining assembly code has stabilized, and high-level languages no longer may lay claim to the remaining segment.

Criteria for Evaluating the Quality of Machine Optimization

The main criteria for evaluating the quality of code are *performance*, *compactness*, and the *time* required to develop the code. In principle, it is impossible to optimize the program by all three criteria simultaneously. In particular, when you align code and data structures by even addresses, the program's performance improves, but its size increases.

Generally, performance has priority over program size. Today, when the amount of RAM physically installed on a computer is hundreds of megabytes and the size of the hard disk is hundreds of gigabytes, compact code is no longer crucial. However, some users still care about the number of megabytes required for a program. Because of this, almost all contemporary compilers support at least two optimization modes: *maximum speed* and *minimum space.*

I will limit this discussion to the compromise mode of *maximum optimization,* an attempt to achieve the maximum speed at the minimum size. This mode is used in most code; therefore, it is of the most interest here.

Note that manipulating the keys responsible for fine-tuning the optimizer can change the test results significantly, both favorably and unfavorably. However, this is a different topic; it would compare fine-tuning skills, rather than optimizing ones.

It is important to understand that precise evaluation of *general* optimization quality based on *particular* operations is impossible. For example, the difference in the performance of code generated by Microsoft Visual C++ and by Borland C++ will vary depending on whether constant division occurs within the program being optimized. You know that Microsoft Visual C++ can replace constant division with multiplication (which is dozens of times faster), but that Borland C++ cannot.

If no specific examples are possible, only an approximate evaluation can be made of the compilers' quality. This topic was covered in detail at the beginning of this chapter. This section will focus on the average quality of machine optimization and will use typical algorithms as examples.

Of course, the idea of typical algorithms is subjective. Some programmers consider the Fourier transform to be a typical and illustrative example; others might never encounter real-number arithmetic. The examples that follows are far from representative; nevertheless, they provide some food for thought.

Methods of Evaluating the Quality of Machine Optimization

The task of evaluating the quality of machine-code optimization is more complicated than it may seem. First, it is necessary to separate the compiler from its working environment, libraries, and so on. For example, comparing the size of the compiled "Hello, World!" program with that of its assembler implementation is incorrect. Particularly, calls such as `printf("xxx");` will be compiled into code such as `PUSH offset xxx\CALL printf\POP EAX`. More thorough optimization is hardly imaginable!

Pay special attention to the size of the object file created by the compiler. Is it significantly larger than the object file of assembler implementation? After all required libraries are linked, the size of the compiled file will increase dozens of times, but the size of the assembler module will be practically the same. Nevertheless, this phenomenon has nothing to do with the compiler! The compiler encountered the call to `printf`, and it included this call in the object file. If you output the string directly, using the appropriate function of the operating system API (found in the implementation of the assembly code), the executable file will become dozens of kilobytes smaller.

This *environment* also is known as the *Run Time Library* (RTL). It comprises service functions called by the compiler. Although RTLs are an integral part of the compiler, they have nothing to do with the quality of code generation; from the compiler's standpoint, they are no different from normal library functions.

Redundancy of built-in library functions and RTL will be obvious in small projects. For example, the output of the "Hello, World!" string doesn't use a hundredth of the `printf` capabilities. However, in programs that comprise several thousands of code lines, the relationship between useful and service functions becomes normal, and the efficiency factor of libraries goes to 1.

Thus, comparing the efficiencies of an assembler and a compiler in an example with library functions is a blatant error. Only implementations that never call external code must be considered. Otherwise, you won't be comparing machine and manual optimization; rather, you will be comparing the quality of libraries (mainly written in the assembler). Comparing the sizes of the resulting object files also is useless; besides the code, these files contain tons of external information. In the examples that follow, the amount of such information is dozens of times the size of machine code!

Only a disassembler can produce a pattern that reflects the real situation. Start the disassembler, load a file (an object file or an executable file), and subtract the function's starting address from its ending address. The difference will be the size of the code under investigation.

Performance measurements are even simpler; it is sufficient to measure the function's execution time. However, there is one peculiarity. To estimate the quality of code generation, rather than the computer's performance, it is necessary to minimize side effects when possible.

First, when the function is called, all data that it processes must be in L1 cache; otherwise, the slowness of RAM will neutralize differences in the performance of the code being tested.

Second, the size of the data being processed must be large enough to mask the overhead produced by calling functions, passing arguments, reading measurements from the performance counter, and so on. The following examples process 4,000 `int` elements. This produces a stable and reproducible result. Saturation is achieved at 1,000 elements, after which, overhead ceases to play a noticeable role.

Comparative Analysis of the Main Compilers

Consider three algorithms: *copying the memory block, searching for the minimum number within a set*, and *bubble sorting*. The choice of algorithm is not random. Programmers traditionally prefer to implement copying operations (like comparison and memory-searching operations) in the "naked" assembler, because Intel 80x86 microprocessors support special machine instructions oriented toward these tasks.

Particularly, memory copying is performed using the REP MOVS command, analogous to the memcpy function. Unfortunately, C/C++ languages do not provide constructions equivalent to the REP MOVS machine command. You can call the memcpy function, but the comparisons in this section do not use library functions! (In addition, recall that the memcpy function, with rare exceptions, is implemented in assembler, rather than in C.) With a pure programming language, there is only one way to solve this task: Copy the array within a loop, element by element.

The problem with this approach is that compilers do not yet understand the physical form of the program being compiled. I know of no contemporary compilers capable of recognizing even an obvious copying algorithm. The compiler will translate the program literally into machine language, preserving the loop and all temporal variables used to pass data. The resulting code will be far from optimal. An assembler would produce better performance and size; it would even leave the compiler far behind if compared using a criterion such as development time.

This makes it interesting to determine the compiling efficiency of code guaranteed to be nonoptimal. This section will allow you to evaluate the suitability of an assembler for tasks that the processor provides with hardware support (when equivalent constructions are lacking in the high-level programming language).

Searching for a minimum number is a simple algorithm, which easily fits within several lines of code in an assembler and in a high-level language. Such a small space doesn't give the compiler an opportunity to reveal itself in all its glory. It would be interesting to determine the amount of redundant code added by the compiler. The amount of useful code is quite small; therefore, this example will be sensitive to even microscopic portions of "garbage."

Sorting is a typical example of the code created by programmers. It is suitable for evaluating the average optimization quality of specific compilers.

The task of comparing compilers is simple. However, comparing a compiler to a human is more difficult. The question immediately arises: Who should be compared with the compiler? A computing guru? Would this comparison be representative? After all, this is not a theoretical discussion about the superiority of human intellect over machine. This is a search for practical ways to solve problems that programmers with average skills encounter during their daily activities. Can such a programmer hope that some guru will come to help? Quite unlikely! The programmer probably will need to handle the coding.

For this reason, I intentionally wrote the assembler programs at the end of this chapter as average code. Because the target processor isn't specified, I only used basic optimization techniques, without optimal planning of the command flow. Nevertheless, these programs represent optimized assembly code corresponding to the code produced by a programmer with average skills. (If you want to become a guru, try to improve the quality of this code.)

Well, a "typical programmer" has been determined. Now, it is time to choose a compiler. Select the "required minimum" of Microsoft Visual C++ 6.0, Borland C++ 5.5, and Watcom C++ 10.0.

Discussion of the Test Results

Running tests of the three algorithms on Intel Pentium III 733 and AMD Athlon 1400 proves that the code-generation quality of contemporary compilers is rather high (Figs. 4.3 and 4.4). On average, the performance of the compiled programs was only 20% to 30% lower than that of the optimized assembly code. This value is rather impressive (especially because the sample assembly program is far from perfect). Hey, who said that machine optimization is only slightly lower than manual optimization? What would they say now?

Nevertheless, the performance gap (with rare exceptions) is not large enough to accommodate a statement that transferring the program to assembly code resulted in quantitative changes.

As expected, the most significant performance gap occurred with memory copying. However, this gap was reduced significantly because of an increase in the clock rate of the processor. On Pentium III 733, the smallest lag was about 31%; on Athlon 1400, it was 9%! The latter measurement doesn't need any comments — Microsoft's compiler rules, and life is fine. The high clock rate of contemporary processors, combined with the power of contemporary compilers, removes the need for assembly inserts. Of course, not all compilers are equally efficient. For example, Watcom showed surprisingly low results in this test. Borland confidently upheld its position on the Intel processor, but it generated slightly nonoptimal code on AMD.

After searching for the minimum number, the results from all three compilers were equally good. Microsoft Visual C++ built an elegant code, close to ideal, but did not obtain the desired 100% result because of a regrettable fortuity: The starting point of the loop hit the `0x4013FF` address, the worst one from the microprocessor's point of view. Because of this, each iteration was fined with several penalty clocks, which, in the long run, produced heavy losses. However, the code generated by the compiler ran efficiently enough.

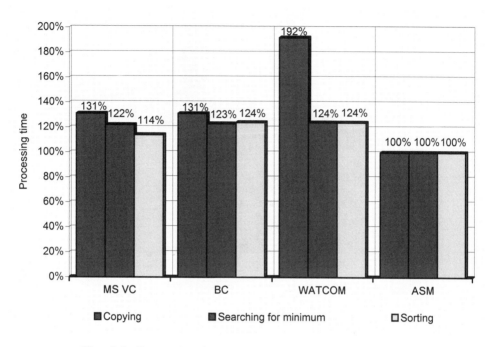

Fig. 4.3. Comparing the quality of machine-code generation
(performed on Intel Pentium III 733)

Note that, even the most insignificant change to a program (including the elimination of redundant code) can degrade performance (sometimes quite noticeably). In this respect, most compilers are unbelievably dumb. They do not align any jumps, or they align all jumps. This unjustifiably increases the program's size and sometimes drastically degrades the performance. (This happens if the program ceased to fit within cache as a result of the increase in its size.) The correct solution is to align only frequently executed jumps, such as loops. Alas, this feature is not implemented in any compilers I am familiar with.

The situation is more favorable for sorting. Microsoft Visual C++ is only 13% or 14% behind the assembler code. Borland C++ follows with the smallest gap (15% and 24% for Athlon 1400 and Pentium III 733). The last position is taken by Watcom, on par with Borland on Pentium, but far behind it on Athlon. This compiler is not to blame for its low result; Watcom was created long ago, when processors and optimization techniques were quite different. Generally, Watcom is a good but obsolete compiler. The love that some of fans feel for their compilers should not be blind. Generally, Watcom is no longer the best choice.

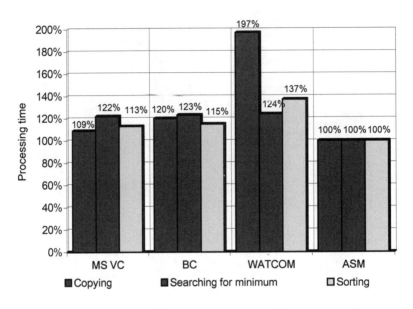

Fig. 4.4. Comparing the quality of machine-code generation
(performed on AMD Athlon 1400)

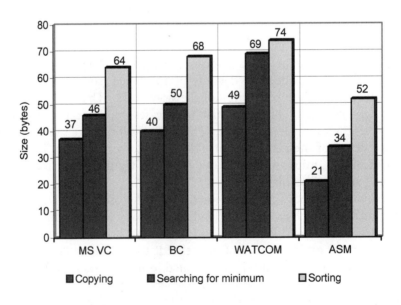

Fig. 4.5. Comparing the quality of machine-code generation (size)

Now, compare the size of the compiled code with that of the assembler code. The first thing that should strike you is the gap between Microsoft Visual C++ and its competitors (Fig. 4.5). Nevertheless, this compiler is behind the "manual" code. This gap rapidly increases as the solved tasks become simpler.

The competitors' results are significantly worse. Generally, transferring the program to assembly code cuts its size approximately in half.

Demonstration of Machine Optimization Quality

This discussion of machine optimization quality would be incomplete without illustrative examples. Performance counters are too abstract. They provide food for thought, but they do not explain *why* compiled code is worse than code written in the assembly language. Most people won't believe this until they see it for themselves!

Consider the assembly code generated by the compiler. For brevity, I will provide one example: the result of compiling the bubble-sorting program using Microsoft Visual C++. It is unlikely that you will improve this code significantly without suffering serious brain damage. If you are not a qualified assembly programmer, don't be upset. I have provided detailed comments in the listings. (Hopefully, even beginners can guess that the compiler didn't create these.)

Listing 4.1. Compiling the Bubble-Sorting Program Using Microsoft Visual C++

```
.text:004013E0 ;              S U B R O U T I N E
.text:004013E0
.text:004013E0
.text:004013E0 c_sort       proc near        ; CODE XREF: sub_401420+DA↓p
.text:004013E0
.text:004013E0 arg_0        = dword ptr  8
.text:004013E0 arg_4        = dword ptr  0Ch
.text:004013E0
.text:004013E0     push   ebx
.text:004013E0;   The EBX register is saved. The function must store
.text:004013E0;   the modified registers; otherwise,
.text:004013E0;   the program would crash.
.text:004013E0;
.text:004013E1     mov    ebx, [esp+arg_4]
.text:004013E1;   The rightmost argument, the number of elements,
.text:004013E1;   is loaded into EBX. A programmer would do the same.
```

```
.text:004013E1;   Local variables are addressed directly via ESP.
.text:004013E1;   This saves one register (EBP) for other purposes.
.text:004013E1;   Programmers can't quite do this. Addressing via ESP
.text:004013E1;   requires the location of the local variables
.text:004013E1;   to be recalculated every time the stack top is moved
.text:004013E1;   (i.e., when arguments are passed). This is very tedious
.text:004013E1;   and inconvenient for humans.
.text:004013E1;
.text:004013E5   push    ebp
.text:004013E6   push    esi
.text:004013E6;   Two more registers are saved. A programmer could use
.text:004013E6;   the PUSHA command, which saves all general-purpose registers.
.text:004013E6;   This would be shorter, but it would increase
.text:004013E6;   the program's demand for free space in the stack and
.text:004013E6;   decrease the execution speed.
.text:004013E6;
.text:004013E7   cmp     ebx, 2
.text:004013E7;   The value of the n argument is compared to the constant 2.
.text:004013E7;
.text:004013EA   push    edi
.text:004013EB   jl      short loc_40141B
.text:004013EB;   Code optimization starts here for early models of PMMX.
.text:004013EB;   The comparison of the EBX contents and the analysis
.text:004013EB;   of the result are separated by the command that stores
.text:004013EB;   the EDI register. PMMX could couple the commands
.text:004013EB;   if they had data dependence. In this case, such optimization
.text:004013EB;   is redundant because the processor tries to predict
.text:004013EB;   the branch direction long before its actual execution.
.text:004013EB;   Nevertheless, command shift is not an obstacle.
.text:004013EB;
.text:004013ED   mov     ebp, [esp+0Ch+arg_0]
.text:004013ED;   The value of the leftmost argument, the pointer to
.text:004013ED;   the sorted array, is loaded into EBP. Only compilers use
.text:004013ED;   this method to address arguments; programmers can't use it.
.text:004013ED;
.text:004013F1
.text:004013F1 loc_4013F1:                  ; CODE XREF: C_Sort+39↓j
.text:004013F1;   The loop is started from the odd address. This is
.text:004013F1;   unfortunate; it has a negative effect on performance.
.text:004013F1;
.text:004013F1   xor     esi, esi
.text:004013F1;   The logical XOR is executed over the ESI register,
.text:004013F1;   clearing the register. Programmers also can do this!
```

```
.text:004013F1;
.text:004013F3    cmp      ebx, 1
.text:004013F6    jle      short loc_40141B
.text:004013F6;   These commands are redundant. For a human, it is obvious that
.text:004013F6;   if EBX >= 2, it is always >= 1. For the compiler,
.text:004013F6;   this isn't obvious. It has turned the ascending for loop
.text:004013F6;   into a descending do/while loop with a postcondition.
.text:004013F6;   (Descending loops with postconditions are implemented
.text:004013F6;   more efficiently than ascending loops on x86 processors.)
.text:004013F6;   However, to do so, the compiler had to be sure that the loop
.text:004013F6;   executes at least once. Therefore, it inserted an additional
.text:004013F6;   (and, in this case, redundant) check into the code.
.text:004013F6;   Regardless, this check doesn't take a long time to complete.
.text:004013F6;
.text:004013F8    lea      eax, [ebp+4]
.text:004013F8;   EBP is added quickly to 4. The result is sent to EAX.
.text:004013F8;   Few programmers know this trick; most of them
.text:004013F8;   implement this task in two steps:
.text:004013F8;   MOV EAX, EBX\ADD EAX, 4
.text:004013F8;
.text:004013FB    lea      edi, [ebx-1]
.text:004013FB;   One is subtracted from EBX. The result is sent to EDI.
.text:004013FB;
.text:004013FE

.text:004013FE loc_4013FE:                  ; CODE XREF: C_Sort+35↑j
.text:004013FE    mov      ecx, [eax-4]
.text:004013FE;   Oops! The command at the beginning of the loop crosses
.text:004013FE;   the 0x10-byte boundary, which results in delays.
.text:004013FE;   This instruction loads the src[a-1] cell into
.text:004013FE;   the ECX register.
.text:004013FE;
.text:00401401    mov      edx, [eax]
.text:00401401;   The src[a] cell is loaded into EDX.
.text:00401401;
.text:00401403    cmp      ecx, edx
.text:00401403;   ECX (src[a-1]) is compared to EDX (src[a]).
.text:00401403;   This could be implemented in a shorter way, as
.text:00401403;   CMP ECX, [EAX], which removes the MOV EDX, [EAX] command.
.text:00401403;   A shorter code is unnecessary; [EAX] is needed to exchange
.text:00401403;   variables, and this command would appear there.
.text:00401403;
.text:00401405    jle      short loc_401411
```

```
.text:00401405;   Go to the loc_401411 branch if ECX <= EDX;
.text:00401405;   otherwise, exchange cells.
.text:00401405;
.text:00401407    mov     [eax-4], edx
.text:0040140A    mov     [eax],   ecx
.text:0040140A;   Cells are exchanged. This could be implemented via
.text:0040140A;   XCHG, which would be several bytes shorter. However,
.text:0040140A;   the XCHG instruction has problems; it doesn't work faster
.text:0040140A;   on all processors.
.text:0040140A;
.text:0040140C    mov     esi, 1
.text:0040140C;   ESI (the F flag) is set to 1.
.text:0040140C;   A programmer could reduce this code by several bytes to
.text:0040140C;   MOV ESI, ECX. (ECX > EDX, ECX !=0, if EDX >= 0.)
.text:0040140C;   Compilers cannot do these transformations. Nevertheless,
.text:0040140C;   algorithmic optimization has nothing to do with
.text:0040140C;   the quality of code generation.
.text:0040140C;
.text:00401411 loc_401411:                    ; CODE XREF: C_Sort+25↑j
.text:00401411    add     eax, 4
.text:00401411;   EAX (a) is increased by 4 (sizeof(int)).
.text:00401411;
.text:00401414    dec     edi
.text:00401414;   The loop counter is decreased by 1. (The compiler
.text:00401414;   has turned an ascending loop into a descending one.)
.text:00401414;
.text:00401415    jnz     short loc_4013FE
.text:00401415;   A jump is made to the loop start, as long as EDI
.text:00401415;   does not equal 0. Some people use LOOP here, which is
.text:00401415;   more compact but runs much slower.
.text:00401415;
.text:00401417    test    esi, esi
.text:00401417;   The F flag is checked for equality to 0.
.text:00401417;
.text:00401419    jnz     short loc_4013F1
.text:00401419;   The loop is repeated until F equals 0.
.text:0040141B
.text:0040141B loc_40141B:
.text:0040141B    pop     edi
.text:0040141C    pop     esi
.text:0040141D    pop     ebp
.text:0040141E    pop     ebx
.text:0040141E;   All modified registers are restored.
```

```
.text:0040141E;
.text:0040141F    retn
.text:0040141F;  The function returns control.
.text:0040141F;
.text:0040141F C_Sort          endp
.text:0040141F
```

Creating Protective Code in the Assembler

Undeniably, the best practice for creating protective mechanisms is to use a "naked" assembler and the maximum number of tricks. The efficiency of the assembler is secondary; the goal is to frustrate and confuse the hacker. Compilers generate predictable code, and most professional hackers know the individual attitudes of each compiler. The assembler places few limits on the flight of the coder's fancy, allowing the coder to implement almost any idea. Polymorphous, encrypted, self-modifying code; anti-debugging and anti-disassembling techniques... This list can be continued infinitely. The advisability of the using specific protective mechanisms is a topic for a different discussion. Here, I will concentrate on the ways of implementing these mechanisms.

First, it is necessary to distinguish a *trick* (an original idea or a nontraditional programming technique) from *undocumented features* of the processor and operating system. When expertly used, tricks are harmless and never create problems. A classic trick is decrypting the program, using a disposable notepad, returned by the rand function. Because the rand function always returns the same sequence, it is suitable for dynamic encryption/decryption of a program. If the disassembler can't recognize rand in the compiled program, the hacker will have to guess how this protection is organized and how it works. Can any problems result from implementing such a trick? There are none.

In contrast, here is an example of a "dirty hack" based on undocumented features: In Windows 95, the region of address space from 0xC0000000 to 0xF0000000, which stores low-level system components, is available to applications. This simplifies the struggle with debuggers and various monitors. On Window NT, however, the first attempt to access this area will throw an exception and subsequently close the violating application. As a result, the user cannot run the protected program under Windows NT. This is the reason most people don't like the assembler. However, is the assembler to blame? If you do not use undocumented features (or only use them cleverly), no problem will result!

Recently, a trend has developed that abandons the assembler even in protective mechanisms. Many tricks can be implemented well in high-level programming languages. In particular, dynamic code decryption (as well as the execution of code within the stack) can be implemented in pure C/C++. To achieve this, it is sufficient to obtain the pointer to the function (permitted in C), after which, you can do whatever you want with its contents. Note that it is not necessary to go down to the level of a naked assembler. In addition, high-level languages simplify the development of polymorphous generators and virtual machines (Turing machines, Petri networks, Pierce arrows, etc.). The only thing that shouldn't be implemented is self-modifying code. This is possible if you are bound to a specific compiler (you need to know how each code line is translated), but this practice is considered bad manners. Besides, the labor costs for creating self-modifying code on high-level languages are significantly higher than those for performing the same task on an assembler.

The possibility of creating protective mechanisms in pure C/C++ makes most old-school hackers writhe; they simply do not want to hear anything about it. (By the way, I share this position.) Traditions and habits are quite obstinate. But change can't be helped! Can you understand that programming in a naked assembler is beautiful? Creating protective mechanisms directly in machine code causes satisfaction that can't be expressed in words!

This is programming for the sake of programming: The coder is satisfied not only with the final result, but also with the process of achieving it.

Assembly Programming as a Creative Activity

The computer long ago ceased to be a machine for a small pack of technical elite. Day by day, its mystique rapidly turns into that of a toaster or a similar household appliance. Today's programmers, turning from the hardware and even the code-grinding algorithms, often rely on the mouse and visual panel with components. Writing a program has become as easy as preparing a can of soup. This situation has its advantages, but for a specific category of individuals, life is a constant search and everlasting challenge. What practical value comes from summiting Everest?

The less effort you spend to achieve the result, the less you value it. Visual programming is too simple to become really interesting. However, the higher the level of the programming language, the more rules and regulations you have to observe, and the fewer possibilities you will have for self-expression. Artists are different from their environments; each of their works bears a part of their vision of the world, a small particle of their individuality.

The assembler is the best tool for "probing" computer hardware, an excellent arena for intellectual struggle, and the perfect diversion for usefully spending the hours free from your main job.

There are lots of assembler puzzles, ranging from "write a program 1 byte shorter than that written by your colleague" to "create a self-learning chess program that takes no more than 2 KB." Most demo programs are written in an assembler, as well as "crackme" code. All of the above can be implemented using high-level languages, which would take you significantly less time and would produce programs equal in efficiency to those produced by assembly code. However, doing so would not be as interesting.

Because of this, if you encounter people devoted to the assembler who despise high-level languages, don't hurry to change their minds. Nine times out of ten, they love the assembler not for its supposed advantages, but for its lack of such advantages. Rarely do they want to demonstrate their superiority. If so, don't try to make them change their minds — they will change them on their own with the years.

Conclusion

The assembler is alive, and it will live eternally. The current situation, in which high-level languages hold the leadership, is a temporary phenomenon. It's simply the calmness before the storm. And the storm will come — don't doubt it. If not today, then tomorrow programmers will have to solve new problems and accomplish new tasks, consuming the entire CPU power and requiring more. The most important thing is to be prepared to offer your knowledge and skills when most companies urgently need qualified assembler specialists. (Programmers with a working knowledge of the half-forgotten Fortran are very popular now. Most scientific applications are written in FORTRAN, but specialists that can maintain them are rare because the new generation tends to use C.)

If you are not working for money, program in the assembler out of interest. Newer Pentium processors are a goldmine in this respect. Believe me, there are lots of things deserving attention.

Grind the code! I wish you good luck and challenging problems.

Source Code

Listing 4.2. C Implementation of the Memory-Copying Algorithm

```
void __cdecl c_cpy(int *src, int *dst, int n)
{
int a; int t;

if (n<1) return; // Nothing to copy

// Copying an array element by element
for (a=0; a<n; a++) dst[a]=src[a];

return;
}
```

Listing 4.3. Assembly Implementation of the Memory-Copying Algorithm

```
_asm_cpy    proc

push    esi                     ;
push    edi                     ; Saving registers
Push    ecx                     ;

mov     esi, [esp+4+3*4]        ; src
mov     edi, [esp+8+3*4]        ; dst
mov     ecx, [esp+8+4+3*4]      ; n

rep     mvsd                    ; Copying one command
pop     ecx                     ;
pop     edi                     ; Restoring registers
pop     esi                     ;

Ret                             ; Exit
_asm_cpy endp
```

Listing 4.4. C Implementation of the Algorithm That Searches for the Minimum

```
int __cdecl c_min(int *src, int n)
{
int a; int t;

if (n<2) return -1; // There's no place to search for the minimum!

// The first element of the array is assigned
// the "conditional minimum" status.
t = src[0];

// Is there an element smaller than the conditional minimum?
// If yes, the status is assigned to it.
for(a=1; a<n; a++) if (t>src[a]) t=src[a];

return t;
}
```

Listing 4.5. Assembly Implementation of the Algorithm That Searches for the Minimum

```
_asm_min   proc

        push    esi                 ; The registers
        push    edi                 ; are saved.

        mov     esi, [esp+8+4]      ; src
        mov     edx, [esp+8+8]      ; n

        cmp     edx, 2              ; Are there elements to search for?
        jb      @exit               ; There are no elements for searching.

        mov     eax, [esi]          ; The "conditional minimum" status
                                    ; is assigned to the first element.
@for:                               ; The loop is started.
        mov     edi, [esi]          ; The current element goes to EDI.
        cmp     eax, edi            ; Are there any smaller elements?
        jb      @next               ; If there are not, the status
        mov     eax, edi            ; is passed to the next element.

@next:
        add     esi, 4              ; Go to the next element.
        dec     edx                 ; The loop counter is decreased by 1.
        jnz     @for                ; The loop is repeated as long as EDX > 0.

@exit:
        pop     edi                 ; The registers
        pop     esi                 ; are restored.
ret
_asm_min endp
```

Listing 4.6. C Implementation of the Bubble-Sorting Algorithm

```
void __cdecl c_sort(int *src, int n)
{
int a; int t; int f;
if (n<2)
return;         // You can't sort less than two elements!

do{
    f=0;   // The sorting flag is set to 0.
```

```
// All elements are checked one by one.
for (a=1; a<n; a++)
    // If the next element is smaller than the previous one,
    // their places are changed, and the sorting flag
    // is set to 1.
    if (src[a-1]>src[a])
    {
        t=src[a-1];
        src[a-1]=src[a];
        src[a]=t;
        f=1;
    }
    // Sorting is repeated until the first "clean" iteration
    // (i.e., without changes) is encountered.
} while(f);
}
```

Listing 4.7. Assembly Implementation of the Bubble-Sorting Algorithm

```
_asm_sort  proc
        mov     edx, [esp+8]        ; n
        cmp     edx, 2              ; Is there anything to sort?
        jb      @exit               ; There is nothing to sort, so exit.

        push    esi                 ; The registers
        push    ebp                 ; are saved.
        push    ebx                 ;

@while:                             ; Main sorting loop
        mov     esi, [esp+4+4*3]    ; src
        mov     edx, [esp+8+4*3]    ; n
        xor     ebp, ebp            ; f := 0

@for:                               ; Loop for checking elements
        mov     eax, [esi]          ; EAX := src
        mov     ebx, [esi+4]        ; EBX := src+1

        cmp     eax, ebx            ; Here, EAX is compared to EBX.
        jae     @next_for           ; If EAX > EBX, go to the next element;
                                    ; otherwise, change their places.

        mov     ebp, ebx            ; The change flag is set to
        mov     [esi+4], eax        ; the "dirty" state.
```

```
        mov     [esi], ebx

@next_for:
        add     esi, 4          ; src+=1;
        dec     edx             ; The loop counter is decreased.
        jnz     @for            ; Elements are checked one by one
                                ; until the counter does not equal 0.

        or      ebp, ebp        ; Is the dirty flag is set? Sorting continues
        jnz     @while          ; until a clean iteration is encountered.

        pop     ebx             ; The registers
        pop     ebp             ; are restored.
        pop     esi             ;
@exit:

        ret                     ; Exit
_asm_sort endp
```

On the CD-ROM

The CPU.CLOCK.SDK directory contains the source code of the demo version of the DO.CPU 1.0 profiler used in this book.

Installation: To install the profiler on your computer, follow the instructions provided in the CPU.CLOCK.SDK\install.txt file. Descriptions of profiler functions are in the CPU.CLOCK.SDK\INCLUDE\DoCPU.h file.

The PIC directory contains the illustrations and diagrams provided in this book.

- ❐ [1].profile — Illustrations from *Chapter 1: Program Profiling*
- ❐ [2].memory — Illustrations from *Chapter 2: RAM Subsystem*
- ❐ [3].cache — Illustrations from *Chapter 3: Cache Subsystem*
- ❐ [4].cmpl — Illustrations from *Chapter 4: Machine Optimization*

The SRC directory contains the source code of programs provided in this book.

- ❐ [1].profile — Source code from *Chapter 1: Program Profiling*
- ❐ [2].memory — Source code from *Chapter 2: RAM Subsystem*
- ❐ [3].cache — Source code from *Chapter 3: Cache Subsystem*
- ❐ [4].cmpl — Source code from *Chapter 4: Machine Optimization*

The README.TXT file describes the contents of the CD-ROM.

Index

Powerful Techniques To Safeguard Your Programming

Hacker Disassembling Uncovered

Learn how to analyze programs using a debugger and disassembler

This guide takes on the programming problem of, having found holes in a program, how to go about disassembling it without its source code. Covered are the hacking methods used to analyze programs with a debugger and disassembler, including virtual functions, local and global variables, branching, loops, objects and their hierarchy, and mathematical operators. Also covered are methods of fighting disassemblers, self-modifying code in operating systems, executing code in the stack, optimizing compilers, and movable code.

Focusing on analyzing and optimizing programs, as well as creating the means of protecting information, this book:

☐ Presents an overview of the basic concepts in hacking methods, disassembling and debugging processes

☐ Identifies key structures of high-level languages

☐ Provides guidance on using the disassembler and the debugger together

☐ Outlines the difficulties related to protecting programs

AUTHOR Kris Kaspersky   ISBN 1-931769-22-2   PRICE $39.95   PUB DATE July release

PAGES 592 pp   SOFTCOVER 7.375 x 9.25